The English republican tradition and eighteenth-century France

Manchester University Press

STUDIES IN EARLY MODERN EUROPEAN HISTORY

This series aims to publish
challenging and innovative research in all areas
of early modern continental history.
The editors are committed to encouraging work
that engages with current historiographical
debates, adopts an interdisciplinary
approach, or makes an original contribution
to our understanding of the period.

SERIES EDITORS

Joseph Bergin, William G. Naphy, Penny Roberts and Paolo Rossi

Already published in the series

Sodomy in early modern Europe
ed. Tom Betteridge

The *Malleus Maleficarum and the construction of witchcraft*
Hans Peter Broedel

Latin books and the Eastern Orthodox clerical elite in Kiev, 1632–1780
Liudmila V. Charipova

*Fathers, pastors and kings:
visions of episcopacy in seventeenth-century France*
Alison Forrestal

*Princely power in the Dutch Republic:
Patronage and William Frederick of Nassau (1613–64)*
Geert H. Janssen, trans. J. C. Grayson

*Power and reputation at the court of Louis XIII: the career of Charles d'Albert,
duc de Luynes (1578–1621)*
Sharon Kettering

Popular science and public opinion in eighteenth-century France
Michael R. Lynn

*Catholic communities in Protestant states:
Britain and the Netherlands c.1570–1720*
eds Bob Moore, Henk van Nierop, Benjamin Kaplan and Judith Pollman

Religion and superstition in Reformation Europe
eds Helen Parish and William G. Naphy

*Religious choice in the Dutch Republic: the reformation of
Arnoldus Buchelius (1565–1641)*
Judith Pollmann

Witchcraft narratives in Germany: Rothenburg, 1561–1652
Alison Rowlands

Authority and society in Nantes during the French Wars of Religion, 1559–98
Elizabeth C. Tingle

*The great favourite:
The Duke of Lerma and the court and government of Philip III of Spain, 1598–1621*
Patrick Williams

The English republican tradition and eighteenth-century France

Between the ancients and the moderns

RACHEL HAMMERSLEY

Manchester University Press

Copyright © Rachel Hammersley 2010

The right of Rachel Hammersley to be identified as the author of this work has been asserted by her in accordance with the Copyright, Designs and Patents Act 1988.

Published by Manchester University Press
Altrincham Street, Manchester M1 7JA, UK
www.manchesteruniversitypress.co.uk

British Library Cataloguing-in-Publication Data is available

Library of Congress Cataloging-in-Publication Data is available

ISBN 978 1 7849 9137 1   paperback

First published by Manchester University Press in hardback 2010

This edition first published 2016

The publisher has no responsibility for the persistence or accuracy of URLs for any external or third-party internet websites referred to in this book, and does not guarantee that any content on such websites is, or will remain, accurate or appropriate.

Printed by Lightning Source

For John and Thomas

Contents

Acknowledgements	*page* ix
Abbreviations	xii
Introduction	1

I Real Whigs and Huguenots — 13

1 From English republicans to British commonwealthmen — 14
2 The Huguenot connection — 33

II Bolingbroke and France — 53

3 Viscount Bolingbroke: an atypical commonwealthman — 54
4 Bolingbroke's French associates — 64
5 A French commonwealthman: the abbé Mably — 86

III Commonwealthmen, Wilkites and France — 99

6 The commonwealth tradition and the Wilkite controversies — 100
7 The British origins of the chevalier d'Eon's patriotism — 110
8 The British origins of the baron d'Holbach's atheism — 123
9 The British origins of Jean-Paul Marat's revolutionary radicalism — 137

IV English republicans and the French Revolution — 153

10 Parallel revolutions: seventeenth-century England and eighteenth-century France — 154
11 The comte de Mirabeau and the works of John Milton and Catharine Macaulay — 174
12 The Cordeliers Club and the democratisation of English republican ideas — 185

Conclusion	198
Appendix: French translations of English republican works, 1652–1801	205
Bibliography	208
Index	231

Acknowledgements

This book is the fruit of more than ten years work. It was, in fact, the book that I originally wanted to write for my DPhil thesis. However, for that purpose I ended up producing a much narrower study. Having completed the thesis, which subsequently appeared as *French Revolutionaries and English Republicans*, and having been lucky enough to be awarded a Leverhulme Special Research Fellowship, I turned back to my original, more ambitious, idea. The relatively long duration of this project means that I have accumulated a large number of debts along the way, and it is a pleasure to be able to record them in print here.

This project could not have been undertaken or completed without the support of various agencies, institutions and individuals. The Leverhulme Trust and the University of Sussex funded my Special Research Fellowship between 2002 and 2004. I would also like to thank my then colleagues at Sussex for providing me with such a stimulating environment in which to work on the project. Newcastle University awarded me an Arts and Humanities Research Fund Grant in the summer of 2005, which made it possible for me to carry out research in Britain, France and Holland. The Arts and Humanities Research Council and Newcastle University funded a period of a year's leave in 2007–8, which provided me with the opportunity to finish the research and write up the book. I am extremely grateful to all of these bodies for their support. I would also like to thank my colleagues at Newcastle for making the University such a fantastic place to work and, more specifically, for fruitful conversations, friendship and for covering teaching and other duties for me during my absence.

The research for this volume has been carried out at libraries and archives in Britain, France and beyond, and I am grateful to the librarians and archivists at the following institutions for their assistance: University of Sussex Library; Robinson Library, Newcastle University; The National Archives; the Historical Manuscripts Commission; the British Library; the London Library; Senate House Library, London University; the Institute of Historical Research; the Huguenot Library; the Special Collections department at the Library of University College London; Cambridge University Library; the Special Collections department at the Brotherton Library, University of Leeds; the Special Collections department at the John Rylands University Library, Manchester; Tyne and Wear Archives Service; the National Library of Scotland; the Archives Nationales; the Bibliothèque Nationale; the Bibliothèque Historique de la Ville de Paris; the Special Collections department at the Library of the University of Leiden; the Special

Collections department (History of the Book) at the Library of the University of Amsterdam and Houghton Library at Harvard University.

The research carried out in foreign institutions was made more pleasant by the hospitality of Fabrice Bensimon, Nathalie Caron, and Ann Thomson in France; Hanneke Booy and Jan-Rouke Kuipers in Holland; and Phyllis Weliver in the United States. I am also grateful to Oliver Parry and Nathan Perl-Rosenthal for photocopying documents on my behalf and to Kate Davies for lending me her microfilm copy of the Catharine Macaulay Graham Papers.

At various stages of the project I have discussed my ideas with colleagues and friends and I am very grateful for their input. In particular I would like to thank: David Armitage; Helen Berry; Colin Brooks; Ian Bullock; Simon Burrows; Fergus Campbell; Peter Campbell; Malcolm Chase; Kate Davies; Saul Dubow; Anne Goldgar; John Gurney; Martyn Hammersley; John Hodgson; Maurice Hutt; Colin Jones; Gary Kates; Pierre Lurbe; Olivier Lutaud; Jeremy Popkin; Wendy Robins; Michael Sonenscher; Ann Thomson; Elizabeth Tuttle; Martin van Gelderen; Randolph Vigne; Phyllis Weliver; Richard Whatmore; Donald Winch; Blair Worden; Brian Young and members of the Republicanism Reading Group at Newcastle University, in particular Ruth Connolly, Jennifer Richards and Michael Rossington. I have also benefited greatly from written communications with Keith Michael Baker, Kent Wright and Justin Champion.

Some of the ideas presented here were explored and tested in papers at various seminars and conferences in Britain, France, Italy and the United States. I am grateful to the audiences on all these occasions for offering helpful comments and insights.

Articles based on certain aspects of this research have been published, or will be published, elsewhere. In particular, the fruits of Chapter 2 will appear in a volume on Anglo-French intellectual and cultural exchange edited by Ann Thomson, Simon Burrows and Edmond Dziembowski, with Sophie Audidière, which will be published by Studies on Voltaire and the Eighteenth Century. Some of the findings of Chapter 7 will be included in an edited collection on the chevalier d'Eon, entitled *The Chevalier d'Eon and his worlds: gender, espionage and politics in the eighteenth century*, edited by Simon Burrows, Jonathan Conlin, Valerie Mainz and Russell Goulbourne, to be published by Continuum in 2010. Finally, an earlier version of Chapter 9 was published as 'Jean-Paul Marat's *The Chains of Slavery* in Britain and France, 1774–1833' in the *Historical Journal* 48 (2005), pp. 641–60. I am grateful to all of the editors and publishers involved for permission to reproduce some of that material here.

In the closing stages of the project several people gave up time in their own busy schedules to read and comment on the draft manuscript. I am grateful to Colin Jones, John Gurney, Martyn Hammersley, Michael Sonenscher and Blair Worden for reading the entire manuscript and to Simon Burrows, Justin Champion, Jonathan Scott and Richard Whatmore for reading particular sections. Their comments and suggestions have undoubtedly made this a better book. It goes without saying that any errors that remain are my own.

ACKNOWLEDGEMENTS

My family have, as always, been unstinting supporters of my work. I am particularly grateful to my parents for all their help (financial and moral) over the years. Other family members, not least my brother and my grandparents, have also supported me in numerous ways. Finally, I would like to thank my husband John and our son Thomas. John's own research and his knowledge of and approach to history have been a constant source of inspiration to me. His contributions to this project in terms of the sacrifices he has made, the references he has found for me, and the hours he has spent discussing these ideas with me are immense, and it will never be possible for me to repay them in full. Thomas's contribution has been to bring joy and laughter to our lives and to remind me that there is more to life than work. This book is dedicated to them in gratitude, friendship and love.

Abbreviations

AN	Archives Nationales, Paris
BL	British Library, London
BN	Bibliothèque Nationale, Paris
GLC	Gilder Lehrman Collection
HL	Huguenot Library, London
JRL	John Rylands University Library, Manchester
NLS	National Library of Scotland, Edinburgh
ODNB	*Oxford Dictionary of National Biography*
PML	The Pierpont Morgan Library, New York
PMP	Prosper Marchand Papers
TNA	The National Archives
TWAS	Tyne and Wear Archives Service
ULBL	University of Leeds Brotherton Library
UoL	University of Leiden Library

Introduction

Introduction

On 3 September 1751 the French statesman René-Louis Voyer de Paulmy, marquis d'Argenson wrote in his journal that

> There blows from England a philosophical wind of free and anti-monarchical government. Already minds have been penetrated and one knows the extent to which opinion governs the world. It could be that this government is already formed in some heads, ready to be implemented at the earliest opportunity. Perhaps the revolution will occur with less conflict than we think ... Today all the orders are discontented at once ... Everywhere there is combustible matter. A riot could turn into a revolt, and a revolt into a total revolution – involving the election of true tribunes of the people, comices, communes; depriving the king and his ministers of their excessive power to do harm.[1]

D'Argenson's assessment of the political situation in France in the mid-eighteenth century is significant not only on account of his prescient warnings about where events were heading, but also for his suggestion that the French were importing ideas of liberty and republicanism from across the Channel.

At first sight d'Argenson's suggestion might seem unlikely. Eighteenth-century Britain and France were, after all, very different in character. In particular, their political and religious establishments were in sharp contrast to one another. Yet in some ways these differences meant that each was fascinated by the other – whether motivated by a desire for emulation or competition. The political situation in Britain had been transformed as a result of the events of the seventeenth century and, in particular, the English Revolution of 1640–60 and the Glorious Revolution of 1688–89, as well as by the Act of Union with Scotland in 1707. Consequently, the British in the early eighteenth century had a reputation for liberty and even revolution.[2] France's political situation was altered (albeit much less dramatically) by the death of Louis XIV in 1715. While the system of absolute government remained in place, the demise of the

Sun King and his replacement, not by an adult monarch but by his five-year-old great-grandson Louis XV and a Regency initially under the duc d'Orléans, provided the French with fresh opportunities to criticise absolutism and, consequently, brought a new interest in alternative systems of government.[3] In this context interest in the British system increased dramatically, and under the influence of Voltaire and Montesquieu it came to be seen by some as constituting a favourable alternative to that which existed in France.[4] The peaks and troughs of anglophilia and anglophobia in eighteenth-century France have been explored at length, and it is evident that the picture is by no means clear or coherent.[5] Nonetheless, French interest in Britain does appear to have been strong throughout the period, and it was this interest that provided the context in which English writings, and especially those associated with the seventeenth-century revolutions and the liberty that had arisen out of them, proved to be of interest and relevance to the French.

Curiously, despite the wealth of research that has been undertaken on the emergence and development of republican ideas during the early modern period, relatively little attention has been paid to the traffic in ideas reported by d'Argenson. The English influences on French republicanism have not been fully investigated, or sufficiently acknowledged.[6] In part, this may be due to the particular perspectives of those who have studied early modern republicanism – especially in its anglophone and francophone manifestations.

The republican tradition and Europe[7]

Our current sense of the geography of the republican tradition has been strongly shaped and coloured by J. G. A. Pocock's seminal work *The Machiavellian Moment*.[8] The trajectory he traced ran from ancient Greece, via Renaissance Italy and seventeenth- and eighteenth-century Britain, on to North America; and in his later assessment of the impact of the book he was explicit that what he had been describing was the movement of republican ideas away from continental Europe.[9] It is perhaps not surprising that among the works on early modern republicanism that have been published since the appearance of *The Machiavellian Moment* in 1975, those concerned with English and American republicanism predominate.[10]

Yet, even at the time at which he was writing, there were already those who believed that Pocock's perspective was too narrow in its focus on North America as the terminus of the republican trajectory in the eighteenth century.[11] Several years prior to the appearance of Pocock's book, Franco Venturi had published a series of lectures he had given at Cambridge University, under the title *Utopia and Reform in the Enlightenment*, in which he set out to examine the impact of republican ideas on the development of Enlightenment thought.[12] Venturi's republican tradition was much broader than that of Pocock. He challenged the conventional view that during the eighteenth century republicanism was primarily viewed in terms of its ancient legacy, and instead placed emphasis on the more recent experiences of the Italian, Flemish and German cities and of Holland, Switzerland, England and Poland.[13] Venturi even paid some attention to the influence of English republican ideas in France, though his account of that influence was necessarily sketchy and brief.

Since the publication of *The Machiavellian Moment*, further research has been carried out on the development of republican thought in a number of European countries, including Italy, Poland and Germany.[14] Early modern Dutch republicanism has received particularly thorough attention in the works of Ernst Kossman, Eco Haitsma Mulier, Martin van Gelderen, Wyger Velema and others.[15] Moreover, some attention has started to be paid to the exchange of republican ideas among European countries.[16] Much of this work was brought together in the two volumes entitled *Republicanism: A Shared European Heritage*, edited by Martin van Gelderen and Quentin Skinner, which appeared in 2002.[17] These volumes place the European dimension of early modern republicanism centre stage. Organised under six separate headings ('The Rejection of Monarchy', 'The Republican Citizen', 'The Republican Constitution', 'Republicanism and Political Values', 'The Place of Women in the Republic', and 'Republicanism and the Rise of Commerce'), the essays explore republican thought and practice in various European countries, including The Netherlands, England, Poland, Germany, Italy, Spain and France. Nevertheless, the predominant emphasis here is on the development of native republican traditions in particular European states, rather than on the influence that republican ideas from one nation have exerted on others.[18] More striking still is the synoptic nature of some of the contributions to the volumes that deal with France itself, important and influential though they are.[19] While this partly reflects the purpose and nature of the volumes, it is also indicative of the fact that it is only relatively recently that historians have begun to examine the emergence and development of republican ideas in pre-revolutionary France.

Republicanism in eighteenth-century France

Traditional accounts of eighteenth-century French republicanism have tended to focus on the distinctiveness of the French example, and to see it as confined to the period of the Revolution itself; the implication being that French republicanism owed little to earlier forms and models, and that it was more or less invented during the late 1780s and early 1790s. This view is reflected in Claude

Nicolet's book *L'Idée républicaine en France*, the chronological parameters of which are 1789 and 1924.[20] The common assumption, Nicolet acknowledged, is that there was no theory or doctrine of republicanism in France prior to the Revolution. While Nicolet questioned this assumption, insisting that republican government was discussed in pre-revolutionary France, he chose not to devote much attention to it in his book. A similar perspective is offered in the volume *Révolution et République. L'exception française* edited by Michel Vovelle.[21]

During the 1990s, this traditional account found new expression in the works of those who have identified the emergence of a modern form of republicanism in late eighteenth-century France. This was first explored in two collections of essays (one French, the other English) that appeared in the early 1990s: François Furet and Mona Ozouf's *Le Siècle de l'avènement républicain*, which was published in 1993; and Biancamaria Fontana's *The Invention of the Modern Republic*, which appeared in 1994.[22] Fontana described the aim of her book as being to clarify the nature of what John Dunn had called the modern or 'bourgeois liberal republic' that had emerged out of the French Revolution. She characterised this form of government as combining a representative constitutional political system with a free-market economy 'committed to the promotion of private property and individual interest'.[23] On her account it was the American Revolution that had demonstrated the possibility of republican government in a large state, and it was this model that had prompted the development of modern republicanism in France. However, for the most part, the essays in the volume (as in that edited by Furet and Ozouf) focus on the period of the Revolution itself. Indeed, in her own contribution to the volume, 'The Thermidorian Republic and its Principles' (a French version of which also appeared in the collection edited by Furet and Ozouf), Fontana argued that it was between July 1794 and November 1799 that the modern republic, based on a wide popular electorate and on constitutional guarantees and therefore suited to large territorial states and advanced commercial societies, was first developed in France.[24]

Since the publication of these two volumes, the nature of this modern form of republicanism, and the process of its development in late eighteenth-century France, have been explored in more detail in the works of several authors, most notably Richard Whatmore and James Livesey.[25] In *Republicanism and the French Revolution: An Intellectual History of Jean-Baptiste Say's Political Economy*, Whatmore focuses on the circle of figures around Say – and in particular on key members of the Brissotin/Girondin faction such as Jacques-Pierre Brissot and Etienne Clavière. Whatmore demonstrates how, inspired by their opposition to the 'classical republicanism' of some of their contemporaries, they drew on the models and experiences of both the Genevan and the American republics in order to create a form of republican government that would be both workable and durable in the circumstances of the modern world. In particular, their version of republicanism was designed to be applicable in a large, modern nation state and to be compatible with both commerce and civilisation. While he focuses on a slightly different cast of characters, the story told by Livesey in *Making Democracy in the French Revolution* is very similar. He offers an account of the development of a new form of 'democratic republicanism', which was particularly suited to the needs of commercial society, during the period of the Directory (1795–99).

Alongside this work on the development of modern republicanism, the last twenty years have also seen the emergence of an interest in the development of classical republican ideas in pre-revolutionary France. Building on older studies that explored the republican character of the political theory of Montesquieu and, more especially, Rousseau,[26] Keith Michael Baker and Kent Wright have incorporated other figures into the canon, building up a picture of what amounts, they claim, to a French branch of the classical republican tradition.[27] Moreover, Baker and Wright have also gone on to suggest that it was this strain of classical republicanism that came to fruition in the Jacobin republic of virtue, as well as informing the political theory of Emmanuel-Joseph Sieyès and other leading revolutionaries.[28]

In several influential articles, Baker has identified a number of eighteenth-century francophone writers whose works, he believes, are best understood in classical republican terms, and who can be related directly to the broader republican tradition as outlined by Pocock and others.[29] The figures discussed by Baker include not only those who are well known, such as Gabriel Bonnot de Mably, Rousseau, Jean-Paul Marat and Maximilien Robespierre, but also more obscure characters including Henri de Boulainvilliers and Guillaume-Joseph Saige. According to Baker, the writings of these figures display key features of the classical republican tradition, including an appeal back to ancient models and texts; a concern with the relationship between political liberty and civic virtue on the one hand and between despotism and luxury on the other; and a sense that politics is about the assertion of the will, and that to be legitimate a political system must have been accepted by the will of the citizen body.

Wright has furthered our understanding of this French classical republican tradition not only by producing a book-length study of Mably, but also by offering his own synoptic account of its development during the course of the eighteenth century, which is centred on the theme of ancient constitutionalism. Wright's account endorses Baker's cast of characters, though it also adds Montesquieu to the picture. Moreover, Wright largely shares Baker's understanding of the nature of classical republicanism. In his book on Mably he describes the central themes of this type of republicanism as being 'the celebration of the self-governing and self-defending citizenries of ancient Sparta and Rome, the fixation on the problem of the stability and durability of political communities, [and] the deployment of the vocabulary of "virtue", "fortune", and "corruption".[30]

While all of this work has greatly enriched our understanding of eighteenth-century French republicanism, the binary division into classical and modern variants does not do justice to its complexity. For example, the accounts of modern republicanism seem to imply that it was only with the American Revolution that French thinkers became aware of the possibility of building a republic in a large modern state, and that it was only during the Revolution itself that the problems involved in combining republican government with a commercial economy were properly explored. Yet, as Venturi had made clear, there were other examples of large modern republics with which eighteenth-century French thinkers were familiar. And, as Michael Sonenscher's recent work has demonstrated, the idea of combining republican politics with a modern political economy was also one that had had a long history in pre-revolutionary France.[31]

The conception of classical republicanism as set out by Baker and Wright is equally problematic. While they acknowledge the influence of English republican ideas in France – not least on Mably – they have not paid sufficient attention to the extent of this influence or to its distinctive nature. It is this influence, above all, which undermines the possibility of any neat division between classical and modern republicanism in the French context.

Early modern republicanism

Some of the difficulties associated with existing accounts of French republicanism can be overcome if we think in terms not of two but rather of three distinct strands of republican thought in eighteenth-century France.[32] On this account, classical republicanism would be divided into two separate branches – 'ancient republicanism' and 'early modern republicanism'. The former is reflected most clearly in the writings of Robespierre and Saint-Just – though it is also presented as an ideal (albeit not a viable) form of government in the works of Montesquieu, Rousseau and Mably.[33] Under the heading of early modern republicanism we can place both the more practical proposals of these three figures as well as the writings of early eighteenth-century Huguenots, and of individuals such as Boulainvilliers and Marat. This early modern strand of republicanism was no more homogeneous than either the ancient or modern varieties, and it developed gradually over the course of the century. It also shared certain features in common with both the ancient and the modern strands. Nonetheless, it is possible to identify several distinguishing characteristics.

In the first place, for early modern republicans English republican works and ideas (and in some cases political models) were more important than ancient or American examples and texts.[34] The reason for this was that the English sources provided answers to what was the fundamental question for early modern republicans – how republican institutions and practices (which would secure liberty, the ultimate goal for most of these writers) could be made workable in the context of a large, nation state. In some cases this also required incorporating republican elements within a monarchical framework, though these writers were staunch opponents of any kind of tyrannical or despotic behaviour on the part of a prince or government ministers.

Secondly, many early modern republicans concerned themselves not just with political liberty but also with religious liberty, and believed the two to be closely interrelated. This led them to advocate freedom of religious belief and to adopt a distinctive view of the relationship between religion and politics. Also involved here was the tendency of many of these figures to show sympathy with deist or freethinking ideas.

Thirdly, the moral philosophy of early modern republicans tended to be rather different from that of their ancient and modern counterparts. In particular, many were pessimistic about human nature, accepting that human beings are necessarily motivated by the passions and by self-interest. Consequently, rather than seeking to suppress these impulses they looked instead for means of directing and using them in order to produce the kind of behaviour that was required for republican government.[35]

On these, and other matters, French early modern republicans shared much in common with their counterparts across the Channel – the British commonwealthmen – whose beliefs have been described in detail by Caroline Robbins.[36] Like them, they both drew on earlier seventeenth-century republican ideas and adapted them to suit their own circumstances.

It is the aim of this book, then, to offer an account of the French uses of English republican ideas during the course of the eighteenth century, and how these generated what I have referred to as French early modern republicanism. Attention will be paid both to the means by which English republican works were disseminated in France and to the uses to which they were put by key French figures. It will be argued that these English ideas – and their distinctive mixture of political, religious and moral thought – exercised a considerable influence in eighteenth-century France, impacting on both the Enlightenment and the French Revolution.

The book is divided into four parts, each of which is subdivided into several chapters. The first chapter in each part is intended to set out the British context and ideas at play, while the subsequent chapters explore their dissemination and application in France. In Part I, the distinctive nature of the British commonwealth tradition is explored, the connections between its exponents and French Huguenot refugees examined and the role that these Huguenots played in bringing English republican ideas to the attention of a French audience investigated.

Part II focuses on the figure of Henry, viscount Bolingbroke and considers his extensive French connections and his contribution to the development of theories of government that incorporated both republican and monarchical elements – on both sides of the Channel. Among those influenced by Bolingbroke were Montesquieu and Mably, both of whom drew on English republican ideas in order to produce a workable eighteenth-century alternative to the ancient republican models that they saw as ideal but impractical.

The chronological focus of Part III is the turbulent period of the 1770s, when despotic behaviour on the part of both the British and the French authorities led to a revival of republican ideas on both sides of the Channel – and especially among the friends and acquaintances of John Wilkes.

Finally, Part IV is concerned with the Revolution itself. It challenges conventional views by seeking to demonstrate that throughout the 1790s a number of French revolutionaries, from across the political spectrum, looked to English models and ideas to help them to make sense of their own experiences and to chart a course for the future. Moreover, it argues that the various versions of republicanism that were propounded and put into practice during the course of the Revolution were built on ideas that had been circulating in France since the beginning of the century.

Notes

1 R. L. Voyer de Paulmy, marquis d'Argenson, *Journal et mémoires du marquis d'Argenson*, ed. E. J. B. Rathery (Paris: Mme Veuve Jules Renouard, 1856–67), VI, p. 464 (3 September 1751). D'Argenson had expressed similar sentiments in December 1750: 'See today how many educated and philosophical writers there are. A wind has been blowing from England for some years on these matters. These are combustible issues.' ibid., VI, p. 320 (21 December 1750). The same passages also appear in the Jannet edition: R. L. Voyer de Paulmy, marquis d'Argenson, *Mémoires et journal inédit du marquis d'Argenson* (Paris: P. Jannet, 1857–58), V, p. 346 and III, p. 384. The translations throughout are my own.
2 M. Goldie, 'The English System of Liberty', in M. Goldie and R. Wokler (eds), *The Cambridge History of Eighteenth-Century Political Thought* (Cambridge: Cambridge University Press, 2006), pp. 40–78.
3 For an overview of this period of French history see C. Jones, *The Great Nation: France from Louis XV to Napoleon* (Harmondsworth: Penguin, 2002).
4 See in particular Voltaire, *Letters Concerning the English Nation* (Oxford: Oxford University Press, 1994) and Montesquieu, *The Spirit of the Laws*, ed. A. Cohler et al. (Cambridge: Cambridge University Press, 1989), especially pp. 156–66.
5 F. Acomb, *Anglophobia in France, 1763–89: An Essay in the History of Constitutionalism and Nationalism* (Durham, NC: Duke University Press, 1950); J. Grieder, *Anglomania in France, 1740–1789: Fact, Fiction and Political Discourse* (Geneva: Droz, 1985); E. Dziembowski, *Un nouveau patriotisme français, 1750–1770: La France face à la puissance anglaise à l'époque de la guerre de Sept Ans* (Oxford: Voltaire Foundation, 1998).
6 Throughout this book the terms 'English republicanism' and 'the English republican tradi-

tion' are used as shorthand to refer to the body of English-language works with which I am concerned, which include both those seventeenth-century works normally identified by the label 'English republicanism' and the eighteenth-century works by the 'British commonwealthmen'. This decision has been made out of a desire for clarity and brevity, it is not intended to downplay the contributions of Scottish, Irish and Welsh writers to this tradition.

7 The very notion of a 'republican tradition' has itself come under scrutiny in recent years. My focus in this Introduction is on setting out the historiographical context to the book and it is the use of this terminology within the historiography that has determined my adoption of it here. This is not to say that I am unaware of, or even unsympathetic to, some of the criticisms that have been levelled against the concept. However, as rethinking the terminology is not the central purpose of this volume I have chosen to reserve direct engagement with this issue for the Conclusion.

8 J. G. A. Pocock, *The Machiavellian Moment: Florentine Political Thought and the Atlantic Republican Tradition* (Princeton: Princeton University Press, 1975). See also J. G. A. Pocock, 'Afterword', in *The Machiavellian Moment: Florentine Political Thought and the Atlantic Republican Tradition* (Princeton: Princeton University Press, 2003 [1975]), pp. 553–83.

9 J. G. A. Pocock, 'The Machiavellian Moment Revisited: A Study in History and Ideology', *Journal of Modern History* 53 (1981), pp. 71–2.

10 Accounts of English republicanism include: B. Worden, 'Classical Republicanism and the Puritan Revolution', in H. Lloyd-Jones et al. (eds), *History and Imagination: Essays in Honour of H. R. Trevor-Roper* (London: Duckworth, 1981), pp. 182–200; B. Worden, 'The Commonwealth Kidney of Algernon Sidney', *Journal of British Studies* 24 (1985), pp. 1–40; J. Scott, *Algernon Sidney and the English Republic, 1623–1677* (Cambridge: Cambridge University Press, 1988); J. Scott, *Algernon Sidney and the Restoration Crisis, 1677–1683* (Cambridge: Cambridge University Press, 1991); A. C. Houston, *Algernon Sidney and the Republican Inheritance in England and America* (Princeton: Princeton University Press, 1991); B. Worden, 'English Republicanism', in J. Burns and M. Goldie (eds), *The Cambridge History of Political Thought, 1450–1750* (Cambridge: Cambridge University Press, 1991), pp. 443–75; B. Worden, 'Marchamont Nedham and the Beginnings of English Republicanism, 1649–56', 'James Harrington and *The Commonwealth of Oceana*, 1656', 'Harrington's *Oceana*: Origins and Aftermath, 1651–1660', and 'Republicanism and the Restoration, 1660–1683', all in D. Wootton (ed.), *Republicanism, Liberty, and Commercial Society, 1649–1776* (Stanford: Stanford University Press, 1994), pp. 45–193; Q. Skinner, *Liberty Before Liberalism* (Cambridge: Cambridge University Press, 1998); D. Norbrook, *Writing the English Republic: Poetry, Rhetoric and Politics, 1627–1660* (Cambridge: Cambridge University Press, 1999); J. Scott, *Commonwealth Principles: Republican Writing of the English Revolution* (Cambridge: Cambridge University Press, 2004); V. B. Sullivan, *Machiavelli, Hobbes, and the Formation of a Liberal Republicanism in England* (Cambridge: Cambridge University Press, 2004) and P. A. Rahe, *Against Throne and Altar: Machiavelli and Political Theory under the English Republic* (Cambridge: Cambridge University Press, 2008). On American republicanism see: B. Bailyn, *The Ideological Origins of the American Revolution*, rev. edn (Cambridge, MA: Belknap, 1967, 1992); G. S. Wood, *The Creation of the American Republic, 1776–1787* (Chapel Hill, NC: University of North Carolina Press, 1969); R. E. Shalhope, 'Republicanism and Early American Historiography', *William and Mary Quarterly* (1982), pp. 334–56; D. T. Rodgers, 'Republicanism: The Career of a Concept', *Journal of American History* 79 (1992), pp. 11–38; J. O. Appleby, *Liberalism and Republicanism in the Historical Imagination* (Cambridge, MA: Harvard University Press, 1992); P. A. Rahe, *Republics Ancient and Modern: Classical Republicanism and the American Revolution* (Chapel Hill, NC: University of North Carolina Press, 1992); A. Gibson, 'Ancients, Moderns, and Americans: The Republicanism-Liberalism Debate Revisited', *History of Political Thought* 21 (2000), pp. 261–307.

11 Several reviews of Pocock's works noted his failure to address the European dimension. See for example F. Gilbert's review of *The Machiavellian Moment* in the *Times Literary Supplement* (19 March 1976), pp. 307–8 and Judith Shklar's review of *The Political Works of James Harrington*, in *Political Theory* 6 (1978), pp. 558–61.

12 F. Venturi, *Utopia and Reform in the Enlightenment* (Cambridge: Cambridge University Press,

1971).
13 Ibid., p. 18.
14 Very little of this work is available in English, but see the relevant articles in M. van Gelderen and Q. Skinner (eds), *Republicanism: A Shared European Heritage*. Vol 1: *Republicanism and Constitutionalism in Early Modern Europe*. Vol. 2: *The Values of Republicanism in Early Modern Europe* (Cambridge: Cambridge University Press, 2002).
15 For English-language accounts of Dutch republicanism see: E. Haitsma Mulier, 'The Language of Seventeenth-Century Republicanism in the United Provinces: Dutch or European?' in A. Pagden (ed.), *The Languages of Political Theory in Early Modern Europe* (Cambridge: Cambridge University Press, 1987), pp. 179–95; M. van Gelderen, *The Political Thought of the Dutch Revolt, 1555–1590* (Cambridge: Cambridge University Press, 1992) and the relevant chapters in van Gelderen and Skinner, *Republicanism*, Vols 1 and 2.
16 See in particular the work of E. Haitsma Mulier on the Dutch interest in the Venetian model and Jonathan Scott on relations between England and the Netherlands. E. Haitsma Mulier, *The Myth of Venice and Dutch Republican Thought in the Seventeenth Century* (Assen: Van Gorcum, 1980); Scott, *Algernon Sidney and the English Republic*; Scott, *Algernon Sidney and the Restoration Crisis*; J. Scott, *England's Troubles: Seventeenth-Century English Political Instability in European Context* (Cambridge: Cambridge University Press, 2000) and Scott, *Commonwealth Principles*.
17 Van Gelderen and Skinner, *Republicanism*, 1 and 2.
18 The contributions by Scott, van Gelderen and Bödeker are obvious exceptions. David Wootton has criticised the confused and ahistorical treatment of republicanism offered in these volumes. See his review in *English Historical Review* 120 (2005), pp. 135–9.
19 J. K. Wright, 'The Idea of a Republican Constitution in Old Régime France', in van Gelderen and Skinner, *Republicanism*, 1, pp. 289–306; M. Sonenscher, 'Republicanism, State Finances and the Emergence of Commercial Society in Eighteenth-Century France – or from Royal to Ancient Republicanism and Back', in van Gelderen and Skinner, *Republicanism*, 2, pp. 275–91.
20 C. Nicolet, *L'Idée républicaine en France* (Paris: Gallimard, 1982).
21 M. Vovelle (ed.), *Révolution et république. L'exception française* (Paris: Éditions Kimé, 1994). The volume does include several articles on the influence exercised by ancient republicanism, two on the American republican model and one on English influences, but the overall emphasis is on the distinctiveness of the French experience.
22 F. Furet and M. Ozouf (eds), *Le Siècle de l'avènement républicain* (Paris: Gallimard, 1993); B. Fontana, *The Invention of the Modern Republic* (Cambridge: Cambridge University Press, 1994).
23 Fontana, *Invention of the Modern Republic*, p. 2.
24 Ibid., pp. 118–19.
25 R. Whatmore, *Republicanism and the French Revolution: An Intellectual History of Jean-Baptiste Say's Political Economy* (Oxford: Oxford University Press, 2000); J. Livesey, *Making Democracy in the French Revolution* (Cambridge, MA: Harvard University Press, 2001).
26 On Montesquieu see D. Lowenthal, 'Montesquieu and the Classics: Republican Government in *The Spirit of the Laws*', in J. Cropsey (ed.), *Ancients and Moderns: Essays on the Tradition of Political Philosophy in Honor of Leo Strauss* (New York: Basic Books, 1964), pp. 258–87; N. O. Keohane, 'Virtuous Republics and Glorious Monarchies: Two Models in Montesquieu's Political Thought', *Political Studies* 20 (1972), pp. 383–96; J. N. Shklar, 'Montesquieu and the new republicanism', in G. Bock et al. (eds), *Machiavelli and Republicanism* (Cambridge: Cambridge University Press, 1990), pp. 265–79; and D. Carrithers, 'Not So Virtuous Republics: Montesquieu, Venice and the Theory of Aristocratic Republicanism', *Journal of the History of Ideas* 52 (1991), pp. 245–68. On Rousseau see: R. A. Leigh, 'Jean-Jacques Rousseau and the Myth of Antiquity in the Eighteenth Century', in R. R. Bolgar (ed.), *Classical Influences on Western Thought, AD 1650–1870* (Cambridge: Cambridge University Press, 1971), pp. 155–68; M. Viroli, 'The Concept of *Ordre* and the Language of Classical Republicanism in Jean-Jacques Rousseau', in Pagden, *Languages of Political Theory*, pp. 159–78; M. Viroli, *Jean-Jacques Rousseau and the 'Well-Ordered Society'* (Cambridge: Cambridge University Press, 1988); J. Hope Mason, 'Individuals in Society: Rousseau's Republican Vision', *History of Political Thought* 10 (1989), pp. 89–112; M.

M. Goldsmith, 'Liberty, Virtue, and the Rule of Law, 1689–1770', in Wootton, *Republicanism*, pp. 197–232; R. Wokler, 'Rousseau and his Critics on the Fanciful Liberties we have Lost', in R. Wokler (ed.), *Rousseau and Liberty* (Manchester: Manchester University Press, 1995), pp. 189–212; R. Wokler, *Rousseau* (Oxford: Oxford University Press, 1995); and H. Rosenblatt, *Rousseau and Geneva: From the* First Discourse *to the* Social Contract, *1749–1762* (Cambridge: Cambridge University Press, 1997).

27 K. M. Baker, *Inventing the French Revolution: Essays on French Political Culture in the Eighteenth Century* (Cambridge: Cambridge University Press, 1990); K. M. Baker, 'Transformations of Classical Republicanism in Eighteenth-Century France', *Journal of Modern History* 78 (2001), pp. 32–53; J. K. Wright, *A Classical Republican in Eighteenth-Century France: The Political Thought of Mably* (Stanford: Stanford University Press, 1997); J. K. Wright, 'The Idea of a Republican Constitution in Old Régime France', in van Gelderen and Skinner, *Republicanism*, 1, pp. 289–306.

28 Baker, 'Representation Redefined' and 'Fixing the French Constitution', in Baker, *Inventing the French Revolution*, pp. 224–51 and 252–305; Baker, 'Transformations'; Wright, 'Idea of a Republican Constitution'.

29 Baker, 'A Script for a French Revolution: The Political Consciousness of the Abbé Mably' and 'A Classical Republican in Eighteenth-Century Bordeaux: Guillaume-Joseph Saige', in Baker, *Inventing the French Revolution*, pp. 86–106 and 128–52; Baker, 'Transformations'.

30 Wright, *Classical Republican in Eighteenth-Century France*, p. 18.

31 M. Sonenscher, *Before the Deluge: Public Debt, Inequality and The Intellectual Origins of the French Revolution* (Princeton and Oxford: Princeton University Press, 2007), especially p. 166; M. Sonenscher, *Sans-Culottes: An Eighteenth-Century Emblem in the French Revolution* (Princeton and Oxford: Princeton University Press, 2008), especially pp. 3–4.

32 Some recent commentators on the republican tradition seem to suggest that we would be better to do away with the concept of 'republicanism' altogether, or, at the very least, reduce it to a much narrower definition. See in particular Blair Worden, 'Republicanism, Regicide and Republic: The English Experience', in van Gelderen and Skinner, *Republicanism*, 1, pp. 307–27. See also David Wootton's review of those two volumes in *The English Historical Review* 120 (2005), pp. 135–9; and D. Wootton, 'The True Origins of Republicanism: The Disciples of Baron and the Counter-Example of Venturi', in M. Albertone (ed.), *Il repubblicanismo moderno: L'idea di repubblica nella riflessione storica di Franco Venturi* (Naples: Bibliopolis, 2006), pp. 271–304. While there are undoubtedly problems with the way in which the term has been employed, my view is that it is too deeply embedded in the historiography simply to discard it and that the solution to the problem lies not in narrowing the definition, but in broadening it out by recognising that different variants of republican thought have existed at different points in time.

33 The influence of ancient models and ideas in late eighteenth-century France, and especially during the Revolution, has been explored in some detail. See H. T. Parker, *The Cult of Antiquity and the French Revolutionaries: A Study in the Development of the Revolutionary Spirit* (Chicago: University of Chicago Press, 1937); C. Mossé, *L'Antiquité dans la Révolution française* (Paris: Albin Michel, 1989); M. Raskolnikoff, *Des Anciens et des modernes* (Paris: Presse Universitaire de Paris-Sorbonne, 1990); M. Raskolnikoff, *Histoire romaine et critique historique dans l'Europe des lumières* (Strasbourg: AECR, 1992); P. Vidal-Naquet, *Politics Ancient and Modern*, trans. J. Lloyd (Cambridge: Polity, 1995).

34 It is undoubtedly also the case that republican models and writings from other European countries (not least those of the Dutch) exercised an influence in eighteenth-century France. However, owing to constraints of space and a desire for some degree of coherence, it has not been possible to explore the full range of these influences here. On Dutch influences on the Enlightenment more generally see J. Israel, *Radical Enlightenment: Philosophy and the Making of Modernity, 1650–1750* (Oxford: Oxford University Press, 2001).

35 One dimension of early modern republican thought that I have not explored in much detail here is the economic. Less attention has been devoted to it partly because I believe it was

less central to the thought of many of the figures discussed here than political, religious and moral ideas, and partly because that aspect of eighteenth-century French political thought has recently been explored in detail by Michael Sonenscher. See Sonenscher, *Before the Deluge* and Sonenscher, *Sans-Culottes*.

36 C.A. Robbins, *The Eighteenth-Century Commonwealthman: Studies in the Transmission, Development, and Circumstance of English Liberal Thought from the Restoration of Charles II until the War with the Thirteen Colonies* (Indianapolis: Liberty Fund, 2004 [1987, 1959]).

Part I
Real Whigs and Huguenots

1
From English republicans to British commonwealthmen

Introduction

The eighteenth-century British commonwealthmen present a problem for any historical account of the republican tradition. In many ways they were central to that tradition. They saw themselves as heirs of the republican writers of mid-seventeenth-century England: they republished their books, quoted from their works and applied their principles and ideas to their own circumstances and concerns. Indeed, it was largely because of the commonwealthmen that those ideas were kept alive in the eighteenth century.[1] The problem is that the majority of them firmly rejected the idea of kingless government. For example, in his manifesto for the early commonwealth movement, *The Principles of a Real Whig*, which appeared as a preface to the 1721 edition of his translation of Hotman's *Franco-Gallia*, Robert Molesworth wrote:

> But there is one very great discouragement under which both I, and all other writers and translators of books tending to the acquiring or preserving the public liberty, do lie: and that is, the heavy calumny thrown upon us, that we are all *Commonwealthsmen*; which (in the ordinary meaning of the word) amounts to *haters of kingly* government; not without broad, malicious insinuations, that we are no great friends of the present.[2]

Similarly, in his Preface to *Cato's Letters*, Thomas Gordon sought to clarify the political persuasion of his late co-author John Trenchard:

> As passionate as he was for Liberty, he was not for a Commonwealth in *England*. He neither believed it possible, nor wished for it. He thought that we were better as we were, than any practicable Change could make us, and seemed to apprehend that a neighbouring Republick was not far from some violent Shock.[3]

These statements would seem to place the commonwealthmen firmly outside the republican camp as defined by some influential scholars.[4] From the perspective of the commonwealthmen themselves, however, the terms 'republican' and 'commonwealthsman' appear to have been more loosely defined. Having made the comment about commonwealthsmen being seen as haters of kingly government Molesworth went on to question that understanding of the term:

> A true *Whig* is not afraid of the name of a *Commonwealthsman*, because so many foolish people, who know not what it means, run it down: The *anarchy* and *confusion* which these nations fell into near sixty years ago, and which was *falsly* called a *Commonwealth*, frightening them out of the true construction of the word. But queen *Elizabeth*, and many other of our best princes, were not scrupulous of calling our government a *Commonwealth*, even in their solemn speeches to *parliament*. And indeed if it be not one, I cannot tell by what name properly to call it: for where in the very *frame* of the *constitution*, the good of the *whole* is taken care of by the *whole* (as it is in our case) the having a *king* or *queen* at the head of it, alters not the case; and the softening of it by calling it a *limited monarchy*, seems a kind of contradiction in terms, invented to please some weak and doubting persons.[5]

Similarly, in the issue of *Cato's Letters* for 15 July 1721, Gordon justified his decision to quote from the works of Algernon Sidney:

> I know it is objected that he is a Republican; and it is dishonestly suggested that I am a Republican, because I commend him as an excellent Writer, and have taken a Passage or two out of him. In answer to this, I shall only take Notice, That the Passages which I take from him are not Republican Passages, unless Virtue and Truth be Republicans: That Mr. *Sidney's* Book, for the Main of it, is eternally true, and agreeable to our own Constitution, which is the best Republick in the World, with a Prince at the Head of it: That our Government is a Thousand Degrees nearer a-kin to a Commonwealth (any Sort of Commonwealth now subsisting, or that ever did subsist in the World) than it is to Absolute Monarchy: That for myself, I hope in God, never to see any other Form of Government in *England*, than that which is now in *England*; and that, if this be the Stile and Spirit of a Republican, I glory in it, as much as I despise those who take base Methods to decry my Writings, which are addressed to the common Sense and Experience of Mankind.[6]

These passages suggest that the commonwealthmen did not view the distinction between government with a king and government without as the central concern. Though they were aware of the apparent contradiction, they clearly believed that the principles and ideas of the mid-seventeenth-century republicans were applicable and relevant in the monarchical context in which they found themselves. Thus in order to understand the commonwealth position it is necessary to put on one side the issue of constitutional forms and to focus instead on the principles, values and practical measures that the commonwealthmen saw as uniting them with the republicans of the mid-seventeenth century.[7]

This approach has, of course, been adopted by previous scholars in this field. In her pioneering account, Caroline Robbins emphasised the specific political measures adopted by the commonwealthmen, in particular 'shorter parliaments, fewer placemen, a national militia, and greater religious liberty'.[8] Yet these measures were simply the outer manifestations of a much deeper set of political, religious and moral beliefs that characterised the commonwealth position. If we take account of these deeper principles, then a 'thicker description' of the British commonwealth tradition is possible. J. G. A. Pocock's magisterial *The Machiavellian Moment* offered precisely this kind of thick description.[9] The analysis of the commonwealthmen offered here is deeply indebted to that book, though there will be several points where my account diverges from Pocock's.

'Liberty, civil and religious'

The fundamental value around which the ideas of the commonwealthmen revolved was liberty. Its importance to them is reflected in the fact that when they sought to justify their publications they often did so by appealing to liberty. For example, Molesworth explained his decision to translate François Hotman's sixteenth-century Huguenot text, *Franco-Gallia*, in the following terms:

> [T]he chief motive which induces me to send abroad this small treatise is a sincere desire of instructing the only possessors of true liberty in the world, what right and title they have to that liberty; of what a great value it is; what misery follows the loss of it; how easily, if care be taken in time, it may be preserved.[10]

Similarly, Gordon justified his translation of Tacitus's works by suggesting that the account of tyranny offered there would awaken in the reader 'just zeal for the preservation of his own British Liberty'.[11] Quick as they were to stress the importance of liberty, the commonwealthmen were less forthcoming in defining exactly what they meant by it. Nonetheless, it is possible to tease out certain elements of the concept.

To a large degree the commonwealthmen appear to have adopted what Quentin Skinner has called the neo-Roman concept of liberty.[12] Essentially they were concerned with the protection of basic civil liberties, such as freedom of speech, the protection of private property, and freedom from arbitrary arrest. Such liberties were threatened not only when they were actually violated, but as long as those in power were in a position to violate them. Thus, the means of protecting such liberties was through the adoption of the rule of law.[13] It was also essential that the citizens themselves were given a role in making legislation (thereby ensuring that they were only required to obey laws to which they had consented).[14] As Moyle and Trenchard declared in *An Argument, Shewing, that a Standing Army is inconsistent with a Free Government*: 'No Man can be imprisoned, unless he has transgressed a Law of his own making'.[15] This was also the reason why Toland insisted in *The Danger of Mercenary Parliaments* that: 'On Parliaments, on free and frequent Parliaments, depend the whole Wealth and Power, all the Liberty and Property of the *British* World'.[16]

A ruler who ruled according to his own will, rather than on the basis of the rule of law, was a tyrant. On this account an absolute monarch was by definition a tyrant, regardless of how he behaved.[17] Historians writing about the commonwealthmen have suggested that the late seventeenth and early eighteenth centuries witnessed a shift away from an emphasis on an absolute monarch as the main threat to liberty, and toward a concern with corruption.[18] While there is certainly an element of truth in this, the Standing Army Controversy of the 1690s, and indeed Gordon's decision to publish his translation of Tacitus in 1728–31, suggest that, despite the revolution settlement, the fear of tyranny and absolute monarchy had not gone away. Not only were the Jacobites an ever-present threat at this time, but it was acknowledged that even William III needed to be restrained, despite his credentials as an agent of liberty. In fact, the tendency for a monarch to become absolute or tyrannical was simply one manifestation of corruption.[19]

While civil liberty was certainly important to the commonwealthmen, this was only one half of the picture. They also placed great emphasis on the need for religious liberty and saw the two as intertwined. The religious dimension of seventeenth-century English republicanism, and of the commonwealth tradition, was for a long time treated as subordinate to their political aspects.[20] The recent work of Jonathan Scott and Justin Champion has done much to correct this.[21] It is now clear that the commonwealthmen, like their seventeenth-century predecessors, were as concerned about religious issues as they were about political ones. The third Earl of Shaftesbury, Toland, Anthony Collins, Trenchard, and Gordon all published works that were devoted to religious topics, and religious themes were also discussed at length in other commonwealth works, including those of Molesworth and Walter Moyle.[22]

The nature of the religious beliefs of the commonwealthmen was not always in line with those of the seventeenth-century republicans, as Blair Worden's work on the toning down of Edmund Ludlow's Puritanism in the published version of his *Memoirs* has made clear.[23] Yet in some ways the rabid anticlericalism and freethinking views of the commonwealthmen can be seen as direct developments of seventeenth-century ideas.[24] Indeed, on the issue of religious liberty, the views of the commonwealthmen were directly in line with those of their seventeenth-century predecessors. In *The Readie and Easie Way* John Milton had declared that: 'The whole freedom of man consists either in spiritual or civil libertie.'[25] And in *A System of Politics* James Harrington had described 'liberty of conscience without civil liberty, or civil liberty without liberty of conscience' as 'but liberty by halves'.[26] These sentiments seem very similar to those of the commonwealthmen. For example, in his pamphlet *Priestianity* Gordon wrote: 'Is not the Liberty of the Mind preferable to the Liberty of the Body? If therefore we have preserved the One from Foreign Enemies at the Expence of our Blood and Treasure, we ought to secure the Other from Domestick Invaders.'[27]

The commonwealthmen stretched beyond many of their seventeenth-century predecessors, however, with regard to the range of beliefs that they were prepared to tolerate.[28] In his *Principles of a RealWhig*, Molesworth called for toleration not just of Quakers, Socinians and Presbyterians, but also of Pagans, Turks and Jews.[29] Similarly Trenchard and Gordon in *The Independent Whig* called for extensive toleration, and insisted on the importance of freedom of thought in religious matters: 'but that we are to enquire before we believe, and to be convinced before we assent ... our Judgment ought to be at no Man's Service, nor our Minds controuled in religious Matters, but by God alone; for as no Man's Soul can be saved by Proxy, so no Man ought to exercise his Faith by Proxy.'[30]

Just as civil liberty was threatened by tyrannical behaviour on the part of a ruler, so religious liberty was put at risk by tyrannical behaviour on the part of the Church and its clergy. Thus, anticlericalism was central to the commonwealth position. In line with Harrington and Henry Neville (and also Milton and Marchamont Nedham), though not with all seventeenth-century republicans, the commonwealthmen adopted an Erastian position.[31] It was their contention that religion had the potential to be used for positive political and moral ends. However, for this to be realised religion had to be subordinated to the state and kept entirely under its control. The problem with the Christian Church was that it was no longer under state control, but had developed power and authority of its own.[32] This was, of course, particularly true of the Catholic Church, and the commonwealthmen were outspoken opponents of popery, but they were also critical of the power and authority exercised by the Church of England. They claimed that, in order to maintain power, priests engaged in tyranny and oppression, stifling religious liberty by cultivating superstition and ignorance among the population.[33] Moreover, political and religious tyranny often reinforced each other. As Gordon explained in setting out the agenda for *The Independent Whig*:

> I shall shew what a shameful Hand ... [the priests] have always had in bringing and keeping Mankind under Tyranny and Bondage to such princes as would divide the Spoil with them. In such Case, it was a Point of Conscience, and a religious Duty, for Subjects to be miserable Slaves; and Damnation but to strive to be Happy.[34]

Similarly, Moyle declared: 'And indeed in all Ages it hath been a current Maxim of arbitrary Princes, to engage the Authority of the Church to support their Tyranny.'[35]

Virtue, passion and self-interest

Virtue has long been seen as a crucial component of English republicanism. Indeed, according to some recent accounts a moral philosophy centred on the pursuit of virtue was at the core of sixteenth and seventeenth-century English republicanism.[36] Moreover, liberty and virtue have generally been seen as mutually reinforcing. Just as liberty was essential if the citizens were to be provided with the opportunity to practise virtue, so the practice of virtue would help to secure liberty. In this context virtue tended to be associated with the rule of reason and, in a political sense, with putting the public good before one's own private interests. Thus, corruption occurred when one or more members of the State began to act in his/their own interests rather than in the public interest. A monarch who put his/her private interests before those of the public good was by definition a tyrant – this was precisely what the Stuarts had done in the seventeenth century. But liberty could also be placed in jeopardy by ministers acting in their own interests and even by citizens who were motivated more by making a profit for themselves than by acting for the good of all.[37] On the face of it, there is evidence to suggest that the commonwealthmen recognised the importance of virtue and sought to promote it. For example, Gordon insisted that the purpose of his discourses on Tacitus was not just 'to maintain the cause of Liberty, and shew its blessings' but also to 'display the sad consequences of public corruption, with the beauty and benefit of public virtue'.[38] However, digging a little deeper it becomes clear that the issue is rather more complex.

Despite their emphasis on virtue, republican writers had always recognised the difficulties associated with practising it.[39] However, in the late seventeenth century, the idea began to emerge that the practice of virtue was not just difficult but impossible. Thinkers such as the duc de la Rochefoucauld and Blaise Pascal in France and Thomas Hobbes in England stressed the tendency for human beings to act on the basis of their passions rather than of reason, and posited self-interest as the key motivating force within human nature.[40] Most seventeenth-century English republicans – including Milton, Henry Vane and Algernon Sidney – remained distanced from these debates and continued to believe in the possibility of virtue, at least among an elite minority.[41] They placed emphasis, as republicans before them had done, on the importance of education as a means of encouraging virtuous behaviour. Nedham and Harrington, however, took a different line. As both Scott and Rahe have argued, Nedham's writings display at least some sympathy with Machiavelli's 'interest theory', according to which free states are more likely to be governed in the public interest, whereas monarchies tend to operate according to particular interests.[42] This was also characteristic, as Scott has argued, of Dutch republicanism as reflected in the work of the De la Courts.[43] The position adopted by Harrington constituted an even sharper break with republican virtue.[44] Again drawing on Machiavelli, but also as a careful – and in many ways sympathetic – reader of Hobbes, Harrington was largely convinced by the idea that human beings tend to act on the basis of their passions and self-interest rather than that of reason and virtue.[45] Yet instead of abandoning the idea of virtue altogether he sought material and constitutional solutions to the problem.

The theory for which Harrington is perhaps best known is that 'empire follows the balance of property' or, in other words, that political power has to be based on the possession of land. On this basis Harrington insisted that the form of government that is appropriate for a particular state depends on the distribution of land within it. According to this interpretation the corruption and decline of a political system was as much a material as a moral issue – it arose from the possession of power being out of line with the distribution of property. Thus one crucial way in which corruption could be prevented was by adopting the appropriate form of government for the society concerned and introducing measures (such as an agrarian law) to ensure that the correct distribution of land would be maintained over time.[46]

Despite the importance that Harrington accorded to the balance between power and property, he recognised that it alone would not produce a virtuous republic. In addition, he was concerned with what he called the 'superstructure' – the orders of the constitution. He believed that through careful construction of the political system, self-interest could actually be used to produce virtuous behaviour:

> But it may be said that the difficulty remains yet; for be the interest of popular government right reason, a man doth not look upon reason as it is right or wrong in itself, but as it makes for him or against him; wherefore unless you can show such orders of a government as, like those of God in nature, shall be able to constrain this or that creature to shake off that inclination which is more peculiar unto it and take up that which regards the common good or interest, all this is to no more end than to persuade every man in a popular government not to carve himself of that which he desires most, but to be mannerly at the public table, and give the best from himself unto decency and the common interest.[47]

Harrington illustrated how such 'orders of a government' might work with his story of the two girls dividing a cake between them. One girl was to cut the cake, while the other would have first choice as to which piece she wanted: 'If this be but once agreed upon, it is enough; for the divident dividing unequally loses, in regard that the other takes the better half; wherefore she divides equally, and so both have right.'[48] This particular idea was to be translated into the political sphere through the establishment of a bicameral legislature in which the upper house or senate would devise legislation, but it would be up to the lower house to accept or reject the laws proposed. This was just one of many constitutional mechanisms (most of which were drawn from the Venetian constitution) that Harrington incorporated into his system so as to ensure that the self-interested actions of the citizens of Oceana would be transformed into virtuous behaviour.

The commonwealthmen appear to have shared Harrington's views on these matters. It was Neville who first adopted Harrington's account of the material causes of corruption. In *Plato Redivivus* he described the alteration of property as the '*Unica corruptio politica*' [the only form of political corruption].[49] In *An Essay Upon the Constitution of the Roman Government* Moyle was even more emphatic about the material (rather than moral) causes of corruption:

> These Periods and Revolutions of Empires are the natural Transmigrations of Dominion, from one Form of Government to another; and make the common Circle in the Generation and Corruption of all States. The Succession of these Changes POLYBIUS knew from Experience, but not from their true and natural Causes: for he plainly derives these Alterations from moral Reasons; such as Vices and Corruption, the Oppression and Tyranny of their Governors, which made the People impatient of the Yoke, and fond of new Forms; and not from the Change of the only true Ground and Foundation of Power, *Property*.
>
> [...]
>
> Thus it appears that Land is the true Center of Power, and that the Ballance of Dominion changes with the Ballance of Property; as the Needle in the Compass shifts its Points just as the great Magnet in the Earth changes its Place. This is an eternal Truth, and confirm'd by the Experience of all Ages and Governments; and so fully demonstrated by the Great HARRINGTON in his OCEANA, that 'tis as difficult to find out new Arguments for it, as to resist the Cogency of the old.[50]

Even Trenchard and Gordon accepted the implications of this argument in insisting that the maintenance of freedom depended on an equal distribution of property.[51]

Commonwealth writers also drew on Harrington's ideas about self-interest. They agreed with him that rather than expecting human beings to behave virtuously and in accordance with reason, it was necessary to accept that they tended to be motivated by their passions and in accordance with self-interest.[52] As Gordon explained in *Cato's Letters*:

> Here therefore lies the source of all the evil which men suffer from men, that every man loves himself better than he loves his whole species, and more or less consults himself in all that he does. He naturally pursues what is pleasant or profitable in his own eyes, though in doing it he entail misery upon multitudes.[53]

Similarly, in an earlier issue of the journal, Gordon had referred explicitly to the duc de la Rochfoucauld's ideas about self-interest:

> Of all the Passions which belong to human Nature, *Self-love* is the strongest, and the Root of all the rest; or, rather all the different Passions are only several Names for the several Operations of Self-love; *Self-love*, says the Duke of *Rochefoucault*,

> *is the Love of one's self, and of every Thing else for one's own Sake: It makes a Man the Idolater of himself, and the Tyrant of others.* He observes, that Man is a Mixture of Contrarieties, imperious and supple, sincere and false, fearful and bold, merciful and cruel: He can sacrifice every Pleasure to the getting of Riches, and all his Riches to a Pleasure: He is fond of his Preservation, and yet sometimes eager after his own Destruction: He can flatter those whom he hates, destroy those whom he loves.
>
> [...]
>
> This is a Picture of Mankind; and they who say it is a false one, ought to shew that they deserve better.[54]

In particular the commonwealthmen noted that power was a corrupting force. For example, both Gordon and Toland acknowledged the tendency for even the most virtuous of men to become corrupt once in a position of power.[55] The commonwealthmen also joined Harrington in believing that rather than simply abandoning virtue one should look to the passions and self-interest to provide, if not virtue itself, then at least the semblance of it. As Gordon explained in *Cato's Letters*:

> The only way therefore of dealing with mankind, is to deal with their passions; and the founders of all states, and of all religions, have ever done so: the first elements, or knowledge of politics, is the knowledge of the passions; and the art of governing, is chiefly the art of applying to the passions.[56]

In following Harrington by breaking with the traditional republican attitude to virtue, the commonwealthmen were venturing into new territory. They were moving away from the neo-Stoic moral philosophy (which aimed at virtue and focused on harmonising private passions with the public good) that was traditionally associated with the republican tradition, and toward a neo-Epicurean position (where the aim was happiness and the passions were pitted against each other in order to produce positive results).[57] This shift was never complete (though some commonwealth writers went further down the neo-Epicurean road than others) and both neo-Stoic and neo-Epicurean elements can be identified within commonwealth works. Essentially, the commonwealthmen appear to have occupied the border areas between the two moral positions and this is one reason why moral concerns, and the relationship between morality and politics, were of such great concern to them.[58]

The commonwealthmen not only followed Harrington in their analysis of the relationship between reason and passion and their belief that the passions ought to be used rather than suppressed, they also accepted Harrington's belief that constitutional measures offered one important means by which the passions might be governed and self-interest transmuted into virtuous behaviour.[59] The centrepiece of these constitutional measures was the mixed and balanced constitution.

The mixed constitution

The idea of the mixed constitution as a means of protecting liberty and slowing the inevitable process of decay and corruption had a long history within the republican tradition.[60] The seeds of the idea were present in Aristotle's political typology, and the concept was fully developed by Polybius in the second century BC.[61] The theory was that a system made up of a mixture of monarchy, aristocracy and democracy would enjoy the advantages of each of those simple forms, without suffering their disadvantages. This traditional idea was, however, modified by Harrington, who presented the mixed constitution as a means of transforming self-interest into virtue. In the Preliminaries to *Oceana* he described the mixed constitution as 'the doctrine of the ancients', having already explained that the key distinction between ancient and modern prudence was that the former was aimed at 'common right or interest' and involved 'the empire of laws and not of men', whereas in the latter 'some man, or some men, subject a city or a nation, and rule it according unto his or their private interest' which could be described as 'the empire of men and not of laws'.[62] Since Harrington's aim in *Oceana* was the reintroduction of ancient prudence in the modern world, it is not surprising that his own constitution also took the form of a mixed system: 'the commonwealth consisteth of the senate proposing, the people resolving, and the magistracy executing, whereby partaking of the aristocracy as in the senate, of the democracy as in the people, and of the monarchy as in the magistracy'.[63] Within such a system each element would perform a task appropriate to it. The careful constitutional design would ensure that the self-interested behaviour of each of the individual parts would result in a virtuous whole. In his 1659 pamphlet *A Discourse Upon this Saying*, Harrington offered a striking illustration of how such a system might work:

> [A]t *Rome* I saw one, which represented a kitchen, with all the proper Utensils in Use and Action. The cooks were all Cats and Kitlings, set in such frames, so ty'd and so ordered, that the poor Creatures could make no Motion to get loose, but the same caused one to turn the Spit, another to baste the Meat, a third to scim the Pot and a fourth to make Green-Sauce. If the Frame of your Commonwealth be not such, as causeth every one to perform his certain Function as necessarily as did the Cat to make Green-sauce, it is not right.[64]

That the commonwealthmen saw Britain's mixed constitution in this light is reflected in the fact that they described it in Harringtonian terms. As Molesworth explained in *The Principles of a Real Whig*: 'Our constitution is a government of *laws*, not of *persons*.'[65] For them, as for Harrington, the construction of a carefully mixed system, and the maintenance of a proper balance between the different elements, could serve to create virtuous behaviour out of self-interested action. Hence, the commonwealthmen tended to express their concerns about corruption in terms of threats to the balanced constitution rather than of lapses of virtue. As Gordon explained in the Preface to *Cato's Letters*:

> The same Principles of Nature and Reason that supported Liberty at *Rome*, must support it here and every where, however the Circumstances of adjusting them may vary in different Places; as the Foundations of Tyranny are in all Countries, and at all Times, essentially the same; namely, too much Force in the Hands of one Man, or of a few unaccountable Magistrates, and Power without a Balance: A sorrowful Circumstance for any People to fall into.[66]

Most of the issues discussed by the commonwealthmen in their pamphlets can be understood in these terms. Most obviously, the Harringtonian influence explains their obsession with the encroachment of the executive over the legislature through the use of places and pensions.[67] In his pamphlet *The Danger of Mercenary Parliaments* Toland condemned the filling of parliament with those who owed their places to the court precisely in terms of the threat it posed to the balanced constitution, asking: 'Whether a Parliament can be a true Balance where all the Weight lies only in one Scale?'[68]

The commonwealth concern with balance also explains their attitude toward the Church. Just as the powers wielded by the monarch and those held by each of the legislative assemblies needed to be kept within very clear and specific bounds in order that they did not encroach on each other, so the powers of the Church were also to be carefully limited. The authority of the Church lay in the spiritual realm. The maintenance of a proper balance required that it did not extend its powers beyond this jurisdiction. This was why the commonwealthmen were so critical of the growth of the political power of the Church over the centuries, and insisted that the clergy should be stripped of their political functions and that the Church should be entirely subordinated to the State.[69] Subordinating the Church to the State also meant that religion could itself be used to induce people to behave virtuously out of a concern for their own self-interest. In his *Essay Upon the Constitution of the Roman Government*, Moyle showed how the civil religion introduced by Romulus and perfected by Numa had been designed to fulfil this end. He and others, including Shaftesbury and Toland, hoped that the Church of England could be reformed to produce a similar effect.[70] In this argument they referred, directly or indirectly, to Harrington and his notion of a civil religion.[71]

The Standing Army Controversy of the 1690s can also be viewed in this light. In seeking to maintain the standing army after the signing of the Peace of Ryswick in 1697, William III was disturbing the balance of power, not only by extending his own powers in a way that was reminiscent of absolute monarchs, but also in denying the citizen body one of their rightful roles within the constitution – that of participating in the citizen militia. Harrington had, of course, included a citizen militia as the main military force in *Oceana*; and it is easy to see how it could work to check self-interested behaviour, just as Harrington's bicameral legislature was supposed to do. If the monarch had to rely on a citizen army then he/she would automatically be constrained to engage only in conflicts that were in the interests of the common good. If he/she failed to do so, he/she ran the risk that the soldiers would mutiny. In their 1697 contribution to the standing army debate Moyle and Trenchard explained that the armed force of the nation ought to be made up of the same elements as its government so that it would be more or less 'impossible' for the army 'to act to the disadvantage of the Constitution, unless we could suppose them to be Felons *de se*'.[72] The same view was expressed in Toland's pamphlet *The Militia Reform'd*. In justifying the idea that the freemen ought to form the armed force of the nation he said: 'That the latter can never be dangerous to our Liberty and Property at home, and will be infinitely more effectual against an Enemy attacking or invaded by us, I am now going to prove'.[73]

Just as a citizen militia could be used to check and control military power, so the commonwealthmen advocated various measures by which those citizens who did not hold political office were able to maintain control over those who did. These included frequent elections and short terms of office,[74] but also the liberty of the press (so that abuses of power could be publicly exposed) and the encouragement of a spirit of vigilance among the population.[75] Even when not actually exercising political power themselves, the ordinary citizens were expected to watch over their rulers and to take action if they believed liberty to be under threat. Gordon, writing in *Cato's Letters*, explained the role that the spirit of vigilance (or as he described it the 'Spirit of Jealousy and Revenge') would play:

> To this Spirit of Jealousy and Revenge, was formerly the *Roman* Commonwealth beholden for the long Preservation of its Liberty; the *Venetian* Commonwealth owes its Preservation to the same Spirit; and Liberty will never subsist long where this Spirit is not: For if any Crimes against the Publick may be committed with Impunity, Men will be tempted to commit the greatest of all; I mean, that of making themselves Masters of the State; and where Liberty ends in Servitude, it is owing to this Neglect.[76]

Ultimately, the citizens had the right to overthrow the government if they believed it was behaving tyrannically. On this issue the commonwealthmen were drawing on writers such as Milton and Sidney rather than Harrington, who rejected resistance theory.[77] The events of 1688–89 were an example of this 'right of revolution' being exercised, and though the commonwealthmen were cautious about suggesting that it might actually be used again, they certainly hoped that the threat of revolution would serve to keep the government in check.[78]

Despite their evident debt to Harrington, there was, of course, one crucial respect in which the mixed constitution of the commonwealthmen differed from that of Harrington. Despite his terminology, Harrington had been clear that the monarchical element within the mixed constitution should not be fulfilled by a king or queen, and made explicit his view that kingless government was not only best for England in the 1650s, but also that it was objectively superior. The commonwealthmen, by contrast, set their mixed constitution firmly within a monarchical context in which the monarchical role would be played by an actual king or queen and the aristocratic element by the House of Lords. This move away from Harrington was made explicit in the publisher's preface to Neville's *Plato Redivivus*:

> *Oceana* was written (it being thought Lawful so to do in those times) to evince out of these Principles, that *England* was not capable of any other *Government* than a *Democracy*. And this Author out of the same Maxims, or Aphorisms of Politicks, endeavours to prove that they may be applied naturally and fitly, to the redressing and supporting one of the best *Monarchies in the World*, which is that of *England*.[79]

To support their argument the commonwealthmen appealed to the 'gothic' liberty of England's Saxon invaders and to the mixed constitution that they had established. As Molesworth explained:

> My notion of a *Whig*, I mean of a real *Whig* (for the nominal are worse than any sort of men) is, that he is one who is exactly for keeping up to the strictness of the true old *Gothic constitution*, under the *three estates* of *king* (or *queen*) *lords* and *commons*; the *legislature* being seated in all three together, the *executive* entrusted with the first, but accountable to the whole body of the people, in case of mal-administration.[80]

This was, of course, in marked opposition to Harrington's stance – for him, the invasion of the Saxons marked the beginning of the rise of modern prudence. However, though he blamed them for introducing monarchical government, he did acknowledge that under them: 'the lower sort of the people had right unto session in parliament'.[81] Moreover, his main criticisms of the gothic monarchy were directed against the post-Conquest regime not that of the Saxons.[82]

The repositioning of Harrington's mixed constitution within a monarchical context, and the associated appeal to 'gothic liberty', was originally made in the aftermath of the Restoration, but it was given new force with the Glorious Revolution of 1688–89.[83] For many of the commonwealthmen the 1689 settlement marked a return to the original gothic balance, after it had been upset by the tyranny of the Stuarts.[84] William III had been chosen by the representatives of the people, and his powers were to be carefully constrained. Toland's optimistic sense of the place of liberty within the new system was reflected, as Justin Champion has noted, in the frontispiece to his edition of Harrington's works. There, the figure of liberty takes centre stage between two portraits – one of Junius Brutus and one of William III. Moreover, Champion has suggested that this 'marriage of republican hero and regal authority' reflected 'the editorial ambitions of the entire volume'.[85]

Conclusion

It is clear that the commonwealthmen were much more closely in line with the seventeenth-century republican tradition than their rejection of kingless government would initially suggest. They may not have been republicans according to the narrow constitutional definition of the term, but they did continue to endorse many of the underlying values of their republican forebears. In their emphasis on the concept of liberty and their concern with both civil and religious freedoms, they were following directly in the earlier tradition. Moreover, it was the shared emphasis on liberty of conscience that allowed Toland and his associates to smooth over some of the other ways in which their own religious views differed from those of the mid-seventeenth-century writers. Similarly, although their assertion that what was essential was virtuous behaviour (rather than actual virtue) – and their associated conviction that it could be achieved by material and constitutional means – marked a break with the republican tradition more generally, it was a break that had already been made by Harrington.

The commonwealthmen were not concerned with creating an ideal state.[86] Nor were they advocating a return to the small city-state republics of antiquity. Rather their main concern was to ensure that liberty was protected and maintained within the circumstances of the late seventeenth and early eighteenth centuries. This meant incorporating republican elements within a monarchical framework and within the context of a large nation state. It also meant taking seriously the tendency of human beings to act on the basis of their passions and private interests rather than according to reason and in the interests of the common good – and finding means for using the passions and interests of individuals to encourage virtuous behaviour.

The real achievement of the commonwealthmen was to bring the works and ideas of the mid-seventeenth-century republicans to the attention of a new generation and to render their ideas applicable in the very different circumstances of eighteenth-century Britain. Yet this was not all they achieved; for, though it has been little noted by historians, they were also instrumental in bringing those same ideas to the attention of a European audience. Exploring how this happened will be the main focus of the remaining chapters of this book.

Notes

1 C. A. Robbins, *The Eighteenth-Century Commonwealthman: Studies in the Transmission, Development, and Circumstance of English Liberal Thought from the Restoration of Charles II until the War with the Thirteen Colonies* (Indianapolis: Liberty Fund, 2004 [1987, 1959]).
2 R. Molesworth, *The Principles of a Real Whig; contained in a preface to the famous Hotoman's Franco-Gallia, written by the late Lord-Viscount Molesworth; and now reprinted at the request of the London Association* (London: J. Williams, 1775), p. 5. On the uses of the term 'commonwealth' in early modern England see J. Scott, 'What Were Commonwealth Principles?', *Historical Journal* 47 (2004), pp. 591–2.
3 J. Trenchard and T. Gordon, *Cato's Letters; or Essays on Liberty, Civil and Religious, and other Important Subjects*, 3rd edn (London: W. Wilkins, 1733), I, p. lv.
4 Though they differ in other respects, both Quentin Skinner and Blair Worden hold this position. See B. Worden, 'Republicanism, Regicide and Republic: The English Experience' in M. Van Gelderen and Q. Skinner (eds), *Republicanism: A Shared European Heritage* (Cambridge: Cambridge University Press, 2002), 1, pp. 307–27 and Q. Skinner, *Liberty Before Liberalism* (Cambridge: Cambridge University Press, 1998).
5 Molesworth, *Principles of a Real Whig*, pp. 5–7. It should be noted that Molesworth's critique of the actual commonwealth of the mid-seventeenth century was not inconsistent with a reverence for the republican works produced at the time – since some of them were themselves critical of the existing system.
6 Trenchard and Gordon, *Cato's Letters*, II, p. 28.
7 Since it was dealt with comprehensively by Robbins I do not intend to devote space here to a discussion of who the commonwealthmen were or the personal connections between them. Suffice to say that the focus here will be on Robbins's first generation of commonwealthmen, the Real Whigs. Central among this group (most of whom were acquainted with each other) were Sir Robert Molesworth, Anthony Ashley Cooper – the third Earl of Shaftesbury, John Toland, Walter Moyle, John Trenchard and Thomas Gordon.
8 Robbins, *Eighteenth-Century Commonwealthman*, pp. 372–3.
9 J. G. A. Pocock, *The Machiavellian Moment: Florentine Political Thought and the Atlantic Republican Tradition* (Princeton: Princeton University Press, 1975), Part Three.
10 Molesworth, *Principles of a Real Whig*, p. 5.
11 T. Gordon, *The Works of Tacitus With Political Discourses Upon That Author*, 3rd edn (London, 1753), 5, p. 9. For similar claims see Trenchard and Gordon, *Cato's Letters*, I, pp. x, xix, xxvi.
12 See Skinner, *Liberty Before Liberalism*.
13 In his discourses on Tacitus, Gordon made much of the distinction between princes who rule according to the laws and those who do not. See in particular Gordon, *Works of Tacitus*, IV, pp. 227–34 and 241–8.
14 Of course, the extent of citizen involvement in legislation required by the commonwealthmen was much more limited than that which would have been expected by many neo-Roman theorists.
15 [W. Moyle and J. Trenchard], *An Argument, Shewing, that a Standing Army is inconsistent with A Free Government, and absolutely destructive to the Constitution of the English Monarchy* (London, 1697), p. 2.
16 [J. Toland], *The Danger of Mercenary Parliaments* (London, 1722), p. v. The work had originally been published, with the support of Shaftesbury, in 1695.
17 To illustrate this Gordon pointed out that even the worst of the Roman Emperors had begun their reigns well. Gordon, *Works of Tacitus*, IV, pp. 193–4.
18 See in particular B. Worden, *Roundhead Reputations: The English Civil Wars and the Passions of Posterity* (London: Allen Lane, 2001), p. 13 and J. G. A. Pocock, 'Machiavelli, Harrington and English Political Ideologies in the Eighteenth Century', *William and Mary Quarterly*, 3rd ser., 22 (1965), pp. 549–83.
19 For more discussion of this see the section 'Virtue, passion and self-interest' later in this chapter.

20 Robbins did acknowledge the prevalence of dissenters among the commonwealthmen and noted their emphasis on religious liberty and toleration. However, she devoted less space to analysing their religious than their political ideas. The role of religion is also underplayed in Pocock's account in *The Machiavellian Moment*.
21 J. Scott, *England's Troubles: Seventeenth-Century English Political Instability in European Context* (Cambridge: Cambridge University Press, 2000); J. Scott, *Commonwealth Principles: Republican Writings of the English Revolution* (Cambridge: Cambridge University Press, 2004); Scott, 'What Were Commonwealth Principles?', especially pp. 594–6; J. A. I. Champion, *The Pillars of Priestcraft Shaken* (Cambridge: Cambridge University Press, 1992); J. Champion, *Republican Learning: John Toland and the Crisis of Christian Culture, 1696–1722* (Manchester: Manchester University Press, 2003); and J. Champion, '*Some Forms of Religious Liberty*: Political Thinking, Ecclesiology and Freedom in Early Modern England', unpublished paper 2008. I am grateful to Justin Champion for providing me with a copy of this paper.
22 A. A. Cooper, third Earl of Shaftesbury, *A Letter Concerning Enthusiasm, to My Lord* ***** (1708), in *Characteristicks of Men, Manners, Opinions, Times*, 4th edn (London, 1727), I, pp. 3–55. On Toland's many religious writings see Champion, *Republican Learning*, especially Part III. A. Collins, *A Discourse of Freethinking* (London, 1713). The religious writings of Trenchard and Gordon included not just the journal *The Independent Whig*, but also a number of pamphlets. J. Trenchard, *A Natural History of Superstition* (London, 1709); T. Gordon, *An Apology for the Danger of the Church* (London, 1719); *Priestianity: or a view of the disparity between the Apostles and the modern inferior clergy* (London, 1720); *The Creed of an Independent Whig* (London, 1720). These pamphlets were presumably of more than just ephemeral interest, since Richard Baron published a three-volume collection of those written by Gordon, under the title *A Cordial for Low Spirits*, in 1763.
23 B. Worden, 'Introduction' to E. Ludlow, *A Voyce from the Watch Tower, V: 1660–1662* (London: Royal Historical Society, 1978), pp. 1–80; B. Worden, 'Whig history and Puritan Politics: the *Memoirs* of Edmund Ludlow revisited', *Historical Research*, 75 (2002), pp. 209–37 and Worden, *Roundhead Reputations*.
24 And even of earlier Machiavellian ideas. On this see P. A. Rahe, *Against Throne and Altar: Machiavelli and Political Theory under the English Republic* (Cambridge: Cambridge University Press, 2008).
25 [J. Milton] *The Readie and Easie Way to establish a free commonwealth; and the excellence thereof compar'd with the inconveniencies and dangers of admitting Kingship in this Nation*, 2nd edn (London: Printed for the Author, 1660), p. 87. For a convincing account of Milton's unorthodox religious views see Rahe, *Against Throne and Altar*, pp. 139–74.
26 J. Harrington, *A System of Politics*, in, *The Commonwealth of Oceana and A System of Politics*, ed. J. G. A. Pocock (Cambridge: Cambridge University Press, 1992), p. 282.
27 [Gordon] *Priestianity*, p. xiv.
28 For a detailed consideration of the concept of toleration during this period see J. Marshall, *John Locke, Toleration and Early Enlightenment Culture* (Cambridge: Cambridge University Press, 2006).
29 Molesworth, *Principles of a Real Whig*, p. 9. Catholics were not to be tolerated, but the reasons for this were political rather than religious. In *Nazarenus* Toland also argued in favour of toleration for Jews and Muslims on the grounds that they, together with Christians, were all part of a single religious tradition. J. Toland, *Nazarenus: or Jewish, Gentile, and Mahometan Christianity*, 2nd edn (London, 1718), pp. 5, 30, 40 and 61.
30 J. Trenchard and T. Gordon, *The Independent Whig: or, a defence of primitive Christianity, and of our ecclesiastical establishment…* 6th edn (London, 1732), p. 52. Similarly, in the Preface to the third edition of *Cato's Letters* Gordon claimed that Trenchard 'saw "Enemies to Liberty of Conscience" as "Enemies to human Society"'. Trenchard and Gordon, *Cato's Letters*, I, p. li. Shaftesbury's support for toleration was expressed in Cooper, *A Letter Concerning Enthusiasm*, p. 17.
31 For a detailed discussion of the religious positions of the seventeenth-century English republicans see Scott, *Commonwealth Principles*, pp. 41–62. Rahe has argued that Milton also adopted

a strongly anticlerical position and has presented Nedham as an Erastian. Rahe, *Against Throne and Altar*, pp. 139–74 and pp. 185 and 209–10.
32 Toland, *Nazarenus*; Trenchard and Gordon, *Independent Whig*.
33 See Trenchard's *Natural History of Superstition*; J. Toland, *Letters to Serena* (London, 1704), Letter 1 and Toland, *Nazarenus*, p. xv.
34 Trenchard and Gordon, *Independent Whig*, p. 43. See also p. 102.
35 W. Moyle, *An Essay Upon the Constitution of the Roman Government*, in *The Works of Walter Moyle Esq* (London: Darby &c., 1726), p. 50. See also p. 25. The same argument is also made in R. Molesworth, *An Account of Denmark, as it was in the year 1692*, 5th edn (Glasgow: R. Urie and Company, 1745), p. xx and in Toland, *Nazarenus*, p. xvi.
36 This is particularly a feature of the work of Jonathan Scott. See especially J. Scott, 'Classical Republicanism in Seventeenth-century England and the Netherlands', in Van Gelderen and Skinner (eds), *Republicanism*, 1, pp. 61–81 and Scott, *Commonwealth Principles*, pp. 170–90.
37 Trenchard and Gordon, *Cato's Letters*, especially I, pp. 14, 25.
38 Gordon, *The Works of Tacitus*, V, p. 10.
39 For a detailed account of Machiavelli's distinctive take on virtue and its impact on his republicanism see Rahe, *Against Throne and Altar*, especially pp. 19–55 and his earlier work P. A. Rahe, *Republics Ancient and Modern: Classical Republicanism and the American Revolution* (Chapel Hill, NC: University of North Carolina Press, 1992). See also V. B. Sullivan, *Machiavelli, Hobbes, and the Formation of a Liberal Republicanism in England* (Cambridge: Cambridge University Press, 2004), especially pp. 31–79.
40 P. Force, *Self-Interest Before Adam Smith: A Genealogy of Economic Science* (Cambridge: Cambridge University Press, 2003). See also A. O. Hirschman, *The Passions and the Interests: Political Arguments for Capitalism Before its Triumph* (Princeton: Princeton University Press, 1977), pp. 9–68.
41 In fact, Vickie Sullivan has offered a different interpretation of Sidney, suggesting that in the *Discourses* he actually moves away from Aristotle's emphasis on the cultivation of reason and toward a more Machiavellian focus on the passions. Sullivan, *Machiavelli, Hobbes*, especially pp. 199–226.
42 Scott, *Commonwealth Principles*, p. 177–8; Rahe, *Against Throne and Altar*, pp. 183–4 and 235–7. Similarly Vickie Sullivan has emphasised Nedham's concern with individual rights and liberties and his belief that the passions are the driving force behind human behaviour. Sullivan, *Machiavelli, Hobbes*, especially pp. 113–43.
43 Scott, 'Classical Republicanism', especially pp. 68–71.
44 My interpretation of this aspect of Harrington's thought is similar to that offered by Scott in *Commonwealth Principles*, pp. 181–4. For Pocock's response to this kind of interpretation of Harrington, see Pocock, 'Afterword', in *Machiavellian Moment*, pp. 567–8.
45 For the direct link back to Machiavelli's innovation of separating *virtù* from morality see Rahe, *Against Throne and Altar*, especially pp. 324–8. The most detailed account of Harrington's debt to Hobbes is A. Fukuda, *Sovereignty and the Sword: Harrington, Hobbes and Mixed Government in the English Civil Wars* (Oxford: Oxford University Press, 1997). See also Rahe, *Against Throne and Altar*, pp. 321–46 and Sullivan, *Machiavelli, Hobbes*, pp. 165–73.
46 Eric Nelson pays particular attention to this aspect of Harrington's thought, and its subsequent influence, in E. Nelson, *The Greek Tradition in Republican Thought* (Cambridge: Cambridge University Press, 2004).
47 Harrington, *Commonwealth of Oceana*, p. 22.
48 Ibid., p. 20. See also J. Harrington, *A Discourse Upon This Saying: The Spirit of the Nation is not yet to be trusted with Liberty; lest it introduce Monarchy, or invade the Liberty of Conscience*, in *The Oceana and Other Works of James Harrington*, ed. J. Toland (London, 1737), pp. 602–3.
49 H. Neville, *Plato Redivivus: Or, A Dialogue Concerning Government, Wherein by Observations drawn from other Kingdoms and States both Ancient and Modern, an Endeavour is Used to Discover the Present Politick Distemper of our own with the Causes, and Remedies*, 3rd edn, in *The Oceana of James Harrington, Esq; and his other works* ... (Dublin, 1737), pp. 572–3. Much of the second day's discussion in *Plato Redivivus* is taken up with the argument that the balance of property

determines political power, and the recent decay of the English constitution is also explained in these terms.
50 Moyle, *Constitution of the Roman Government*, pp. 71–3.
51 'A free People are kept so, by no other Means than an equal Distribution of Property; every Man, who has a Share of Property, having a proportionable Share of Power; and the first Seeds of Anarchy (which, for the most part, ends in Tyranny) are produced from hence, that some are ungovernably rich, and many more are miserably poor; that is, some are Masters of all Means of Oppression, and others want all the Means of Self-defence.' Trenchard and Gordon, *Cato's Letters*, I, p. 11. According to Gordon, who wrote this issue, the collapse of the South Sea Bubble posed a threat to liberty in England because it had drained money from the people.
52 It must be noted that this view was not shared by all commonwealthmen. The third Earl of Shaftesbury, for example continued to believe in the possibility of reason and virtue. Nonetheless he too endorsed the notion of balance as essential in order for reason to prevail. Shaftesbury in Cooper, *Letter Concerning Enthusiasm*, p. 18. For Shaftesbury's views on virtue see: M. B. Gill, 'Shaftesbury's Two Accounts of the Reason to Be Virtuous', *Journal of the History of Philosophy* 38 (2000), pp. 529–48.
53 Trenchard and Gordon, *Cato's Letters*, II, p. 54. See also Gordon's account of Trenchard's awareness of the frailties of human nature in the preface to the 3rd edn, I, pp. xxxiv–xlii and pp. 25–7. Vickie Sullivan has also emphasised this aspect of *Cato's Letters*, though her interpretation is somewhat different from mine. Sullivan, *Machiavelli, Hobbes*, esp. pp. 227–57. Even Neville acknowledged that 'passion' is 'as natural to man as reason and virtue'. Neville, *Plato Redivivus*, p. 590.
54 Trenchard and Gordon, *Cato's Letters*, I, p. 239.
55 Gordon, *Works of Tacitus*, IV, pp. 193 and 239–40; [Toland], *Danger of Mercenary Parliaments*, pp. 10–11.
56 Trenchard and Gordon, *Cato's Letters*, II, pp. 47–8. See also issues 38, 39, 40, 43, and 44 more generally.
57 Gordon certainly saw the ultimate aim as being happiness rather than virtue. See for example Gordon, *Works of Tacitus*, IV, p. 247. Similarly, in *Cato's Letters* Gordon was explicitly critical of the neo-Stoic position. Trenchard and Gordon, *Cato's Letters*, II, pp. 44–5. See also Hirschman, *Passions and Interests*; Force, *Self-Interest Before Adam Smith*.
58 According to John Robertson, neo-Epicureanism as developed by Pierre Bayle and others was central to the development of Enlightenment ideas. Thus the commonwealthmen might also be understood as adapting classical republican ideas in line with Enlightenment views. J. Robertson, *The Case for the Enlightenment: Scotland and Naples, 1680–1760* (Cambridge: Cambridge University Press, 2005).
59 See for example Toland's Appendix to his *Nazarenus*, p. 7.
60 Though it should be noted that Scott has downplayed its significance within English republicanism, presenting Harrington as exceptional in this respect. Scott, 'Classical Republicanism' and Scott, *Commonwealth Principles*, pp. 131–50.
61 The case for the mixed constitution was also made by Cicero in his *De Republica*. Cicero, *De Republica*, trans. C. Walker Keyes (Cambridge, MA and London: Harvard University Press and William Heinemann, 1977), Book 1. The mixed constitution is, of course, central to the accounts of the republican tradition offered by both Fink and Pocock. Z. S. Fink, *The Classical Republicans: An Essay in the Recovery of a Pattern of Thought in Seventeenth-Century England* (Evanston, IL: Northwestern University Press, 1945); Pocock, *Machiavellian Moment*.
62 Harrington, *Oceana*, pp. 8–9.
63 Ibid., p. 25.
64 Harrington, *Discourse*, p. 608.
65 Molesworth, *Principles of a Real Whig*, p. 8.
66 Trenchard and Gordon, *Cato's Letters*, I, p. xxviii. See also [Moyle and Trenchard], *An Argument*, pp. 3–4.
67 Molesworth, *Principles of a Real Whig*, p. 12.

68 [Toland], *Danger of Mercenary Parliaments*, p. 4.
69 Moyle, *Essay*, pp. 18, 35–7; Trenchard and Gordon, *Cato's Letters*, p. lii; Trenchard and Gordon, *Independent Whig*.
70 Moyle, *Essay*, p. 17. Toland, *Nazarenus*, p. xiv. See also Champion, *Pillars of Priestcraft*, p. 191.
71 Shaftesbury referred directly to Harrington in Cooper, *A Letter Concerning Enthusiasm*, p. 17. On Harrington's civil religion see M. A. Goldie, 'The Civil Religion of James Harrington', in A. Pagden (ed.), *Languages of Political Theory in Early Modern Europe* (Cambridge: Cambridge University Press, 1987), pp. 197–224 and Champion, *Pillars of Priestcraft*, especially pp. 170–95.
72 [Moyle and Trenchard], *An Argument*, p. 4.
73 J. Toland, *The Militia Reform'd; or an easy scheme of furnishing England with a constant land force, capable to prevent or to subdue any forein Power; and to maintain perpetual Quiet at Home, without endangering the Publick Liberty* (London: John Darby, 1698), p. 17.
74 On frequent elections see Neville, *Plato Redivivus*, p. 636; Molesworth, *Principles of a Real Whig*, p. 12; [Toland], *Danger of Mercenary Parliaments*, pp. v–vi.
75 The liberty of the press is presented in these terms by Trenchard and Gordon in *Cato's Letters*. The need for a 'spirit of vigilance' among the population was also emphasised by Nedham and Sidney, who in turn were drawing upon Machiavelli. See Scott, *Commonwealth Principles*.
76 Trenchard and Gordon, *Cato's Letters*, I, p. 7. It is important to note that this spirit of vigilance was inspired not by virtue, but by self-interest.
77 Scott, *Commonwealth Principles*, p. 110.
78 Gordon invoked this idea in his account of Caesar. Gordon, *Works of Tacitus*, IV, p. 196. See also, pp. 221 and 247–8: 'To conclude, if Princes would never encroach, Subjects would hardly ever rebel; and if the former knew that they would be resisted, they would not encroach.'
79 Neville, *Plato Redivivus*, p. 551.
80 Molesworth, *Principles of a Real Whig*, p. 6. The same ideas are also present in Molesworth, *Account of Denmark*, pp. xvi–xviii and 30. Indeed, the purpose of this work was to demonstrate how Denmark had been transformed from a free state on this model to an absolutist monarchy. It was also for this reason that Molesworth chose to translate Hotman's *Franco-Gallia*.
81 Harrington, *Oceana*, p. 50.
82 Ibid., pp. 52ff. Significantly, in his account of the gothic monarchy in *Plato Redivivus*, Neville described the original system as well balanced and suggested that corruption only arose after the Norman Conquest. Neville, *Plato Redivivus*, pp. 581ff.
83 Pocock, of course, makes much of this transformation. See Pocock, 'Machiavelli, Harrington' and Pocock, *Machiavellian Moment*, especially pp. 401–22.
84 Molesworth, *Principles of a Real Whig*, p. 7.
85 Champion, *Republican Learning*, p. 106.
86 As the English Gentleman declared at the end of Neville's *Plato Redivivus*, 'If you ask me whether I could have offer'd any thing that I thought better than this, I will answer you as *Solon* did a Philosopher, who askt him whether he could not have made a better Government for *Athens*? Yes, but that his was the best, that the People would or could receive.' In this respect too they were continuing the attitude of the seventeenth-century English republicans, who were also concerned with practical possibilities. It was simply the case that what was practically possible in 1656 was rather different from what was practically possible in the aftermath of 1660.

2
The Huguenot connection

Introduction

The commonwealth tradition that was presented in Caroline Robbins's pioneering account was resolutely British.[1] Among its main protagonists were natives of each of the four component nations (England, Wales, Scotland and Ireland) and in *The Eighteenth-Century Commonwealthman* she even devoted an entire chapter each to the Irish and Scottish contributions. The concerns of Robbins's commonwealthmen were predominantly British too, from securing a Protestant succession to removing placemen and pensioners from the House of Commons. Robbins did, of course, acknowledge that those commonwealth ideas had gone on to exercise an important influence upon the revolutionary generation in America (a fact that has been explored in detail by others) but even here the story remained an exclusively anglophone one.[2]

Yet, on closer scrutiny, even Robbins's first generation of commonwealthmen appear to have been a far more cosmopolitan group than either her account, or those of many subsequent scholars, would suggest.[3] These Real Whigs regularly travelled abroad, they were well acquainted with international affairs and they built up and maintained friendships and associations with foreigners. In particular they enjoyed close connections with French Huguenots, who had fled into exile following Louis XIV's revocation of the Edict of Nantes on 22 October 1685. Of the 200,000 refugees who left France, the majority fled to the Dutch Republic – which was renowned for its policy of religious toleration – or to Protestant England.[4] Though there was much debate and disagreement within the European Huguenot community over issues such as the right of resistance and the legitimacy of absolutist rule, the Huguenot associates of the Real Whigs had their own reasons for supporting civil and religious liberty against absolutism and Catholicism. As members of a huge francophone diaspora, they were also ideally placed to facilitate the exchange and dissemination of ideas across Europe and beyond. This chapter will focus on the small group of Huguenot exiles who, in alliance with the Real Whigs, played a crucial role in bringing English republican and commonwealth works to the attention of the French-speaking world.

The Real Whigs and Europe

English republicans had always had close links with continental Europe. Not only had many travelled in Europe during their youth, but several, including Ludlow and Sidney, fled into exile and lived there for many years. Moreover, some of their works were directly shaped by European events and debates. Milton's *Pro populo anglicano defensio* was written in response to the pamphlet *Defensio regia* by one of Europe's leading Protestant scholars, the Frenchman Claude Saumaise (Claudius Salmasius). Milton wrote his work in Latin precisely so that it would be accessible to a European audience and, according to Joseph Dedieu, copies were burned in both Paris and Toulouse, which only served to increase French interest in the work.[5] In addition, another of Milton's works, *Eikonoklastes*, was translated into French in 1652.[6] Similarly, Sidney's *Court Maxims* was written during his stay in the Netherlands. It was addressed to the Dutch republican leader Johan De Witt, with the intention of securing his backing for an English republican insurrection.[7] Moreover English republicans, including Milton and Sidney, were profoundly influenced by the French monarchomach theorists of the sixteenth century, and during the 1650s parallels and connections were drawn with the Fronde in France.[8]

The Real Whigs maintained and built on these links. They were remarkably cosmopolitan in both their associations and their outlook. They frequently travelled on the Continent and were closely associated with foreigners – particularly Dutch radicals and French Huguenots. For example, Anthony Ashley Cooper, later the third Earl of Shaftesbury, was in Holland in 1698–99 and again in 1703–4. His associates there included the English Quaker Benjamin Furly, but also Dutch figures such as John Van Twedde and Huguenots including Pierre Bayle. Shaftesbury also offered protection and financial support to Huguenots based in London – not least the influential biographer and journalist Pierre Desmaizeaux.[9] Similarly, Shaftesbury's friend and protégé John Toland had studied at Leiden University, and made several trips to the continent in the early eighteenth century. He too had close connections with both Dutch and French figures, and spoke fluent French.[10] Toland's friend Anthony Collins also spoke French and, once again, he made regular visits to the continent and kept up correspondence with a number of foreign friends.[11] Like Shaftesbury, Toland and Collins were both closely associated with Desmaizeaux and they were also involved with the *Chevaliers de la Jubilation*, an organisation that was itself cosmopolitan.[12]

Given these associations, it is perhaps not surprising that the Real Whigs appear to have been almost as concerned about continental issues as they were about British ones. Securing civil and religious liberty in Britain was undoubtedly important to them, but they were equally concerned with securing a Protestant alliance in Europe that would curb the expansionist policies of Louis XIV. Following the signing of the Treaty of Ryswick in September 1697, there was a brief cessation of hostilities between Britain and France. Yet, far from welcoming the peace, Anthony Ashley Cooper (who was consistently anti-French throughout his life) campaigned for a renewal of war.[13] The Real Whigs were also closely associated with Prince Eugene of Savoy and Baron Hohendorf, and followed the former's anti-French military campaigns with interest.[14] Moreover, to the Real Whigs these were not separate issues, but all part of a single Protestant and anti-absolutist concern. For these reasons, I suggest that the Real Whigs of the late seventeenth and early eighteenth centuries were not simply reviving England's 'Good Old Cause' and manipulating it to fit their own circumstances and concerns, as Robbins suggested, they were also expanding that cause and applying it not just to Britain but to Europe as a whole.

Practical political action – whether by influencing the decisions of the House of Lords as Shaftesbury attempted, or by gaining the ear of the rich and powerful as Toland did – was obviously one means of pursuing the cause, but the Real Whigs also recognised the importance of influencing public opinion and therefore of writing and publishing. This was reflected not just in their own extensive publications, but also in their campaign to republish a number of mid-seventeenth-century English republican works between 1697 and 1700.[15] As with their practical political campaigns, there appears to have been an important European dimension to their publishing projects. Not only did they produce works that looked to European examples and issues, but they were also keen to ensure that their works circulated on the continent as well as in Britain.[16] Consequently, they employed booksellers in Holland to publish their Latin works, they tried to ensure that their publications were reviewed in the francophone press, and they even had some of their works translated into French.[17] Their Huguenot friends and acquaintances were ideally placed to disseminate their works and ideas among French-speakers. Indeed, the French-language Huguenot journals that were in circulation at the turn of the century were one of the main vehicles for this dissemination.

Reviews in the Huguenot press

It was Pierre Bayle who popularised the idea of French-language Huguenot journals, with his establishment of *Nouvelles de la république des lettres* in 1684.[18]

The genre proved popular and Bayle's journal was soon joined by others, including Jean Le Clerc's *Bibliothèque universelle et historique* in 1686 and Henri Basnage de Beauval's *Histoire des ouvrages des savans* in 1687.[19] Bayle ceased editing his journal in 1687, but in 1699 it was revived under the editorship of Jacques Bernard.

Born in 1658, Bernard was a French Protestant minister who had been forced to flee France in 1683, having demonstrated against the destruction of his church by soldiers.[20] After spending some time at Geneva and Lausanne, Bernard settled in Holland where he made his living preaching and teaching. Bernard's first involvement with Huguenot journals came in 1691, when he was invited by Le Clerc to take over the editorship of the *Bibliothèque universelle et historique*. He edited *Nouvelles de la république des lettres* from 1699 until 1710 – and again between 1716 and his death two years later. As a journal editor, Bernard was very much at the heart of the European Huguenot network and was in touch with many of its members, including the bookseller Prosper Marchand and Desmaizeaux.[21]

Bernard appears to have had a particular interest in the works of the English republican tradition, and even claimed to have met Ludlow during his time at Lausanne.[22] Under his editorship *Nouvelles de la république des lettres* included lengthy, knowledgeable and largely favourable reviews, written by Bernard himself, of most of the works of the republican canon. His reviews of both Sidney's *Discourses Concerning Government* and Toland's edition of *Harrington's Oceana and Other Works* immediately followed their publication in England.[23] The former ran to eighty-two pages and had to be serialised over three issues.[24]

These same works were also reviewed in the other great Huguenot journal that was in print at the turn of the century, Basnage de Beauval's *Histoire des ouvrages des savans*.[25] Born into a distinguished Norman Protestant family in 1656, Basnage de Beauval moved to Holland in 1687.[26] Both he and his journal had a reputation for moderation and impartiality. Not surprisingly, therefore, the reviews of English republican works that appeared in *Histoire des ouvrages des savans* were shorter and less enthusiastic than those in Bernard's journal. Nonetheless, between 1698 and 1702 Basnage de Beauval reviewed Ludlow's *Memoirs*, Toland's edition of Milton's works and Sidney's *Discourses*, and in doing so he helped to make these works known to a francophone audience.[27]

J. H. Broome claimed that Desmaizeaux was close to both Bernard and Basnage de Beauval, and has suggested that he may have been responsible for much of the English material in both *Nouvelles de la république des lettres* and *Histoire des ouvrages des savans*.[28] However, while Desmaizeaux certainly drew Bernard's attention to Toland's edition of Harrington's works, the reviews of Ludlow and Sidney appeared before Bernard was in touch with Desmaizeaux.[29] Similarly, the reviews of English republican works in Basnage de Beauval's journal appeared before 1705, when Broome suggests Desmaizeaux may have become his English correspondent.

The reviews of English republican works continued to appear in Huguenot journals well into the eighteenth century. When an extended version of Toland's edition of Harrington's political works was published in 1737 it prompted a review in one of the main Huguenot journals of the time, the *Bibliothèque britannique*.[30] Milton's complete works were also reviewed there in 1740.[31] This journal was a collaborative effort involving the publisher Pierre, or Pieter, De Hondt, who was based at The Hague, together with Jacques Bernard's son Jean-Pierre, Desmaizeaux and other London-based Huguenots.[32] As its title suggests it was one of a number of eighteenth-century Huguenot journals that focused exclusively on English works. The works of early eighteenth-century commonwealthmen also caught the attention of Huguenot reviewers.[33] Perhaps prompted by the interest in English republican works and ideas evident in the French-language journals, several members of the Huguenot diaspora chose to translate certain of those works into French, so as to make them more accessible to a European audience.[34]

The Huguenot translations

Of the seventeenth-century English republican works, Ludlow's *Memoirs* was translated into French between 1699 and 1707 and Sidney's *Discourses* in 1702. Though the works of Milton and Harrington were not translated at this stage, they too continued to attract European – and particularly Huguenot – attention.[35] In addition to the reviews of the works of both men that appeared in Huguenot journals, both authors were included (together with Ludlow, Sidney, Moyle, Shaftesbury, Collins, Toland and Trenchard) in Jacques Georges de Chauffepié's continuation of Bayle's *Dictionnaire Historique et Critique*, which appeared from 1750.[36] Moreover, copies of *Harrington's Oceana and Other Works* were sent to the continent by Shaftesbury, and both Bernard and Benjamin Furly (the Rotterdam-based English Quaker) appear to have owned copies.[37] Moreover, a detailed account of Harrington's life and works, which was clearly based on Toland's edition, appeared in the *Encyclopédie* under the heading 'Rutland'.[38] Interestingly, it was the work of one of the most prolific contributors to the project, the Chevalier de Jaucourt – who was also of Huguenot descent. Works by the Real Whigs themselves were also translated into French. Between 1694 and 1759 works by Molesworth, Toland, Collins, Shaftesbury and Gordon all appeared. The translation, publication and distribution of many of these works were carried out by a small group of Huguenots, who were close friends and associates of the Real Whigs.

The translations of Sidney's *Discourses* (1702) and Shaftesbury's *Letter Concerning Enthusiasm* (1709) were the work of Pierre Auguste or Peter Augustus Samson.[39] Descended from a Protestant family who it is thought came originally from the Ile de Ré,[40] Samson was living in Holland, probably at The Hague, by the early eighteenth century and was apparently fluent in English and Flemish as well as French.[41] In addition to the works by Sidney and Shaftesbury, he was also responsible for the translation of Jonathan Swift's edition of the letters of Sir William Temple (1711) and was the author of a three-volume history of William III (1703–4).[42]

Significantly, Samson appears to have been a key figure within the Real Whig-Huguenot network. According to the correspondence between Bernard and Desmaizeaux, the former already knew of Samson in 1700.[43] By 1708 he was also known to Toland. P. Augustus Samson appears as the dedicatee of Toland's *Origines Judaicae*, which was published that year. This work attacked Christian understandings of Moses and the Israelites, and instead presented the Hebrew republic in civic humanist terms.[44] Toland began his dedication 'To the learned and honourable P. Augustus Samson, sends health, John Toland' and concluded it: 'Farewell, my dear Augustus, and continue that affection and esteem for me, which I have invariably felt for yourself.' He also noted that Samson had been convinced by his argument in *Adeisidaemon* of the political origins and purposes of religion.[45] Interestingly, *Adeisidaemon*, which was bound in with *Origines Judaicae*, was dedicated to Collins. The fact that the two works were bound together might suggest that Samson was a close acquaintance not just of Toland, but also of Collins.

Samson was also closely associated with another key figure within the Huguenot network: Charles Levier, who had a bookshop at The Hague.[46] In 1726 Samson, who was then working as a translator, secretary and secret agent for Horatio Walpole (the younger brother of Sir Robert), collaborated with Levier over the printing and distribution of a response to a work known as the 'Analyse', an analysis of the Treaty of Hanover.[47] It was a sensitive job, and Samson's belief that Levier was someone who could be trusted would suggest that they had known each other for some time. The friendship certainly continued long afterward, despite the fact that Samson settled in England in 1726.[48] Following Levier's death in 1734, Samson kept up his association with Levier's son, to whom he offered fatherly advice.[49] Both Samson and Levier were associated with Marchand, and Levier was also close to the Rotterdam booksellers Gaspard Fritsch and Michel Böhm, and to Collins.[50] In addition, Levier was a member of the *Chevaliers de la Jubilation*,[51] and was responsible for publishing the 1719 edition of the infamous *Traité des trois imposteurs*, having made a copy of it in Furly's library in 1711.[52] Moreover, the published catalogue of the works held in Levier's shop at the time of his death reveals that he was one of those who distributed the French translations of English republican works on the Continent. The list includes Ludlow's *Memoirs* and Sidney's *Discourses* as well as Toland's *Adeisidaemon/Origines Judaicae* and Samson's biography of William III.[53]

Levier was not the only bookseller involved in distributing these works. Another key figure was Thomas Johnson, an English bookseller based at The Hague, who was responsible for publishing a number of Toland's works as well as Samson's translation of Shaftesbury's *A Letter Concerning Enthusiasm*. In addition to these works, Johnson also stocked one of the French translations of Molesworth's *An Account of Denmark*, the translation of Ludlow's *Memoirs*, Samson's translation of Sidney's *Discourses* and his history of the life of William III.[54] Johnson was a correspondent of Levier and, like him, was associated with other members of the Real Whig-Huguenot network. According to Margaret Jacob, he was involved with the *Chevaliers de la Jubilation*, publishing the *Journal littéraire*, which she associates with the group, from 1713 until 1722.[55] He has also been implicated as a co-editor alongside Levier of the *Traité des trois imposteurs*.[56] It was another bookseller, the Huguenot Paul Marret, who was the translator of Ludlow's *Memoirs*.[57] Marret had a shop in Beurs-straat in Amsterdam. Beyond this little is known about him, or about the translation, though after his death his widow published Michel de la Roche's B*ibliothèque angloise*.[58]

Another member of the Real Whig-Huguenot network who produced important translations of English works was Jean Rousset de Missy.[59] Born into a French Protestant family in 1686, he had fled France and settled at The Hague in 1704, later moving to Amsterdam. Throughout his life he remained a staunch opponent of French absolutism and an admirer of the British political system. He collaborated with Levier over the 1719 publication of the *Traité des trois imposteurs*, and was also associated with Marchand, Toland and Collins. In 1706 he published a translation of Collins's *A Discourse of Free Thinking* together with Toland's *A Letter from an Arabian Physician*.[60] Most significantly, in 1755 Rousset de Missy published a French translation of John Locke's *Two Treatises of Government*.[61] As Margaret Jacob has demonstrated, this edition was composed in the light of Dutch politics of the mid-eighteenth century, and in particular the failure of the Dutch Revolution of 1747 (in which Rousset de Missy had been a leading figure). It was based on the 1691 translation, generally attributed to the Huguenot David Mazel, but Rousset de Missy added a new preface and notes, which highlighted the threat posed to liberty by a ruling oligarchy (such as that which was then in power in the Netherlands), radicalised the work and emphasised its republican elements. This edition was reprinted several times during the eighteenth century and exercised an important influence in France.[62]

By far the most influential commonwealth works translated into French during the eighteenth century were Gordon's discourses on Tacitus and Sallust. Like Shaftesbury and Toland, Gordon was an associate of Desmaizeaux, who arranged for his friend – another Huguenot, Pierre Daudé – to translate Gordon's discourses (though not his editions of the writings of Tacitus and Sallust themselves) into French.[63]

Pierre Daudé was born in the Auvergne in 1681, but moved to London in 1725 to join his father Jean Daudé and his maternal uncle Pierre Daudé senior – an important figure in London's Huguenot community.[64] Daudé's correspondence with Desmaizeaux, which covers the period between 1732 and 1744, reveals that they were close friends, that Daudé was part of Desmaizeaux's 'cotterie' [sic], and that both men were involved with the Bibliothèque britannique.[65] Unlike his uncle, Pierre Daudé junior appears to have lived in England out of choice rather than necessity and was able to travel back and forth across the Channel. In a letter written to Desmaizeaux from Paris in January 1744, he announced his intention to live and die in London, but as a foreigner not a naturalised Englishman.[66] Indeed, far from sharing the committed Protestantism of his uncle, Daudé junior appears to have been a freethinker. In a letter written from Paris in October 1733 he declared with delight: 'Freethinking is very rife in this town and a northerly wind hath blown down a great spirit of freedom in any respect.'[67] Moreover, in another letter dated February 1734, he referred explicitly to his own 'incredulité'.[68]

Daudé was clearly working on the translation of Gordon's *Tacitus* from as early as 1732 and he appears to have finished it by December 1733, though it would be almost ten years before the translation was published. Daudé discussed the publication problems with Desmaizeaux:

> It does not appear that the printing of Mr Gordon's discourse will be allowed without some retrenchment ...: the problem lies in the mass of blood. It is therefore necessary to endeavour to do something; to make the manuscript valuable to a bookseller in Holland, and see whether our friend de Hondt would like to do this business, the question is to find a sure way of making it valuable to an honest man who can make good use of it.[69]

Daudé's translation of Gordon's *Discourses on Tacitus* finally appeared in 1742, having been published by the Amsterdam bookseller, and friend of Desmaizeaux, François Changuion.[70] Despite the problems involved in publishing it, the translation was apparently a success. During a trip to France in 1744 Daudé noted that it was selling well, and announced that he was about to begin working on an edition of Gordon's discourses on Sallust, which eventually appeared in 1759.[71]

The Huguenot interpretation: continuities

Not surprisingly, the French translations of English republican works – and the reviews of them in Huguenot journals – reflect at least some of the concerns of the Real Whigs with whom the Huguenot translators and reviewers were associated. In the French reviews and translations, Ludlow, Sidney, Harrington, Locke and Gordon are all presented as enemies of arbitrary, tyrannical government (and of the Catholicism that was associated with it), and as supporters of liberty and Protestantism. In his review of the French translation of Ludlow's *Memoirs*, Bernard insisted, on the basis of his own conversation with Ludlow, that the succession of James II had thrown Ludlow into a melancholy due to its implications for the Protestant religion and for liberty in England.[72]

Liberty appears to have been the key value for these Huguenots, just as it was for the Real Whigs. In the preface to his translation of Sidney's *Discourses*, Samson explained that the value of Sidney's work lay in the fact that it dealt with a matter 'of no little importance', namely liberty:

> [T]hat liberty is the most advantageous, that liberty is the most precious treasure that men can possess on earth; that they must do all they can to assure possession of it, and that it is up to them to change the form of their government, if they believe that it is necessary to maintain and affirm this precious liberty without which all the other goods of the world must be considered only as gilded chains, which are no less heavy than normal chains.[73]

Samson insisted that Sidney's work offered the best defence of liberty available. Moreover, Sidney had demonstrated his ardent love for liberty not just in his writings, but also in his behaviour throughout his life: 'mortal enemy of slavery, zealous defender of the privileges, or rather, of the rights of his country, he believed it to be his duty to sacrifice everything to prevent the one and to assure possession of the others'.[74] As proof of his principles, Samson made reference to the epigram that Sidney had supposedly written in the visitor's book of the University of Copenhagen: 'This hand, enemy to tyrants / By the sword seeks calm peacefulness with liberty.'[75]

Samson's other works reflected similar ideas. His choice of William III as the subject for a biography is significant. Not only had William been celebrated by the Real Whigs as the restorer of English liberties, but he was also the central figure in the Protestant alliance against the absolutist and expansionist policies of Louis XIV. Moreover, the detail of that book again betrayed Samson's own commitment to liberty and to the rights of the people. The book discussed not only William III himself, but also his forebears. In particular, William of Nassau was presented as having played a similar role on behalf of the Dutch to that played by his descendant on behalf of the English in 1688–89. Samson repeatedly described the Dutch as groaning under the yoke of Spanish tyranny, and presented William of Nassau as the man who liberated them from this oppression.[76] Of him and his associates Samson said:

> I don't believe that one can tire of reading of the heroic actions of these great men, who are so recommendable to posterity owing to the generous efforts they have made to maintain the rights of the people and to assure for them the enjoyment of the richest present they have received from heaven.[77]

In his review of the work, Bernard said of Samson himself: '[F]ull of respect for the sovereign who governs according to the laws, he is so in love with liberty that he appears to be horrified by the least shadow of tyranny.'[78]

It was this same love of liberty and hostility toward tyranny that Daudé identified as the central theme behind Gordon's life and works. In the brief 'Avertissement' to his translation of the *Discourses on Tacitus* he referred to Gordon's great reputation in England that had arisen from his political writings: 'where he is acknowledged as having much penetration, an exquisite judgement, and a great zeal for the liberty of his country'.[79]

Unsurprisingly, the Huguenots also appear to have shared the Real Whig emphasis on religious as well as civil liberty, and the sense that the two were closely intertwined. The printers who produced Samson's translation of Sidney's *Discourses*, Louis and Henri Van Dole, made much of the theme of liberty in their dedication, and particularly emphasised the religious aspect of it. The book was dedicated to the nobles of the states of Holland and West Friesia, who had granted a patent for the work. Acknowledging that Sidney's book was concerned with liberty, they suggested the appropriateness of its being published at The Hague, describing Holland and West Friesia as 'un Azile assûré' for those persecuted elsewhere and referring to the tendency of foreigners to come to the country because of the liberty, and particularly the liberty of conscience, that was offered there.[80] Liberty of conscience was also a central theme of one of the other works translated by Samson, Shaftesbury's *A Letter Concerning Enthusiasm*.[81]

Though they associated Protestantism with liberty and were firm supporters of a European Protestant alliance, the personal religious views of many of these Huguenots, like those of their British associates, strayed beyond what was considered orthodox. Desmaizeaux's enthusiasm for freethinking and deist ideas is well documented.[82] The involvement of Rousset de Missy, Levier and Johnson with the *Traité de trois imposteurs* suggests that they too were that way inclined. Moreover Silvia Berti has suggested, on the basis of Levier's papers and a reference in Marchand's *Dictionnaire historique*, that he was a committed Spinozist.[83] Samson's freethinking tendencies are reflected in his translation of Shaftesbury's *A Letter Concerning Enthusiasm* and in Toland's dedication to him in *Origines Judaicae*. Finally Daudé, as we have seen, was explicit about his own unbelief.[84]

The Huguenot interpretation: discontinuities

While the French translations and reviews do reflect some of the central concerns of the Real Whigs, there are important differences in the detail of the message that is conveyed – differences that reflect the disparities between the circumstances and priorities of the Huguenots and those of their British counterparts.

In the first place, the French translators and reviewers seem to have been much more comfortable with the label 'republican' than were their British contemporaries, and they readily applied the term to the seventeenth-century figures.[85] Marret described Ludlow as 'ce Chef des Républicains Anglois', while Harrington was labelled a 'grand Républican d'Angleterre' by Bernard and a 'fameux Républicain d'Angleterre' by the reviewer for the *Bibliothèque britannique*.[86] In each case the epithet was clearly intended as a compliment. Bernard was suspected of anti-royalist sentiments himself,[87] and he also identified Samson as a republican: 'Mr Samson has raised the mask, he has made himself known as a good republican in all forms and I would be very surprised if he ever took another side.'[88] The willingness on the part of the Huguenots to use the term 'republican', and even to identify themselves in this way, contrasts sharply with the anxieties expressed by the Real Whigs, but it can be easily explained.[89] Marret, Bernard and Samson were all based in Holland at this time – a country that was itself a republic. Consequently they did not need to employ coded language or play down any evidence of republicanism, nor did they need to fit the ideas of the seventeenth-century English figures into a monarchical framework.

A pro-Dutch perspective was also of more general importance to these Huguenot writers. Marret was keen to exonerate the Dutch from the hostile accusations Ludlow had levelled against them in his *Memoirs*. In his 'Avertissement' to the third volume of the *Memoirs*, Marret challenged what he called Ludlow's 'unjust accusation' that the Estates General of the United Provinces had betrayed some of his compatriots.[90] Similarly, in his review of Sidney's *Discourses*, Bernard highlighted Sidney's own praise for the government of the United Provinces: 'He strongly exalts the form of government of the United Provinces, and maintains that it is difficult to find another in the world, which can be compared to it.'[91] Rousset de Missy went so far as to use Locke in support of Dutch resistance, and his own Dutch sympathies were always clear. Samson too appears to have been ardently pro-Dutch. This is reflected most clearly in his *History of William III* – the real hero of which sometimes appears to be not William but De Witt. In his review of the work, Bernard declared: 'Mr Samson is almost always the apologist for the Estates General and for the Estates of Holland. He demonstrates wherever possible, by incontestable facts, the purity and the sincerity of all their intentions.'[92] Moreover, Samson himself stressed the liberty-loving and republican characteristics of the Dutch – characteristics that he clearly admired. He described the Flemish and above all the Hollanders and Friesians as 'people who are passionate about their liberty'.[93]

Samson's love of Holland, and his commitment to the maintenance of a strong Protestant alliance to keep the French government in check, also helps to explain one aspect of his life and work that does not fit so easily with his associations with the Real Whigs – his employment by Horatio Walpole. As Prime Minister, Robert Walpole was a key target for the anger and hostility of the British commonwealthmen of the 1720s and 1730s.[94] When viewed from a British perspective, therefore, the willingness of the translator of Sidney's *Discourses* to work for Horatio Walpole – who, in turn, worked closely with his brother – seems inexplicable. However, from a European perspective the apparent contradiction is more easily explained. Horatio Walpole's efforts to shore up a strong Protestant alliance (coupled with his obvious affection for Holland) was far more important to Samson than the behaviour of Walpole's brother as British Prime Minister.

This also points to a deeper distinction between the interpretation of the commonwealth tradition offered by the Real Whigs and that of their French sympathisers. Though the fear of tyrannical or absolutist government remained a concern in Britain, at least as long as the Jacobites remained a threat, the revolution settlement was seen as having gone a long way toward averting this problem, and the focus turned instead to maintaining the appropriate balance within the existing mixed constitution. By contrast, for the Huguenots tyrannical government – as personified by Louis XIV and his successors – remained the primary concern. The ministerial corruption under Walpole was far less significant than the continuing threat of French tyranny. Thus the Huguenots placed much less emphasis than did their British counterparts on the importance of a mixed and balanced constitution, and much more emphasis on the anti-absolutist elements of the republican tradition, and especially on the people's right of resistance against a tyrannical or arbitrary ruler. This is reflected in the particular English republican works that they chose to translate – Ludlow's *Memoirs*, Sidney's *Discourses* and Gordon's *Tacitus* and *Sallust* rather than Harrington's *Oceana*. It is also evident from their own comments. In the preface to his translation of Sidney's *Discourses*, Samson was insistent that the crucial means of securing the basic rights and liberties of the people was to allow them to resist a tyrannical ruler and to choose their own form of government. Speaking of Sidney he said: 'he had in view establishing the rights of the people, showing them that they are born free, and that it was up to them to establish whatever form of government they believed to be the most advantageous for them.'[95]

The other aspect of the British commonwealth tradition that received only limited treatment in the Huguenot works was scepticism about the possibility of virtue, and the suggestion that material and constitutional mechanisms could be used to produce virtuous behaviour out of self-interested motives. In this respect it is interesting to note the enthusiasm among the Huguenots for the works of Shaftesbury, who remained much more positive than some of his associates about the potential of human beings to act in accordance with reason and virtue. In addition to Samson's edition of Shaftesbury's *A Letter Concerning Enthusiasm*, Desmaizeaux began, though never completed, a translation of Shaftesbury's *Enquiry Concerning Virtue*.[96] Bernard did note Harrington's ideas on balancing powers so as to avoid corruption in his review of Harrington's works,[97] and there were of course hints at this idea in Gordon's discourses, but the emphasis of the Huguenots was on opposing tyranny rather than on building a workable republic, and so these ideas were less relevant to them. Nonetheless, as will become clear in Part II, this aspect of the commonwealth tradition was picked up by other French figures in the first half of the eighteenth century.

Conclusion

The Huguenot connection was one means by which commonwealth ideas came to play an important role in continental European political thought. The Real Whigs, who were themselves deeply concerned about European affairs, were closely associated with a network of Huguenot writers, translators and booksellers. It was via the translations and reviews produced by these French Protestant exiles that the key works of the English republican tradition entered France and became known to a francophone audience. Moreover, the impact of the Huguenot adoption and adaptation of the English republican tradition was not limited to their own generation. As will become clear in the chapters that follow, their translations reappeared at various points during the eighteenth century and continued to exercise an influence, impacting on both the Enlightenment and the French Revolution.

Notes

1 C. A. Robbins, *The Eighteenth-Century Commonwealthman: Studies in the Transmission, Development, and Circumstance of English Liberal Thought from the Restoration of Charles II until the War with the Thirteen Colonies* (Indianapolis, IN: Liberty Fund, 2004 [1987, 1959]).

2 B. Bailyn, *The Ideological Origins of the American Revolution*, rev. edn (Cambridge, MA: Belknap, 1992 [1967]); G. S. Wood, *The Creation of the American Republic, 1776–1787* (Chapel Hill, NC: University of North Carolina Press, 1969); R. E. Shalhope, 'Towards a Republican Synthesis: The Emergence of an Understanding of Republicanism in American Historiography', *William and Mary Quarterly* (1972), pp. 49–77; J. G. A. Pocock, *The Machiavellian Moment: Florentine Political Thought and the Atlantic Republican Tradition* (Princeton: Princeton University Press, 1975), pp. 506–52; R. E. Shalhope, 'Republicanism and Early American Historiography', *William and Mary Quarterly* (1982), pp. 334–56; D. T. Rodgers, 'Republicanism: The Career of a Concept', *Journal of American History*, 79 (1992), pp. 11–38; P. A. Rahe, *Republics Ancient*

and Modern: Classical Republicanism and the American Revolution (Chapel Hill, NC: University of North Carolina Press, 1992); A. Gibson, 'Ancients, Moderns and Americans: The Republicanism-Liberalism Debate Revisited', History of Political Thought 21 (2000), pp. 261–307.

3 In fact, in her Foreword to the Atheneum Edition of The Eighteenth-Century Commonwealthman, published in 1968, Robbins herself recognised the limitations of her own study and acknowledged the possibility of European comparisons. Robbins, Commonwealthman, pp. xi–xii. Moreover, the European connections of the Real Whigs have received some attention from Margaret Jacob and Justin Champion. See M. C. Jacob, The Radical Enlightenment: Pantheists, Freemasons and Republicans (London: George Allen & Unwin, 1981); J. Champion, Republican Learning: John Toland and the Crisis of Christian Culture, 1696–1722 (Manchester: Manchester University Press, 2003); J. Champion, '"The Forceful, Full, Energetic, Fearless Expression of Heretical Thoughts": Rethinking Clandestine Literature and the European Reading Public, 1680–1730'. I am grateful to Justin Champion for providing me with a copy of this paper.

4 R. D. Gwynn, Huguenot Heritage: The History and Contribution of the Huguenots in Britain (London: Routledge & Kegan Paul, 1985), p. 23.

5 J. Dedieu, Montesquieu et la tradition politique anglaise en France: les sources anglaises de l'esprit des lois (Geneva: Slatkine Reprints, 1971 [1909]), p. 17n.

6 J. Milton, Eikonoklastes, ou réponse au livre intitulé Eikon Basilike, ou le portrait de sa sacrée majesté durant sa solitude et ses souffrances (London: G. Du Gard, 1652). See also Dedieu, Montesquieu, p. 17n.

7 On the circumstances in which the Court Maxims was written, and Sidney's European connections more generally see J. Scott, 'Classical Republicanism in Seventeenth-century England and the Netherlands', in M. van Gelderen and Q. Skinner (eds), Republicanism: A Shared European Heritage. Vol. 1: Republicanism and Constitutionalism in Early Modern Europe (Cambridge: Cambridge University Press, 2002), pp. 61–81.

8 J. H. M. Salmon, The French Religious Wars in English Political Thought (Oxford: Clarendon, 1959).

9 British Library (BL): Desmaizeaux Papers, Add. MS. 4288 fols. 95–103, 'Letters from Shaftesbury to Desmaizeaux'. Robert Molesworth is also said to have employed Huguenots on his Yorkshire estates. See Robbins, Commonwealthman, p. 109.

10 M. C. Jacob, 'John Toland and the Newtonian Ideology', Journal of the Warburg and Courtauld Institutes 32 (1969), pp. 307–31; Jacob, Radical Enlightenment; Champion, Republican Learning.

11 University of Leiden (UoL) Prosper Marchand Papers (PMP), March. 2 (unfoliated), 'Anthony Collins, à Charles Levier, 11 septembre (n.y.), 5 janvier 1713, 10 octobre 1713'.

12 On the Chevaliers de la Jubilation see Jacob, Radical Enlightenment. For a critique of Jacob's account of this group see C. Berkvens-Stevelinck, 'Les Chevaliers de la Jubilation: Maçonnerie ou libertinage? A propos de quelques publications de Margaret C. Jacob', Quaerendo 13 (1983), pp. 50–73 and 124–48. For Jacob's response see M. C. Jacob, 'The Knights of Jubilation: Masonic and Libertine. A Reply', Quaerendo 14 (1984), pp. 63–75.

13 The National Archives (TNA): Shaftesbury Papers, PRO/30/24/20, 'Letters between Anthony Ashley Cooper, third Earl of Shaftesbury and Benjamin Furly'.

14 Champion, Republican Learning, especially p. 7.

15 On these republications see B. Worden, Roundhead Reputations: The English Civil Wars and the Passions of Posterity (London: Allen Lane, 2001), especially pp. 9–179 and Champion, Republican Learning, especially pp. 93–115.

16 Though its ultimate lessons were aimed at the British, Molesworth's An Account of Denmark demonstrated extensive knowledge of that country, and the work had implications for Europe as a whole. Moreover, in his Preface Molesworth explicitly noted the benefits of knowledge of the history and institutions of other countries. R. Molesworth, An Account of Denmark, as it was in the year 1692, 5th edn (Glasgow: R. Urie and Company, 1745). Many other commonwealth works also invoked other European examples. The tyranny experienced by the French under Louis XIV and his successors was a frequent trope. See for example T. Gordon, The Works of Tacitus With Political Discourses Upon That Author, 3rd edn (London, 1753), IV, p. 246.

17 In addition to the translations (which will be discussed in detail later in this chapter), Toland produced a number of manuscript works in French for Prince Eugene and Baron Hohendorf. See Champion, *Republican Learning*, especially pp. 3, 48 and 169.
18 *Nouvelles de la république des lettres*, ed. P. Bayle (March 1684) Preface, unpaginated. On *Nouvelles de la république des lettres* see: J. Sgard (ed.), *Dictionnaire des journaux, 1600–1789* (Paris: Universitas, 1991), II, pp. 940–3.
19 On these journals see: H. J. Reesink, *L'Angleterre dans les périodiques français de Hollande, 1684–1709* (Paris, 1931) and Dedieu, *Montesquieu*, pp. 35–69.
20 M. M. Haag, *La France Protestante ou vies des protestants français* (Paris: Joël Cherbuliez, 1861), II, pp. 204–6; J. Sgard, M. Gilot and F. Weil (eds), *Dictionnaire des journalistes (1600–1789)* (Grenoble: Presses Universitaires de Grenoble, 1976), pp. 34–8.
21 UoL PMP: March. 2, 'Jacques Bernard à P. Marchand, 27 novembre 1709'; BL: Add. MS. 4281 fols. 80–160, 'Letters from J. Bernard to P. Desmaizeaux, 1700–1709'.
22 *Nouvelles de la république des lettres*, ed. J. Bernard (February 1699), p. 147.
23 Ibid. (March, April, May 1699), pp. 243–69, 426–56 and 553–79; (September 1700), pp. 243–63.
24 Bernard also reviewed the French translations of both Ludlow's *Memoirs* and Sidney's *Discourses*. Ibid. (February 1699), pp. 145–74; (March 1702), p. 347.
25 On *Histoire des ouvrages des savans* see: Sgard, *Dictionnaire des journaux*, I, pp. 543–5.
26 Haag, *La France Protestante*, II, pp. 3–16.
27 *Histoire des ouvrages des savans*, ed. H. Basnage de Beauval, XV, pp. 271 and 521–33; XVI pp. 78–88 and 242–8; and XIX, pp. 63–75.
28 J. H. Broome, 'An Agent in Anglo-French Relationships: Pierre Des Maizeaux, 1673–1745' (University of London PhD Thesis, 1949), pp. 22, 95–6 and 115–17.
29 BL: Add. MS. 4281 fols. 80, 92–3.
30 *Bibliothèque britannique, ou histoire des ouvrages des savans de la Grande-Bretagne* (July–September 1737), pp. 408–30.
31 Ibid. (October–December 1740), pp. 48–86. The focus of this review was on the political works in the volume, the other works were dealt with in separate reviews.
32 On this journal see Sgard, *Dictionnaire des journaux*, I, pp. 170–3 and F. Beckwith, 'The *Bibliothèque Britannique*, 1733–47', *The Library: Transactions of the Bibliographical Society* 12 (1931), pp. 75–82. See also Haag, *La France Protestante*, II, pp. 206–7.
33 *Bibliothèque britannique*, I (April–June 1733), pp. 36–58 and I (July–September 1733), pp. 251–93; *Bibliothèque raisonnée des ouvrages des savans de l'Europe*, VIII, pp. 345–68 and IX, pp. 243–79. See also Dedieu, *Montesquieu*, pp. 37 and 286 n.2.
34 That claim is made explicitly in A. Sidney, *Discours sur le gouvernement, par Algernon Sidney, … traduits de l'anglois par P. A. Samson* (The Hague, 1702), I, Preface, unpaginated.
35 In addition to the 1652 edition of Milton's *Eikonoklastes*, *Paradise Lost* was translated in 1729 and *Paradise Regained* in 1730.
36 J. G. de Chauffepié, *Nouveau Dictionnaire historique et critique pour servir de supplement ou de continuation au dictionnaire historique et critique de Mr. Pierre Bayle* (Amsterdam, 1750).
37 TNA: PRO/30/24/20 f. 13; BL: Add. MS. 4281 f. 93.
38 J. D'Alembert, et al. (eds), *Encyclopédie, ou dictionnaire raisonnée des sciences, arts et des metiers, par une société des gens de letters* (Stuggart, 1967) XIV, pp. 446–7.
39 Sidney, *Discours sur le gouvernement*; A. A. Cooper, 3rd Earl of Shaftesbury, *Lettre sur l'enthousiasme*, trans. P. A. Samson (The Hague: T. Johnson, 1709).
40 Haag, *La France Protestante*, IX, pp. 134–5.
41 *Nouvelles*, ed. Bernard (February 1703), p. 159.
42 J. Swift, *Lettres de Mr le Chevalier G. Temple, et autres Ministres d'état, tant en Angleterre que dans les paies étrangers*, trans. P. A. Samson (The Hague, 1711); P. A. Samson, *Histoire du Règne de Guillaume III* (The Hague, 1703–4).
43 BL: Add. MS. 4281 f. 92.
44 J. Toland, *Dissertationes Duae: Adeisidaemon et Origines Judaicae* (The Hague, 1708/9). An

English-language manuscript version is held at the John Rylands Library [JRL] in the Christie Collection, 3. f. 38. See also Champion, *Republican Learning*, pp. 174–5.
45 Toland, *Dissertationes Duae*, pp. 101–3. JRL: Christie, 3. f. 38, dedication, unpaginated.
46 In TNA: Secretaries of State: State Papers Foreign, France, SP78/184 fols. 193–5, 'Address of Charles Levier at the Hague', Levier's address is given as Korte Begijne Straat, but a number of undated letters sent to him by Saint-Hyacinthe are addressed to Le Spuystraat. UoL PMP: March. 2, 'Saint-Hyacinthe à Ch. Levier, 7 lettres'. Levier also worked for a time in Rotterdam.
47 TNA: SP78/184, fols 193, 195, 196, 211, 213, 215, 222, 230, 231. 'Arrangements for printing and publishing the "Analyse"'. Samson had been working for Walpole for more than ten years by this point. He was originally recruited in 1715, when Walpole was appointed as a plenipotentiary in negotiations taking place at The Hague. See *An Honest Diplomat at The Hague: The private letters of Horatio Walpole 1715–1716*, ed. J. J. Murray (Bloomington: IN Indiana University Press, 1955), pp. 67, 95–6 and 107. In 1723 he accompanied Walpole to Paris and in December 1726 he travelled with him to England. TNA: SP78/184 f. 276. Samson was still in touch with Walpole years later. See: BL: Add. MS. 32750 f. 527, 'Letter from P. A. Samson to H. Walpole (1727)' and UoL PMP: March. 2, 'P. A. Samson à Ch.[sic] Levier, 18 janvier 1737 (v.s.)'.
48 On 20 January 1726/7, the marriage took place of Peter Augustus Sampson to Anne de Charmes at the Charterhouse Chapel in Finsbury, and on 13 February 1727/8 he was granted denization by King George II, BL: Add. MS. 36128 f.76, 'Peter Augustus Samson Denization'. He was described in the certificate as living in the parish of St Martin's in the Fields in Middlesex. It was at the Church of St Martin's in the Fields, on 11 March 1729, that Samson's son Michael Lawrence Samson was christened. Samson became involved in London's Huguenot community and in 1740 he was elected as one of the directors of the French Protestant Hospital (La Providence), The Huguenot Library (HL): A1/1 'Minutes of the Court's Quarterly and Extra-Ordinary Meeting, 1718–1779', 9 April and 2 July 1740, 21 February 1740/1, 6 October 1742, 5 October 1743. Samson's will, originally written in March 1746 and proved on 16 November 1748, indicates that by this time he, his wife and son were living in a farm known as Baynards or Barnards Place in the Sussex parish of West Hoathly, TNA: Prob 11/766, fols. 66–7, 'Will of Peter Augustus Samson, translated out of the French'.
49 UoL PMP: March. 2, 'P. A. Samson à Ch.[sic] Levier, 18 janvier 1737 (v.s)'.
50 For the association between Samson and Marchand see UoL PMP: March. 2, 'P. A. Samson à Ch. [sic] Levier, 18 janvier 1737 (v.s.)'. Levier's links to Marchand are evident throughout the Marchand papers, which also incorporate those of Levier himself. Details on Levier's relationship with Fritsch and Böhm, with whom he worked for a time, can be found in UoL PMP: March. 2, 'Gaspar Fritsch à Ch. Levier, 27 mai 1711 & 7 août 1714'; March. 29: 1, fols 7–12, 'Mémoire instructif concernant le Procès ... contre les sieurs Gaspard Fritsch, Michel Böhm, et Charles Levier'. Collins's letters to Levier were particularly affectionate, March. 2, 'Anthony Collins à Charles Levier, 11 septembre [n.y.], 5 janvier 1713, 1 octobre 1713'.
51 See UoL PMP: March. 2, 'Fritsch à Marchand, 17 octobre 1711' in which Fritsch signs himself 'Le Grand Maistre' and 'Gaspar Fritsch à Ch. Levier, 7 août 1714' in which Fritsch refers to 'La Société de M. Boyd'. See also Jacob, *Radical Enlightenment*, p. 144.
52 UoL PMP: March. 2, 'Fritsch à Marchand, 7 novembre 1737' and Fritsch à Marchand, 17 janvier 1740'. See also S. Berti, 'The First Edition of the *Traité des trois imposteurs*, and its Debt to Spinoza's *Ethics*', in M. Hunter and D. Wootton (eds), *Atheism from the Reformation to the Enlightenment* (Oxford: Clarendon, 1992), pp. 183–220, and Champion, *Republican Learning*, p. 171.
53 C. Levier, *Catalogus Librorum Bibliopoli Caroli Levier* (The Hague, 1735), pp. 203, 236, 296.
54 This information comes from a catalogue of books sold in Johnson's shop that was appended to Toland's *Relations des cours de Prusse et Hannovre* (1706). In fact, several separate translations of Molesworth's work appeared between 1694 and 1790 (not all comprised the whole work). See P. Ries, 'Robert Molesworth's "Account of Denmark": A Study in the Art of Political Publishing and Bookselling in England and on the Continent Before 1700', *Scandinavica* 7 (1968), pp. 108–25.

55 Interestingly Bernard, Desmaizeaux and Marchand were all associated with the *Journal littéraire* at some point. Sgard, *Dictionnaire des journaux*, II, pp. 693–5.
56 Berti, 'First Edition of the *Traité des trois imposteurs*, p. 194n; Jacob, *Radical Enlightenment*, pp. 184 and 188.
57 In the 'Avertissement du Libraire' to the third volume Marret made clear that he was not just the publisher, but also the translator of the work. E. Ludlow, *Nouveaux Mémoires d'Edmond Ludlow …*, ed. P. Marret (Amsterdam, 1707), 'Avertissement du Libraire', unpaginated.
58 Sgard, *Dictionnaire des journaux*, I, p. 169.
59 On Rousset de Missy see Jacob, *Radical Enlightenment*; M. C. Jacob, 'In the Aftermath of Revolution: Rousset de Missy, Freemasonry, and Locke's *Two Treatises of Government*', in *L'Età dei lumi: Studi storici sul settecento Europea in onore di Franco Venturi* (Naples: Jovene Editore, 1985), I, pp. 487–521 and Berti, 'First Edition of the *Traité des trois imposteurs*'.
60 Berti, 'First Edition of the *Traité des trois imposteurs*', p. 194 and A. Thomson, 'Le *Discourse of Freethinking* d'Anthony Collins et sa traduction française', *La Lettre clandestine*, no. 9 (2000), pp. 95–116.
61 Like the earlier French translation on which it was based, Rousset de Missy's version comprised only Locke's *Second Treatise*.
62 J. Locke, *Du Gouvernement civil, où l'on traite de l'origine, des fondemens, de la nature, du pouvoir et des fins des sociétés politiques par L.C.R.D.M.A.D.P*, [J. Rousset de Missy] (Amsterdam: J. Schreuder and P. Mortier, 1755), especially pp. xv–xviii. See also, Jacob, 'In the Aftermath of Revolution'; Jacob, *Radical Enlightenment*, p. 85 and K. M. Baker, *Inventing the French Revolution: Essays on French Political Culture in the Eighteenth Century* (Cambridge: Cambridge University Press, 1990), p. 90.
63 BL: Add. MS. 4283 fols. 61–2, 'Pierre Daudé to Desmaizeaux, 16 August (n.y.)'. Though no letters from Gordon appear among the Desmaizeaux papers, the connection between them is clear from Desmaizeaux's correspondence with De la Motte. BL: Add. MS. 4286 fols. 248–9 and 271. See also Broome, 'An Agent', pp. 152, and 281–3.
64 On his death in 1733 Pierre Daudé senior left money to various Huguenot charities and institutions. See TNA: Prob 11/656, 'Will of Pierre Daudé Senior'; HL: E2/12, 'Daudé, Pierre: original codicil, signed and sealed 8 September 1733, to his will of August 1733' and 'Receipt for £200 bequest'; HL: M2/11/1–7, 'Papers concerning the Daudé bequest'; HL: A1/1 'Minutes of the Court's Quarterly and Extra-Ordinary Meeting, 1718–1779', 3 October 1733. Perhaps due to his bequest, Pierre Daudé senior was highly regarded by the authorities of the French Protestant Hospital. His portrait still hangs in the Hospital, which is now based at Rochester. Judge Dumas, 'Huguenot History written in the Portraits and Pictures at the French Hospital', *Proceedings of the Huguenot Society of London* 14 (1929–33), pp. 326–32. I owe this information to Randolph Vigne. For more information on the lives of both uncle and nephew see Haag, *La France Protestante*, IV, pp. 207–8.
65 BL: Add. MS. 4283 fols. 39–68 'Pierre Daudé to Desmaizeaux'. Daudé's involvement with the *Bibliothèque britannique* earned him an entry in the *Dictionnaire des journalistes*. However, that article has little more to say about him. Sgard et al., *Dictionnaire des journalistes*, p. 109.
66 BL: Add. MS. 4283 f. 54. Daudé did not fulfil his aim of dying in London. Though his will was drawn up there in 1750 – at which point he was described as an inhabitant of the Parish of St Ann, Westminster – the codicil was produced in Paris, just days before his death in the spring of 1754. It refers specifically to what Daudé wanted to happen if he died in Paris. Unlike his uncle, Daudé junior appears to have left the majority of his fortune not to Protestant charities but to relations and friends – mostly in France. Interestingly, the codicil also gives specific instructions as to what should be done with Daudé's extensive collection of books, TNA: Prob 11/809, 'Will of Pierre Daudé junior'.
67 BL: Add. MS. 4283 f. 49. Interestingly, Daudé's idea of a wind of freedom blowing from the north is very similar to ideas expressed by the Marquis d'Argenson in his *Memoirs*. See the Introduction to this book.
68 BL: Add. MS. 4283 f. 58.

69 BL: Add. MS. 4283 f. 49.
70 For Desmaizeaux's friendship with Changuion see Broome, 'An Agent', pp. 457–8.
71 BL: Add. MS. 4283 fols. 53–4. The success of Gordon's discourses in France was also noted by the Abbé Prévost who claimed that 'Gordon's political discourses are highly esteemed'. Quoted in Dedieu, *Montesquieu*, p. 287.
72 *Nouvelles*, ed. Bernard (February 1699), p. 146.
73 Sidney, *Discours*, I, Preface, unpaginated.
74 Ibid.
75 Ibid.
76 Samson, *Histoire du Règne de Guillaume III*, I, p. 3.
77 Ibid., I, pp. 2–3.
78 *Nouvelles*, ed. Bernard (February 1703), pp. 160–1.
79 T. Gordon, *Discours Historiques, Critiques et politiques sur Tacite, traduits de l'anglois de Mr Th. Gordon*, trans. P. Daudé (Amsterdam: François Changuion, 1751), pp. v–vi.
80 Sidney, *Discours*, I, Dedication, unpaginated.
81 A. A. Cooper, third Earl of Shaftesbury, *A Letter Concerning Enthusiasm, to My Lord ****** (1708), in his *Characteristicks of Men, Manners, Opinions, Times*, 4th edn (1727), I, pp. 3–55.
82 Broome, 'An Agent', esp. pp. 145–211; J. H. Broome, 'Bayle's Biographer: Pierre Desmaizeaux', *French Studies* 60 (1955) p. 1–17; J. H. Broome, 'Pierre Desmaizeaux, Journaliste: Les nouvelles littéraires de Londres entre 1700 et 1740', *Revue de littérature comparée* 29 (1955), pp. 184–204.
83 Berti, 'First Edition of the *Traité des trois imposteurs*', pp. 195–6.
84 Haag suggests that Daudé was also the translator of *De fide et officiis Christianorum* by Thomas Burnet and the author of *Sybilla capitolina, Publii Virgilii Maronis Poëmation interpretatione et notis illustratum*, a critique of the bull Unigenitus. Haag, *La France Protestante*, p. 208. Burnet, though not irreligious, was suspected of being so by some contemporaries. S. Mandelbrote, 'Burnet, Thomas (c.1635–1715)', *Oxford Dictionary of National Biography* (Oxford: Oxford University Press, 2004; online edition, January 2008), www.oxforddnb.com/view/article/4067, accessed 26 February 2008.
85 Of course, this was not true of all Huguenots. The Huguenot historian Paul de Rapin Thoyras disowned Sidney's republicanism. Worden, *Roundhead Reputations*, p. 151.
86 Ludlow, *Nouveaux Mémoires*, 'Avertissement du Libraire', unpaginated; *Nouvelles*, ed. Bernard (September 1700), p. 244; *Bibliothèque britannique* (July–September 1737), p. 409. See also Dedieu, *Montesquieu*, pp. 37 and 58.
87 Sgard et al., *Dictionnaire des journalistes*, p. 35.
88 *Nouvelles de la république des lettres*, ed. Bernard (February 1703), p. 181.
89 On the Real Whig concerns about the terms 'republican' and 'commonwealthsman' see Chapter 1 above.
90 Ludlow, *Nouveaux Mémoires*, 'Avertissement du Libraire', unpaginated.
91 *Nouvelles*, ed. Bernard (April 1700), pp. 448–9.
92 Ibid. (February 1703), pp. 161–2.
93 Samson, *Histoire du Règne de Guillaume III*, I, p. 30.
94 Robbins, *Commonwealthman*, pp. 7 and 267. In fact, the relationship between the Real Whigs and Walpole appears to have been more complex than Robbins suggests, since Samson was not alone in working for the Walpoles. Shortly after John Trenchard's death in 1723 Thomas Gordon took up a post as first commissioner of the wine licences under Walpole, and the first volume of his edition of Tacitus (devoted to the *Annals*) was dedicated to him. Some historians have explained this by saying that Gordon sold out after Trenchard's death. (I. Kramnick, *Bolingbroke and His Circle: The Politics of Nostalgia in the Age of Walpole* (Ithaca and London: Cornell University Press, 1992 [1968]), pp. 116–18 and 243.) However, his translation of Tacitus's *Histories* was dedicated to Frederick, Prince of Wales – the focal figure of the opposition to Walpole – and those to Tacitus's *Germania* and *Agricola* were also to figures who opposed Walpole in the late 1720s and 1730s. Moreover, the content of his later works – not least his discourses on Tacitus and Sallust – suggests that his underlying political principles remained the same even if he no longer saw Walpole as a serious threat.

95 Sidney, *Discours*, I, Preface, unpaginated.
96 Add. MS. 4288 fols. 95–103, 'Letters from Shaftesbury to Desmaizeaux'.
97 In his review of Harrington's works, Bernard referred to Harrington's mixed system and noted his suggestion that government is based on an equilibrium of power between those who govern and those who are governed, and that when that equilibrium fails, the government becomes corrupt. *Nouvelles*, ed. Bernard (September 1700), p. 258.

Part II
Bolingbroke and France

3

Viscount Bolingbroke: an atypical commonwealthman

Introduction

The Real Whigs and their Huguenot associates were not the only ones responsible for disseminating English republican ideas in early eighteenth-century France. Given his French connections and influence, Henry St John, Viscount Bolingbroke played an equally important role as a conduit for the transfer of these ideas across the Channel.

On the face of it, Bolingbroke would seem to have had little in common with the Real Whigs.[1] He was a Tory, and even had Jacobite links, entering into negotiations with the Old Pretender in 1713 and serving as his Secretary of State for a short time on his arrival in France in 1715. Moreover, on a number of issues his views reflected this political affiliation. During his time as an MP in the early eighteenth century he favoured (and worked for) peace with France, and was involved in promoting legislation against the dissenters.[2]

If one looks beneath the surface, however, it is clear that Bolingbroke had important affinities with the commonwealthmen.[3] Indeed, he acknowledged the association himself. In *A Dissertation upon Parties* he explained how, since the Glorious Revolution, the older division between Whigs and Tories had been superseded by that between Court and Country.[4] The Country Party, Bolingbroke acknowledged, was made up of an alliance of Tories and Old (or Real) Whigs.[5] There is also some evidence to suggest that Bolingbroke had personal links to the Real Whig-Huguenot network. Margaret Jacob claimed that he had got to know Prosper Marchand and some of his associates when he was in the Netherlands and that he 'endorsed their society' (the *Chevaliers de la Jubilation*).[6] Similarly, Dennis Fletcher suggested that Bolingbroke's nonconformist background would have made it easy for him to link up with the Huguenot exiles who met at the Rainbow Coffee House in London, and also noted the definite connections between Bolingbroke and certain members of the Huguenot diaspora such as David Durand and Thémiseul de St. Hyacinthe.[7] Whatever the extent of these connections, Bolingbroke certainly made reference to the writings of central republican figures – including Cicero, Harrington and Sidney – in his works.[8] Most significantly, the values that he emphasised in his political thought were almost identical to those of the commonwealthmen.

'Liberty, civil and religious'

Bolingbroke certainly shared the Real Whig belief that liberty was *the* central political value. He described it as 'the greatest of human blessings' and 'the greatest good of a people', and like them he referred to it in order to justify his works.[9] At the beginning of his *Remarks on the History of England* he suggested that the purpose of the essays in the *Craftsman* was to revive the spirit of British liberty.[10] His understanding of liberty was also similar to theirs in that he believed that liberty is threatened not just by the exercise of tyranny, but by the very possibility of it: 'for tyranny and slavery do not so properly consist in the stripes that are given or received, as in the power of giving them at pleasure, and the necessity of receiving them, whenever and for whatever they are inflicted'.[11] He was, therefore, insistent that the power of a monarch ought to be limited and that he or she should rule according to the constitution and the laws.[12] Bolingbroke appears to have held these views from early in his life. In letters addressed to his friend Sir William Trumbull, while on his grand tour in 1698, he was already expressing his hatred of absolute monarchy, as practised by Louis XIV, and his love of British liberty.[13]

Interestingly, Bolingbroke's insistence on the restraints and limits that ought to be placed on monarchy led him to fear, just as his Real Whig compatriots had done, that his views would be misunderstood and that he would be thought of as a republican in the narrow, constitutional, sense of the word: 'If my readers are ready by this time to think me antimonarchical, and in particular an enemy to the succession of kings by hereditary right, I hope to be soon restored to their good opinion. I esteem monarchy above any other form of government, and hereditary monarchy above elective.'[14]

Bolingbroke also echoed the Real Whigs in emphasising the importance of religious as well as civil liberty and in seeing the two as bound up together. He was critical of religious intolerance and persecution, and attacked the Christian Church for failing to secure liberty of conscience.[15] He also accused the Church of sometimes operating in such a way as to reinforce tyrannical or absolute rule on the part of a monarch. For example, he blamed the contemporary dominance of ideas such as 'the divine institution and right of kings' and the notion that a monarch was entitled to absolute power on 'an old alliance between ecclesiastic and civil policy'.[16]

Bolingbroke's more general religious views were also strikingly similar to those of the Real Whigs. Like them he was rabidly anticlerical, believing that the Church had been corrupted over time by power-hungry clerics who exploited the ignorance and superstitious beliefs of the population.[17] However, he continued to believe in the political necessity of religion and refused to abandon the idea of organised religion altogether. He remained committed to the basic tenets of Christianity and to the idea of a national Church, but he was insistent that it ought to be kept subservient to the State.[18] Also in line with the Real Whigs was his adoption of an analytical, historical approach to Christian beliefs and texts. He questioned the truth of the Old Testament and traced the doctrines of the immortality of the soul and the distribution of rewards and punishments in the afterlife to Greek and ultimately Egyptian sources.[19] Indeed the similarities between Bolingbroke's religious views and those of the Real Whigs were so striking that William Warburton insisted that most of his religious ideas were borrowed directly from the writings of Anthony Collins, Matthew Tindal and John Toland.[20]

Virtue, passion and self-interest

On the issue of virtue Bolingbroke again appears to have followed the Real Whigs in adopting the Harringtonian, rather than the conventional republican, line. Like them he accepted the importance of virtuous behaviour, but remained unconvinced that genuine virtue was possible for the majority of human beings. He acknowledged, for example, the tendency for even the best of people to become corrupted, particularly when holding a position of power:

> A man of sense and virtue both will not fall into any great impropriety of character, or indecency of conduct: but he may slide or be surprised into small ones, from a thousand reasons, and in a thousand manners, which I shall not stay to enumerate. Against these, therefore, even men, who are incapable of falling into the others, must be still on their guard, and no men so much as princes.[21]

Moreover, he explicitly accepted the fact that human beings tend to operate on the basis of passion rather than reason, and self-interest rather than virtue. In *A Dissertation upon Parties*, for example, he described self-love as 'the strongest spring in the human, nay in the whole animal system'.[22] Bolingbroke had explored this idea at some length in his *Reflections Concerning Innate Moral Principles*. In that work, in which he argued against the idea that compassion is innate in human beings, he emphasised the tendency for humans to act in pursuit of pleasure and avoidance of pain.[23] The role of reason was to govern these innate springs and to direct them toward proper objects. However, he was aware that reason was not always as fully developed or operative in individual human beings as it ought to be: 'Our Reason is imperfect, and consequently our Virtue is so.'[24] He therefore acknowledged that it was up to rulers to ensure that the passions were controlled and directed toward virtue.[25] Moreover, he suggested that the best means of doing so would be to use passion to curb passion and to create a system in which it would be in an individual's self-interest to act virtuously.[26] Thus, like the Real Whigs, Bolingbroke positioned himself on the borderline between neo-Stoicism and neo-Epicureanism.[27]

Bolingbroke also acknowledged the importance of material and constitutional solutions to the problem of the passions. In *A Dissertation upon Parties*, he made use of Harrington's idea that it is property that determines power: 'Property then, and power by consequence, have changed hands, or rather have shifted much in the same hands since the Norman era.'[28] His belief in this Harringtonian maxim was one reason why he worried about the rise of a moneyed interest after the financial revolution of the late seventeenth century. Bolingbroke also emphasised the role that the mixed constitution could play in constraining and shaping passionate and self-interested behaviour: 'We have observed already, that the constitution of the British government supposes our Kings may abuse their power, and our representatives betray their trust, and provides against both these contingencies, as well as human wisdom can provide.'[29]

The mixed constitution

In line with conventional ideas, Bolingbroke described the three simple forms of government (monarchy, aristocracy and democracy) as tyrannical because they are subject to the arbitrary will of the sovereign.[30] Instead he favoured a mixed system in which a proper balance was struck between the monarchical, aristocratic and democratic elements and, like the commonwealthmen, he saw Britain's constitution in these terms:

> It is by this mixture of monarchical, aristocratical and democratical power, blended together in one system, and by these three estates balancing one another, that our free constitution of government hath been preserved so long inviolate, or hath been brought back, after having suffered violations, to its original principles, and been renewed, and improved too, by frequent and salutary revolutions.[31]

The balance was crucial. As Bolingbroke explained in *Remarks on the History of England*: '[I]n a constitution like ours, the safety of the whole depends upon the balance of the parts, and the balance of the parts on their mutual independency on each other.'[32] He went so far as to suggest that as long as the Lords and Commons remained independent they would provide an adequate restraint even on a bad king.[33]

As with the Real Whigs, Bolingbroke insisted that both Britain's reputation for liberty, and the mixed constitution that secured it, had their roots in Saxon times:

> A spirit of liberty, transmitted down from our Saxon ancestors, and the unknown ages of our government, preserved itself through one almost continual struggle, against the usurpations of our princes, and the vices of our people…
>
> Let us justify this conduct by persisting in it, and continue to ourselves the peculiar honour of maintaining the freedom of our Gothic institution of government, when so many other nations, who enjoyed the same, have lost theirs.[34]

It was this ancient Saxon constitution that had been threatened by the behaviour of the Stuarts, but restored in 1688–89. Bolingbroke's attitude toward the 1689 settlement was typically ambiguous. On the one hand he believed that it had brought the constitution back to its first principles and had removed the threat of prerogative power.[35] It was thus 'brought nearer than any other constitution ever was, to the most perfect idea of a free system of government'.[36] On the other hand, Bolingbroke was critical of the financial revolution that had followed the political one, and he believed that the latter had not gone far enough.[37] In particular, in its current state, there was insufficient protection against the influence of the Crown over Parliament, while the extent of control that the people could exercise over their representatives was too restricted. Thus, in Bolingbroke's eyes, the threat of the prerogative had been replaced by the threat of corruption.[38] This was precisely the focus of the latter part of *A Dissertation upon Parties*:

> But nothing of this kind was done at the Revolution. Pleased that the open attacks on our constitution were defeated and prevented, men entertained no thought of the secret attacks that might be carried on against the independency of Parliaments; as if our dangers could be but of one kind, and could arise but from one family. Soon after the Revolution, indeed, men of all sides, and of all denominations … began to perceive not only that nothing effectual had been done to hinder the undue influence of the crown in elections, and an over-balance of the creatures of the court in Parliament, but that the means of exercising such an influence, at the will of the crown, were unawares and insensibly increased, and every day increasing. In a word, they began to see that the foundations were laid of giving as great power to the crown indirectly, as the prerogative, which they had formerly dreaded so much, could give directly, and of establishing universal corruption.[39]

The task now was to perfect the constitution by taking action to prevent corruption, just as it had been taken against the prerogative.[40] The means of doing so was to secure 'the freedom of elections, and the frequency, integrity and independency of Parliaments'.[41] This would be done by ensuring that fresh elections be held on a regular basis (Bolingbroke favoured annual – or at least triennial – parliaments[42]) and by bringing an end to the system of places and pensions.[43]

Bolingbroke also placed emphasis (as the Real Whigs had done) on the need for a spirit of liberty among the population, which would animate the popular vigilance that was required.[44] From as early as 1716, when he wrote *Reflections upon Exile*, Bolingbroke had been aware that the people 'are always the surest instruments of their own servitude',[45] but as time went on he became more and more concerned that in Britain the spirit of liberty had been lost. Hints at these concerns can be found in *A Dissertation upon Parties*,[46] but they took centre stage in his later works, especially: *On the Spirit of Patriotism*, *The Idea of a Patriot King* and *Some Reflections on the Present State of the Nation*. In part the spirit of vigilance had declined as a result of the effects of the financial revolution, but Bolingbroke placed particular blame on the actions of Robert Walpole. In *The Idea of a Patriot King* he accused Walpole of having debased the sentiments of the people:

> from the love of liberty, from zeal for the honour and prosperity of their country, and from a desire of honest fame, to an absolute unconcernedness for all these, to an abject submission, and a rapacious eagerness after wealth, that may sate their avarice, and exceed the profusion of their luxury.[47]

And he expressed deep pessimism about Britain's prospects for the future: 'In a word, will the British spirit, that spirit which has preserved liberty hitherto in one corner of the world at least, be so easily or so soon reinfused into the British nation? I think not.'[48] It would certainly take time, and by this point Bolingbroke believed that the only real hope lay in a Patriot King: 'Nothing can so surely and so effectually restore the virtue and public spirit essential to the preservation of liberty and national prosperity, as the reign of such a prince.'[49] The Patriot King would restore the spirit of liberty: 'by rendering public virtue and real capacity the sole means of acquiring any degree of power or profit in the state, he will set the passions of their hearts on the side of liberty and good government.'[50] Thus even here, it was a matter of using the passions and self-interest to produce virtuous behaviour.

Conclusion: a European outlook

It would seem that despite his Tory credentials Bolingbroke's political thought had much in common with that of the Real Whigs. Indeed, it would not seem an exaggeration to describe Bolingbroke himself as a commonwealthman. Moreover, in addition to expressing views very similar to theirs, Bolingbroke also appears to have shared their cosmopolitan outlook. His works included numerous examples drawn from the history of other European countries, which revealed the depth of his knowledge in this area. His expertise on French history and politics was particularly strong and he engaged directly in the controversial contemporary debates concerning French history.[51] Bolingbroke's works also became well known in France. The first translations of them appeared in the

1730s and by 1754 almost all of his major works were available in French.[52] The enthusiasm for his works among the French was no doubt partly inspired by Bolingbroke's own very personal connections with France.

In total Bolingbroke spent more than a quarter of his life in France. He first fled there in March 1715, soon after the accession of George I when he (correctly) feared that the Whigs, who had just come to power, were about to take action against him. He stayed until 1725, by which time a pardon had been secured and the Act of Attainder that had been issued against him in 1715 reversed (though he was still unable to take up his seat in the House of Lords). He returned to France again in May 1735 (following a bitter press campaign against him led by Walpole) and remained there until 1744.

During his first stay in France, in 1719, Bolingbroke had secretly married Marie-Claire de Marcilly, the widowed marquise de Villette (a public ceremony followed in 1722). Both on his own account and through her, Bolingbroke established connections, and in many cases friendships, with a wide range of French figures including both *philosophes* such as Voltaire and political figures – especially those involved in foreign affairs and diplomacy such as the marquis de Torcy, and the French ambassador to Britain Chavignard de Chavigny.[53] Of particular relevance to the impact of his political thought in France were his connections with Henri de Boulainvilliers and with members of the Entresol Club.

Notes

1 He was not included as a commonwealthman in Caroline Robbins's study. See also I. Kramnick, *Bolingbroke and his Circle: The Politics of Nostalgia in the Age of Walpole* (Ithaca and London: Cornell University Press, 1992 [1968]), p. 2.
2 This is despite having apparently attended a Dissenting Academy himself.
3 A number of historians have noted his use of classical republican and commonwealth ideas. See for example J. G. A. Pocock, 'Machiavelli, Harrington and English Political Ideologies in the Eighteenth Century', *William and Mary Quarterly*, 3rd series, 22 (1965), pp. 549–83; Q. Skinner, 'The Principles and Practice of Opposition: The Case of Bolingbroke versus Walpole', in N. Mc Kendrick (ed.), *Historical Perspectives: Studies in English Thought and Society in Honour of J. H. Plumb* (London: Europa Publications, 1974), pp. 113–28; D. Armitage, 'Introduction' to Bolingbroke, *Political Writings*, ed. D. Armitage (Cambridge: Cambridge University Press, 1997), pp. vii–xxiv; D. Armitage, 'A Patriot for Whom? The Afterlives of Bolingbroke's Patriot King', *Journal of British Studies* 36 (1997), pp. 397–418. Kramnick also noted the similarities between Bolingbroke's works and those of the Real Whigs: see Kramnick, *Bolingbroke and His Circle*, pp. 236–60. Even Dickinson noted Bolingbroke's debt to Charles Davenant, Harrington and the neo-Harringtonians, in H. T. Dickinson, *Bolingbroke* (London: Constable, 1970), pp. 184–5 and 190–2.
4 To some degree this was prescriptive rather than descriptive, since Bolingbroke was seeking to create a Country alliance through his writings.
5 Bolingbroke, *A Dissertation upon Parties*, in *Political Writings*, pp. 8–9. It is also significant that Bolingbroke's writings were picked up by later commonwealthmen.
6 M. C. Jacob, *The Radical Enlightenment: Pantheists, Freemasons and Republicans* (London: George Allen & Unwin, 1981), p. 148. See also, E. R. Briggs, 'The Political Academies of France in the Early Eighteenth Century; with Special Reference to the Club de l'Entresol, and to its Founder, the Abbé Pierre-Joseph Alary' (University of Cambridge PhD Thesis, 1931).
7 D. J. Fletcher, 'The Intellectual Relations of Lord Bolingbroke with France' (MA Thesis,

University of Wales, 1953), pp. 3–5. In fact, Bolingbroke's own stepmother was from a French-Swiss Huguenot family and supposedly kept up her Huguenot links. Dickinson, *Bolingbroke*, p. 3; R. A. Barrell, *Bolingbroke and France* (Lanham, New York, London: University Press of America, 1988), p. 3. On the Rainbow Coffee House see S. Harvey and E. Grist, 'The Rainbow Coffee House and the Exchange of Ideas in Early Eighteenth-century London', in A. Dunan-Page, *The Religious Culture of the Huguenots, 1660–1750* (Aldershot: Ashgate, 2006), pp. 163–72.
8 Cicero is referred to repeatedly throughout his works, and Bolingbroke's Patriot King is supposed to rule on the basis of the ideas set out in Cicero's *De Officiis*. Harrington's works are alluded to in several places including in *A Dissertation upon Parties*, pp. 69 and 98, and Sidney is quoted on pp. 46–7.
9 Bolingbroke, *On the Spirit of Patriotism*, in *Political Writings*, p. 195; and *Idea of a Patriot King*, in ibid., p. 244.
10 [Bolingbroke], *Remarks on the History of England* (London: R. Francklin, 1743), pp. xiv and 1–17.
11 Bolingbroke, *Dissertation upon Parties*, in *Political Writings*, p. 127. See also p. 90 where he quoted Richard Hooker's maxim that 'to live by one man's will became the cause of all men's misery'. Quentin Skinner acknowledged Bolingbroke's debt to the neo-Roman tradition himself in *Liberty Before Liberalism* (Cambridge: Cambridge University Press, 1998), pp. 12 and 72.
12 Bolingbroke, *Dissertation upon Parties*, in *Political Writings*, pp. 83 and 91. He defined tyranny simply as 'monarchy without any rule of law'. Bolingbroke, *Idea of a Patriot King* in ibid., p. 242.
13 Historical Manuscripts Commission, *Reports on the Manuscripts of the Marquess of Downshire, preserved at Easthampstead Park, Berks* (London: HMSO, 1924), Volume I: Papers of Sir William Trumbull, Part II, p. 777, 'Henry St. John to Sir William Trumbull, 1698, May 23, o.s.' and p. 782, 'Henry St. John to Sir William Trumbull (received) 1698, July 31'. See also Fletcher, 'Intellectual Relations', p. 7 and H. Dickinson, 'St John, Henry, styled first Viscount Bolingbroke (1678–1751)', *Oxford Dictionary of National Biography* (Oxford: Oxford University Press, 2004; online edition, May 2006), www.oxforddnb.com/view/article/24496, accessed 10 March 2008. The presence of these beliefs at this early stage, and in Bolingbroke's private correspondence, challenges Quentin Skinner's interpretation that his adoption of Real Whig language was part of a propaganda campaign rather than reflecting his own genuine beliefs: see Skinner, 'Principles and Practices of Opposition'.
14 Bolingbroke, *Idea of a Patriot King*, in *Political Writings*, pp. 226–7.
15 Bolingbroke, *Dissertation upon Parties*, in ibid., p. 17. However, it should be noted than in his earlier political career he had been involved in drafting bills against the practice of occasional conformity, which had allowed the dissenters to hold political office. Dickinson, 'St John, Henry', *ODNB*.
16 Bolingbroke, *Idea of a Patriot King*, in *Political Writings*, p. 224.
17 Henry St John, Lord Viscount Bolingbroke, *Letters on the Study and Use of History* (London: A. Millar, 1752), pp. 122–30 and pp. 174–6. See also Fletcher, 'Intellectual Relations', pp. 137–9.
18 Henry St John, Lord Viscount Bolingbroke, 'Essay the Fourth: Concerning Authority in Matters of Religion', in *Works of the Late Right Honourable Henry St. John, Lord Viscount Bolingbroke* (London, 1809), VII, p. 274; *Lettres historiques, politiques, philosophiques et particulières de Henri Saint-John, Lord Vicomte Bolingbroke, depuis 1710 jusqu'en 1736…*, ed. Grimoard (Paris: Dentu, 1808), I, pp. 180–1.
19 'Fragments, or Minutes of Essays: XXIX', in Bolingbroke, *Works*, VIII, pp. 60–5.
20 Montesquieu, *Correspondance de Montesquieu*, ed. F. Gebelin and A. Morize (Paris: Librairie Ancienne Honoré Champion, 1914), II, p. 505, 'Warburton à Montesquieu, London, Bedford-Row, Feb. 9, 1754'.
21 Bolingbroke, *Idea of a Patriot King*, in *Political Writings*, pp. 281–2.
22 Bolingbroke, *Dissertation upon Parties*, in ibid., p. 34. See also Bolingbroke, 'Fragments, or Minutes of Essays: XXII', in *Works*, VIII, p. 8.
23 Henry St. John, Lord Viscount Bolingbroke, *Reflections Concerning Innate Moral Principles* (London, Bladon, 1752), pp. 5 and 31.

24 Ibid., p. 83.
25 Bolingbroke, *Dissertation upon Parties*, in *Political Writings*, p. 48.
26 Bolingbroke, *Innate Moral Principles*, p. 65.
27 In his 'Reflexions upon Exile' of 1716, Bolingbroke declared that 'in truth there is not so much difference between stoicism reduced to reasonable intelligible terms and genuine orthodox epicurism, as is imagined'. Bolingbroke, 'Reflections upon Exile', in *Letters*, II, p. 277. See also Fletcher, 'Intellectual Relations', p. 35.
28 Bolingbroke, *Dissertation upon Parties*, in *Political Writings*, p. 155. See also p. 98.
29 Ibid., p. 111. See also p. 164. 'In short, these two orders [the Lords and the Commons], according to the present constitution ... have no temptation, and scarce the means, of invading each other: so that they may the better, and the more effectually, employ their vigilance, and unite their efforts, whenever it shall be necessary, against the encroachments of the crown, from whose shackles they have both emancipated themselves, whether the attempts to impose these shackles again are carried on by prerogative, or by the more formidable enemy of liberty, corruption.'
30 Ibid., p. 127.
31 Ibid., pp. 125–6.
32 Bolingbroke, *Remarks*, p. 80.
33 Bolingbroke, *Dissertation upon Parties*, in *Political Writings*, p. 124.
34 Ibid., pp. 82–3. See also pp. 113–15.
35 Ibid., p. 78.
36 Ibid., p. 116.
37 Ibid., p. 97.
38 Nonetheless, he remained a sharp opponent of a standing army. Ibid., p. 92. This issue was also central to the parliamentary campaign against Walpole pursued by Bolingbroke's associates in the early 1730s. See Skinner, 'Principles and Practices of Opposition', pp. 96–7.
39 Bolingbroke, *Dissertation upon Parties*, in *Political Writings*, pp. 172–3. See also pp. 52 and 135.
40 Ibid., p. 162.
41 Ibid., p. 101.
42 Ibid., p. 105. Indeed, the whole 'Letter' from which this quotation comes was published separately, as *The Craftsman Extraordinary; Or, The Late Dissertation on Parties Continued; In Which the Right of the People to Frequent Elections of their Representatives is Fully Considered*, in the context of the campaign to repeal the Septennial Act. Interestingly, in the issue of *The Craftsman* for 16 March 1734, frequent elections was presented as the means of ensuring a rotation of office-holders, which was described as 'the very essence of Harrington's *Oceana*': *The Craftsman*, ed. Caleb D'Anvers [Bolingbroke et al.] (London: R. Francklin, 1731–37), XII, p. 65 (402, 16 March 1734). See also Kramnick, *Bolingbroke and His Circle*, p. 29.
43 Bolingbroke, *Dissertation upon Parties*, in *Political Writings*, pp. 93 and 124–5. As with the standing army, this was also a central issue in the parliamentary campaign. See Skinner, 'Principles and Practices of Opposition', pp. 97–8.
44 Bolingbroke, *Dissertation upon Parties*, in *Political Writings*, p. 151.
45 Bolingbroke, 'Reflections upon Exile', in *Letters*, II, p. 249.
46 Bolingbroke, *Dissertation upon Parties*, in *Political Writings*, p. 167.
47 Bolingbroke, *Idea of a Patriot King*, in ibid., p. 220.
48 Ibid., p. 220.
49 Ibid., p. 222.
50 Ibid., p. 251.
51 See for example Bolingbroke, *Dissertation upon Parties*, in ibid., pp. 143–52.
52 Various extracts from *The Craftsman*, including the whole of *A Dissertation upon Parties*, were translated in the 1730s. By 1754 *Remarks on History*, *A Letter on the Spirit of Patriotism*, *The Idea of a Patriot King*, *Letters on the Study and Use of History*, *Letter to Sir William Windham* and *Considerations on the Present State of Great Britain* had all been translated. Extracts from and reviews of his works also appeared in Huguenot journals. See for example *Bibliothèque britannique*,

XXI (September–December 1743), Article II and XXII (January–March 1744), Article V. *Bibliothèque raisonnée des ouvrages des savans de l'Europe*, XLIII (October–December 1749), pp. 243–67 and *Journal britannique*, I (January-February 1750). According to the marquis d'Argenson even the Dauphin was familiar with Bolingbroke's works. R. L. Voyer de Paulmy, marquis d'Argenson, *Journal et mémoires du marquis d'Argenson*, ed. E. J. B. Rathery (Paris: Mme Veuve Jules Renouard, 1856–67), VI, pp. 152 and 206 (18 February 1750). The influence of Bolingbroke's ideas in France has been investigated by both Fletcher and Barrell. Fletcher, 'Intellectual Relations'; D. J. Fletcher, 'The Fortunes of Bolingbroke in France in the Eighteenth Century', *Studies on Voltaire and the Eighteenth Century*, ed. T. Besterman, 47 (Geneva, 1966), pp. 207–32; 'Bolingbroke and the Diffusion of Newtonianism in France', *Studies on Voltaire and the Eighteenth Century*, ed. T. Besterman, 53 (Geneva, 1967), pp. 29–46; '*Le Législateur* and the Patriot King: A Case of Intellectual Kinship', *Comparative Literature Studies* 6 (1969), pp. 410–18; Barrell, *Bolingbroke and France*.

53 It is striking how many of those who translated Bolingbroke's works were involved in diplomacy. The dedicatory letter to his *Dissertation upon Parties* was translated by Chavigny's successor as French ambassador to Britain, Bussy, and the whole work was then translated by Etienne de Silhouette, who had also been involved in diplomatic missions in England. Similarly, Bolingbroke's *Letter to Sir William Windham* was translated as *Mémoires Secrets* by Jean-Louis Favier who had been sent on several diplomatic missions, including acting as secretary to the French ambassador at Turin, before becoming involved with the system of parallel diplomacy known as the *Secret du roi*. On Favier see J. Flammermont, 'J.-L. Favier: sa vie et ses écrits', *La Révolution française* 36 (1899), pp. 161–84, 258–76 and 314–35 and Chapter 7 below. In addition, both English and French versions of *The Craftsman* were available to French diplomats and are still held today in the archives of the Quai d'Orsay. Fletcher, 'Intellectual Relations', pp. 112, 250; Fletcher, 'Fortunes', pp. 218–19.

4

Bolingbroke's French associates

Introduction

Previous research into Bolingbroke's French connections has tended to focus on two important and interrelated areas. First, his association with and influence on well-known figures, most notably Voltaire and Montesquieu, and secondly his role in disseminating and popularising Newtonian ideas in France.[1] Much of this research was carried out in the 1940s and 1950s, before the theories about republicanism and the commonwealth tradition had been fully developed. Perhaps for this reason, Bolingbroke's role in disseminating those ideas in France has never been fully explored. This chapter will focus on this hitherto neglected aspect of Bolingbroke's influence in France. In particular, attention will be paid to Bolingbroke's associates at the Club de l'Entresol, many of whom were struggling with similar questions and coming up with similar solutions to his, and to two of his French acquaintances, Henri de Boulainvilliers and Montesquieu, both of whose ideas are such that they could even be described as proponents of a French version of the commonwealth tradition.[2]

Henri de Boulainvilliers

It was probably via his second wife, Madame de Villette, that Bolingbroke became acquainted with Boulainvilliers, the aristocratic historian and political writer, who was apparently an old friend of hers.[3] Bolingbroke certainly seems to have come to know Boulainvilliers early in his stay in France. In a letter to his friend the abbé Alary, dated 2 February 1718, he referred to Boulainvilliers in a way that suggests he was a mutual friend.[4] Dennis Fletcher, who carried out a detailed study of Bolingbroke's relations with France, insisted that there could be little doubt that Bolingbroke frequented Boulainvilliers's circle.[5] And Bolingbroke was certainly responsible for popularising some of Boulainvilliers's ideas among an English-speaking audience. Letter XV of his *A Dissertation upon Parties* included a summary of Boulainvilliers's views on French history.[6] As well as his links to Bolingbroke, Boulainvilliers may also have been associated with the Real Whig-Huguenot network. Margaret Jacob claimed that he was in contact with radical circles in the Netherlands,[7] while Ira Wade went so far as to suggest that he was the author of the manuscript version of the *Traité des Trois Imposteurs/ La Vie et L'Esprit de Spinosa*, a number of copies of which were in circulation in the early eighteenth century.[8] Subsequent scholars have questioned Wade's assertion, and the most recent study of the *Traité* demonstrates decisively that Boulainvilliers was not involved.[9] Nevertheless, the fact that he could have been suspected of being the author reflects the affinity between his ideas and those of the Real Whig-Huguenot circle.

Boulainvilliers is best known as the architect of what has come to be described as the *thèse nobiliaire*. This theory, and its counterpart the *thèse royale*, emerged in the final years and immediate aftermath of Louis XIV's reign, and as direct responses to it. The *thèse nobiliaire* and *thèse royale* offered competing accounts of the nature and origins of France's constitution and on the basis of these put forward rather different proposals for the reform of the French state. Advocates of the *thèse nobiliaire* argued that the French monarchy was German in origin, and called for a strengthened role for the nobility within the polity. Against them, proponents of the *thèse royale* insisted that the French monarchy had grown out of Roman rule, and they focused their attention on a strong absolute monarchy that would cultivate and rely on widespread popular support. Boulainvilliers developed the *thèse nobiliaire* in several works that circulated in manuscript form during his lifetime.[10] In those works he sought to demonstrate that the Francs, who had conquered Gaul at the time of the collapse of the Roman Empire, had been a free and equal warrior people who had chosen their kings and shared in rule with them. The system had been corrupted over time, particularly under Charles Martel and Pepin (Pippin), but was restored under Charlemagne – for whom Boulainvilliers had great admiration.[11] Through his historical analysis, Boulainvilliers sought to demonstrate that absolutism had been a much later innovation within the French polity. On this basis he argued that the nobility ought to reclaim their traditional role within the French government, and he argued for the restoration of the assemblies of the nation.

Given the character of the intellectual milieu in which they operated, where ideas were discussed informally and works circulated in manuscript form, it is difficult to be certain about the nature and direction of any influence exercised by the Real Whigs and Bolingbroke on Boulainvilliers or by him on them.[12] Nonetheless, the connections between them undoubtedly help to explain the marked affinity that can be detected between Boulainvilliers's ideas and those of the British commonwealth tradition. This affinity touches several different aspects of his thought.

In the first place there are noticeable similarities between Boulainvilliers's *political* views and those of the British commonwealthmen. He, like them, placed particular emphasis on the value and importance of liberty. As he explained in his *Histoire de l'ancien gouvernement de la France*: 'Originally the *French* were all free and perfectly equal and independent, both in general and as individuals', and he suggested that they fought so long and hard against the Romans and Barbarians precisely in order to secure 'this precious *Liberty* which they regarded as the dearest of all their goods'.[13] Boulainvilliers also combined a strong critique of tyrannical and even absolutist government with an acceptance of monarchy,[14] and he saw the mixed government of medieval Europe as an ideal means of balancing and checking the power of the monarch:

> [I]t is difficult not to praise the foresight of our ancestors and not to agree with them that the most desirable form of government is that in which the supreme authority is tempered by a council that is equally wise, disinterested and necessary. Such, in fact, as that which the incomparable Charlemagne gave his confidence to and made part of his power.[15]

Central to this system, and essential for the preservation of liberty, was the holding of general assemblies of the nation at which the nobility played a role in the establishment of the laws.[16] For example, in *Lettres historiques sur les parlements* Boulainvilliers described the role that the assemblies had played in the early French monarchy: 'It is true that [the early French kings] were not absolute masters, that there survives no order from the earliest times of the monarchy, which was not characterised by the consent of the General Assemblies of the *Champ de Mars* or *Champ de Mai*, where they had been drawn up.'[17] That the assemblies were supposed to be independent of the king was made clear by Boulainvilliers's suggestion that they began to be corrupted under Charlemagne's son Louis who, though still showing deference to their right and authority, began to try to persuade them to think as he did rather than learning from their advice.[18]

More specifically, just as with the writings of the British commonwealthmen, a number of distinctively Harringtonian ideas can be identified in Boulainvilliers's work. For example, he endorsed the notion of land as the basis of political power. It was their ownership of land that gave the Francs the right to participate in determining the affairs of the nation and it was important to him that they owned their land directly, not via their king.[19] Moreover, when explaining the problems faced by the successors of Charles the Bald in the late ninth century, Boulainvilliers noted that in their attempts to strengthen the power of the monarchy they had failed to take account of the fact that the majority of the land was owned not by them, but by the seigneurs.[20] It was this emphasis on land as the basis of power that led Boulainvilliers to stress the political role and significance of the nobility. In this respect his ideas were close to those of Bolingbroke, of whom it has been said that his 'most rooted political belief was his conviction that the landed gentry were the backbone of the political nation and the natural leaders of society'.[21] Moreover, in emphasising the role that the landed nobility ought to play in government both Boulainvilliers and Bolingbroke were attacking the rise of 'moneyed men' within the political sphere and the corruption of society that it entailed.[22]

Boulainvilliers also appears to have shared Harrington's belief that there were two sides to citizenship – the military and the political – and that the same people should exercise both. On Boulainvilliers's account, what distinguished the Francs from the Gauls was precisely their involvement in both military service and political office.[23] When Charles Martel sought to increase his own power he did so by depriving the Francs of their military and political roles – he filled his armies with foreigners and adventurers and stopped holding the *Champ de Mars* assemblies.[24] Moreover, in Boulainvilliers's eyes military service was not just a right that belonged to the Francs; he was also quick to acknowledge the advantages of a citizen militia over an army made up of foreigners and adventurers.[25]

Yet, despite these Harringtonian echoes, Boulainvilliers, just like the British commonwealthmen, reversed the chronology of Harrington's account by locating his ideal system in the gothic past. Like them he was appealing to the notion of an ancient constitution. Moreover, like them he also noted that this system was common to much of Europe in the period after the fall of the Roman Empire.[26] There is also a more direct link. Boulainvilliers's account of French history shared much in common with François Hotman's sixteenth-century Huguenot resistance tract, *Franco-Gallia*.[27] It was Hotman who had pioneered the idea of using an historical account of the ancient constitution of France as a means of justifying the form the constitution ought to take in the present. In particular, he sought to use the fact that according to the ancient constitution the monarch was simply a magistrate appointed to serve the Estates General, to argue for the limitation of royal power, and the importance of the role of that assembly, in the present. As was demonstrated in Chapter 1, Hotman's work was also an important source for the account of British history offered by the commonwealthmen. Indeed it was considered so important that Robert Molesworth chose to produce a translation of it in 1711. Moreover, Molesworth emphasised the affinity between Hotman's ancient constitutionalism and the Real Whig position by prefacing the 1721 edition of his translation with his pamphlet *The Principles of a Real Whig*.

This is not to say that Boulainvilliers's account of French history was identical to that of British history offered by the commonwealthmen. For one thing, the mixed system celebrated by the British writers comprised a monarchical, an aristocratic and a democratic element (King, Lords and Commons), whereas Boulainvilliers's emphasis was simply on the power of the monarch being tempered and controlled by assemblies of the nobility. According to Boulainvilliers, the French equivalent of the Commons – the Third Estate – was made up of descendants of the Gauls, whose subject status had meant that they did not enjoy political rights.[28] Bolingbroke himself was aware of this difference and used it to stress Britain's superiority over France.[29]

Not only did Boulainvilliers's political views resemble those of the commonwealthmen, but also he had a similar religious outlook (despite the obvious confessional differences).[30] Like them he acknowledged the relationship between civil and religious tyranny. For example, in his *Histoire de l'ancien gouvernement de la France* he described how Pepin (Pippin) had made an alliance with the clergy and had increased their role in government in order to strengthen his own power and reduce that of the nobility.[31] Moreover, his criticism of Charlemagne's son Louis, on the grounds that he had more respect for ministers than religion, echoes the anticlericalism of the commonwealthmen.[32] More broadly, Boulainvilliers appears to have shared the commonwealth understanding of religion as a human invention, which could be put to positive political ends, but which had more often been employed for the benefit of rulers and priests.[33] Like them, Boulainvilliers also favoured a rational and simple religion, and engaged in comparative religious studies, writing on the Jewish and Egyptian religions and, in his *La Vie de Mahomed*, on Islam.[34] He was also an admirer, though not a direct follower, of Spinoza and one of those who disseminated his ideas in France.

Finally, Boulainvilliers appears to have shared certain elements of the moral philosophy of the British commonwealthmen. Like them he accepted the Polybian notion of the tendency of all human institutions to decay,[35] and like them he emphasised the role played by the passions and self-interest within human nature.[36] He described how when the king's heart became divided between his own personal interests and those of the state – 'and when, consequently, he acts by the motivation of his passions' – those under him would also start to act on the basis of their own personal interests: 'they would accustom themselves at first to the same principles of personal interest, of scorn or indifference for the common good and of desire for the satisfaction of individual passions'.[37] Moreover, there is evidence to suggest that Boulainvilliers drew on the Harringtonian solution to the problem of the passions. He appears to have favoured the idea of constructing the political system in such a way that the self-interested actions of individuals could have a positive effect on society. According to Boulainvilliers, one of the advantages of the system of government introduced by Charlemagne was that it did just that:

> Moreover, this order rendered the men who were owners of their goods, interested in the conservation of all. It employed toward this end the liveliest passions in nature, such as love of oneself and of one's well-being, and love of one's children and kin.[38]

The classical republican or civic humanist character of Boulainvilliers's political thought has been noted by several scholars in recent years, as has his indebtedness to English ideas.[39] As has been demonstrated here, however, it is possible to go further than this since not only Boulainvilliers's political thought but also his religious and moral ideas were in line with those of the British commonwealthmen. Boulainvilliers is best understood, therefore, not simply as a classical republican, but rather as an early modern republican or a French exponent of the commonwealth tradition.

The Club de l'Entresol

The founder of the Club de l'Entresol, the abbé Pierre-Joseph Alary, was a friend of both Boulainvilliers and Bolingbroke.[40] Moreover, there is evidence to suggest that the works and ideas of both men were discussed within the Club.[41] Bolingbroke owed his friendship with Alary to the same source to which he owed that with Boulainvilliers – his wife, Madame de Villette.[42] Bolingbroke's extensive correspondence with Alary dates from at least February 1718, and the content of the earliest surviving letter between them suggests that the two men had already met prior to this point.[43] Moreover, the frequency of the letters and the tone in which they were written are redolent of a deep friendship.

While Bolingbroke's relations with Alary are well documented, the extent of his involvement with the Club de l'Entresol is less clear. The marquis d'Argenson made no mention of Bolingbroke in his account of the Club.[44] Yet, it has been suggested that Bolingbroke was in fact involved in its establishment in 1723.[45] The evidence on which this claim is based are two letters that Bolingbroke wrote to Alary on 13 July and 6 October 1723, in which he referred to 'our little academy' and 'our little society'.[46] Bolingbroke was also friendly with other members of the Club including the marquis de Torcy and the marquis de Matignon.[47] Thus, however limited Bolingbroke's direct involvement with the Club, he could easily have exercised an influence on its members via Alary and others.

The Club de l'Entresol met every Saturday between 5 and 8pm in the apartment that Alary rented from a member of the *Paris Parlement*, Charles-Jean-François Hénault, on the place Vendôme. It was the position of the apartment, on the mezzanine floor of the building, which gave the Club its name.[48] The focus of the Entresol was explicitly political. As d'Argenson explained, the attendees 'occupied themselves there with the affairs of the time and with modern political history'.[49] Each of the regular members of the Club was expected to carry out research into a different topic and then present a paper on it at the meetings. The rest of the time during meetings was devoted to catching up on and discussing the latest news (political and literary) as gleaned from newspapers and from members. Despite the nature of the topics covered, the discussions were said to be free: 'We debated without any reservation, and with a just confidence, all matters of importance that were being discussed in the world.'[50] Indeed, it was probably this freedom of speech on sensitive political topics that eventually brought about their downfall.[51]

Accounts of the Club de l'Entresol have tended to focus on the divisions between members, and in particular the distinction between those who favoured the *thèse nobiliaire* and those who endorsed the *thèse royale*.[52] While these divisions were undoubtedly important, the emphasis placed on them has led scholars to overlook the equally important ideas that held the members of the Club together. On the most basic level they were, of course, united in their interest in politics and foreign affairs and their concern with reform. More specifically, they also appear to have adopted a historical approach to contemporary political issues. In addition there were a number of common themes and historical models to which members of the Club repeatedly turned. For example, a number of them were interested in studying the decline and fall of once powerful states, and particularly of Rome.[53] Most significant for our purposes, however, is the fact that various members of the Club displayed an interest in forms of government that combined republican and monarchical elements, and several of them were particularly influenced by the British constitution.

A number of the research topics described by d'Argenson touch on the idea of mixed forms of government. The comte de Verteillac: 'was charged with writing on mixed governments, that is to say on combinations of aristocracy, democracy and monarchy. He had already finished Switzerland, Poland and la Moscovie. The comte d'Autri had to write in the same vein on the diverse governments of Italy'.[54] Similarly, several members of the Club were charged with investigating the gothic system of government and its key institutions. They included Alary himself, who was working on German history, and Lastre d'Oby who planned a complete history of the Estates-General and the *Parlements*.[55] The latter died soon after joining the Club and so his work was never completed, but other members also appear to have been interested in this topic. D'Argenson recalled how, during the time when they were meeting in Alary's apartment in the Bibliothèque du Roi, they would sometimes read manuscripts from the King's collection instead of listening to each other's works, and he specifically mentioned one occasion when they read a manuscript on the Estates-General.[56]

Developing a system that combined republican and monarchical elements was also central to many of the published works and reform proposals of members of the Club. In his *Relations du royaume des Féliciens*, the marquis de Lassay was explicit about this. In describing the origins of his fictional Félicien state, he explained that its wise legislator had been the Roman Lelius, 'who having known from his own experience the defects of republican government and being not unaware of how dangerous monarchical government is, composed a mixture of the two'.[57] Under Lelius's system royalty was hereditary, but the king was effectively 'the head of their Republic, because he placed such limits on royalty that the kings were strictly speaking only the protectors of the laws and of liberty'.[58] The king's role was simply to ensure that the laws were obeyed and to exercise mercy in individual cases.[59] The King governed together with two Councils, whose members were chosen by the deputies of the nation for their wisdom and virtue. In addition, the Estates of the Realm, comprising deputies of the entire nation, would meet once every six years and were charged with examining the King's conduct as well as having to consent to the declaration of war or the settling of peace.[60] Across the realm, government was administered locally, though always in accordance with the national laws.[61] Lassay himself noted the similarity between the Félicien system and that of the British,[62] and he even went so far as to describe the state, in terms reminiscent of Harrington, as: 'a place where one is governed by laws rather than by men'.[63]

The idea of combining republican and monarchical elements was not just reflected in the reform proposals of those like Boulainvilliers and Lassay, who favoured the *thèse nobiliaire*, but was also evident in the works of the Club's main proponent of the *thèse royale*, the marquis d'Argenson, though he proposed a mixture of a rather different kind. D'Argenson's major work was his *Considérations sur le gouvernement ancien et présent de la France*. Though it was not published until 1764, d'Argenson had written the work during the 1730s and it circulated in manuscript form from the end of the decade. The 'Notice sur la vie' to the Jannet edition of d'Argenson's *Mémoires* even suggested that it was in Entresol meetings that he first conceived of his plan for the work, and that he read sections of it to the Club.[64] Whether or not this was the case, the aim and nature of the work certainly suggest that it owed something to discussions held at the Entresol. D'Argenson's explicit purpose was to demonstrate the imperfections of feudal government and to refute Boulainvilliers's call for the restoration of the power of the old nobility.[65] In order to do so d'Argenson, in typical Entresol style, set out to examine the different governments of Europe. Despite their differences on other matters, d'Argenson was almost as explicit as Lassay about the need to combine republican and monarchical elements. Having noted, in the midst of his account of the Dutch state, the good standard of public works under republican governments, d'Argenson asked: 'Are the springs that produce this effect in republics absolutely antithetical to royalty?'[66] Like other members of the Entresol, d'Argenson was well aware of the problems of unrestrained monarchical power, and he criticised the desire of absolute monarchs to govern everything by their own agents.[67] Against the supporters of strict absolutism, d'Argenson insisted that political liberty and monarchical power could coexist, and he suggested that monarchical authority ought to be balanced: 'that which must balance it is the council of reason, that which must aid it is the interest of the people, recognised and driven by the people, ordered and authorised by the public power'.[68] This language of balance is reminiscent of that adopted by the commonwealthmen; like Lassay, d'Argenson even used the Harringtonian phrase about obeying laws not men.[69] However, in contrast to Lassay, d'Argenson firmly rejected mixed government on the British model. Rather, he characterised his proposals, which involved a strong and powerful monarch and a system of popular administration at a local level, as a unique combination of democratic and monarchical rule.[70] Indeed, the title of the manuscript version of the work was 'Jusques où la démocratie peut être admise dans le gouvernement monarchique'.

While at least some members of the Entresol showed a certain interest in the British constitution, most members of the Club appear to have shared Bolingbroke's concern that the British state in the early eighteenth century was threatened by corruption and decline. Moreover, their analyses of the faults within the British system were very similar to his. For example, Lassay drew a parallel between the British Parliament and the Félicien Estates of the Realm, but he noted that there was one important difference between them: 'that intrigue in elections, that money received and given, were crimes punished so rigorously by the Féliciens that such cases were rare and punishment always certain. The kings never got involved in these elections and they would risk much in doing so'.[71] Though he differed from Lassay in firmly rejecting the British model, the marquis d'Argenson's account of the constitutional developments on the other side of the Channel also appears to have owed much to the *Craftsman*.[72] In particular, d'Argenson emphasised the corruption that money had wrought within the British system. As he explained in his *Considérations*: 'The habit of loving money corrupts equally the manners and the politics of England.'[73]

In addition to expressing political views that shared something in common with the outlook of Bolingbroke and other British commonwealthmen, there is also evidence to suggest that members of the Club de l'Entresol held similar views to theirs on both religion and moral philosophy. A number of members of the Club, including d'Argenson, Michael Ramsay and Lévesque de Champeaux have been described as holding freethinking views.[74] However, it is the religious ideas of the marquis de Lassay, as reflected in his *Relation du royaume des Féliciens*, that are most instructive in this respect. Lassay described the religion of the Féliciens in some detail. Like the commonwealthmen, he proposed a system in which the doctrines were so simple that they could easily be accepted by all: 'Without admitting either books or revelation they worship a supreme Being and seek to practise virtue. That is their religion.'[75] Though regular public worship was required, it too was simple, and beyond these basic requirements liberty of conscience was endorsed: 'they leave men to think as they wish, without believing themselves to be charged with the care of their consciences'.[76]

Fletcher suggested that the primacy of the passions in determining human behaviour was probably much discussed by Bolingbroke when he was in exile,[77] and it has been suggested that his *Reflections concerning innate moral principles* was actually written for the Entresol, having been prompted by a discussion that had taken place there.[78] There is also evidence that other members of the club picked up on these ideas. In *Relation du royaume des Féliciens* Lassay suggested that the political system was organised in such a way that it was in the interests of the Féliciens to behave virtuously.[79] The role played by the passions and self-interest was also a constant preoccupation in d'Argenson's *Considérations*, and the system that he proposed in that work again stressed the benefits for the state that would follow from allowing people to pursue their own interests.[80] Though he believed self-interest to be a fundamental spring to human behaviour, d'Argenson did not believe it to be incompatible with concern for others, as long as the manners of the state were not corrupted by inequality and luxury. Where this had occurred (as he believed was the case in France) he, like Bolingbroke in *The Idea of a Patriot King*, placed his hopes in an enlightened monarch who would bring about a return to simpler customs and manners.[81]

Thus, though the differences between d'Argenson's *thèse royale* proposals and the *thèse nobiliaire* sympathies of other members of the Club de l'Entresol were undoubtedly important, the ideas that they shared are just as interesting and significant. In particular, members of the Club were some of the first thinkers in France to suggest that a combination of republican and monarchical elements might offer the best means of reforming the French state. In this, and in their ambiguous attitude toward the British constitution and religious and moral ideas, they shared much in common with Bolingbroke and with the British commonwealth tradition more generally. The same can be said of another important figure whose name has been linked to the Club de l'Entresol, the baron de Montesquieu.[82]

Montesquieu

In a letter to his friend William Warburton written in July 1752, Montesquieu referred to Bolingbroke, who had died the previous December. While acknowledging that they had become acquainted over thirty years before, Montesquieu played down the significance of the relationship: 'I have not had the pleasure of obtaining the good grace of this famous Lord. We have known each other for thirty years. This acquaintance has not been at all successful.'[83] Despite comments such as this, historians have long speculated on the influence Bolingbroke exerted on his French contemporary, noting several striking parallels between their ideas. As early as 1909, Joseph Dedieu suggested that Montesquieu had been profoundly influenced by a number of English thinkers including Bolingbroke, Thomas Gordon and, to a lesser extent, Algernon Sidney.[84] Subsequently, Dennis Fletcher acknowledged that Bolingbroke and Montesquieu were concerned with similar problems, in particular the relationship between environment and national character, and the tendency for political systems to decay over time.[85] Robert Shackleton famously argued that Bolingbroke was the source of Montesquieu's theory of the separation of powers.[86] However, it is possible to go further than Dedieu, Fletcher or Shackleton, since these similarities were, in fact, symptomatic of a deeper affinity. Montesquieu did not simply borrow particular ideas from Bolingbroke – rather, he engaged in a transformation of Harrington's thought along very similar lines to that enacted by the commonwealthmen.

Eric Nelson has recently suggested that Montesquieu drew on Harringtonian ideas.[87] In particular, Nelson emphasises the striking similarities between Montesquieu's account of Roman history, as reflected in his *Considérations sur les causes de la grandeur des Romains et de leur décadence*, and *An Essay on the Constitution and Government of the Roman State* by the British commonwealthman and committed neo-Harringtonian Walter Moyle.[88] On the basis of his analysis, Nelson challenges those who have suggested that Montesquieu was simply concerned with analysing different types of political system rather than with making normative judgements about them, and insists that Montesquieu in fact demonstrated a clear preference for republican government:

> That the President ... makes clear that his Greek republics cannot be brought into being in 'the dregs and corruption of modern times' does not negate his basic point. True, the 'political men' who lived in ancient Greece 'recognized no other force to sustain [the city] than virtue' while 'those of today speak to us only of manufacturing, commerce, finance, wealth, and even luxury'. But that disparity only reinforces Montesquieu's conviction that republics alone gave men the chance to live in accordance with their true natures.[89]

Yet this passage begs an obvious question. If Montesquieu did not believe his ideal republic to be applicable in the modern world, what was the next best thing? What advice did Montesquieu have to offer to his contemporaries concerning the form of government most suited to the large states of modern Europe? One answer might be the English constitution, as described by Montesquieu in Book 11 of *The Spirit of the Laws*. What is important here is that Montesquieu's depiction of the English constitution was also distinctively neo-Harringtonian.

We know for certain that Montesquieu owned a copy of Harrington's *The Commonwealth of Oceana*.[90] However, Montesquieu's treatment of Harrington in *The Spirit of the Laws* appears almost as scathing as his treatment of Bolingbroke in his letter to Warburton. Harrington's name appears just twice in the work.

The first reference to him comes at the end of the chapter 'On the constitution of England':

> Harrington, in his *Oceana*, has also examined the furthest point of liberty to which the constitution of a state can be carried. But of him it can be said that he sought this liberty only after misunderstanding it, and that he built Chalcedon with the coast of Byzantium before his eyes.[91]

Montesquieu's second reference to Harrington appeared at the end of Book 29. In referring to the way in which the laws tend to be affected by the 'passions and prejudices' of the legislator, he said: 'Harrington saw only the republic of England, while a crowd of writers found disorder wherever they did not see a crown.'[92] While Montesquieu's aim was certainly to criticise Harrington's work, the strength of his critique owed much to the fact that Montesquieu shared many of Harrington's principles.

The similarities between Montesquieu's ideas and those of Harrington are clear throughout Book 11 of *The Spirit of the Laws*. Like Harrington, Montesquieu was particularly concerned with liberty, the threat posed to it by the exercise of power and the means by which it could be secured. In his *Pensées* Montesquieu described liberty as 'that good which makes it possible to enjoy other goods'.[93] In Book 11 of *The Spirit of the Laws* he noted that liberty 'is only present when power is not abused'. This presented him with a problem, since 'it has eternally been observed that any man who has power is led to abuse it'.[94] Moreover, Montesquieu, like Harrington, acknowledged that the solution to this problem lies in the constitution: 'So that one cannot abuse power, power must check power by the arrangement of things. A constitution can be such that no one will be constrained to do the things the law does not oblige him to do or be kept from doing the things the law permits him to do.'[95] Significantly, one of the passages from Bolingbroke's *Craftsman* that Montesquieu copied into his *Spicilège* notebook expressed precisely this idea: 'From the *Craftsman*. The government is good when the laws are such that they necessarily produce virtue and can turn even bad men into good ministers.'[96]

While Montesquieu seems to have accepted that Harrington had correctly identified the problem, and the general means of solving it, he did not accept the details of his solution. He thought that the existing English constitution itself offered a better means of protecting liberty against the abuses of power than the model constitution set out by Harrington in *Oceana*. In particular, Montesquieu rejected Harrington's suggestion that what was required was kingless government. Writing during the Interregnum, Harrington had sought to show that England in the mid-seventeenth century was not suited to monarchical government. The mixed and balanced constitution that he proposed, though incorporating monarchical, aristocratic and democratic elements, did not include a king or queen. By contrast Montesquieu, writing in eighteenth-century France, was adamant that a monarch was an essential component of a mixed and balanced system. Only a monarch, Montesquieu insisted, could properly perform the executive function:

> The executive power should be in the hands of a monarch, because the part of the government that almost always needs immediate action is better administered by one than by many, whereas what depends on legislative power is often better ordered by many than by one.[97]

Moreover, having a hereditary monarch would also ensure a clear distinction between the executive and legislative functions:

> If there were no monarch and the executive power were entrusted to a certain number of persons drawn from the legislative body, there would no longer be liberty, because the two powers would be united, the same persons sometimes belonging and always able to belong to both.[98]

In failing to acknowledge this, Harrington had made the common mistake, noted by Montesquieu at the beginning of Book 11, of confusing 'the power of the people' with 'the liberty of the people' and therefore assuming that liberty was better protected in a republic than in a monarchy. Consequently, in attempting to find a means of protecting liberty against the abuse of power, Harrington had looked to the small city-state republics of antiquity and renaissance Italy. In Montesquieu's opinion he could have found a model better suited to the large states of the modern world if he had turned not to Greece and Rome, but to medieval Europe: 'If one wants to read the admirable work by Tacitus, *On the Mores of the Germans*, one will see that the English have taken their idea of political government from the Germans. This fine system was found in the forests.'[99] That this German model (not the Greek city-state) served as the basis of Montesquieu's favoured form of government (at least for practical purposes) is made clear in the subsequent chapter:

> Soon the civil liberty of the people, the prerogatives of the nobility and of the clergy, and the power of the kings, were in such concert that there has never been, I believe, a government on earth as well tempered as that of each part of Europe during the time that this government continued to exist; and it is remarkable that the corruption of the government of a conquering people should have formed the best kind of government men have been able to devise.[100]

Thus, both Harrington and Montesquieu recognised that a proper balance of powers was essential if liberty was to be protected, but, unlike Harrington, Montesquieu believed that the monarchical element was best performed by a king or queen and that the aristocratic element should be represented by a hereditary aristocracy. Consequently, on Montesquieu's account, the English constitution provided the balance that was necessary for liberty to be protected.

This was why Montesquieu was able to describe Britain as 'a nation where the republic hides under the form of monarchy' and as 'an absolute government over the foundation of a free government',[101] and it was why he accused Harrington of having built Chalcedon when he had the coast of Byzantium before his eyes.[102]

Montesquieu's accusation was more than a little unfair, however, since what he was referring to when he spoke of the English constitution was the post-1688 settlement, whereas what Harrington had actually had before his eyes was the English constitution as it operated under Charles I. While it is true that the English political system of the 1630s and 1640s could be characterised as a mixed and balanced system – as it was in *His Majesty's Answer to the Nineteen Propositions*, drafted by Viscount Falkland and Sir John Colepeper in 1642 – the way in which it had operated in practice did not conform to the ideal.[103] To take the most obvious example, during the 1630s Charles I had managed to reign for eleven years without calling Parliament and during that time had introduced a number of extra-parliamentary means of raising revenue. On the basis of what he said in *The Spirit of the Laws*, Montesquieu would have had to acknowledge that this behaviour posed a threat to liberty:

> If the legislative body were not convened for a considerable time, there would no longer be liberty. For one of two things would happen: either there would no longer be any legislative resolution and the state would fall into anarchy; or these resolutions would be made by the executive power, and it would become absolute.
>
> [...]
>
> If the executive power enacts on the raising of public funds without the consent of the legislature, there will no longer be liberty, because the executive power will become the legislator on the most important point of legislation.[104]

It is perhaps to be expected that not all eighteenth-century commentators were convinced by Montesquieu's attempt to distance himself from Harrington. In his *Éloge de Montesquieu*, published in 1786, Jean-Jacques Rutledge drew a close parallel between the two men and suggested that, although he had sought to hide it, Montesquieu had been profoundly influenced by Harrington.[105] Rutledge insisted that the differences between the two men on forms of government could easily be explained by the circumstances in which they were writing. Had Montesquieu lived in Harrington's time and place he: 'would have had the same ideas as him. He would have produced similar writings and very probably would have suffered a fate similar to that of the unfortunate Gentleman of the Bedchamber to Charles I'. And if Harrington had been born in Guyenne a century later he would have: 'followed the same course and fulfilled the same role as the illustrious Montesquieu'.[106] In particular Rutledge sought to argue that the circumstances in which Montesquieu lived had prevented him from being open about his true position.

Montesquieu's sympathetic critique of Harrington's *Oceana* in Book 11 of *The Spirit of the Laws* was not, of course, original. Rather, Montesquieu followed with striking precision the moves that had already been made by British commonwealthmen writing in the late seventeenth and early eighteenth centuries. They too had sought to apply Harrington's principles to the monarchical setting of the post-1688 constitutional settlement. In order to do so they, like Montesquieu, had turned to the Germanic model of a mixed monarchy.[107]

Montesquieu also echoed the British commonwealthmen in recognising that while the English constitution might – in theory – offer the best means available of protecting political liberty, in practice it was not immune to corruption. Montesquieu hinted at this at the end of his chapter 'On the constitution of England', where he said: 'It is not for me to examine whether at present the English enjoy this liberty or not. It suffices for me to say that it is established by their laws, and I seek no further.'[108]

Conclusion

I have tried to show that what we find on both sides of the Channel in the first half of the eighteenth century is the adaptation of seventeenth-century English republican ideas into a form that was more appropriate for eighteenth-century circumstances. No doubt partly influenced by Bolingbroke and his predecessors, Boulainvilliers and various members of the Club de l'Entresol expressed political, religious and moral ideas that were remarkably similar to those put forward by the British commonwealthmen.

Several of the figures discussed here appear to have combined reverence for the small republican governments of antiquity with a recognition that such governments simply were not viable in the very different circumstances of modern Europe. In these conditions a mixed and balanced system, like that which existed (at least in theory) in Britain after 1688, offered the next-best thing. It provided a means by which republican elements might be maintained within a monarchical framework in such a way that political liberty could be protected. Given the central role played by Montesquieu in promoting this idea, we can perhaps expand upon Judith Shklar's observation that Montesquieu 'set the terms in which republicanism was to be discussed' in the second half of the eighteenth century.[109] Not only did Montesquieu provide the seeds and terms of the ancient republican tradition that went on to influence Jacobin thought to such devastating effect but, also, he was one of the key figures in the transmission of the English republican or commonwealth tradition to eighteenth-century France.

While Montesquieu's focus in Book 11 of *The Spirit of the Laws* was on England, and while he was (as his Preface made clear) cautious about the idea of reforming political systems, and especially of applying ideas from one time or place to another, the lessons that could be learned were not without relevance elsewhere in Europe. The English constitution offered a means by which some of the advantages of the republican systems of the ancient world could be incorporated within the large states of modern Europe. Moreover, the fact that the origins of the English constitution could be traced back to the Germanic institutions that had spread across Europe at the time of the fall of the Roman Empire suggested that the model could perhaps be similarly revived in other eighteenth-century European states, not least France.[110] Montesquieu never did anything more than hint at this idea, but in the works of one of his contemporaries, we find the explicit development of a commonwealth reform programme for France.

Notes

1. D. J. Fletcher, 'The Intellectual Relations of Lord Bolingbroke with France' (MA Thesis, University of Wales, 1953); D. J. Fletcher, 'The Fortunes of Bolingbroke in France in the Eighteenth Century', *Studies on Voltaire and the Eighteenth Century*, ed. T. Besterman, 47 (Geneva, 1966), pp. 207–32; D. J. Fletcher, 'Bolingbroke and the Diffusion of Newtonianism in France', *Studies on Voltaire and the Eighteenth Century*, ed. T. Besterman, 53 (Geneva, 1967), pp. 29–46; D. J. Fletcher, '*Le Législateur* and the Patriot King: A Case of Intellectual Kinship', *Comparative Literature Studies* 6 (1969), pp. 410–18; R. Shackleton, 'Montesquieu, Bolingbroke, and the Separation of Powers', *French Studies* 3 (1949), pp. 25–38; R. Shackleton, *Montesquieu: A Critical Biography* (Oxford: Oxford University Press, 1961); R. Barrell, *Bolingbroke and France* (Lanham, MD: University Press of America, 1988). There has been some debate over Bolingbroke's relationship with Voltaire. Torrey downplayed Bolingbroke's influence over his French acquaintance, but others, including Fletcher, have suggested that the influence was significant. N. L. Torrey, *Voltaire and the English Deists* (New Haven, CT: Yale University Press, 1930), especially pp. 135–53.
2. There is, of course, also a story to be told about Bolingbroke's influence on the development of the idea of patriotism in France. However, since this topic has recently received attention from other scholars, and since it does not relate directly to the focus of this study, I have not dwelt on it here. See E. Dziembowski, *Un Nouveau Patriotisme français, 1750–1770: La France face à la puissance anglaise à l'époque de la guerre de Sept Ans* (Oxford: Voltaire Foundation 1998) and P. R. Campbell, 'The Language of Patriotism in France, 1750–1770', *E-France: An On-Line Journal of French Studies* 1 (2007), pp. 1–43, www.reading.ac.uk/e-france/Campbell%20%20 Language%20of%20Patriotism.htm.pdf. Similarly, Michael Sonenscher has noted the influence of Bolingbroke's views on public credit in France. M. Sonenscher, *Before the Deluge: Public Debt, Inequality, and the Intellectual Origins of the French Revolution* (Princeton and Oxford: Princeton University Press, 2007), pp. 182–3.
3. Fletcher, 'Intellectual Relations', p. 40.
4. Bolingbroke, *Lettres historiques, politiques, philosophiques et particulières de Henri Saint-John, Lord Vicomte Bolingbroke, depuis 1710 jusqu'en 1736…*, ed. Grimoard (Paris: Dentu, 1808), II, p. 453.
5. Fletcher, 'Intellectual Relations', p. 131. See also Fletcher, 'Fortunes', p. 221.
6. Bolingbroke, *A Dissertation upon Parties*, in Bolingbroke, *Political Writings*, ed. D. Armitage (Cambridge: Cambridge University Press, 1997), pp. 143–51.
7. M. C. Jacob, *The Radical Enlightenment: Pantheists, Freemasons and Republicans* (London: George Allen & Unwin, 1981), pp. 146, 223. Interestingly, Jacob insists on page 223 that Boulainvilliers was not a republican. While this may be true in the narrow constitutional sense of the word, his political position, as will be demonstrated below, was remarkably similar to that of the Real Whigs.

8 I. O. Wade, *The Clandestine Organization and Diffusion of Philosophic Ideas in France from 1700 to 1750* (Princeton: Princeton University Press, 1938).
9 S. Berti, 'The First Edition of the *Traité des trois imposteurs*, and its Debt to Spinoza's *Ethics*', in M. Hunter and D. Wootton (ed.), *Atheism from the Reformation to the Enlightenment* (Oxford: Clarendon Press, 1992), pp. 183–220.
10 See in particular H. comte de Boulainvilliers, *Histoire de l'ancien gouvernement de la France, avec XIV Lettres historiques sur les parlements où états généraux* (Amsterdam and The Hague, 1727). On Boulainvilliers and his works see R. Simon, *Henry de Boulainviller: historien, politique, philosophe, astrologue, 1658–1722* (Paris: Boivin & C., [1941]); M. Ozouf and F. Furet, 'Two Historical Legitimations of Eighteenth-century French Society: Mably and Boulainvilliers', in F. Furet (ed.), *In the Workshop of History* (Chicago: University of Chicago Press, 1984), pp. 125–39; and H. A. Ellis, *Boulainvilliers and the French Monarchy: Aristocratic Politics in Early Eighteenth-Century France* (Ithaca and London: Cornell University Press, 1988).
11 See for example Letter II in *Lettres historiques sur les parlements*, in Boulainvilliers, *Histoire de l'ancien gouvernement*, Part II, pp. 209–50.
12 Barrell certainly believed that the two men had influenced each other. Barrell, *Bolingbroke and France*, esp. pp. 58 and 68. Isaac Kramnick insisted that Bolingbroke was influenced by Boulainvilliers, suggesting that in the latter's *thèse nobiliaire* he found a 'frame of reference' in which to 'analyze his own society'. I. Kramnick, *Bolingbroke and his Circle: The Politics of Nostalgia in the Age of Walpole* (Ithaca and London: Cornell University Press, 1992 [1968]), pp. 16–17.
13 Boulainvilliers, *Histoire de l'ancien gouvernement*, Part I, pp. 26–7. Interestingly, the English translation of Boulainvilliers's *Lettres historiques sur les parlements où états généraux* which appeared in 1739 stressed Boulainvilliers's emphasis on liberty. The title page stated that the work had been translated 'for the Use and Instruction of such BRITISH Lovers of LIBERTY, as cannot read the ORIGINAL', while in the preface Boulainvilliers himself was labelled 'a passionate Adorer of Liberty' (p. xxvii) and his work was described as demonstrating how the French had descended from being the freest nation in Europe to their current position of slavery (p. xxviii). Moreover, the translation was dedicated to Frederick, Prince of Wales, for the instruction of whom Bolingbroke's *The Idea of a Patriot King* was probably written and who was also the dedicatee of Thomas Gordon's translation of Tacitus' *Histories*. H. comte de Boulainvilliers, *An Historical Account of the Antient Parliaments of France, or States-General of the Kingdom. In Fourteen Letters*, ed. C. Forman (London: J. Brindley, 1739).
14 Boulainvilliers, *Histoire de l'ancien gouvernement*, Part II, pp. 252–3.
15 Ibid., Part II, pp. 254–5.
16 Ibid., Part I, p. 57. Describing the decline of the Estates General and the means by which it could be revived were two of the central aims of the *Lettres historiques sur les parlements*: ibid., Part II, pp. 169–70.
17 Ibid., Part II, p. 215.
18 Ibid., Part II, p. 269.
19 Ibid., Part I, p. 50.
20 Ibid., Part I, p. 97.
21 H. Dickinson, 'St John, Henry, styled first Viscount Bolingbroke (1678–1751)', *Oxford Dictionary of National Biography* (Oxford: Oxford University Press, 2004; online edition, May 2006), www.oxforddnb.com/view/article/24496, accessed 10 March 2008. See also H. T. Dickinson, *Bolingbroke* (London: Constable, 1970). Bolingbroke's faith in the nobility is made particularly clear in *A Letter on the Spirit of Patriotism*, so it is perhaps not a coincidence that this work was written while he was in France, in 1736.
22 For Boulainvilliers's critique of the usurpation of birth and virtue by wealth and royal favour see: Ellis, *Boulainvilliers and the French Monarchy*, pp. 27 and 66 and H. A. Ellis, 'Genealogy, History, and Aristocratic Reaction in Early Eighteenth-Century France: The Case of Henri de Boulainvilliers', *Journal of Modern History* 58 (1986), p. 414–51, especially pp. 444–6.
23 Boulainvilliers, *Histoire de l'ancien gouvernement*, Part I, p. 39.
24 Ibid., Part I, pp. 98–9.

25 Ibid., Part I, pp. 41–3. In the preface to the English translation of the *Lettres historiques sur les parlements où états généraux*, the link between the decline of liberty and the establishment of a standing army – typical of the Standing Army debate of the 1690s – was emphasised: 'From this View of Parliamentary Power, he leads to others of its declining State, and so from Scene to Scene, unto the Establishment of a *perpetual Army*, and then Good-night to all Remains of Liberty! A *Standing Army*, I don't say an *annual one*, in a free Nation is a Paradox.': Boulainvilliers, *Historical Account of the Antient Parliaments of France*, pp. xxix–xxx.
26 Boulainvilliers, *Histoire de l'ancien gouvernement*, Part II, pp. 251–2.
27 On Hotman's text see Q. Skinner, *The Foundations of Modern Political Thought*. Vol. 2: *The Age of Reformation* (Cambridge: Cambridge University Press, 1978), pp. 310–15.
28 Of course, Boulainvilliers's ideas can be interpreted as reflecting a threefold mixture of monarchy, aristocracy and democracy if the Council of State is seen as representing the aristocratic element and the Frankish nobility the democratic. However, this is still a rather different model from that of the British.
29 Bolingbroke, *Dissertation upon Parties* in *Political Writings*, pp. 143–9. See also Fletcher, 'Intellectual Relations', p. 200.
30 On Boulainvilliers's religious views see Simon, *Henry de Boulainviller*, pp. 321–57.
31 Boulainvilliers, *Histoire de l'ancien gouvernement*, Part I, p. 99 and Part II, pp. 247–8.
32 Ibid., Part I, pp. 84–8.
33 Simon, *Henry de Boulainviller*, p. 332.
34 H. comte de Boulainvilliers, *La Vie de Mahomed* (London [Amsterdam]: P. Humbert, 1730). On this work see D. Venturino, 'Un prophète "philosophe"? Une *Vie de Mahomed* à l'aube des lumières', *Dix-huitième siècle* 24 (1992), pp. 321–31.
35 Boulainvilliers, *Histoire de l'ancien gouvernement*, Part II, p. 324.
36 Ellis, *Boulainvilliers and the French Monarchy*, p. 207; V. Buranelli, 'The Historical and Political Thought of Boulainvilliers', *Journal of the History of Ideas* 18 (1957), pp. 480–1.
37 Boulainvilliers, *Histoire de l'ancien gouvernement*, Part I, p. 120. This was not the only place in which Boulainvilliers suggested that the behaviour of the prince had an important impact on the character of the nation. See also Part II, pp. 244–245. There is a similarity here to Bolingbroke's arguments in *The Idea of a Patriot King*.
38 Boulainvilliers, *Histoire de l'ancien gouvernement*, Part I, p. 109. See also Part II, pp. 184–5 on the cultivation of a love of one's country.
39 Ellis, *Boulainvilliers and the French Monarchy*; Ellis, 'Genealogy, History, and Aristocratic Reaction', p. 449; J. K. Wright, 'The Idea of a Republican Constitution in Old Régime France', in M. van Gelderen and Q. Skinner (eds), *Republicanism: A Shared European Heritage*. Vol. 1: *Republicanism and Constitutionalism in Early Modern Europe* (Cambridge: Cambridge University Press, 2002), pp. 289–306. In her account of Boulainvilliers in *Philosophy and the State in France*, Nannerl Keohane also noted Boulainvilliers's borrowing of English constitutionalism. N. O. Keohane, *Philosophy and the State in France* (Princeton: Princeton University Press, 1976), pp. 348–9.
40 On Alary and the Club de l'Entresol see E. R. Briggs, 'The Political Academies of France in the Early Eighteenth Century; with Special Reference to the Club de l'Entresol, and to its Founder, the Abbé Pierre-Joseph Alary' (University of Cambridge PhD Thesis, 1931); N. Childs, 'New Light on the Entresol, 1724–1731: The Marquis de Balleroy's "Histoire Politique de l'Europe", *French History* 4 (1990), pp. 77–109 and N. Childs, *A Political Academy in Paris, 1724–1731: The Entresol and its Members* (Oxford: Voltaire Foundation, 2000).
41 Most of Boulainvilliers's works were first published in the 1720s and 1730s, at the time when the Club de l'Entresol was meeting. It is perhaps not surprising, therefore, that its members were familiar with, and discussed, Boulainvilliers's ideas.
42 Bolingbroke, *Lettres historiques*, ed. Grimoard, I, pp. ix–x; Fletcher, 'Intellectual Relations', p. 40.
43 Bolingbroke, *Lettres historiques*, ed. Grimoard, II, pp. 439–42. Almost all of the surviving letters to Alary from Bolingbroke were reprinted in Grimoard's collection.
44 D'Argenson, 'Mémoire, pour servir à l'histoire des conferences politiques, tenues à l'*Entresol*,

depuis 1724, jusqu'en 1731', printed in Bolingbroke, *Lettres historiques*, ed. Grimoard, III, pp. 458–85. See also the very similar 'Histoire des conférences de l'Entresol, tenues, chez M. l'abbé Alary de 1724–1731' in R. L. Voyer de Paulmy, marquis d'Argenson, *Mémoires et journal inédit du marquis d'Argenson* (Paris: P. Jannet, 1857–58), I, pp. 87–115.

45   Childs, *Political Academy*, p. 87. See also Barrell, *Bolingbroke and France*, p. 29.
46   'Chargez-vous de mes très humbles compliments à toute notre petite académie. Si je ne comptais pas les revoir dans le mois prochain, je serais inconsolable. Ils ont confirmé mon gout pour la philosophie; ils ont fait reviver celui que j'avais autrefois pour les belles lettres: que je leur suis obligé.' Bolingbroke, *Lettres historiques*, ed. Grimoard, III, p. 193 (Grimoard actually gives the date as 13 July 1724, but this is corrected in the addendum). 'Mille tendres compliments à notre petite société.' Ibid., III, p. 206.
47   Bolingbroke worked with the marquis de Torcy in the negotiations that led to the Peace of Utrecht. Some of the letters between them appear in Grimoard's collection. Bolingbroke mentioned Matignon as a friend in a letter addressed to Madame de Ferriol in February 1718. Ibid., II, pp. 459–60. Significantly, Barrell suggests that Bolingbroke also became friendly with another member of the Club, the marquis de Lassay. Barrell, *Bolingbroke and France*, p. 17. During his second period of exile in France Bolingbroke appears to have been in touch with d'Argenson himself.
48   Alary moved house more than once during the lifetime of the Club. In his final apartment in the Bibliothèque du Roi a mezzanine was constructed especially for the Club. D'Argenson, 'Mémoire', in Bolingbroke, *Lettres historiques*, ed. Grimoard, III, p. 475.
49   Ibid., III, p. 458.
50   Ibid., III, p. 472. See also d'Argenson, *Mémoires et journal inédit*, I, p. 68.
51   For d'Argenson's account see *Lettres historiques*, ed. Grimoard, III, pp. 476–85 and his 'Histoire', in *Mémoires et journal inédit*, pp. 102–15, which also includes several letters relating to the downfall of the Club. See also Childs, *Political Academy*, pp. 125–35.
52   Childs has also drawn a further distinction among supporters of the *thèse nobiliaire* between those who saw the revival of the provincial assemblies and the Estates General as the basis for reform and those who focused instead on strengthening the power of the *parlements*. Childs, *Political Academy*, p. 17.
53   Bolingbroke expressed his own interests in this theme in a letter to Alary dated 26 April 1722: 'Once this is done I would like to work on Roman history, conjointly with that of my country, following an idea that has long been turning round in my head. The history of France will also come into it a lot, and that of Greece a little.' National Library of Scotland (NLS): 3419, f. 40, 'Letter from Bolingbroke to Alary, 1722'. Reprinted in Bolingbroke, *Lettres historiques*, ed. Grimoard, III, p. 164. The decline of states was also a particular interest of Lévesque de Champeaux (Childs, *Political Academy*, p. 102) and it was, of course, the central theme of Montesquieu's *Considérations sur les causes de la grandeur des Romains et de leur decadence*. See also Childs, *Political Academy*, Chapter 11.
54   D'Argenson, 'Mémoire', in Bolingbroke, *Lettres historiques*, ed. Grimoard, III, p. 466.
55   Ibid., III, pp. 464 and 467.
56   Ibid., III, p. 475.
57   Marquis de Lassay, *Relation du royaume des Féliciens, peuples qui habitent dans les terres australes; dans laquelle il est traité de leur origine, de leur religion, de leur gouvernement, de leurs moeurs, & de leurs coutumes*, in *Recueil de differentes choses, par M. le Marquis de Lassay* (Lausanne: Marc-Michel Bousquet, 1756), p. 387.
58   Ibid., pp. 385–6.
59   Ibid., pp. 399–400.
60   Ibid., pp. 399 and 409.
61   Ibid., p. 410.
62   Ibid., p. 396.
63   Ibid., p. 348. See also p. 441.
64   D'Argenson, *Mémoires et journal inédit*, I, p. ciii. For background on Argenson and this work

see N. O. Henry, 'Democratic Monarchy: The Political Theory of the Marquis d'Argenson' (Yale PhD Thesis, 1968) and her account of him in Keohane, *Philosophy and the State in France*, pp. 376ff.
65. R. L. Voyer de Paulmy, marquis d'Argenson, *Considérations sur le gouvernement ancien et present de la France* (Amsterdam: Rey, 1764), pp. 1, 29, 121, 140. A note on the manuscript version made this aim explicit. See Childs, *Political Academy*, pp. 185–6.
66. D'Argenson, *Considérations*, p. 62. In the 'Notice sur la vie' to the Jannet edition of d'Argenson's *Mémoires et journal inédit*, it was suggested that d'Argenson had a secret affection for the federal republican government of the United Provinces. *Mémoires et journal inédit*, I, pp. xlvi–ii.
67. D'Argenson, *Considérations*, p. 28.
68. Ibid., pp. 120–1.
69. Ibid., p. 289. Whether or not he was familiar with Harrington's works, d'Argenson certainly knew that of Sidney. In his journal he offered a refutation of it on the grounds that 'It is the best thing that has been written against the power of a single person' and that it had, therefore, to be refuted by anyone wishing to defend monarchical government. D'Argenson, *Mémoires et journal inédit*, V, pp. 271–6.
70. D'Argenson set out his reform proposals in Chapter 7 of his work, D'Argenson, *Considérations*, pp. 207–50. A body of popular magistrates would be established at the head of each community. These magistrates would represent the community and be responsible for policing public works, the encouragement of manufacturing and financial administration within their locality. Significantly these popular magistrates were to be replaced annually by mixture of election and appointment.
71. Lassay, *Relation du royaume des Féliciens*, p. 403.
72. Fletcher, 'Intellectual Relations', p. 112. As Fletcher noted, d'Argenson had studied and even made translations of extracts from *The Craftsman*, which are still held in the Archives of the Quai d'Orsay.
73. D'Argenson, *Considérations*, p. 40. See more generally pp. 36–41.
74. Nannerl Keohane described d'Argenson as a 'free-thinker'. Keohane, *Philosophy and the State in France*, p. 378. On Michael Ramsay and Lévesque de Champeaux see Fletcher, 'Intellectual Relations', pp. 50–65 and Childs, *Political Academy*, p. 117.
75. Lassay, *Relation du royaume des Féliciens*, p. 486. See also p. 395.
76. Ibid., p. 486.
77. Fletcher, 'Intellectual Relations', p. 154.
78. Bolingbroke referred in the work to the conversation that had prompted it and the eighteenth-century editor of his works, David Mallet, suggested that it had been written 'for the use of a noble club at Paris of which he was a member'. Bolingbroke, *Reflections Concerning Innate Moral Principles* (London: Bladon, 1752), pp. 5 and 84.
79. Lassay, *Relation du royaume des Féliciens*, p. 349.
80. See Keohane, *Philosophy and the State in France*, pp. 380–2.
81. Although Bolingbroke does not appear to have still been associated with the Entresol once d'Argenson was a member, there is clear evidence that the Frenchman knew Bolingbroke's works. On 29 May 1750 d'Argenson wrote in his journal: 'Bolingbroke has written a very well known work that has excited kings to patriotism. But this is not all. This quality must also be found in ministers, otherwise the government degenerates into tyranny.' D'Argenson, *Mémoires et journal inédit*, III, p. 332.
82. The extent of Montesquieu's relationship with the Entresol is unclear. The only direct evidence of his involvement is the fact that the nineteenth-century collector Matthieu Villenave claimed that a copy of Montesquieu's *Dialogue de Sylla et d'Eucrate* was found among Alary's papers. According to d'Argenson, members deposited with Alary manuscript copies of the papers they had read at meetings. Montesquieu was also known to be friendly with a number of members of the Club, including the marquis de Lassay, the Matignons and Lévesque de Champeaux. Briggs, Shackleton and Childs all conclude that he probably was associated with the Club and that he attended at least some meetings between 1724 and 1728. Briggs, 'Political Academies

of France', pp. 138–40; Shackleton, *Montesquieu*, pp. 63–7; Childs, *Political Academy*, pp. 81–6 and 191–6.
83 *Autographes de Mariemont*, ed. M. J. Durry (Paris, 1955–59), II, pp. 499–502, 'Montesquieu to Warburton, 4 July 1752'.
84 J. Dedieu, *Montesquieu et la tradition politique anglaise en France: les sources anglaises de l'esprit des lois* (Geneva: Slatkine Reprints, 1971 [1909]).
85 Fletcher, 'Intellectual Relations', pp. 205–43.
86 Shackleton, 'Montesquieu, Bolingbroke, and the separation of powers'. See also Barrell, *Bolingbroke and France*, pp. 72–8. The influence between Bolingbroke and Montesquieu did not just flow in one direction. Several issues of the *Craftsman* imitated Montesquieu's *Lettres Persanes*. See *The Craftsman*, ed. Caleb d'Anvers (London: R. Francklin, 1731–37), II, pp. 6–14 (46 and 47, 20 and 27 May 1727); V, pp. 152–8 (172, 18 October 1729) and IX, pp. 144–9 (311, 17 June 1732). See also Kramnick, *Bolingbroke and His Circle*, pp. 21 and 69.
87 E. Nelson, *The Greek Tradition in Republican Thought* (Cambridge: Cambridge University Press, 2004), pp. 129, 159–60 and 172–4.
88 As Nelson notes, this influence was originally spotted by Bertrand Barère, who produced a translation of Moyle's work in 1801. W. Moyle, *Essai sur le gouvernement de Rome*, trans. B. Barère (Paris: Imprimerie de Marchant l'aîné, an X [1801]), pp. v–viii. Nelson, *The Greek Tradition*, p. 136.
89 Nelson, *The Greek Tradition*, p. 193.
90 Montesquieu, *Catalogue de la bibliothèque de Montesquieu*, ed. L. Desgraves (Geneva: Droz, 1954), p. 169 – no. 2376.
91 Montesquieu, *The Spirit of the Laws*, ed. A. Cohler et al. (Cambridge: Cambridge University Press, 1989), p. 166.
92 Ibid., p. 618.
93 Montesquieu, *Pensées*, in *Pensées, Le Spicilège* (Paris: Robert Laffont, 1991), no. 1574. As Shackleton noted, Montesquieu had already demonstrated his interest in the English conception of liberty in *Lettres persanes*: 'Usbek alludes to the English view that unlimited power is illegitimate, and Rica explains that in England liberty has been born from the flames of discord and sedition.' Shackleton, *Montesquieu*, p. 119.
94 Montesquieu, *Spirit of the Laws*, p. 155.
95 Ibid., pp. 155–6.
96 Montesquieu, *Le Spicilège*, in *Pensées, Le Spicilège* (Paris: Robert Laffont, 1991), no. 525, p. 818. The same entry in Montesquieu's notebook also included a reference to the issue of the *Craftsman* for 13 June 1730 (the beginning of *Remarks on the History of England*): 'The love of power is natural. It is insatiable almost constantly whetted never cloyed by possession.' [Bolingbroke], *Remarks on the History of England* (London: R. Francklin, 1743), p. 9.
97 Montesquieu, *Spirit of the Laws*, p. 161.
98 Ibid., p. 161.
99 Ibid., pp. 165–6. As Montesquieu well knew, Harrington had explicitly rejected 'Gothic monarchy' as offering an unequal balance.
100 Ibid., pp. 167–8.
101 Ibid., pp. 70 and 330.
102 Though close to each other, Chalcedon and Byzantium lay on opposite sides of the Bosphorus. Though the town of Chalcedon was built first, its situation and natural resources were far inferior to those of its later neighbour. Thus, Montesquieu was suggesting that Harrington's constitutional model was close to, but inferior to, the existing English constitution, which would have better fulfilled his aims.
103 [L. Carey, viscount Falkland and J. Colepeper], *His Majesties Answer to the Nineteen Propositions of Both Houses of Parliament* (London, 1642). On this text see J. G. A. Pocock, *The Machiavellian Moment: Florentine Political Thought and the Atlantic Republican Tradition* (Princeton: Princeton University Press, 1975), pp. 361–6.
104 Montesquieu, *Spirit of the Laws*, pp. 161 and 164.

105 J. J. Rutledge, *Éloge de Montesquieu* (Paris, 1786), p. 19. On Rutledge see R. Hammersley, *French Revolutionaries and English Republicans: The Cordeliers Club, 1790–1794* (Woodbridge: Boydell and Brewer for the Royal Historical Society, 2005), esp. pp. 86–115.
106 Ibid., pp. 19–20.
107 There is also evidence to suggest that Montesquieu shared some of the religious and moral ideas of the commonwealthmen. His *Lettres Persanes* contains anticlerical views that have been likened to those of Trenchard and Gordon. Pocock, *Machiavellian Moment*, p. 475. And although he insisted that virtue was essential to republics, his account of the operation of honour in monarchies sounds very similar to Harrington on the manipulation of self-interest in order to produce virtuous behaviour: 'You could say that it is like the system of the universe, where there is a force constantly repelling all bodies from the center and a force of gravitation attracting them to it. Honor makes all the parts of the body politic move; its very action binds them, and each person works for the common good, believing he works for his individual interests.' Montesquieu, *Spirit of the Laws*, p. 27.
108 Montesquieu, *Spirit of the Laws*, p. 166.
109 J. Shklar, 'Montesquieu and the New Republicanism', in G. Bock, Q. Skinner and M. Viroli (eds), *Machiavelli and Republicanism* (Cambridge: Cambridge University Press, 1990), p. 265.
110 Montesquieu did, of course, offer his own version of the *thèse nobiliaire* conception of French history in Books 30 and 31 of *The Spirit of the Laws*. Moreover, while he was opposed to the idea of simply imposing the British model in France, his conception of monarchy undoubtedly owed something to these ideas. On his unwillingness simply to adopt the British model see S. Tomaselli, 'The Spirit of Nations', in M. Goldie and R. Wokler (eds), *The Cambridge History of Eighteenth-Century Political Thought* (Cambridge: Cambridge University Press, 2006), pp. 9–39. On Montesquieu's distinctive conception of monarchy see Sonenscher, *Before the Deluge*, pp. 95–172.

5
A French commonwealthman: the abbé Mably

Introduction

Gabriel Bonnot de Mably is one of the central figures in the accounts of eighteenth-century French classical republicanism offered by Keith Baker and Kent Wright.[1] Their groundbreaking studies transformed our understanding of Mably and placed him at the centre of accounts of eighteenth-century French republicanism and the intellectual origins of the French Revolution. Yet, the classical republican label does not quite do justice to the complexity of Mably's ideas. As in the case of Montesquieu, two distinct republican positions can be identified within Mably's works. Though his ideal form of government was in line with the ancient republican tradition, his proposals for the reform of contemporary states were those of a commonwealthman.

Mably and the ancient republican tradition

Benjamin Constant's condemnation of Mably in his famous lecture 'De la liberté des anciens comparée à celle des modernes' is well known.[2] Constant cast Mably, alongside Jean-Jacques Rousseau, as one of the key exponents of the ancient concept of liberty in eighteenth-century France.[3] It was their ideas, Constant insisted, that had shaped Jacobin republicanism and encouraged Robespierre and his colleagues to try to impose ancient political ideas in the very different circumstances of the modern world. While Constant was no doubt right that Jacobin republicanism was inspired by the writings of Rousseau and Mably, he misrepresented their own views on this subject. Though both thinkers idealised the city-states of antiquity and their republican forms of government, neither believed that the ancient system could simply be applied to eighteenth-century France.

Rousseau made it quite clear in *The Social Contract* that his injunction that sovereignty should neither be alienated nor represented meant that it could only function properly within a small state: 'All things considered, I do not see that among us the Sovereign can henceforth preserve the exercise of its rights unless the City is very small.'[4] Moreover, when he did attempt to adapt his ideas for a larger state, in his *Considerations on the Government of Poland*, he produced something that looked very different from the Jacobin Republic of the 1790s.[5] Furthermore, it was not just the size of the French state that was problematic for Rousseau – he also believed that corruption was too far advanced in France for republican morality to take hold.[6]

Two of the central tenets of Mably's ancient republicanism were his anti-monarchism and his emphasis on the importance of material equality. In *Observations sur les Grecs* he directly linked the emergence of liberty and independence in Greece to the abolition of monarchical government:

> No sooner had some towns thrown off the yoke, than all Greece wanted to be free. A people does not content itself with governing itself by its own laws. Whether concerned that their own liberty might suffer from the dangerous example of tyranny among their neighbours, or whether this enthusiasm is typical of the first moments of revolution, these peoples offered their support to all who wished to bring down kings. The love of independence became, from this point, the distinguishing characteristic of the Greeks.[7]

Mably also insisted that ancient-style republicanism could only operate in states in which there was a certain degree of equality – where the difference between the richest and the poorest was not too great.[8] Consequently, he believed that the rise of wealth and luxury was the most common cause of corruption within states:

> What good would his [Lycurgus'] establishment of order have been if the taste for riches and the love of luxury, which are always found together and which are always linked to the inequality of citizens because they make some tyrants and others slaves, had been allowed to silently unbalance the harmony of the government?[9]

Lycurgus had recognised this and so he had not only divided the land equally among the citizens, but also introduced a number of measures aimed at maintaining that equality. These included banning the use of gold and silver, imposing a system of collective meals and education, prohibiting any commerce with foreigners, and instituting a law forbidding the citizens from taking up arms – except in their own defence.[10] Significantly, Mably insisted that Sparta's decline was prompted by Lysander's reversal of Lycurgus' policies, not least his reintroduction of gold and silver.[11] It was this belief in equality as a key basis for republicanism that was behind the description of an ideal state, incorporating the abolition of private property and the establishment of a community of goods, that was proposed by Milord Stanhope, one of the central characters in *Des Droits et des devoirs du citoyen*.[12]

While the republicanism of the ancient city-states – and especially that of Lycurgus' Sparta – certainly came closest to Mably's ideal form of government, he insisted that the immediate establishment of an ancient-style republic in modern states such as Britain or France would not work.[13] The central reason for this was that the nature and character of those states and their peoples were not suited to such a system.[14] As Milord Stanhope explained:

> If you were a brave people, without luxury, without avarice, without weakness such that the words arbitrary power made you tremble, I would speak to you in a completely different language. I have taken note of the fact that a love of money is at the heart of all your thoughts, and that you have sought honours for yourselves by covering yourselves with ignominy. I have fitted my remedies to your temperament. It is because all idea of equality shocks you that you are so accustomed to the abuses of despotism … In short, it is because you are hardly worthy of being free, that I want you to become so only gradually and not to aspire straightaway to a government that is too perfect.[15]

Thus, Stanhope was quite clear that his idea of establishing a republic based on a community of goods on a desert island was merely a daydream, and not something he believed could be successfully imposed among the citizens of modern Europe. When Stanhope's French companion expressed enthusiasm for the establishment of the ideal state, he responded negatively:

> Who would want to follow us? Who would want to travel far from his country to search for a happiness that he would despise there if he found it under his hand? We have come to such a point of corruption that extreme wisdom must seem extreme folly, and effectively is so. If we do not have completely new men, whom we can turn into citizens according to our will, how would we succeed in changing their ideas? How would we cut out from their hearts the roots of these numerous passions which are constantly renewed and which have been rendered unshakeable by education and habit?[16]

Similarly, when the Frenchman, newly converted to republicanism, began proposing the abolition of hereditary monarchy following the example of the Romans, Stanhope counselled restraint and caution:

> [Y]ou have become a republican as proud and zealous as any I know in England. But, we must respect thrones and try not to run after a beautiful chimera, as we did two days ago when you wished to set sail for my desert island. Royalty is without doubt a vice in government, but it is necessary in a nation that has lost its primitive ideas of simplicity and equality, and is incapable of recovering them. With the unequal distribution of ranks, titles, riches, fortunes and dignities that there are in France, England and Sweden, is it possible to think there as one thinks in Switzerland?[17]

A FRENCH COMMONWEALTHMAN: THE ABBÉ MABLY 89

Thus, while he may have been an ancient republican in theory, when it came to proposing means of reforming the large states of modern Europe Mably adopted a rather different position – that of a commonwealthman.

Mably and the British commonwealth tradition

Most of Mably's works that dealt with contemporary politics and political reform were written during the 1750s and 1760s. This was a turbulent period in France, dominated on the international stage by the Seven Years War and domestically by conflicts between the Crown and the *parlements*, in particular the debate over the *billets de confession*. In 1749 the Archbishop of Paris, Christophe de Beaumont, ordered that the sacrament of the last rites be refused to anyone who failed to produce a *billet de confession* – a declaration of their faith signed by a priest who had subscribed to the anti-Jansenist Papal Bull, Unigenitus. The aim of this decree was to root out Jansenism, but its effect was to pit the ecclesiastical authorities against the *parlements*, because the *Paris Parlement* responded to the Archbishop's decree by declaring it unlawful and insisting that it should not be obeyed. This dispute was compounded by the response to Machault d'Arnouville's attempt, as Controller-General of Finances, to introduce a new *vingtième* tax in 1750, to help to pay off the nation's war debt. The Assembly of the Clergy sought to preserve its traditional immunity from taxation and refused to contribute. Machault initially stood his ground, but Louis XV's desire to keep the clergy on-side in the Jansenist debate forced him to give way in December 1751. Once again the *Paris Parlement* reacted angrily to this decision. These affairs cemented the role of the *parlements* as the opponents of ecclesiastical and royal despotism, but they were also significant in highlighting the impotence of the King, and in marking a key moment in the rising importance of public opinion within the French nation.[18]

These events appear to have prompted a renewed French interest in English republican ideas. The 1750s witnessed the publication, or republication, of French translations of a large number of works associated with the British commonwealth tradition.[19] Samson's translation of Sidney's *Discourses Concerning Government* was republished in 1755, the same year in which Rousset de Missy's republicanised version of Locke's *Second Treatise of Government* appeared. Daudé's translation of Gordon's discourses on Tacitus was reissued in 1749 and 1751, with his translation of Gordon's discourses on Sallust appearing for the first time in 1759. Denis Diderot's translation of Shaftesbury's *An Inquiry Concerning Virtue*, which had first appeared in 1745, was republished in 1751. Finally, most of the French translations of Bolingbroke's works appeared or reappeared during the 1750s, including *Lettres sur l'esprit de patriotisme, sur l'idée d'un roy patriote et sur l'état des parties qui divisoient l'Angleterre* (1750); *Lettres sur l'histoire* (1752); *Mémoires secrets de Mylord Bolingbroke sur les affaires d'Angleterre* ... (1754); *Testament politique de milord Bolingbroke* (1754); and *Réflexions politiques sur l'état présent d'Angleterre* (1754).[20]

The influence of British Commonwealth ideas on Mably's thought is particularly evident in *Des Droits et des devoirs du citoyen*.[21] Not only is one of the two main characters, Milord Stanhope, clearly supposed to be a contemporary British commonwealthman,[22] but there is also internal evidence that Mably had read several of the French translations of British commonwealth works.[23] There are also echoes of Bolingbroke's ideas in Mably's work, not least in his concern about the influence of the Crown over Parliament and about the impact of the rise of wealth and luxury.

Through Stanhope, Mably offered an analysis of the British system that was typical of the commonwealth tradition. A certain degree of admiration for the British constitution was combined with a concern that the Revolution of 1688–89 had not gone far enough, and a sense that in practice it was being threatened by corruption. Stanhope voiced the standard commonwealth calls for an end to places and pensions, for the introduction of frequent elections, and for a citizen militia rather than a standing army.[24] He also expressed their belief that riches and luxury were threatening to undermine the British constitution: 'What a host of calamities avarice and prodigality are preparing in England, said Milord. Her riches will be the death of her.'[25] There is even a hint that Mably had some sympathy for the religious views of the commonwealthmen, including their anticlericalism, their belief in toleration and their sense of the political value of religion.[26] Indeed, he had Stanhope refer to a comment from Thomas Gordon's discourses on Tacitus, which was characteristically scathing about the Church.[27]

Of greater significance than this, however, is the fact that Mably not only echoed the commonwealth attitude toward eighteenth-century Britain, he also suggested that the British model offered the key to the reform of the French state. Mably's decision to structure his work as a dialogue, in which an Englishman instructed a Frenchman in political philosophy, was deliberate and added a symbolic dimension to the point that he was seeking to make.

> We English, for example, have up to the present held ideas that are unclear concerning royal power, and under the name of *prerogative* we have left too much authority to the prince to be able, one day, to raise a perfect republic on the ruins of royalty. We are not worthy of governing ourselves as the Romans did. You French are even further behind us in this respect, and in order to make your way safely you must initially aspire only to the kind of liberty that we enjoy. That is to say, you should seek to re-establish the assembly of your ancient Estates-General.[28]

Later, in the sixth letter of the work, Stanhope offered a more detailed account of the means by which this 'révolution ménagée' (as he described it) might occur.[29] He suggested that the *Paris Parlement* should take the opportunity of a conflict with the Court, such as that which had recently occurred over the attempt to impose the new *vingtième*, to spark the reform process. By standing its ground and refusing to consent to the Court's demands, the *Paris Parlement* would gain the support of the other *parlements* and of the nation as a whole. It would then be in a position to convoke the Estates-General. Once established, that body ought immediately to secure its own continued existence by fixing for itself regular meetings and outlawing its dissolution or interruption during deliberations.

Thus Mably's reform proposals, like those of both Boulainvilliers and the British commonwealthmen, were rooted in a belief in the ancient constitution and the liberty associated with it.[30] Like them, Mably believed that the key to future reform lay in a return to the gothic institutions of the past. However, Mably's proposals went beyond those of both Boulainvilliers and the British commonwealthmen. Where Boulainvilliers had sought to extend political rights only as far as the nobility, Mably also included a central role for the commons or Third Estate.[31] In this respect he was in line with the British commonwealthmen, but on the question of geography he even exceeded their proposals. Despite their cosmopolitanism, their practical reform proposals had tended to remain focused on Britain itself. Mably, by contrast, not only applied these ideas to France, but also was able to use his appeal to the gothic past to conceive of a republic that embraced much of Western Europe, along the lines of the Frankish Empire under Charlemagne.[32]

The moral question

It is not only on purely political matters that Mably's views resemble those of the British commonwealthmen. Like them, he was also deeply concerned about the relationship between morality and politics. Mably shared the conventional republican view that all human institutions are inevitably subject to decline and decay over time: 'Everything becomes distorted, everything deteriorates, everything becomes corrupted.'[33] Even the best laws, he insisted, would become 'worn by the rust of time'.[34] Mably's concern about this Polybian tendency is reflected in the fact that he favoured Spartan stability and durability over both the democracy of Athens and the expansionism of Rome. In this respect he can be placed alongside other supporters of Sparta – and its modern counterpart Venice – such as James Harrington, Henry Neville and Walter Moyle.

On the question of virtue, Mably, like the commonwealthmen, occupied the borderlands between neo-Stoicism and neo-Epicureanism. His views on this subject are brought out most clearly in three dialogues produced during the 1760s and 1770s: the highly successful *Entretiens de Phocion, sur le rapport de la morale avec la politique*; and two less well-known works, *Principes de morale* and *Du cours et de la marche des passions dans la société*.[35] In the former work, which focused on the issue of how a love of country and of freedom might be rekindled within a nation that had become corrupted by greed and luxury, the eponymous hero is forced to counter the neo-Epicurean arguments voiced by one of his young companions, Aristias.[36] In the opening dialogue Phocion describes the means by which Lycurgus had succeeded in establishing a successful system among the Spartans:

> Instead of consulting their prejudices, he consulted only nature. He descended to the torturous depths of the human heart and penetrated the secrets of providence. His laws were designed to restrain the passions. Accordingly, they tended only to develop and affirm those same laws that the author of nature prescribed for us, through the ministry of that reason with which we have been endowed, and which is the supreme and only infallible magistrate of human beings.

> At these words, my dear Cleophanes, Aristias, who was steeped in the doctrines of our Sophists, could not resist interrupting Phocion. What are these mysterious laws that reason imposes on us? he asked. Why stifle the passions, whose healthy fire gives movement and life to society? Does not nature, which imperiously orders us to run relentlessly toward happiness, clearly make known to us her will and our destination by this attraction of pleasure or this hint of pain with which she arms everything around us?[37]

Phocion's response sought a middle way between the neo-Stoic and the neo-Epicurean positions:

> To wish to destroy the passions is to go further than the author of nature. They are his creation and, like him, are immortal. But he orders us to temper them, to regulate them, to direct them by the councils of reason, since it is only by this means that they can lose their venom, and contribute to our happiness.[38]

In his second dialogue on this subject, *Principes de morale*, Mably was even more explicit.[39] The work describes three conversations between the author and his friends Ariste, Eugène and Théante, held in the Jardin de Luxembourg in Paris. The first of their three conversations is devoted to the passions and the Stoic and Epicurean positions are discussed directly. The conclusion reached is that both positions are problematic and that what is required is something between the two:

> Stoicism is not the philosophy of men. It supposes us to be completely different from how we are ...
> The contrary philosophy which mistrusts the right of our reason, which

exaggerates those of our sense and would reduce us to the instinct of animals is no less false and the consequences of it infinitely more dangerous. The one ignores our weakness, the other our dignity: the truth is placed between these two opinions.[40]

Thus, according to Mably both reason and passion had a role to play within the individual and the state. Like the Epicureans, he acknowledged that people are motivated by their desire for pleasure and their dislike of pain,[41] and accepted that the passions perform a useful function. As he explained in *Principes de morale*:

> No one is more persuaded than I that they have been given to us for our happiness.
> ...
> I sense that without the assistance of the passions, my reason would freeze, and would be reduced to a crude instinct. Why would I complain of feeling passions? It would mean complaining about being intelligent and sensitive. On this basis I am convinced that I must love them, that is to say seek my happiness. It is impossible for me to separate myself from this self-love; and I must flee from pain as I fly toward the pleasure that calls me.[42]

However, he did not follow the Epicureans in accepting that the passions should be given free reign. Rather, he insisted that they needed to be carefully directed and controlled, and like the Stoics he believed that it was reason that ought to perform this function.

At the same time, like the commonwealthmen, Mably was concerned that human reason was too weak to act alone.[43] As he explained in *Principes de morale*, and in *Du Cours et de la marche des passions*, which was effectively a continuation of it,[44] only a small proportion of people in any society would be capable of keeping their reason in control at all times.[45] Consequently, he believed that it was necessary for laws and institutions to be constructed in such a way that they strengthened and reinforced the reason of individual citizens. As Phocion explained, promoting the love of virtue ought to be 'the sole object of legislators, laws and magistrates'.[46] Mably returned to this idea in *Du Cours et de la marche des passions*:

> I could give you a thousand other examples, my dear pupil, and all of them would prove that the passions that are the most ardent ..., the most impetuous ... and the most impatient ... are tamed and even become great virtues in a government that is well enough constituted to contain them within just bounds, or rather to direct them by the love of glory, of the patrie and of liberty to the greatest good of the patrie.[47]

Though Mably placed some emphasis on the idea that laws ought to forbid and punish bad behaviour, he was more interested in encouraging good behaviour. Indeed he even endorsed the idea of appealing to people's self-interest in order to encourage them to behave virtuously. For example, when describing the use that might be made of the love of glory Phocion said: 'Learn by what resources the practice of duties, even those that appear the most austere, can become agreeable and even delicious.'[48] Similarly, Phocion endorsed the use of the religious doctrine that vice will be punished and virtue rewarded in the afterlife, as a means of encouraging people to check their passions and to cultivate virtue.[49] This was why, despite his emphasis on reason, Mably was able to accept that in certain circumstances the doctrine of countervailing passions could prove useful.[50] At the end of *Entretiens de Phocion*, Phocion himself declared:

> Are all your efforts in vain? There remains a final means open to politics; it is to make use of the passions themselves to gradually weaken and ruin their empire.
>
> At these words, my dear Cleophanes, our new initiate to the secrets of wisdom could not prevent himself from smiling as he looked at me. The passions, he said, are therefore sometimes useful? Yes, my dear Aristias, replied Phocion, like these poisons that medicine sometimes converts into remedies.[51]

Just as was the case with politics, so Mably believed that the solution to the problem of the passions ought to be adapted to suit the circumstances of the times. Though he admired the laws of Lycurgus, he recognised that the simple morality of the ancient Spartans was not suitable for the large states of modern Europe.[52] In this context, the mixed system of government offered better protection against the excesses of the passions than the austere morality of Lycurgus: 'It is easy … in a mixed government to establish between the different powers a sort of equilibrium which, in containing the passions one by another, leaves more power to reason, and [allows it to] extend knowledge and develop talent.'[53] As a good commonwealthman, however, Mably was clear that even this solution was far from perfect. It would be difficult to get the balance absolutely right, it would require the maintenance of a spirit of vigilance among the population and, like all other human things, it would be subject to decay and corruption.[54]

Conclusion

Constant was right in suggesting that for both Rousseau and Mably the republicanism of the ancient city-states constituted the ideal form of government. He was wrong, however, in blaming them for the attempt to impose ancient ideas and practices in eighteenth-century France, since neither thinker believed such a strategy would be workable. Moreover, Constant also did them a disservice in failing to acknowledge that their views on how to bring about reform in the large nation-states of the modern world were rather different from one another. Mably's solution shared much in common with the views and concerns of the British commonwealthmen, not least their suggestion that the best means of bringing about reform was to revive the key institutions of Europe's gothic monarchies. On the vexed question of the relationship between morality and politics, Mably was again in line with the commonwealthmen in seeking a middle way between neo-Stoicism and neo-Epicureanism.

Mably's significance for the history of the early modern republican tradition lies in two key areas. In the first place, he not only analysed the strengths and weaknesses of the British constitution in commonwealth terms, but also self-consciously went on to propose a commonwealth reform package for France. Secondly, he engaged in a radicalisation of the early modern republican tradition. The early modern republicans of the early eighteenth century (both British and French) had been relatively conservative in their appeal back to a past golden age, in their firm rejection of kingless government and in their emphasis on the importance of property ownership as the basis for political participation. Mably's writings reflect the beginnings of a shift to a more forward-looking, anti-monarchical and democratic position. What is all the more interesting is that this subtle shift within the early modern republican tradition did not just take place in France in the mid-eighteenth century. It is also evident in the works of commonwealthmen in Britain and among opponents of the British Crown across the Atlantic in America.

Notes

1. K. M. Baker, 'A Script for a French Revolution: The Political Consciousness of the abbé Mably', in K. M. Baker, *Inventing the French Revolution: Essays on French Political Culture in the Eighteenth Century* (Cambridge: Cambridge University Press, 1990), pp. 86–106; J. K. Wright, *A Classical Republican in Eighteenth-Century France: The Political Thought of Mably* (Stanford: Stanford University Press, 1997) and J. K. Wright, 'The Idea of a Republican Constitution in Old Régime France', in M. van Gelderen and Q. Skinner (eds), *Republicanism: A Shared European Heritage*. Vol. 1: *Republicanism and Constitutionalism in Early Modern Europe* (Cambridge: Cambridge University Press, 2002), pp. 289–306.
2. B. Constant, 'The Liberty of the Ancients Compared with that of the Moderns', in Constant, *Political Writings*, ed. B. Fontana (Cambridge: Cambridge University Press, 1988), pp. 309–28. Kent Wright opened his monograph on Mably with a description of the lecture, Wright, *Classical Republican*, pp. 1–2. It is also mentioned by Eric Nelson in his brief discussion of Mably in E. Nelson, *The Greek Tradition in Republican Thought* (Cambridge: Cambridge University Press, 2004), p. 177.
3. Constant, 'Liberty of the Ancients', pp. 318–20.
4. J. J. Rousseau, *The Social Contract*, in *The Social Contract and other later political writings*, ed. V. Gourevitch (Cambridge: Cambridge University Press, 1997), pp. 115–16.
5. Rousseau, *Considerations on the Government of Poland*, in ibid., pp. 177–260.
6. Indeed, Rousseau has recently been presented as more typical of the 'moderns' than of the 'ancients'. See M. Sonenscher, *Before the Deluge: Public Debt, Inequality and the Intellectual Origins of the French Revolution* (Princeton and Oxford: Princeton University Press, 2007), especially pp. 222–53. See also R. Tuck, *The Rights of War and Peace: Political Thought and the International Order from Grotius to Kant* (Oxford: Oxford University Press, 1999), pp. 197–207 and P. Riley, 'Rousseau, Fénelon, and the Quarrel between the Ancients and the Moderns', in P. Riley (ed.), *The Cambridge Companion to Rousseau* (Cambridge: Cambridge University Press, 2001), pp. 78–93.
7. G. Bonnot de Mably, *Observations sur les Grecs* (Geneva, 1749), pp. 9–10. It should be noted,

however, that in line with other republicans, Mably did not completely dismiss the inclusion of a monarchical element within a mixed system of government. In his account of Sparta (which was, in his view, the best of the ancient city-states) he praised Lycurgus' decision simply to reduce the powers of Sparta's kings rather than removing them completely, and endorsed his creation of a Senate of the wisest and most experienced citizens. Ultimately he declared: 'The republic of Lycurgus was therefore composed of the most advantageous elements of all the different forms of government.' Ibid., p. 21.

8. On this basis Eric Nelson has presented Mably as an exponent of the Greek Tradition. Nelson, *Greek Tradition*, pp. 177–83.
9. Mably, *Observations sur les Grecs*, p. 23.
10. Ibid., pp. 24–7.
11. Ibid., pp. 121–4.
12. G. Bonnot de Mably, *Des Droits et des devoirs du citoyen*, ed. J. L. Lecercle (Paris: Marcel Didier, 1972), pp. 107–13 and especially p. 111.
13. The exception that proved the rule was Switzerland, but Mably was clear that the Swiss republic had developed gradually and that it was very different from other modern European nations. See ibid., pp. 120 and 212 and J. K. Wright, 'Mably and Berne', *History of European Ideas* 33 (2007), pp. 427–39.
14. The need for legislators to take account of the manners and disposition of the people was something Mably had stressed in his *Observations sur les Grecs*: 'A skilful legislator must consult the manners and general spirit [of the people] when giving laws to a great State, because the genius of the nation will be stronger than the legislator.' Cf. Mably, *Observations sur les Grecs*, p. 11.
15. Mably, *Des Droits et des devoirs du citoyen*, pp. 181–2.
16. Ibid., p. 113.
17. Ibid., p. 212.
18. On these events and their significance for Mably see Baker, 'Script for a French Revolution', pp. 88–9 and Wright, *Classical Republican*, pp. 69–70. See also C. Jones, *The Great Nation: France from Louis XV to Napoleon* (Harmondsworth: Penguin, 2002), pp. 148, 227–9; J. Egret, *Louis XV et l'opposition parlementaire, 1715–1774* (Paris: Librairie Armand Colin, 1970) and D. Van Kley, *The Religious Origins of the French Revolution: From Calvin to the Civil Constitution*, 1560–1791 (New Haven: Yale University Press, 1996).
19. Baker, 'Script for a French Revolution', pp. 89–90.
20. For a list of the French translations of English republican works see the Appendix.
21. Baker, 'Script for a French Revolution', p. 88; Wright, *Classical Republican*, esp. pp. 71–2 and 77–80.
22. There has been some disagreement as to the identity of 'Stanhope' (who had supposedly been labelled 'Halifax' in the autograph manuscript). For a discussion of this issue see Lecercle's 'Introduction' to his edition of the work: Mably, *Des Droits et des devoirs du citoyen*, pp. xx–xxiii. See also Wright, *Classical Republican*, p. 71.
23. In the work Mably refers, albeit implicitly, to both Algernon Sidney's *Discourses Concerning Government* and Thomas Gordon's discourses on Tacitus. Mably, *Des Droits et des devoirs du citoyen*, pp. 61–4 and 41 and note 1. See also Baker, 'Script for the French Revolution', pp. 90 and 94.
24. Mably, *Des Droits et des devoirs du citoyen*, pp. 32, 44–8 and 117–20.
25. Ibid., p. 199.
26. Ibid., pp. 92–3.
27. Ibid., p. 41 and note 1. For other hints at Mably's anticlericalism see pp. 160–1. In this respect it is interesting to note Wright's claim that despite his ecclesiastical education, and the lack of firm evidence on the subject, 'the balance of evidence suggests his consistent adherence to a fairly conventional form of deism'. Wright, *Classical Republican*, pp. 23–4, see also p. 188.
28. Mably, *Des Droits et des devoirs du citoyen*, pp. 44–5.
29. Ibid., pp. 152–78.
30. Ibid., pp. 6–7. Mably put forward his own version of the *thèse nobiliaire* in his *Observations sur*

l'histoire de France. On the similarities (as well as the differences) between the *thèse nobiliaire* arguments of Boulainvilliers, Montesquieu and Mably see M. Ozouf and F. Furet, 'Two Historical Legitimations of eighteenth-century French Society: Mably and Boulainvilliers', in F. Furet (ed.), *In the Workshop of History* (Chicago: University of Chicago Press, 1984), pp. 125–39; Wright, *Classical Republican*, pp. 146–8 and Wright, 'Idea of a Republican Constitution'.
31 Ozouf and Furet, 'Two Historical Legitimations', pp. 126, 132, 134–8 and Wright, *Classical Republican*, pp. 146–8.
32 On Mably's vision of a large, federal republic see M. Sonenscher, 'Republicanism, State Finances and the Emergence of Commercial Society in Eighteenth-century France – or from Royal to Ancient Republicanism and Back', in M. van Gelderen and Q. Skinner (eds), *Republicanism: A Shared European Heritage*. Vol. 2: *The Values of Republicanism in Early Modern Europe* (Cambridge: Cambridge University Press, 2002), pp. 279–82. Interestingly, Sonenscher associates this vision with Bolingbroke's 'Patriot King' solution to the debt problem. See also Sonenscher, *Before the Deluge*, pp. 244–50.
33 Mably, *Des Droit et des devoirs du citoyen*, p. 217. The same idea is set out at the beginning of Mably's *Entretiens de Phocion*. G. Bonnot de Mably, *Entretiens de Phocion sur le rapport de la morale avec la politique* (Paris, 1797), p. 20.
34 Mably, *Des Droits et de devoirs du citoyen*, p. 217.
35 Mably, *Entretiens de Phocion*; G. Bonnot de Mably, *Principes de morale*, in *Collection complète des oeuvres de l'Abbé Mably* (Paris: Desbriere, L'An III de la République (1794–95)), X; G. Bonnot de Mably, *Du Cours et de la marche des passions dans la société*, in *Collection complète des oeuvres de l'abbé de Mably* (Paris: Desbriere, L'An III de la République (1794–95)), XV. On *Entretiens de Phocion* see Wright, *Classical Republican*, esp. pp. 80–90 and Wright, 'Mably and Berne'. On *Principes de morale* and *Du Cours et de la marche des passions* see Wright, *Classical Republican*, pp. 187–94. Because my emphasis here is on the affinities between Mably's views on morality and those of the commonwealthmen, my interpretation of these works differs slightly from that of Wright.
36 Aristias was supposedly modelled on the marquis de Chastellux. Wright, *Classical Republican*, pp. 81–2.
37 Mably, *Entretiens de Phocion*, pp. 34–5.
38 Ibid., p. 37.
39 On the harsh reaction to this work see Wright, *Classical Republican*, pp. 187–8.
40 Mably, *Principes de morale*, pp. 298–9. See also pp. 412–13.
41 Mably, *Du Cours et de la marche des passions*, p. 173.
42 Mably, *Principes de morale*, p. 253.
43 As Wright notes, on this point Mably had been influenced by the writings of his brother Condillac. Wright, *Classical Republican*, p. 189.
44 It is set in Poland and involves a conversation between the author and his pupil 'Le Marquis', but reference is made back to *Principes de morale*. Mably, *Du Cours et de la marche des passions*, p. 136.
45 Mably, *Principes de morale*, p. 362; Mably, *Du Cours et de la marche des passions*, pp. 178–9.
46 Mably, *Entretiens de Phocion*, p. 39.
47 Mably, *Du Cours et de la marche des passions*, p. 170.
48 Mably, *Entretiens de Phocion*, p. 87. The same idea is also evident in *Des Droits et des devoirs du citoyen*, pp. 111–2. Also in that work Stanhope suggests that under the scheme he proposes the courtiers and *parlementaires* will be induced by self-interest to behave in the way that is required. He also suggests elsewhere that the members of the Estates-General will need to be constrained in order to ensure that they behave appropriately: 'Make them worthy of the admiration, the confidence and the respect of the nation by putting them in the happy necessity of being almost incapable of making mistakes.' Mably, *Des Droits et des devoirs du citoyen*, pp. 152ff and pp. 192–3.
49 Mably, *Entretiens de Phocion*, pp. 96–7. There is even a hint here that Mably shared the anticlerical views of the British commonwealthmen. In responding to the objection that religion and

virtue do not go together he suggested that those who make this objection: 'call religion what is only superstition or hypocrisy'. Ibid., p. 98.
50 On this doctrine see A. O. Hirschman, *The Passions and the Interests: Political Arguments for Capitalism Before its Triumph* (Princeton: Princeton University Press, 1977) and P. Force, *Self-Interest Before Adam Smith: A Genealogy of Economic Science* (Cambridge: Cambridge University Press, 2003).
51 Mably, *Entretiens de Phocion*, p. 146. He was clear, however, that only certain passions could be used in this way and that they had to be handled very carefully. Ibid., p. 151. See also *Principes de morale*, p. 360 and *Du Cours et de la marche des passions*, pp. 246–7 and 410–13.
52 Mably, *Principes de morale*, p. 456.
53 Mably, *Du Cours et de la marche des passions*, p. 248.
54 Ibid., pp. 249–58.

Part III

Commonwealthmen, Wilkites and France

6

The commonwealth tradition and the Wilkite controversies

Introduction

Bernard Bailyn's *The Ideological Origins of the American Revolution*, which was first published in 1967, transformed conventional understandings of the American Revolution. Based on research undertaken for the publication of a collection of American revolutionary pamphlets, Bailyn's book reasserted the conception of the Revolution as essentially an 'ideological, constitutional, political struggle', and demonstrated the fundamental role played by the British commonwealth tradition in shaping American attitudes in the period leading up to the outbreak of revolution.[1] According to Bailyn, the ideas of that tradition acquired an importance and relevance in colonial America that they had never achieved in Britain, and were transformed into an active revolutionary ideology in the context of the distinctive American experiences of the mid-eighteenth century. Bailyn himself summed up the essence of that revolutionary ideology as follows:

> In the end I was convinced that the fear of a comprehensive conspiracy against liberty throughout the English-speaking world – a conspiracy believed to have been nourished in corruption, and of which, it was felt, oppression in America was only the most immediately visible part – lay at the heart of the Revolutionary movement.[2]

However, it was not just in America that the ideas of the commonwealth tradition proved influential during the 1760s and 1770s. The escalation of the American situation coincided with domestic controversies associated with the colourful journalist and politician John Wilkes. The parallels between these events were evident to contemporaries. As one American correspondent of Wilkes, William Palfrey, put it: 'The fate of Wilkes and America must stand or fall together'.[3] Like the American conflict, the Wilkes controversies raised issues that were central to the British commonwealth tradition, not least the relationship between liberty and authority, the tendency for power to become corrupt, and the importance of representative government and free speech in countering that corruption. Moreover, as we shall see, these themes resonated in France too, against the background of the conflict between the Crown and the *parlements*, and especially the Maupeou Coup. The events of the 1760s and 1770s in America, Britain and France thus breathed new life into the old commonwealth texts and rendered them of relevance once more – on both sides of the Atlantic.

'Wilkes and liberty'

The activities of Wilkes and his supporters coloured British politics throughout the 1760s and 1770s. There were three key controversies in which Wilkes was involved.[4] The first concerned the use of general arrest warrants. On 23 April 1763 the forty-fifth issue of Wilkes's newspaper, the *North Briton*, appeared. In that issue Wilkes attacked the new Prime Minister George Grenville for his commendation of the Peace of Paris and, by implication, cast aspersions against George III. Following its appearance the government issued a general warrant for the arrest of 'the authors, printers and publishers' involved. For various reasons the legality of the warrant was questionable, and the fact that in total forty-nine people (including Wilkes) were arrested prompted public indignation. Wilkes was subsequently linked directly to the *North Briton*, was expelled from Parliament and eventually served time in prison for his involvement. However, the case not only resulted in significant changes to the legal system (including bringing an end to the use of general warrants to arrest individuals), but also brought Wilkes to prominence and gave birth to the cry 'Wilkes and liberty!'

The second controversy involving Wilkes focused on the attempt to exclude him from the House of Commons. Wilkes had been elected as MP for Middlesex in March 1768, but the Commons tried various means to expel him, eventually succeeding in early February 1769 on the grounds of his libellous suggestion that the Massacre on St George's Field, which had taken place on 10 May 1768, had been premeditated. Following this decision, fresh elections were held and Wilkes was twice re-elected – unopposed – as MP for Middlesex, but each time the Commons expelled him the following day. In April 1769 a third election took place. This time Parliament put up its own candidate, Henry Lawes Luttrell, to stand against Wilkes. Despite the fact that Wilkes defeated Luttrell by 1,143 votes to 296 the Commons reversed the decision and voted to admit Luttrell as MP for Middlesex. A petitioning campaign followed – with petitions being sent from across the country opposing the Commons' decision, and Wilkes's role as hero of liberty was confirmed. It was also during this period, on 20 February 1769, that the Society of the Supporters of the Bill of Rights was formed. The aim of the Society was to support Wilkes and to raise money to pay off his debts.

The first chairman of the Society was Sergeant John Glynn, who had acted as Wilkes's lawyer in 1763.

The third controversy involving Wilkes is less well known, but no less important. In 1771 he was involved in a campaign to overturn Parliament's prohibition on the reporting of parliamentary debates in the press. Following Parliament's issuing of legal proceedings against two printers in February 1771, Wilkes decided to pit the authority of the City of London (where he was then an alderman) against that of Parliament. Since the City had the exclusive right of arrest within its boundaries, he and his associates encouraged any printer who was facing prosecution for reporting parliamentary debates to take refuge there. By this means Wilkes and his associates succeeded in quashing arrest warrants against those involved in such publications and in securing the right of the press to publish details of the proceedings of parliament.

The revival of the commonwealth tradition

It was against the background of the American and Wilkite controversies that a number of works from the English republican tradition were republished and read. The republications were largely the work of two men, Thomas Hollis and Richard Baron.[5] Their aims and actions were very similar to those of Toland and his circle who had republished many of the same works at the turn of the century. Indeed, Hollis was a great admirer of the Real Whigs, and especially of Molesworth.[6]

Hollis had originally conceived of his plan to promote liberty and oppose tyranny in 1754.[7] As part of this project he quoted extracts from the works of English republican authors in the press and arranged for a number of them to be republished.[8] Republications for which he was responsible included Toland's *The Life of John Milton* (1761), Sidney's *Discourses Concerning Government* (1763) and Neville's *Plato Redivivus* (1763). Moreover, he also made clear the connections between these works that had already been noted by Toland and his associates. His edition of Sidney's *Discourses* was based on Toland's edition and included his preface. A footnote to the preface read: 'By *John Toland*. Besides the "Discourse concerning Government", he also collected and first published Milton's prose-works; and Harrington's works, "some of them from the original manuscripts".'[9] As well as republishing these works, Hollis was involved in promoting and disseminating them. He sent large numbers to universities, and to various individuals, groups and institutions in Britain, North America, Switzerland, Italy and elsewhere.[10] Alongside the books, Hollis also disseminated prints, medals and coins symbolising liberty. During the 1760s Hollis's attention became increasingly focused on America. He was deeply interested in American affairs and sympathised with the colonists. Not only did he distribute British works favourable to liberty in America, but he also disseminated American writings in Britain, becoming a key mouthpiece for American views.

Baron had begun editing commonwealth works independently, before he met Hollis in 1756, but by the 1760s they were working together. Baron's republications included *The Memoirs of Edmund Ludlow* (1751); a collection of the religious writings of Thomas Gordon entitled *A Cordial for Low Spirits* (1751, 1763); *The Works of John Milton* (1753) and Nedham's *The Excellencie of a Free State* (1767). He described his aim in publishing these works as being 'to strengthen and support' the 'Good old Cause'.[11] To this end he regularly added prefaces to his editions in which he praised their authors, stressed their contribution to the cause of liberty, and pointed out the connections between them and the relevance of their works to the present. For example, at the end of his preface to *The Memoirs of Edmund Ludlow* Baron wrote:

> The editor concludes with wishing, that men of all ranks and orders would endeavour to understand the principles of true liberty, and the just rights of mankind; this being the best, and indeed the only means to dissolve all parties, to heal all divisions, and to unite us all in one common cause; viz. in the promoting the prosperity and happiness of Great Britain, and transmitting down to future ages the blessings we now enjoy.[12]

His preface to *The Works of John Milton* was more pessimistic, but voiced similar sentiments:

> Many circumstances at present loudly call upon us to exert ourselves. Venality and corruption have well-nigh extinguished all principles of Liberty ... One remedy for these evils is to revive the reading of our old Writers, of which we have good store, and the study whereof would fortify our youth against the blandishments of pleasure and the arts of Corruption.
>
> MILTON in particular ought to be read and studied by all our young Gentlemen as an Oracle.[13]

He then went on to associate Milton with Sidney. Finally, in his preface to *A Cordial for Low Spirits*, he explicitly endorsed Gordon's anticlericalism and attacked key Church doctrines, including that of the Trinity.[14]

Alongside the republication of older commonwealth works, new ones also appeared. Key works produced during this period included Obidiah Hulme's anonymously published *An Historical Essay on the English Constitution* (1771), James Burgh's *Political Disquisitions* (1774) and Catharine Macaulay's republican *History of England* (1763–83).[15] The latter focused on the seventeenth century, and constituted a response to David Hume's Tory account of the period. Macaulay was one of a quartet identified by Horace Walpole as 'the chiefs' of a 'very small republican party' that was in existence in the late 1760s.[16] The other figures listed were Macaulay's brother John Sawbridge; his brother-in-law, a merchant called Stephenson; and Thomas Hollis. Interestingly, Wilkes was associated with three of these four alleged republicans.[17]

Wilkes's commonwealth connections

John Sawbridge was a leading figure in the Wilkite movement.[18] He spoke on Wilkes's behalf in Parliament and was a founder member of the Society of the Supporters of the Bill of Rights. In 1771 a split occurred within the Society between those who believed that it ought to take on a more comprehensive political role and those who thought it should continue to exist simply to pay Wilkes's debts. Sawbridge was in the former camp, which was led by John Horne and which seceded to form a separate Constitutional Society in April of that year. Nonetheless, the two groups continued to cooperate during the summer of 1771 over the campaign to secure the right to report on parliamentary debates, and in 1774 Wilkes and Sawbridge agreed to support each other in the mayoral and parliamentary elections. Moreover, according to Wilkes's diary, he continued to dine with Sawbridge, even after April 1771.[19] Wilkes also dined regularly with Macaulay and her husband, and from 1770 Wilkes and the Macaulays were neighbours at Prince's Court in London.[20] Moreover, like her brother, Macaulay identified her own political position with that of Wilkes. Among Wilkes's papers in the British Library there is an undated letter from Macaulay in which she justified her decision to give money to Wilkes's cause and went on to express her own patriotic beliefs – which she associated directly with those of Wilkes:

> You know sir that the admiration of that Patriotic virtue which so eminently flourished in the glorious states of Greece and Rome (and for a short period of time in this Country) always subsisted in my Character. I have not like others stopt at admiration but endeavoured to regulate my own conduct by the most illustrious patterns of antiquity. The only object of my ambition and the honest aim of my life is that I may die with the pleasing consciousness of having in the most profligate times which this unhappy Country ever knew acted … the part of a good citizen.[21]

Both Macaulay and Wilkes were also friendly with Hollis. Macaulay presented a copy of the second volume of her *History* to Hollis in January 1765 and he responded positively.[22] Moreover, on 22 March of that year he bought a collection of pamphlets and tracts concerning the history of England, and especially the period of the civil wars, which he presented 'anonymously to the ingenuous Mrs. Catharine Sawbridge Macaulay, who is now writing that most important period of our history.'[23] He kept up the acquaintance, writing to her in November

1768 and praising her most recent volume.[24] He was also involved in designing a famous print of her dressed as Liberty.[25]

It also appears to have been during the 1760s that Wilkes became acquainted with Hollis, and by the middle of the decade the two men were already exchanging politically significant gifts. Hollis's diary for 14 June 1763 records that he sent a copy of Toland's *Milton* to Wilkes, while an entry for 17 January 1764 refers to a 'gift of Sidney'.[26] It is possible that the latter was a print of the great man, rather than a copy of his *Discourses Concerning Government*, since in a letter written from Naples in March 1765 Wilkes asked his friend Humphrey Cotes to send him, among other things, 'my prints of Hampden, Sidney, &c. given me by Mr Hollis'.[27] The gifts did not just flow one way. In 1768 Wilkes sent Hollis a copy of his recently published introduction to a *History of England*, one of the projects that he had been working on while in Naples.[28] Interestingly this work had a commonwealth character to it. Wilkes blamed Charles I for the outbreak of the Civil War and praised the efforts of the Long Parliament.[29] He offered a positive account of the Glorious Revolution, in particular praising the political and religious liberty that had resulted from it, though he acknowledged that the revolutionaries had not gone as far as they should.[30] He also made reference to commonwealth works, praising Milton's *Defence of the People of England* and quoting from Bolingbroke's *Letters on the Study and Use of History*; and he drew the parallel between Brutus and William of Orange that had been a key trope in the works of Toland.[31] The friendship between Wilkes and Hollis appears to have been maintained into the 1770s. During a trip to the West Country in August 1772, Wilkes met up with Hollis.[32] In a letter to his daughter Polly dated Sunday, 23 August 1772 he said: 'I found there [at Lyme] Mr. Thomas Hollis, and other true friends of liberty; with whom I passed the remainder of the day'.[33] Wilkes and Hollis also made use of the same publishers and printers, including both George Kearsley, the publisher of the *North Briton*, and Wilkes's friend and biographer John Almon.[34]

Though he did not always agree with Wilkes's behaviour, Hollis certainly shared his politics and supported Wilkes's cause.[35] As early as 1763 he was writing in favour of Wilkes and criticising the Government's behaviour toward him.[36] In March 1768 he celebrated Wilkes's election as MP for Middlesex:

> Mr. Wilkes, that wonderful man, has carried his election for the county of Middlesex, with great superiority, and as great decorum in all circumstances, as from the nature of the election could be expected … His election must be a mortification of the most humiliating kind to the favorite; and, to my sense, most seasonable to liberty. If from this time he will but watch against the specks of his own irregularities, he must render prime services to his country, and be transmitted in history a most honorable Englishman to posterity.[37]

Moreover, Hollis was still speaking favourably of Wilkes in December 1773.[38]

Significantly, Hollis appears to have seen the relevance of the works of the commonwealth tradition in the context of the Wilkite controversies. Not only did he send republican works and prints to Wilkes, but, according to Caroline Robbins, in February 1769 he arranged for extracts from Harrington's works to appear in the press as a commentary on Wilkes's expulsion from the House of Commons.[39] Wilkes himself also identified directly with a key figure from the commonwealth tradition. According to Almon, Wilkes drew a parallel between his own case and that of Sidney 'and he therefore admired Sydney almost to enthusiasm'.[40] Wilkes mentioned Sidney's *Discourses* in his *History of England* and it is said that he even considered writing a life of Sidney, possibly at Hollis's suggestion.[41] It is also interesting to note that the Society of the Supporters of the Bill of Rights adopted as their own a number of traditional commonwealth demands. On 23 July 1771 they issued a manifesto in which they set out a number of measures to which any prospective parliamentary candidate wanting their support would have to subscribe. The list included such old favourites as annual parliaments and the exclusion of placemen and pensioners from the House of Commons.[42] Though Wilkes did not draft this document, he is said to have endorsed it.[43] Moreover, he is also credited with having moved the first ever motion for parliamentary reform, calling for a redistribution of parliamentary seats on 21 March 1776.[44]

The situation in France

It was not only in the anglophone world that the 1760s and 1770s were dominated by conflicts that pitted liberty against despotism and corruption. In France, despite some attempt at reconciliation during the 1760s, the long-standing battle between the Crown and the *parlements* continued to simmer.[45] In the region of Brittany in particular, discontent persisted in response to proposed changes to the tax system. In the spring of 1765 most of the members of the *Rennes Parlement* resigned in protest. In response, the government arrested six of those members in the autumn (imprisoning them in the Bastille) and exiled the *Parlement* itself, replacing it with a more subservient body. These moves prompted objections from various quarters, including from the *Paris Parlement*. Louis XV made clear his own position in the debate at the meeting, known as the *Séance de la Flagellation*, held on 2 March 1766:

> It is in my person alone that sovereign power resides ... it is from me alone that my courts hold their existence and their authority ... public order in its entirety emanates from me, and my people forms one with me, and the rights and interests of the nation, of which people are daring to make a body separate from the monarch, are necessarily united with mine and repose only in my hands.[46]

The conflict came to a head in the winter of 1770–71. On 28 November, the King issued an Edict of Discipline, which prohibited the *parlements* from corresponding with one another, or protesting against royal declarations and *lits de justice*, and challenged their claims to represent the nation. Following this, on the night of 19 January 1771 soldiers visited individual members of the *Paris Parlement* and demanded to know whether they would end their opposition. The following night Chancellor René-Nicolas-Charles de Maupeou exiled to the provinces all those *parlementaires* who had refused a reconciliation. Maupeou then went on to abolish the *Paris Parlement* and to replace it with a judicial system that would be more subservient to royal authority. These events were seen to epitomise the corrupt and despotic behaviour of Louis XV's regime and its rejection of representative government – and therefore of liberty. As a result, France too offered fertile ground for the revivification of commonwealth works and ideas.[47]

Conclusion

Of course, Wilkes himself had close links with France. His daughter Polly was educated there from the age of 13 and he fled there himself on Christmas Day 1763 to escape the legal action that he rightly feared would follow the fallout from the *North Briton* case. His conviction (*in absentia*) for libel, and the subsequent declaration of outlawry issued against him, forced him to stay abroad and he spent much of the next four years in Paris. Even after his return to Britain in February 1768, he made frequent trips to France and kept up his correspondence and friendship with a number of French friends. It is perhaps not entirely coincidental that among Wilkes's friends were several who were involved in translating commonwealth works into French.

Notes

1   B. Bailyn, *The Ideological Origins of the American Revolution*, rev. edn (Cambridge, MA: Belknap Press, 1992 [1967]), p. x. The pamphlets themselves were published as *Pamphlets of the American Revolution, 1750–1776*, ed. B. Bailyn (Cambridge, MA: Harvard University Press, 1965), and *The Ideological Origins* was based on the 'General Introduction' to that work.
2   Bailyn, *Ideological Origins*, p. xiii.
3   As quoted in R. Postgate, *That Devil Wilkes* (London: Dobson Books, 1956 [1930]), p. 167. On the parallels and connections between the Wilkite affairs and events in America, and the impact of the Wilkes controversies on American attitudes to Britain, see: P. Maier, 'John Wilkes and American Disillusionment with Britain', *William and Mary Quarterly*, 3rd ser., 20 (1963), pp. 373–95.
4   My account of these affairs is based on: G. Rudé, *Wilkes and Liberty: A Social Study of 1763 to 1774* (Oxford: Clarendon, 1962); P. D. G. Thomas, *John Wilkes: A Friend to Liberty* (Oxford: Oxford University Press, 1996); P. D. G. Thomas, 'Wilkes, John (1725–1797)', *Oxford Dictionary of National Biography* (Oxford: Oxford University Press, 2004; online edition, May 2008), www.oxforddnb.com/view/article/29410, accessed 16 July 2008; and A. H. Cash, *John Wilkes:*

The Scandalous Father of Civil Liberty (Newhaven and London: Yale University Press, 2006).

5 Both men regularly made use of the printer Andrew Millar. On Baron and Hollis see: C. A. Robbins, *The Eighteenth-Century Commonwealthman: Studies in the Transmission, Development and Circumstance of English Liberal Thought from the Restoration of Charles II until the War with the Thirteen Colonies* (Indianapolis, IN: Liberty Fund, 2004 [1987, 1959]), especially pp. 253–64; C. A. Robbins, 'The Strenuous Whig, Thomas Hollis of Lincoln's Inn' and 'Library of Liberty – assembled for Harvard College by Thomas Hollis of Lincoln's Inn', both in B. Taft (ed.), *Absolute Liberty: A Selection from the Articles and Papers of Caroline Robbins* (Hamden, CT: Archon Books, 1982), pp. 168–229; P. D. Marshall, 'Thomas Hollis (1720–74): The Bibliophile as Libertarian', *Bulletin of the John Rylands University Library of Manchester*, 266 (1984), pp. 246–63; and B. Worden, 'Introduction' to M. Nedham, *The Excellencie of a Free State* (Indianapolis, IN: Liberty Fund, forthcoming). I am grateful to Blair Worden for providing me with a copy of this Introduction prior to publication.

6 T. Hollis, *Memoirs of Thomas Hollis*, ed. F. Blackburne (London, 1780), I, pp. 58, 118–9, 235–7 and 475.

7 Ibid., I, p. 60. See also: Robbins, 'The Strenuous Whig', p. 185.

8 Hollis, *Memoirs*, I, pp. 501–2; Robbins, 'The Strenuous Whig', p. 193.

9 A. Sidney, *Discourses Concerning Government* (London: A. Millar, 1763), 'Preface'.

10 Details of the gifts sent appear throughout Hollis, *Memoirs*.

11 J. Milton, *The Works of John Milton, Historical, Political and Miscellaneous* (London: A. Millar, 1753), p. v. For Hollis's own assessment of Baron's character and concerns see Hollis, *Memoirs*, I, pp. 75–6 and II, pp. 573–86.

12 E. Ludlow, *Memoirs of Edmund Ludlow...* (London: A. Millar; D. Browne and J. Ward, 1751), 'Preface to this Edition'.

13 Milton, *Works*, p. iv.

14 T. Gordon, *A Cordial for Low Spirits. Being a collection of curious tracts. By Thomas Gordon, Esq.*, ed. R. Baron (London: Wilkson and Fell, 1763), pp. iii–xxvii.

15 On the works by Hulme and Burgh see Robbins, *Commonwealthman*, pp. 355–60 and C. H. Hay, 'The Making of a Radical: The Case of James Burgh', *Journal of British Studies* 18 (1979), pp. 90–117. On Macaulay see B. Brandon-Schnorrenburg, 'The Brood Hen of Faction: Mrs Macaulay and Radical Politics, 1767–75', *Albion* 11 (1979), pp. 33–45; B. Hill, *The Republican Virago: The Life and Times of Catharine Macaulay, Historian* (Oxford: Clarendon, 1992); J. G. A. Pocock, 'Catharine Macaulay: Patriot Historian', in H. Smith (ed.), *Women Writers and the Early Modern British Political Tradition* (Cambridge: Cambridge University Press, 1998), pp. 243–57 and K. Davies, *Catharine Macaulay and Mercy Otis Warren: The Revolutionary Atlantic and the Politics of Gender* (Oxford: Oxford University Press, 2005).

16 H. Walpole, *Memoirs of the Reign of King George the Third*, ed. D. Le Marchant (London: Richard Bentley, 1845), III, p. 331.

17 The nature of Hollis's 'republicanism' is discussed in some detail in his *Memoirs*. The editor, Francis Blackburne, was insistent that Hollis was not opposed to monarchy: Hollis, *Memoirs*, I, pp. 94, 186, 210–11 and 475. It is also important to note that Wilkes himself was not in favour of republican government in the narrow sense of the term, though interestingly his position was not all that different from that adopted by the Real Whigs at the turn of the century. In a speech given in 1792, in the light of recent events in France, he declared: 'Gentlemen, I am firmly attached to a limited monarchy. I have spent no small part of my life abroad: in countries where the government depended on the will or the caprice of an individual, of a minister, a minion, or a mistress; where no one was secure. // One of the great advantages of our constitution is, that all is clearly defined, and the limits of each branch ascertained. Now in a republican government there is a continued struggle who shall be the greatest. The Roman was the most famous republic; and witnessed the contentions of Marius and Sylla, of Cesar and Pompey, for pre-eminence. But here the line is clearly chalked out by law; no subject can with us be so ambitious, or so mad, as to contend for the sovereign power. We are preserved from all those evils which necessarily attend a republican government.' J. Wilkes, 'Speech to

inhabitants of the Ward of Farrington without, 14 December 1792', in *The Correspondence of the Late John Wilkes*, ed. J. Almon (London: Richard Phillips, 1805), V, p. 158.
18 On Sawbridge see: 'John Sawbridge', in *Biographical Dictionary of Modern British Radicals*, Vol. 1, 1770–1830, ed. J. O. Baylen and N. J. Gossman (Sussex: Harvester Press, 1979), pp. 429–33.
19 BL: Add. MS. 30866, 'J. Wilkes Diaries, 1770–97'.
20 Ibid.
21 BL: Add. MS. 30870 f. 242, 'Catharine Macaulay to John Wilkes'.
22 Hollis, *Memoirs*, I, p. 264. See also p. 210.
23 Ibid., I, p. 264. Hollis sent a further thirty civil war tracts to Macaulay on 18 June 1765. Ibid., I, p. 269.
24 Ibid., I, p. 410.
25 Ibid., I, pp. 221–2 and 503; Robbins, 'The Strenuous Whig', p. 183.
26 As cited in Robbins, 'The Strenuous Whig', p. 201 note 132.
27 Wilkes, *Correspondence*, ed. Almon, II, p. 195.
28 J. Wilkes, *The History of England from the Revolution to the Accession of the Brunswick Line* (London, 1768), in *The Works of the Celebrated John Wilkes, Esq; formerly published under the title of The North Briton, in three volumes* (London, n.d.), I, pp. 3–34. The subsequent volumes, though promised, never appeared.
29 Ibid., pp. 10–11.
30 Ibid., pp. 5 and 18. Though his campaigns tended to focus on political liberty, there is evidence to suggest that Wilkes also endorsed religious liberty. In a speech to Parliament concerning the Dissenters Relief Bill of 20 April 1770 he called for toleration not just of Christians, but also of other religious groups including Muslims and Jews. Thomas, 'Wilkes, John', *ODNB*.
31 Wilkes, *History of England*, pp. 12, 22 and 32–3.
32 BL: Add. MS. 30866 No. 2 f. 11.
33 Wilkes, *Correspondence*, ed. Almon, IV, p. 134.
34 Robbins, 'The Strenuous Whig', pp. 173 and 191–4. On Almon see D. D. Rogers, *Bookseller as Rogue: John Almon and the Politics of Eighteenth-Century Publishing* (New York: Peter Lang, 1986).
35 Hollis, *Memoirs*, I, pp. 289–90.
36 Ibid., II, p. *554.
37 Ibid., I, p. 393.
38 Ibid., I, p. 464.
39 Cited in Robbins, 'The Strenuous Whig', p. 194.
40 Wilkes, *Correspondence*, ed. Almon, IV, p. 219. Wilkes was also frequently compared to Sidney by the Americans, see Maier, 'John Wilkes and American Disillusionment with Britain', p. 376.
41 Wilkes, *History of England*, p. 8. On the idea of Wilkes writing a life of Sidney see: Robbins, 'The Strenuous Whig', p. 172 and P. Karsten, *Patriot-Heroes in England and America: Political Symbolism and Changing Values over Three Centuries* (Madison, WI: University of Wisconsin Press, 1978).
42 As reprinted in F. Junius, *Letters of Junius*, ed. J. Cannon (Oxford: Oxford University Press, 1978), p. 404.
43 Thomas, 'Wilkes, John', *ODNB*.
44 Ibid.
45 On this period see, in particular, D. Echeverria, *The Maupeou Revolution: A Study in the History of Libertarianism: France, 1770–1774* (Baton Rouge, LA: Louisiana State University Press, 1985).
46 As quoted in C. Jones, *The Great Nation: France from Louis XV to Napoleon* (Harmondsworth: Penguin, 2002), p. 263.
47 Parallels between events in England and those in France were also frequently drawn during this period and there was a sense that the *parlementaires* were pushing French politics more into line with that which operated across the Channel. See K. M. Baker, 'Public Opinion as Political Invention', in his *Inventing the French Revolution: Essays on French Political Culture in the Eighteenth Century* (Cambridge: Cambridge University Press, 1990), pp. 167–99 and especially pp. 182–5.

7

The British origins of the chevalier d'Eon's patriotism

Introduction

On 6 June 1771 a humorous article appeared in the *Public Advertiser*. It described the plan to build a new Magdalen institution near Bedlam in London. One part of the hospital would be reserved for ladies of '*Rank* and *Fortune*', but the other part:

> is to be appropriated for the Reception of our *Patriots*, whose *honest* Enthusiasm about *Liberty* and the *Good* of their Country, has quite turned their *poor* Brains; and whose wild Ravings are now become so loud and extravagant as to annoy and disturb all the sober industrious Part of the Community. *Mademoiselle D'Eon* is to be *necessary Woman*, and Lady V——e Matron to the *Fair Penitents*. *Jack Wilkes* is to be Turnkey, and Mr. Catherine Macaulay Keeper of the *Patriots*.[1]

The association drawn here between the colourful French diplomat and author the chevalier d'Eon de Beaumont, John Wilkes and Catharine Macaulay was not distinctive.[2] One of several articles suggesting that Wilkes and d'Eon had had a child together, which also appeared in *The Public Advertiser* – on 17 April 1771, listed 'Mrs Mac____ly' as one of the sponsors.[3] Moreover, there were other articles that linked d'Eon directly to Macaulay, just as there were many that drew parallels between him and Wilkes.[4] There were good reasons for such links to be made. Not only were these three figures directly acquainted with one another, but they also believed themselves to be engaged in a common cause – defending liberty against despotism and corruption. While in England, d'Eon became acquainted with commonwealth works and ideas, which he then applied to the contemporary situation in France. An examination of the British origins of d'Eon's patriotism can thus reveal something about the means by which commonwealth ideas were disseminated in France in the 1760s and 1770s, and the uses to which they were put.

D'Eon in England

D'Eon had arrived in England in 1762 and this first stay lasted fifteen years.[5] Throughout this period he was mired in controversy and his relations with both the French and British authorities were complex and ambiguous. Indeed an account of his time in England reads like the plot of a fantastical espionage novel. The official purpose of his original visit had been to assist the duc de Nivernais in the peace negotiations that brought an end to the Seven Years War. However, from 1756 d'Eon had also been involved with Louis XV's parallel system of diplomacy known as the *Secret du roi*. Thus, in addition to his official commission, d'Eon had also been instructed (in a secret order from Louis XV) to make use of his stay to explore the possibilities for a French invasion of England, and perhaps also to make contacts among opponents of the British government. D'Eon's relations with his own government quickly turned sour (not least because he was spending way beyond his means) and by October 1763 the French Foreign Minister was ordering him to return to France.[6] Unwilling to do so, and protected by the British government's refusal to extradite him, d'Eon began using the diplomatic papers in his possession to bargain with, threaten and even blackmail the French government. In 1764 he published *Lettres, mémoires et négociations particulières du chevalier d'Eon*, which brought together some of the diplomatic correspondence in his possession (though not the papers relating to the *Secret du roi*). In that work d'Eon also accused the French government of plotting to assassinate him. The pressure d'Eon exerted eventually paid off, and in 1765 Louis XV gave him permission to remain in England, and granted him a pension of 12,000 *livres*.

D'Eon's personal life, during his time in England, was no less controversial. From 1770 rumours began to circulate that he was actually a woman. The rumours escalated as people began to use insurance policies to bet on d'Eon's sex. The betting frenzy was only brought to an end in 1777 when a case between two gamblers held at the Court of King's Bench concluded that d'Eon was, in fact, female.[7] D'Eon challenged neither the hearing of the case nor its judgement, and soon after it had been concluded he agreed to dress in women's clothes, though he regarded the French government's demand that he do so on his return to France as evidence of its increasingly despotic behaviour. D'Eon was still living as a woman when he returned to London in 1785, and continued to do so until his death there in 1810. It was only then that the truth was revealed. When she laid out the body, Mrs Cole – who had been d'Eon's landlady for more than a decade – discovered that her supposedly female co-habitant had been a man all along.

D'Eon's commonwealth connections

D'Eon's main connection with British radical and commonwealth circles came via his friendship with Wilkes.[8] Though they were initially critical of one another, the two men had become close friends by 1768, and they regularly dined together from then until d'Eon's return to France in 1777.[9] Moreover, the friendship and meals continued when the now Mademoiselle d'Eon returned to London in the mid-1780s, though it was Polly Wilkes, rather than her father, who generally corresponded with d'Eon during this period.[10] There is also some evidence of a direct personal connection between d'Eon and Macaulay.[11] However, the newspaper articles quoted above depended on the fact that the connections between these figures ran deeper than friendship. Gender was the key theme in parallels drawn between d'Eon and Macaulay, since both were portrayed as occupying a middle ground between the sexes. Indeed, the speculations concerning d'Eon's sex appear to have prompted similar questions to be asked of Macaulay.[12] Though d'Eon's sex was often used for comic effect in the parallels drawn between him and Wilkes – as in the frequent references to them marrying or having children together – the focus of that parallel was more explicitly political. During the 1760s and 1770s both men were presented as champions of liberty in the face of harsh and despotic treatment on the part of their respective governments.[13] In addition, both men were involved in attempting to bring into the public domain details of political documents and debates that had conventionally been deemed secret.

These parallels were not simply imposed from outside, since there is evidence to suggest that d'Eon (like Macaulay) clearly identified with Wilkes, and especially with his love of liberty. In October 1768 d'Eon sent a gift of smoked tongue to Wilkes, who was then in prison, and the accompanying letter included the following passage: 'Monsieur d'Eon will eat with Mr Wilkes in a few days time. In the meantime he would desire that these tongues had the eloquence of Cicero and the refinement of Voltaire, in order that they might praise him in a worthy manner on the anniversary of his birth, which will be regarded in future as that of English liberty.'[14] Macaulay also appears to have acknowledged d'Eon's position as a fellow patriot since, according to Gary Kates, she sent him an annotated copy of the third volume of her *History* in 1768 and asked for his comments on it.[15] Furthermore, d'Eon did not simply talk about his love of liberty, and comment on the works of others; he also contributed directly to the commonwealth tradition. His *Les Loisirs du chevalier d'Eon de Beaumont*, which appeared in 1774, included within it the first French translation of the English republican pamphlet *The Excellencie of a Free State* by the seventeenth-century journalist Nedham.[16] In translating this work d'Eon was both signalling his association with the British commonwealth tradition and demonstrating how the works and ideas associated with that tradition could be applied with equal veracity to the contemporary situation in France.

Marchamont Nedham and *The Excellencie of a Free State*

Originally published during the early 1650s as a series of editorials in the weekly newspaper *Mercurius Politicus*, Nedham's *The Excellencie of a Free State* first appeared as a complete (and anonymous) pamphlet in 1656.[17] It was published by the printer Thomas Brewster who, that same year, also published Harrington's *The Commonwealth of Oceana*. Nedham's editorials had originally been written against the background of the Rump Parliament, but in the 1656 version the focus shifted to the Cromwellian Protectorate, though the content remained much the same. The overall aim of the work was, as the title suggested, to demonstrate the excellence of a free state and to indicate the form that such a state should take. In pursuing this, Nedham was explicitly and uncompromisingly anti-monarchical. He insisted that a free state had to be ruled not by a king, but by the people – or their representatives: 'It is an undeniable rule, *that the people* (that is, such as shall be successively chosen to represent the people) *are the best keepers of their own liberties*.'[18] Following from this, Nedham argued that those who represented the people had to be kept accountable to them, and he proposed the use of regular elections (or as he called it 'revolution') as a means of ensuring that this was the case:

> That since freedom is to be preserved no other way in a commonwealth, but by keeping officers and governors in an accountable state; and since it appears no standing powers can ever be called to an account without much difficulty, or involving a nation in blood or misery. And since a revolution of government in the people's hands hath ever been the only means to make governors accountable, and prevent the inconveniences of tyranny, distraction, and misery; therefore for this, and those other reasons foregoing, we may conclude, that a free state, or government by the people, settled in a due and orderly succession of their supreme assemblies, is far more excellent every way than any other form whatsoever.[19]

Nedham's pamphlet was not included among the seventeenth-century works republished by Toland and his associates at the turn of the eighteenth century. It was revived, however, in 1767 under the editorship of Baron. It was thus set alongside the collection of republican works that were republished and disseminated by Baron and Hollis during the course of the 1750s and 1760s.[20] Moreover, in his preface, which d'Eon included in his translation, Baron set Nedham's pamphlet firmly within the context of other seventeenth-century English republican works:

> On the subject of government, no country hath produced writings so numerous and valuable as our own. It hath been cultivated and adorned by men of greatest genius, and most comprehensive understanding, MILTON, HARRINGTON, SYDNEY, LOCKE, names famous to all ages.
>
> But beside their incomparable writings, many lesser treatises on the same argument which are little known, and extremely scarce, deserve to be read and preserved: in which number may be reckoned the small volume I now give the public, written by MARCHAMONT NEDHAM, a man, in the judgement of some, inferior only to MILTON.[21]

Nedham's pamphlet certainly appears to have had some resonance in the 1760s and 1770s. Hollis sent a copy to America, where it was widely read; and 1774 saw the publication of d'Eon's French translation in his *Les Loisirs*.[22]

D'Eon's *Les Loisirs*

D'Eon's translation of Nedham's *The Excellencie of a Free State* appeared in the sixth volume of his thirteen-volume *Les Loisirs du chevalier d'Eon de Beaumont*. As the title suggested, the work was produced during d'Eon's extensive 'leisure time' following his refusal to return to France in 1763. The work opened with a dedicatory epistle in which d'Eon drew a parallel between the dedicatee (a key figure in the French government throughout the 1760s) and the Roman statesman Scipio, on the grounds that both men were not only adept at handling public affairs but also interested in – and knowledgeable about – culture and science.[23] Scipio had been a close friend of great thinkers such as Polybius and Panaetius, and d'Eon noted that he had held savants in esteem and kept these men near him at all times.[24] The implication was clearly that d'Eon saw himself as playing Polybius or Panaetius to his dedicatee's Scipio:

> The benefits that he gained from their companionship rendered even his leisure time laborious. Moreover no one knew better than he how to use literature to fill the void left by the functions of war or peace. Among arms or among books he ceaselessly exercised either the power of his body through military manoeuvres or the faculties of his mind through the study of literature and politics.[25]

Though d'Eon did not mention it explicitly, Scipio was also greatly admired by Cicero, who had viewed him as the ideal statesman and made him the central character in his *De Republica*.[26]

Thus, the philosophy underpinning *Les Loisirs* was that learning, and particularly the study of other countries, of history and of past works, could be useful to statesmen. However, d'Eon acknowledged that most statesmen rarely had the time to undertake such study. D'Eon had therefore devoted his own leisure time to the gathering together of works that he believed would prove useful to France's rulers:

> Consequently, I believed that I could not spend the leisure time of my exile in the country of liberty more fruitfully than by occupying myself in diverse matters of relevance to the administration of states ... In instructing myself, I could thus become useful to many of my contemporaries who, employed in the ministry, lead a life more active than passive and are more concerned with dealing with current affairs than with instructing themselves on the fundamentals of their business.[27]

The works he had included, d'Eon noted, were concerned primarily with public administration, and his main aim was to offer advice on the reform of the abuses and vices that had been introduced into various parts of the French system – and in particular those relating to finance.[28] The majority of the works included are accounts of specific states ranging from Poland to England's American colonies. For obvious reasons d'Eon devoted particular attention to France and Britain. His translation of Nedham's work was presented as a kind of preface to his accounts of England, Scotland and the English colonies that appeared in volumes seven and eight.

As well as offering some sense of the aims of the work, d'Eon's dedicatory epistle and preliminary discourse also offer some indication of the intellectual context in which d'Eon wanted the work to be read. These sections clearly reflect d'Eon's long-standing promotion of liberty and his concomitant opposition to despotism and tyranny.[29] D'Eon made a number of references to the conventional view of England as a land of liberty (on this he appears to have been echoing Voltaire, a thinker who is referred to explicitly at several points in *Les Loisirs*).[30] D'Eon suggested that it was as a result of living in a free state that he had come to certain conclusions regarding successful administration: 'It is, sir, in the island of philosophy and liberty, where one learns to give praise only to virtue and merit, that my mind freed from prejudices exposes to the public the traits that characterise you.'[31] Similarly, he began his 'Avis du Traducteur' to his translation of Nedham's work itself by describing liberty as the essence of English government.[32]

Alongside his praise of liberty, d'Eon pointed out – in language that undoubtedly owed something to Montesquieu – the dangers of despotic rule. A ruler who dreams only of making his subjects fearful and subordinate to him is, d'Eon insisted, 'the scourge of the human race'. His abuse of power will certainly make him feared: 'but he is hated and detested, and must fear his subjects more than they have reason to fear him'.[33] Rather than ruling by fear, d'Eon counselled, a ruler will prove far more successful if he seeks to make his people happy, and his authority will never be better established than when it is founded on love for his people.[34] Thus d'Eon insisted that the goal of wise politics should be to make the public good preferable to the private good, and that a ruler should inspire in those around him a lively, pure and disinterested love for all human beings. D'Eon attacked the political theories of Niccolo Machiavelli (in *The Prince*) and Thomas Hobbes, accusing them of operating under the false idea that the good of society has nothing in common with the essential good of man, which is virtue. Consequently they had established, as the only maxims of government, 'finesse, tricks, stratagems, despotism, cruelty, injustice, irreligion'.[35] Against them, d'Eon's goal was to secure the exercise of virtue within government. At the same time, however, he was not unaware of the problems involved in maintaining virtuous conduct among those in power: 'Unfortunately, the most virtuous man, on entering the ministry, soon loses the idea of social, Christian and moral virtues.'[36] In response to this problem, he suggested that some forms of government were better suited to maintaining virtue than others:

> In a republic, regardless of human nature, if the minister appears more virtuous, it is because he is constrained by the necessity of obeying the laws and his enlightened conduct makes him fear the censure of patriots, whether his rivals or his enemies.
>
> …There is in monarchical and even aristocratic governments this problem, that almost all those who are involved … imagine that the advantages of their education will suffice and that they have the probity, the knowledge, the prudence and all the merit necessary to govern alone. This belief prevents them from either seeking advice or taking notice of that which the most capable men offer them.[37]

In short, in the preliminaries to his *Les Loisirs,* d'Eon expressed a number of ideas that were typical of the early modern republican tradition. These included an interest in the Roman Republic and its heroes, a love of liberty and hatred of despotism or tyranny, a belief in the importance of virtuous government, concern at the corrupting effects of power, and even an acknowledgement that in certain respects republican government may be preferable to monarchical or aristocratic forms. It seems unlikely that d'Eon shared Nedham's rabidly anti-monarchical views; given his recruitment as a royal spy, his repeated declarations of loyalty to Louis XV and his opposition to the execution of Louis XVI in 1793.[38] However, he may well have agreed with others at the time that representative bodies offered a means by which monarchical authority might be tempered and its despotic tendencies curbed. Such ideas were not unknown in France, and thus more light can be shed on d'Eon's aims and intentions by considering the audience toward which he directed *Les Loisirs* and some of the wider French circles with which he was associated.

D'Eon's French *patriote* connections

D'Eon dedicated *Les Loisirs* to Etienne François de Choiseul, who had been Minister for Foreign Affairs from 1758 until 1761 and had remained the dominant figure in Louis XV's government until 1770. On the face of it Choiseul appears an odd choice of dedicatee, since during the 1760s d'Eon had been directly opposed to key figures within his circle. It was Choiseul's cousin, the duc de Praslin, who had ordered d'Eon to return to France in 1763, and d'Eon's old enemy the comte de Guerchy was a client of his. Indeed it was this Praslin-Pompadour-Choiseul faction at court that d'Eon believed was behind the attempt to assassinate him.[39] The dedication was rendered even more bizarre by the fact that Choiseul had been unceremoniously dismissed from office in December 1770, and was therefore no longer an obvious target for a work aimed at advising the French government.[40] D'Eon's own explanation for the dedication was that it was a kind of peace offering to Choiseul.[41] There may have been more to this than personal reconciliation, however, since there were also political reasons why d'Eon may have wanted to be seen to be making peace with Choiseul in the early 1770s. In the first place, Choiseul was associated with the patriot movement in France. His particular brand of patriotism echoed the ideas of Bolingbroke's *Patriot King* in its attempt to introduce political reform while maintaining a central role for a strong monarch.[42] In particular, he had sought to forge an alliance between the Ministry and the *parlementaires*, who were increasingly claiming a representative role within the French polity. Significantly, Choiseul retained his association with the patriot movement even after his fall from office – becoming, according to Robert and Isabelle Tombs, 'the focus of what was arguably France's first opposition party, public, patriotic and vocal'.[43] There was, however, another important reason for declaring one's support for Choiseul in the early 1770s. The person who took over his role as the dominant figure within Louis XV's government was Chancellor René-Nicolas-Charles de Maupeou, who was then in the midst of his wholesale attack on the growing political power of the *parlements*.[44] Thus in dedicating *Les Loisirs* to Choiseul, d'Eon was perhaps indicating his support for a particular kind of monarchical patriotism and for the representative role of the *parlements*, as well as expressing – in a subtle, but clear fashion – his opposition to the despotic behaviour of Louis XV's government under the leadership of Chancellor Maupeou.[45]

We do not know what Choiseul thought of the work, but it does not appear to have gone entirely unnoticed elsewhere. Hollis apparently sent a copy of *Les Loisirs* to America, and an article in the *London Evening Post* for 23 July 1774 suggested that it had also been read by ministers in Berlin and that Frederick the Great had ordered that the work: 'should immediately be put into execution, for the benefit of the public and of the government'.[46]

Interestingly d'Eon was also not alone among those involved with the *Secret du roi* in criticising certain aspects of Louis XV's government and voicing a degree of admiration for republican forms of government and for English republican ideas. In 1773 the principles behind the *Secret du roi* were set out in a work commissioned and directed by the then head of the movement – and d'Eon's former employer – the comte de Broglie.[47] The author of the work was Jean-Louis Favier, a disciple of Bolingbroke and translator of his *Letter to Sir William Windham*.[48] In his 'Preliminary Discourse' to that translation, Favier had noted the similarities between the British system of government and the ancient republics of Greece and Rome. Noting the tendency for the English nobility to be educated according to Greek and Roman models of eloquence, he went on:

> This imitation is the result of neither enthusiasm nor pedantry, but the necessary consequence of the foundational principles of the British Constitution. Its resemblance with some ancient republics is particularly marked with regard to Rome. The one had its Consuls who were the depositaries of royal authority, but were tempered by division and annual limitation. The other has its King, who is essentially only a single, perpetual and if one wishes hereditary consul. The House of Lords plays almost the same role in this system as the Senate does in that. Finally, the Commons, composed of knights and townsmen, corresponds almost exactly to the *Comitia* or assembly of the people, formed of the equestrian order and the simple citizens.[49]

While Favier was undoubtedly presenting the British/Roman constitution as an alternative preferable to that of the French, he was too careful a reader of Bolingbroke to be unaware of the defects of the British system. It faced, Favier argued, the same problems as those that ultimately destroyed Rome: 'Ambition, venality, and the spirit of party often caused abuses in Rome. London cries out today, louder than ever, against a similar abuse.'[50]

The significance of the republican ideas being voiced by members of the *Secret du roi* was not lost on contemporaries. Looking back to the period of the 1760s and 1770s in his *Letters on a Regicide Peace* of 1796, Edmund Burke suggested that the 'diplomatic politicians' involved in the *Secret du roi* had begun by blaming the Ministry for the decline in French influence on the international stage, but then: 'From quarrelling with the Court, they began to complain of Monarchy itself; as a system of Government too variable for any regular plan of national aggrandizement. They observed, that in that sort of regimen too much depended on the personal character of the Prince.'[51] It was these men, Burke insisted, together with the philosophers (who were aimed at the 'utter extirpation of religion') who were ultimately responsible for bringing about the Revolution in 1789.[52] According to Burke they were avid readers of Machiavelli's *Discourses* and Montesquieu's *Considérations* and on the basis of these works they compared the French monarchy unfavourably with the Roman system.[53]

Given their choice of reading matter, their proposed solution was perhaps not surprising:

> What cure for the radical weakness of the French Monarchy, to which all the means which wit could devise, or nature and fortune could bestow, toward universal empire, was not of force to give life, or vigour, or consistency, but in a republick? Out the word came; and it never went back.
>
> Whether they reasoned right or wrong, or that there was some mixture of right and wrong in their reasoning, I am sure, that in this manner they felt and reasoned. The different effects of a great military and ambitious republick, and of a monarchy of the same description were constantly in their mouths. The principle was ready to operate when opportunities should offer, which few of them indeed foresaw in the extent in which they were afterwards presented; but these opportunities, in some degree or other, they all ardently wished for.[54]

Burke no doubt had reasons to exaggerate the views and influence of these 'diplomatic politicians', and it is interesting that he placed emphasis on the works of Machiavelli and Montesquieu rather than acknowledging the English sources of their ideas. Nonetheless, Burke was right in noting that republican models and ideas were being discussed in mid-eighteenth-century France, even among those who were working for the King. There is also no doubt some truth in his suggestion that these discussions helped to domesticate republican ideas in France, thereby paving the way for the events of the 1790s.

Conclusion

On the face of it, Nedham's republican pamphlet seems an odd work for d'Eon to have included within a collection that was explicitly aimed at offering advice on matters of government and administration to those involved in running the French state in the mid-eighteenth century.[55] However, his use of republican language in his prefatory material, and his dedication of the work to Choiseul, makes clear that he was deliberately positioning himself against the increasingly despotic measures being taken by Louis XV's government under Maupeou, and in support of the kind of patriotic reforms associated with the *parlements*.[56] In this context, Nedham's emphasis on the importance of representative assemblies for securing liberty no doubt had a particular resonance.

D'Eon owed his awareness of Nedham's work, and of the ideas of the English republican tradition more generally, to his long period of exile in Britain. It was during that stay that he began to acknowledge the importance of liberty and virtue and the threat posed to them by despotism and corruption.[57] In this respect, d'Eon's friendship with Wilkes, and the parallels drawn between the experiences of the two men, appear to have been crucial. What makes this all the more significant is that d'Eon was not the only francophone associate of Wilkes to develop an interest in British commonwealth ideas during the late 1760s and 1770s, or to see the relevance of those ideas in a French, as well as a British, context.

Notes

1. University of Leeds, Brotherton Library (ULBL): Brotherton Collection, d'Eon papers, Case 9, File 60, f. 350, 'Newspaper cuttings on d'Eon's political and social career: *Public Advertiser*, 6 June 1771'.
2. The identity of 'Lady V—e' is not clear, but this may have been a reference to Lady Frances Vane, whose sexually explicit 'Memoirs of a lady of quality' had featured in Tobias Smollett's novel *The Adventures of Peregrine Pickle* in 1751. If so, then it reflects a, not uncommon, attempt to associate radical politics with immorality.
3. ULBL: d'Eon papers, Case 9, File 60, f. 332.
4. Ibid., Case 9, File 60, f. 327, '*Gazette and New Daily Advertiser*, 26 March 1771'. A whole host of articles linking d'Eon to Wilkes can be found in Ibid., Case 8, File 58 and Case 9, File 60.
5. For more detailed accounts of d'Eon's stay in England, on which my brief summary is based, see G. Kates, *Monsieur d'Eon is a Woman: A Tale of Political Intrigue and Sexual Masquerade* (New York: Basic Books, 1995) and S. Burrows, *Blackmail, Scandal, and Revolution: London's French libellistes, 1758–92* (Manchester: Manchester University Press, 2006).
6. D'Eon had been hoping to replace Nivernais as French ambassador, but was overlooked in favour of his old enemy the comte de Guerchy.
7. In fact Louis XVI had already made a public announcement to this effect in 1776 and had called for d'Eon's return to France. Kates, *Monsieur d'Eon is a Woman*, pp. 3–4.
8. On the friendship between d'Eon and Wilkes and the parallels drawn between them see: A. Clark, 'The Chevalier d'Eon and Wilkes: Masculinity and Politics in the Eighteenth Century', *Eighteenth-Century Studies* 32 (1998), pp. 19–48; A. Clark, *Scandal: The Sexual Politics of the British Constitution* (Princeton and Oxford: Princeton University Press, 2004), pp. 19–52; J. Conlin, 'Wilkes, the Chevalier d'Eon and the "Dregs of Liberty": an Anglo-French Perspective on Ministerial Despotism, 1762–1771', *English Historical Review* 120 (2005), pp. 1251–88 and Burrows, *Blackmail, Scandal, and Revolution*, pp. 93–4 and 194–5.
9. BL: Add. MS. 30877 f. 67, 'D'Eon to Wilkes, 5 October 1768' and BL: Add. MS. 30866, 'J Wilkes Diaries (1770–1797)'.
10. ULBL: d'Eon papers, Case 6, File 49, 'Letters from John Wilkes and his daughter to La Chevalière d'Eon, 1785–87'.
11. Kates, *Monsieur d'Eon is a Woman*, p. 197.
12. ULBL: d'Eon papers, Case 9, File 60, f. 327.
13. In fact, such parallels were being drawn from as early as 1764. See in particular ibid., Case 8, File 58, f. 38, '*Lloyd's Evening Post*, 5–7 September, 1764' and ibid., f. 43, 'The *St James's Chronicle or, The British Evening-Post*, 11–13 September, 1764'.
14. BL: Add. MS. 30877 f. 67, 'D'Eon to Wilkes, 5 October 1768'.
15. As cited in Kates, *Monsieur D'Eon is a Woman*, p. 197. Macaulay's letter to d'Eon is held among d'Eon's papers at the Bibliothèque municipale de Tonnerre.
16. D'Eon de Beaumont, *Les Loisirs du chevalier d'Eon de Beaumont ancien ministre plénipotentiaire de France, sur divers sujets importans d'administration, &c. pendant son séjour en Angleterre* (Amsterdam, 1774), VI, pp. 137–399.
17. For a detailed account of Nedham and the background to this text see: B. Worden, 'Introduction' to M. Nedham, *The Excellencie of a Free State* (Indianapolis, IN: Liberty Fund, Forthcoming). I am grateful to Blair Worden for providing me with a copy of this Introduction prior to publication.
18. [M. Nedham], *The Excellencie of a Free State. Or, The Right Constitution of a Commonwealth. Wherein all objections are answered, and the best way to secure the people's liberties discovered. With some errors of*

government and rules of policie (London: Thomas Brewster, 1656), p. 24. The italics are Nedham's own.
19 Ibid., pp. 79–80.
20 On these republications see Chapter 6 above.
21 R. Baron, 'Preface to this Edition', in M. Nedham, *The Excellencie of a Free State*, ed. R. Baron (London: A. Millar and T. Cadell, 1767), p. iii.
22 C. A. Robbins, *The Eighteenth-Century Commonwealthman: Studies in the Transmission, Development and Circumstance of English Liberal Thought from the Restoration of Charles II until the War with the Thirteen Colonies* (Indianapolis, IN: Liberty Fund, 2004 [1987,1959]), p. 46 note 22.
23 The choice of dedicatee and the significance of that choice are discussed below.
24 D'Eon, *Loisirs*, I, p. 1.
25 Ibid., I, pp. 2–3.
26 Cicero, *De Republica*, trans. C. Walker Keyes (Cambridge, MA and London: Harvard University Press and William Heinemann, 1977). Interestingly, Ludlow's virtues were also compared with those of Scipio (and Cato) in his *Memoirs*. E. Ludlow, *Memoirs of Edmund Ludlow Esq* ... (London, 1720–22), I, p. iii.
27 D'Eon, *Loisirs*, I, p. 11.
28 Economic policy had been a matter of particular debate in France during the mid-1760s, and d'Eon had already published works on this subject.
29 On D'Eon's hostility to despotism and tyranny see Conlin, 'Wilkes, the Chevalier d'Eon and "the dregs of liberty" and Burrows, *Blackmail, Scandal, and Revolution*, pp. 44–5.
30 D'Eon, *Loisirs*, I, pp. 21 and 25.
31 Ibid., I, p. 4.
32 Ibid., VI, p. 137.
33 Ibid., I, pp. 28–9.
34 Ibid., I, p. 27.
35 Ibid., I, p. 26.
36 Ibid., I, p. 20.
37 Ibid., I, pp. 20–1.
38 On d'Eon's loyalty to Louis XV see Conlin, 'Wilkes, the Chevalier d'Eon and "the dregs of liberty" and Burrows, *Blackmail, Scandal, and Revolution*, pp. 44 and 182.
39 Burrows, *Blackmail, Scandal, and Revolution*, p. 91.
40 Moreover, Kates suggests that d'Eon initially welcomed Choiseul's dismissal – particularly as there was a suggestion that the comte de Broglie (with whom d'Eon was associated) would replace Praslin as Foreign Minister, but the Duc d'Aiguillon was appointed to the post in June 1771. Kates, *Monsieur d'Eon is a Woman*, pp. 193–4.
41 D'Eon, *Loisirs*, I, p. 5.
42 On the development of patriotism in eighteenth-century France and Choiseul's role within that movement see E. Dziembowski, *Un nouveau patriotisme français, 1750–1770: La France face à la puissance anglaise à l'époque de la guerre de Sept Ans* (Oxford: Voltaire Foundation, 1998). On some of the ambiguities and complexities in the use of the language of patriotism at this time see P. R. Campbell, 'The Language of Patriotism in France, 1750–1770', *E-France: An On-Line Journal of French Studies* 1 (2007), pp. 1–43.
43 R. Tombs and I. Tombs, *That Sweet Enemy: The French and the British from the Sun King to the Present* (London: William Heinemann, 2006), p. 159.
44 On the Maupeou coup see D. Echeverria, *The Maupeou Revolution: A Study in the History of Libertarianism: France, 1770–1774* (Baton Rouge, LA: Louisiana State University Press, 1985).
45 Interestingly, d'Eon was not the only one of his circle to express support for Choiseul at this time. Charles-Claude Théveneau de Morande also did so in his *Gazetier Cuirassé*. *Le Gazetier cuirassé: ou anecdotes scandaleuses de la cour de France*, ed. C. Théveneau de Morande (1772), pp. 16–20. I am indebted to Simon Burrows for this information.
46 On the copy of *Les Loisirs* that was sent to America see C. A. Robbins, 'Library of Liberty – assembled for Harvard College by Thomas Hollis of Lincoln's Inn', in B. Taft (ed.), *Absolute*

Liberty: A Selection from the Articles and Papers of Caroline Robbins (Hamden, CT: Archon Books, 1982), p. 219 note 18. The *London Evening Post* article can be found in ULBL: d'Eon papers, Case 8, File 58, f. 76. Interestingly, in an essay entitled 'Of French Principles', which appeared in his posthumously published *Works* in 1798, the Scottish judge and writer John Maclaurin, Lord Dreghorn, described having come across *Les Loisirs*. He was particularly interested to discover the translation of Nedham's work (being previously unaware of it and unable to obtain a copy of the original), which he saw as epitomising the basic principles of the French Constitution. John Maclaurin, Lord Dreghorn, *The Works of the Late John MacLaurin, Esq. of Dreghorn: One of the Senators of the College of Justice* (Edinburgh: Ruthven and Sons, 1798), II, pp. 173–83.

47 J. L. Favier, *Conjectures raisonnées sur la situation de la France dans le système politique de l'Europe*, in *Politique des cabinets de l'Europe, sous les règnes de Louis XV et de Louis XVI* (Paris: Buisson, 1794).

48 On Favier see: J. Flammermont, 'J.-L. Favier: sa vie et ses écrits', *La Révolution française* 36 (1899), pp. 161–84, 258–76 and 314–35; G. Savage, 'Favier's Heirs: The French Revolution and the *Secret du Roi*', *Historical Journal* 41 (1998), pp. 225–58 and M. Sonenscher, 'Republicanism, State Finances and the Emergence of Commercial Society in Eighteenth-century France – or from Royal to Ancient Republicanism and Back', in M. van Gelderen and Q. Skinner (eds), *Republicanism: A Shared European Heritage*. Vol. 2: *The Values of Republicanism in Early Modern Europe* (Cambridge: Cambridge University Press, 2002), pp. 275–91. Ironically, Favier was recommended as a replacement for d'Eon as secretary to Guerchy, the French ambassador in London, in 1764. Interestingly Flammermont, Savage and Sonenscher have all demonstrated the striking similarities between Favier's views (as expressed in the work commissioned by Broglie) and views expressed several years earlier by the abbé Mably in his *Le Droit Public de l'Europe, fondé sur les traités* (1746) and *Principes des négociations* (1757).

49 Bolingbroke, *Mémoires Secrets de Mylord Bolingbroke sur les affaires d'Angleterre*, trans. J. L. Favier (Paris, 1754) pp. ix–x.

50 Ibid., p. xi–xii.

51 E. Burke, *Select Works of Edmund Burke*, Vol. 3: *Letters on a Regicide Peace* (Indianapolis, IN: Liberty Fund, 1999), p. 175. See also Sonenscher, 'Republicanism, State Finances', pp. 277–8.

52 On this Burke referred to the advertisement to the published version of Favier's work which ended: '*Il sera facile de se convaincre, qu'*Y COMPRIS MÊME LA REVOLUTION, *en grande partie,* ON TROUVE DANS CES MÉMOIRES ET SES CONJECTURES LE GERME DE TOUT CE QU'ARRIVA AUJOURD'HUI, & *qu'on ne peut pas sans les avoir lus, être bien au fait des intérêts, & même des vues actuelles des diverses puissances de l'Europe.*' Burke, *Letters on a Regicide Peace*, p. 174 note 1.

53 Ibid., p. 175.

54 Ibid., p. 177.

55 Those who have referred to this translation have had trouble explaining it. See for example Clark, 'The Chevalier d'Eon and Wilkes', p. 35.

56 D'Eon was presumably not being entirely honest when he claimed, in a letter to Broglie, that *Les Loisirs* posed no threat to the French court. I owe this information to Jonathan Conlin.

57 It is worth noting that Kates's explanation for d'Eon's decision to dress as a woman places particular emphasis on d'Eon's desire to remain virtuous in what he regarded as an increasingly corrupt society. Kates, *Monsieur d'Eon is a Woman*, and G. Kates, 'The Transgendered World of the Chevalier/Chevalière d'Eon', *Journal of Modern History* 67 (1995), pp. 558–94.

8

The British origins of the baron d'Holbach's atheism

Introduction

If d'Eon and Favier represented the 'diplomatick politicians', one of the groups to whom Burke attributed responsibility for the outbreak of the French Revolution, then Paul Henri Thierry, baron d'Holbach surely personified the other group: the philosophers aimed at 'the utter extirpation of religion'.[1] Not only was he the host of one of the most notorious salons of the period (at which even religion and politics were freely discussed), but he was also the author of some of the earliest explicitly atheistic works ever to have been published.[2] Moreover, between 1766 and 1776 d'Holbach engaged in a huge anti-religious publishing campaign that sought to undermine religion and its role within morality and politics.[3]

D'Eon, Favier and d'Holbach had more in common, however, than simply being on the receiving end of Burke's ire. Like d'Eon, d'Holbach was a close friend of Wilkes, and in common with both d'Eon and Favier he was responsible for translating works from the English republican tradition into French. Among the dozens of works that he published as part of his anti-religious campaign were a number by early eighteenth-century British freethinkers, many of whom were also Real Whigs.[4]

On the face of it, d'Holbach's decision to translate these works as part of his campaign does not sit easily with conventional interpretations of his thought or of his relationship to the republican tradition. In an article on d'Holbach, which appeared in the *Republicanism* volumes edited by Martin van Gelderen and Quentin Skinner, Jean Fabien Spitz presented d'Holbach as one of the staunchest opponents of republicanism in eighteenth-century France.[5] While Spitz's analysis of d'Holbach's writings is perceptive and convincing, his overall argument is based on the conventional account of eighteenth-century French classical republicanism, which presents both ancient and English republicanism as part of a single tradition. However, if we accept that these two strands in fact constituted two separate republican traditions in eighteenth-century France then the problem resolves itself. D'Holbach was indeed an opponent of the ancient republican tradition – as represented in the ideal forms of Montesquieu, Rousseau and Mably – but he was far more sympathetic to the more moderate (and pragmatic) republicanism of the commonwealthmen. Indeed, as will be demonstrated in this chapter, d'Holbach not only made use of their religious arguments, but also shared some of their moral and political ideas.

D'Holbach's commonwealth connections

The catalogue listing the books that were held in d'Holbach's library on his death reveals that he owned a number of English republican works himself. Among these were most of the religious works that he translated, but also several of the seventeenth-century works that had been republished by Toland at the turn of the century, including Harrington's *The Commonwealth of Oceana* and Samson's French translation of Sidney's *Discourses Concerning Government*.[6] Moreover, he also appears to have been familiar with Thomas Gordon's political (as well as his religious) writings. In the advertisement to his translation of *The Independent Whig* d'Holbach referred to the fact that Gordon was 'known for his commentary on Tacitus and Sallust and for many other works favourable to civil and religious liberty'.[7]

It is not entirely surprising that d'Holbach was familiar with the works of the English republican tradition, given his British contacts and the circles in which he operated. He had actually travelled to Britain in 1765 to stay with his friend the actor and playwright David Garrick, and the timing has led more than one author to suggest that it was during this trip that he decided to translate the English works.[8] However, the origins of d'Holbach's interest in the writings of British freethinkers and commonwealthmen may well have dated back long before 1765, to his time as a student at the University of Leiden in the 1740s. At Leiden, d'Holbach had made a number of British friends, including the poet Mark Akenside and Wilkes. They supposedly formed a club (a kind of forerunner to d'Holbach's salon) at which the free discussion of ideas was encouraged.[9]

During his youth, Akenside expressed commonwealth views – on both religion and politics – and drew heavily on the ideas of the third Earl of Shaftesbury.[10] These views were most clearly expressed in his poem *Pleasures of Imagination*, which he first published (anonymously) at the beginning of 1744, just before he travelled to Leiden to complete his studies.[11] Thomas Hollis was so impressed by Akenside's poem, and the commitment to liberty that it expressed, that he sent him a gift of the bed on which Milton (Hollis's great hero) had died.[12] D'Holbach was presumably also impressed by the poem, since he produced a French translation of it in 1759.[13]

The tone and content of the letters that d'Holbach sent to Wilkes just after the latter had left Leiden in 1746 demonstrate that they were close friends.[14] These letters also reveal that the two men were already discussing political matters and sending each other books at this point. D'Holbach's friendship with Wilkes survived well beyond their school days.[15] They were still writing to each other in the late 1760s, when d'Holbach was engaged in his publishing campaign, and whenever he was in France Wilkes attended d'Holbach's salon.[16] Moreover, in his letters d'Holbach suggested that he had sympathy with Wilkes's cause: 'be persuaded, Dear Sir, that nobody interest's himself in your happiness [more] than myself, and nothing will conduce more to it than your steady attachement to the principles of honour and patriotism.'[17] D'Holbach also appears to have thought that Wilkes would be interested in (and not offended by) his radical religious ideas, since he recommended his own works to him, and asked him to procure copies of those he could not find in Paris.[18]

Not only did d'Holbach have contacts with British commonwealthmen, but he was not alone among his French friends in showing an interest in, and even translating, works from the English republican tradition. Not only did Diderot publish a translation of the third Earl of Shaftesbury's *An Inquiry Concerning Virtue* (the fourth part of his *Characteristicks*) under the title *Principes de la philosophie morale; ou Essai de M. S*** sur le mérite et la vertu* in 1745,[19] but the following year he extended his *Pensées philosophiques* with a piece entitled *De la Suffisance de la religion naturelle*, which drew on the ideas of Toland, Collins and Matthew Tindal among others.[20] Moreover, Diderot also appears to have had an interest in the history of mid-seventeenth-century England. In his *Memoirs*, Samuel Romilly recalled a conversation he had enjoyed with Diderot during a trip to France in 1781. According to Romilly, Diderot had spoken out against the tyranny of the French government and had claimed to have long thought of producing a work on the death of Charles I. Had he lived in England, Diderot confessed, he would have done so, but he did not have the courage to produce such a work in France.[21]

D'Holbach's translations of English works

D'Holbach embarked on his anti-religious publishing campaign in 1766, and from the outset translations of English works played a central role. Of the fifteen works d'Holbach published between 1766 and 1769, just over half were translations of works by British freethinkers.[22] Alongside them d'Holbach published French works previously only circulated in manuscript form and original works of his own.[23]

Given their content, and the severity of France's censorship laws at the time, publishing these works was a dangerous business, and d'Holbach did all he could to disassociate himself from them.[24] Though most of the works were published by Marc Michel Rey in Amsterdam, they were given a false imprint (usually London). Moreover, even those works that had been written by d'Holbach himself were either published anonymously or issued under the names of authors who were no longer alive. His *magnum opus*, *Système de la nature*, appeared under the name of the Frenchman (and associate of the comte de Boulainvilliers) Jean-Baptiste de Mirabaud, while *Christianisme dévoilé*, though actually by d'Holbach himself, was presented as the work of Nicolas Boulanger and as a companion piece to his *Antiquité dévoilée*, which d'Holbach had published in 1766. D'Holbach employed the same kind of trickery with the English works. According to the foreword to *La Contagion sacrée, ou histoire naturelle de la superstition*, it was a translation of a pamphlet by John Trenchard that had appeared in England in 1709.[25] Trenchard did indeed publish a pamphlet in that year under the title *The Natural History of Superstition*.[26] However, d'Holbach's version is not a straightforward translation of the work and contains within it extreme religious views that Trenchard himself would not have endorsed.[27] Indeed, it was one of the works that the *Paris Parlement* condemned to be burned on 18 August 1770. Nonetheless, d'Holbach did not always misrepresent the views of the British authors whose works he translated. For the most part his translations were relatively accurate, even when the views being expressed were not in line with his own.[28]

Early modern republican ideas: religion

It was the religious aspects of Real Whig thought that were the main focus of d'Holbach's interest. In particular what appealed to him was the anticlericalism and toleration of the British freethinkers, as well as the materialism of Toland's *Letters to Serena*.

Anticlericalism was the first topic d'Holbach explored in his anti-religious publishing campaign and he appears to have become completely obsessed with it during 1767. In the course of that year he translated no fewer than seven English works on the subject. His *L'Imposture sacerdotale* comprised translations of six English pamphlets on this theme,[29] while his *De L'Esprit du clergé* was a translation of the first two volumes of Trenchard and Gordon's *The Independent Whig*, which was designed to show 'the infinite Evils brought upon Mankind from Age to Age by the Pride and Imposture of corrupt Ecclesiasticks'.[30] Anticlericalism was also a key theme in d'Holbach's own book *Christianisme dévoilé*, which appeared that year. As he explained in that work: 'Priests of all sects have ever wished to govern mankind, and impose on them their decisions as infallible and sacred. They were always persecutors when in power, involved nations in their fury, and shook the world by their fatal opinions.'[31] D'Holbach was perhaps attracted by the extreme nature of the commonwealthmen's views on this subject. While Trenchard and Gordon were quick to insist that their criticisms were aimed not at all clerics, but only at those who had become corrupt,[32] their condemnation was actually fairly broad:

> Nothing is more evident from History, than that most, if not all, the Improvements and Reformations of Religion have been made, not only without, but in Opposition to these Men [the priests]. There have been near a Million of them kept in constant Pay for the best Part of Seventeen Hundred Years to teach the World by their Precepts, and reform it by their Example; and yet I am persuaded they will not pretend that Religion is plainer, the Scriptures better understood, or that Mankind are more wise or virtuous for all their Instructions. So little have we been benefited by their Labours, and for all the Money they have received! I wish I could not say that the World has gradually decreased in Piety and Virtue, as these its Teachers have advanced in Riches and Power. It is owned by the best of Themselves.[33]

Moreover, they challenged not only the temporal authority of the clergy, but also their spiritual authority to instruct others and interpret Scripture.[34]

Despite the strength of his own atheistic views, d'Holbach also appears to have shared the commonwealthmen's commitment to extensive toleration, and this became a dominant theme of his campaign in 1769 and 1770.[35] As its title suggests, d'Holbach's 1769 volume *De La Tolérance* focused on this issue.[36] The first part of the work consisted of a revision of an earlier French translation of the work *Junii Bruti Poloni, vindiciae pro religionis libertate* (1637), by the Socinian Jan Crell [Crellius].[37] The second part comprised a translation of nine chapters from the third and fourth volumes of Trenchard and Gordon's *The Independent Whig* (d'Holbach's earlier translation of the work having been of only the original two volumes). Both works were concerned with demonstrating the utility of an extremely wide degree of toleration. Indeed, d'Holbach described Crell's work as demonstrating 'the utility, the justice and the necessity of universal toleration'.[38] However, while d'Holbach was serious in his commitment to toleration, he also used the discussion of it as an opportunity to continue his anticlerical theme, and to reiterate and reinforce his attacks on the Church and the clergy. The articles from *The Independent Whig* that appeared in *De La Tolérance* dealt specifically with religious intolerance, especially that exercised by the Church.[39] This theme was also reflected in another translation d'Holbach produced that year, his *De La Cruauté religieuse*, which was based on the third part of an anonymous pamphlet entitled *Considerations Upon War*. Similarly in d'Holbach's own works, an account of the benefits of toleration was often accompanied by an attack on the intolerance of the Church. For example, in *Système de la nature* he attacked the tendency of clerics to persecute those who did not share their religious views, before declaring:

> If he must have his chimeras, let him at least learn to permit others to form theirs after their own fashion; since nothing can be more immaterial than the manner of men's thinking on subjects not accessible to reason, provided those thoughts are not suffered to embody themselves into actions injurious to others: above all, let him be fully persuaded that it is of the utmost importance to the inhabitants of this world to be just, kind, and peaceable.[40]

D'Holbach's materialism centred on his belief that the whole universe was made up of matter in motion. On this topic he explicitly acknowledged his debt to Toland's *Letters to Serena*.[41] In the second chapter of *Système de la nature*, which was entitled 'Of Motion and its Origin' he declared: 'Those [particles] which appear to us to be without motion, are, in fact, only in relative or apparent rest; they experience such an imperceptible motion, and expose it so little on their surfaces, that we cannot perceive the changes they undergo.' Naigeon's footnote to this passage read:

> This truth, which is still denied by many metaphysicians, has been conclusively established by the celebrated Toland, in a work which appeared in the beginning of the eighteenth century, entitled *Letters to Serena*. Those who can procure this scarce work will do well to refer to it, and their doubts on the subject, if they have any, will be removed.[42]

The fact that this work was accessible to a French audience in 1770 was entirely due to d'Holbach himself, who had published a translation of it in 1768 under the title *Lettres philosophiques*.[43]

Of course, d'Holbach went much further in his criticism of religion than any of the British authors whose works he translated. Unlike the Real Whigs, who had believed that religion could perform a useful societal function if organised correctly, he repudiated all forms of it and even denied the existence of a Supreme Being. It was precisely d'Holbach's intention to create a moral system that did not rely on, or have any place for, religion.

The fact that d'Holbach went beyond the views of the British writers necessarily raises the question of why he chose to spend time translating their works. In part it was probably a question of numbers. By including the translations (and the French works that had previously circulated in manuscript form) among his publications, d'Holbach was able to mastermind a more extensive campaign than would have been possible if he had produced only original works of his own. Moreover, the fact that the works d'Holbach published were associated with the names of a whole range of British and French authors may have been intended to add greater authority to the ideas and to enhance the sense of this being a widespread movement, rather than simply reflecting the views of one or two eccentric individuals. In addition, he may have wanted to appeal to as wide an audience as possible. Given his concerns about the negative effects of religion, his primary aim was presumably to encourage people to question religious conventions and institutions rather than necessarily converting them to his own views. Ultimately, however, given the order in which the works appeared, it seems likely that d'Holbach was using the English works as a kind of stepping-stone to help him – and his audience – to reach his more extreme position.

Of the fifteen works published between 1766 and 1769, eight were translations from the English, as compared with just three works of his own, three editions of French manuscripts by other authors, and one work translated from German. In the period 1770 to 1776 the ratio was more or less reversed. Of the sixteen works published during this period, nine had been authored by d'Holbach himself, whereas just five were translations from the English (the last of which appearing in 1772), with one translation each from Spanish and German. Thus, whereas the English translations had dominated during the late 1760s, there was from 1770 a general shift away from translations and editions of the works of others, and toward d'Holbach's own compositions. Given the focus of the English translations, their role within the campaign was presumably to undermine the existing system in order to prepare the way for d'Holbach's own theory as set out in *Système de la nature* and the works that followed. By subjecting the French public to a steady stream of anticlerical works from 1767, d'Holbach perhaps hoped that the ground would have been prepared for his own extreme irreligious views, and his alternative moral system, when they were made public in the early 1770s.

Early modern republican ideas: morality

As has been demonstrated in earlier chapters, the moral position of early modern republicans was ambiguous and complex. Unlike earlier exponents of the republican tradition, they did not simply adopt a neo-Stoic position (according to which virtue was the goal, reason was to dominate, and private passions were to be subordinated to the public good), but rather occupied the murky borderlands between neo-Stoicism and neo-Epicureanism. Rather than simply dismissing the role played by self-interest or the passions, they took account of and even made use of them when constructing their moral and political systems. Indeed, many of them went so far as to suggest that what was required was not virtue itself but the appearance of it, and that this could be achieved through the direction and manipulation of the passions and self-interest that would arise out of a careful construction of the constitution, laws and institutions of the state. It is clear that some exponents of the early modern republican tradition were more convinced by neo-Epicurean ideas than others, but it is significant that republicanism and neo-Epicureanism were not necessarily incompatible.

D'Holbach was clearly on the neo-Epicurean side of the border, but his moral position was not all that different from that expressed in *Cato's Letters* or in the works of Bolingbroke. D'Holbach believed that all bodies are directed toward their own preservation and that self-love and the passions are therefore the primary motivating factors in humans: 'self-love, interest, the passions are the sole motives for [human] actions'.[44] He thought that, ideally, human beings ought to operate on the basis of reason, which would direct them toward more lasting happiness and pleasure, but he acknowledged that very few people are actually capable of acting on this basis and that most would act instead to gratify their immediate passions: 'I shall be told: he [man] ought to have learned to resist his passions; to contract a habit of putting a curb on his desires. I agree to it without any difficulty. But in reply, I again ask, is his nature susceptible of this modification?'[45]

This presented a problem for d'Holbach, since he also believed that in order for society to function effectively the passions of its individual members would have to be controlled. Given that he did not believe that simply ordering people to suppress their natural passions would prove effective, he focused instead on the idea of using those passions to regulate and direct behaviour. In a passage that almost seems to echo *Cato's Letters*, d'Holbach insisted: '*Politics* ought to be the art of regulating the passions of man, and of directing them to the welfare of society.'[46] In reality, however, this had rarely been the case:

> [T]oo frequently it is nothing more than the detestable art of arming the passions of the various members of society against each other to accomplish their mutual destruction and fill with rancorous animosities that association, from which, if properly managed, man ought to derive his felicity. Society is commonly so full of vice because it is not founded upon nature, upon experience, upon general utility, but on the contrary upon the passions, the caprices, the particular interests of those by whom it is governed.[47]

Like the commonwealthmen, d'Holbach was keen to show his readers how the passions might be used more positively. Though he explored other (constitutional) means in his later works,[48] his focus in *Système de la nature* was on shaping the manners of the population and the culture of the society:

> Let the vain project of destroying passions from the heart of man be abandoned; let an effort be made to direct him toward objects that may be useful to himself and to his associates. Let education, let government, let the laws, habituate him to restrain his passions within those just bounds which experience and reason prescribe. Let the ambitious have honours, titles, distinctions, power, when they have usefully served their country; let riches be given to those who covet them, when they shall have rendered themselves necessary to their fellow citizens; let eulogies encourage those who shall be actuated by the love of glory. In short, let the passions of man have a free course, whenever real and durable advantages to society result from their exercise. Let education kindle only those that are truly

beneficial to the human species, let it favour those alone who are really necessary to the maintenance of society. The passions of man are dangerous, only because everything conspires to give them an evil direction.[49]

In other words, rather than simply insisting that people ought to behave virtuously (as republicans in the past had often suggested) it was a question (as Harrington had recognised) of making virtuous behaviour appeal to people: 'In order that man may become virtuous, it is absolutely requisite that he should have an interest or should find advantages in practising virtue.'[50]

Early modern republican ideas: politics

D'Holbach's politics have presented something of an enigma, since twentieth- and twenty-first-century minds can find it difficult to square his extremely radical religious and moral views with what is perceived to be a rather conservative political position. Scholars have noted that he remained committed to monarchical government and firmly rejected the idea of revolutionary change, preferring a process of gradual reform.[51] Yet, while it is true that d'Holbach was not a regicide, a democrat or a revolutionary, concluding from this that he was politically conservative is somewhat disingenuous, since it involves judging him against the standards of the 1790s rather than those of his own time.[52] In fact on political matters, as on religion and morality, d'Holbach appears to have shared much in common with the British commonwealthmen.

As has been demonstrated, for many commonwealthmen the crucial issue was not whether the political system had a monarch at its head, but rather whether it was designed to protect and maintain liberty. They generally agreed that a government ought to operate in the public interest, rather than in the private interests of its rulers, and that it therefore had to be based on the free consent of society and to operate according to the rule of laws not of men. However, a mixed or limited monarchy might be just as successful at achieving these ends as a republic. Moreover, the commonwealthmen also agreed that whatever form of government was adopted, further checks and balances would be required to slow the inevitable tendency toward corruption among those in power. These might include frequent elections, freedom of thought and speech and, ultimately, the right of resistance.[53] Since the population as a whole were just as liable to corruption as those in power, attention also had to be paid to them. Designing the constitution in such a way that they were only required to act in their own interests was Harrington's favoured means, but the commonwealthmen also believed that both education and legislation could be used to shape public opinion and to make passions such as a love of glory work for the public good.[54]

Once again, d'Holbach appears to have shared this commonwealth perspective. He too insisted that government should operate in the interests of the governed not of the governors. As he explained in *Système de la nature:* 'the end of all government [is] the benefit of the governed not the exclusive advantage of the governors.'[55] To secure this he embraced the idea of the rule of law and the subordination of the sovereign to it: 'In short, the experience of all ages will convince nations that man is continually tempted to the abuse of power: that therefore the sovereign ought to be subject to the law, not the law to the sovereign.'[56] He also acknowledged that government had to be based on the free consent of society,[57] thereby endorsing its right to modify the sovereign's powers and even overthrow them altogether if necessary: 'Government only borrows its power from society: being established for no other purpose than its welfare, it is evident that society can revoke this power whenever its interest shall dictate it – change the form of its government – extend or limit the power which it has confided to its chiefs, over whom, by the immutable laws of nature, it always conserves a supreme authority.'[58]

D'Holbach's debt to the political aspect of the commonwealth tradition is most clearly indicated, however, in his book *La Politique naturelle*, which appeared in 1773.[59] Having gone through the advantages and disadvantages of all other forms of government, he turned to what he called 'limited monarchy'. Though he was adamant that a perfect form of government was an impossibility, and that different forms might suit different states, it is clear from his description that this form of government appeared to him to be the best available:

> It is believed that an authority that is balanced in this way places a brake on the abuses of royalty, on the ambitions of the aristocrats and on the hotheadedness of the people. From the mix of these three governments that which is called *mixed or tempered monarchy* is born. It is hoped that by this means the forces of society will be more justly distributed. It is felt that to prevent the abuse that is inseparable from all power, it is necessary to place it in several different hands so as to prevent one of the orders of the state from tipping the balance in its favour. This government is regarded as the masterpiece of the human spirit. The laws invariably apply equally to all members of the society; the monarch himself acknowledges their empire: they bind his hands when he wishes to do wrong and leave him only the happy liberty of doing good. By this means, all citizens are protected against his power. These laws are not subject to the caprices of a sovereign or his court; the people represented by an assembly, whose members they choose, concur in the legislation that it imposes; those citizens who are distinguished by birth, fortune and rank participate in it. Finally [those laws] are adorned with the royal authority that is charged with their execution. Under such a government the laws are only the expression of the public will. The person, the property, the liberty of each individual become sacred objects that no power can touch with impunity.
>
> England provides us with an example of this form of government. If some

human institution seemed able to procure the happiness of a people, this would undoubtedly be it, a government that reunites, balances and tempers all the governments that men have imagined up to the present.[60]

The similarities between this description and the accounts of mixed or balanced government offered by the commonwealthmen are striking.[61] As if this were not enough, d'Holbach then went on to acknowledge that there is no edifice that human passions cannot undermine, and that even this form of government was subject to corruption and decay. His account of how this could happen echoed the critique that the British commonwealthmen had made of their own government:

> A crafty monarch will perhaps make the representatives of the people complicit in their enslavement. What power money has over a greedy nation when it has become its only motive. A monarch who is master of the treasury can easily corrupt miserly citizens. A sovereign who commands mercenary soldiers as a despot, can easily subjugate those whom he cannot seduce. And citizens who are divided offer only a very weak barrier to the designs of an ambitious prince. A venal aristocracy is an uncertain dyke against arbitrary power. Finally a people who are restless and unruly and who mistake unrestrained licence for liberty, can easily throw themselves into chains.[62]

Conclusion

While the baron d'Holbach was extremely unsympathetic to the ancient republican tradition, his views on a range of issues were strikingly similar to those of the British commonwealthmen, whose religious works he translated. Though he certainly ventured further than the Real Whigs in attacking not just the Christian Church, but religion itself, their anticlericalism provided an important staging post on his route, and he echoed their arguments on this and many other issues. On moral matters they were even more closely aligned, since the Real Whigs had already moved in the direction of neo-Epicureanism. Like d'Holbach, many of them had accepted the fundamental role played by self-interest and the passions within human nature, and sought to work with them rather than insisting on their suppression. Similarly, in political terms the commonwealthmen, like d'Holbach, were conservative when compared with the standards of the 1790s. They were not writing in the midst of revolution, but were seeking to propose reforms that would ameliorate and improve upon existing political systems. That is not to say, however, that these ideas did not have revolutionary potential. In fact, in the case of another francophone Wilkite, the British commonwealth tradition provided the foundations for revolutionary radicalism.

Notes

1. E. Burke, *Select Works of Edmund Burke*, Vol. 3: *Letters on a Regicide Peace* (Indianapolis, IN: Liberty Fund, 1999), p. 170. On this see Chapter 7 above.
2. There are surprisingly few works on d'Holbach, his life and work. See: W. H. Wickwar, *Baron d'Holbach: A Prelude to the French Revolution* (London: George Allen & Unwin, 1935); V. W. Topazio, *D'Holbach's Moral Philosophy, its Background and Development* (Geneva: Institut et Musée Voltaire, 1956); J. Vercruysse, *Bibliographie descriptive des écrits du baron d'Holbach* (Paris: Lettres modernes, Minard, 1971); A. C. Kors, *D'Holbach's Coterie: An Enlightenment in Paris* (Princeton: Princeton University Press, 1976); A. Sandrier, *Le Style philosophique du baron d'Holbach* (Paris: Champion, 2004) and M. Curran, 'The Reception of the Works of the Baron d'Holbach in France, 1752–1789' (University of Leeds PhD Thesis, 2005).
3. Though d'Holbach appears to have taken the lead role in the campaign, he was assisted by Denis Diderot and Jacques-André Naigeon.
4. Surprisingly little attention has been paid to this aspect of d'Holbach's thought in anglophone works. Topazio did discuss d'Holbach's use of British ideas, but he focused almost entirely on Thomas Hobbes and John Locke, devoting just a couple of pages to John Toland, Anthony Collins and Thomas Woolston, and not mentioning Thomas Gordon at all. Similarly, Michael Bush in his introduction to volume one of *The System of Nature* makes no mention of Gordon. Topazio, *D'Holbach's Moral Philosophy*, pp. 27–46; M. Bush, 'Introduction' to P. H. T., Baron d'Holbach, *The System of Nature: Volume One,* trans. H. D. Robinson, ed. M. Bush (Manchester: Clinamen Press, 1999), pp. vii–xvi. Interestingly, d'Holbach also exercised an influence back on British thinkers, and especially William Godwin. See: S. Deane, *The French Revolution and Enlightenment in England, 1789–1832* (Cambridge, MA and London: Harvard University Press, 1988), pp. 72–94.
5. J. F. Spitz, 'From Civism to Civility: D'Holbach's Critique of Republican Virtue', in M. van Gelderen and Q. Skinner (eds), *Republicanism: A Shared European Heritage*. Vol. II: *The Values of Republicanism in Early Modern Europe* (Cambridge: Cambridge University Press, 2002), pp. 107–22.
6. P. H. T., baron d'Holbach, *Catalogue des livres de la bibliothèque de feu M. le Baron d'Holbach* (Paris: De Bure, 1789), pp. 50–1.
7. [P. H. T., baron d'Holbach], *De L'Esprit du clergé* (London [Amsterdam]: Marc Michel Rey, 1767), 'Avertissement'.
8. Wickwar, *Baron d'Holbach*, pp. 72–3; Topazio, *D'Holbach's Moral Philosophy*, p. 21.
9. Wickwar, *Baron d'Holbach*, p. 21.
10. There have been suggestions that Akenside became more conservative in later life. On this and other aspects of his life, see: R. Dix, 'Akenside, Mark (1721–1770)', *Oxford Dictionary of National Biography* (Oxford: Oxford University Press, 2004; online edition, October 2006) www.oxforddnb.com/view/article/263, accessed 28 April 2008.
11. M. Akenside, *Pleasures of Imagination: A Poem in Three Books* (London, 1744). Akenside subsequently revised the work several times for later editions. He even rewrote the work completely under the amended title *The Pleasures of the Imagination*, the first book of which appeared in 1757.
12. T. Hollis, *Memoirs of Thomas Hollis*, ed. F. Blackburne (London, 1780), I, pp. 111–12, see also p. 14 and II, pp. 722–6. See also C. A. Robbins, *The Eighteenth-Century Commonwealthman: Studies in the Transmission, Development, and Circumstance of English Liberal Thought from the Restoration of Charles II until the War with the Thirteen Colonies* (Indianapolis, IN: Liberty Fund, 2004 [1987, 1959]).
13. [P. H. T. baron d'Holbach] *Les Plaisirs de l'imagination: poème en trois chants, par M. Akenside*; traduit de l'anglais (Amsterdam and Paris: Arkstée et Merkus and Pissot, 1759).
14. BL: Add. MS. 30867 fols. 14, 18, 19, 20, 21, 'Letters from d'Holbach to Wilkes'.
15. In May 1766 d'Holbach wrote to Wilkes: 'I hope you Know too well the sincere dispositions of my heart as to doubt of the friendship I have vowed to you for life; it has been of too long a duration to be shaken by any circumstances.' BL: Add. MS. 30869 f. 39, 'D'Holbach to Wilkes, 22 May 1766'.

16 BL: Add. MS. 30869 fols. 39, 40, 81, 82, 173, 174, 'D'Holbach to Wilkes, 22 May and 10 September 1766, 10 December 1767'; Add. MS. 30870 fols. 59, 60, 'D'Holbach to Wilkes, 17 July 1768'; Add. MS. 30871 fols.16, 17, 'D'Holbach to Wilkes, 19 March, 1770'.
17 BL: Add. MS. 30869 f. 40, 'D'Holbach to Wilkes, 22 May 1766'.
18 BL: Add. MSS 30871 f. 17 and 30869 f. 174.
19 The loose nature of the translation has led some scholars to suggest that it is more accurate to describe it as an independent work by Diderot that was based on Shaftesbury's original.
20 D. Diderot, *Principes de la philosophie morale; ou Essai de M. S*** sur le mérite et la vertu*, ed. J. Assézat and M. Tourneux and D. Diderot, *De la Suffisance de la religion naturelle*, ed. J. Assézat and M. Tourneux. Both accessed via gallica, http://gallica.bnf.fr/ on 17th December 2008.
21 S. Romilly, *The Memoirs of the Life of Sir Samuel Romilly* (London: John Murray, 1840), I, pp. 63–4.
22 D'Holbach had already established his position as a translator long before 1766. From as early as 1753 he had been translating German scientific works into French and he had translated two works from English into French, Akenside's poem and Jonathan Swift's *History of the Reign of Queen Anne*, prior to 1766.
23 D'Holbach's own works were also influenced by his reading of the English texts. For example Justin Champion notes how he exploited elements of John Toland's *Pantheisticon* for his *Système de la nature*. J. Champion, '"The forceful, full, energetic, fearless expression of heretical thoughts": Rethinking clandestine literature and the European reading public, 1680–1730', p. 8. I am grateful to Justin Champion for providing me with a copy of this paper.
24 Supposedly even some of his closest friends were not aware of his role as author and translator of these works.
25 [P. H. T., baron d'Holbach], *La Contagion sacrée, ou histoire naturelle de la superstition* (London, [Amsterdam]: Marc Michel Rey, 1768), 'Foreword'.
26 J. Trenchard, *The Natural History of Superstition* (London, 1709).
27 Justin Champion claims that elements of Trenchard's original pamphlet were translated in chapters 12 and 13 of d'Holbach's work. J. A. I. Champion, *The Pillars of Priestcraft Shaken: The Church of England and its enemies, 1660–1730* (Cambridge: Cambridge University Press, 1992), p. 161n.
28 See Curran, 'Reception of the Works', pp. 40–1.
29 [P. H. Thierry, baron d'Holbach], *De L'Imposture sacerdotale* (London [Amsterdam]: Marc Michel Rey, 1767).
30 J. Trenchard and T. Gordon, *The Independent Whig: or a defence of primitive Christianity, and of our ecclesiastical establishment...* 6th edn (London, 1732), p. 41. [Holbach], *De L'Esprit du clergé*.
31 P. H. T., baron d'Holbach, *Christianity unveiled; being, an examination of the principles and effects of the Christian Religion* (New York, 1795), p. 220.
32 'I ... design by this Work to illustrate the Beauty of Christianity, by exposing the Deforming of Priestcraft; to distinguish the good Clergy from the bad, by giving to each his Share of Praise or Infamy, according to the different Deeds done by them.' Trenchard and Gordon, *The Independent Whig*, p. 41.
33 Ibid., pp. 50–1.
34 Ibid., pp. 46, 52 and 79. This was also the argument of Toland's *Christianity not mysterious*. On this see J. Champion, *Republican Learning: John Toland and the Crisis of Christian Culture, 1696–1722* (Manchester: Manchester University Press, 2003), p. 82.
35 For more detail on the commitment to extensive toleration expressed by the Real Whigs see Chapter 1 above.
36 [P. H. Thierry, baron d'Holbach], *De La Tolérance* (London [Amsterdam]: Marc Michel Rey, 1769).
37 As d'Holbach explained in his foreword to the work, the earlier translation had been produced by the Arminian Charles Le Cène, in his work *Conversations sur diverses matières de religion* of 1687. D'Holbach was critical of the style of that translation, claiming that it was almost unreadable, and had touched it up so as to make it more accessible. Ibid., 'Avertissement'.
38 Ibid., 'Avertissement'.

39 The issues translated were numbers 55, 56, 57, 61, 62, 63, 64 and 65 from Volume III and number 4 from Volume IV.
40 Holbach, *System of Nature*, p. 5.
41 However, his understanding of matter was not identical to that of Toland. See P. Lurbe, 'Matière, nature, mouvement chez d'Holbach et Toland', *Dix-huitième siècle* 24 (1992), pp. 53–62.
42 Holbach, *System of Nature*, p. 19.
43 [P. H. Thierry, baron d'Holbach], *Lettres Philosophiques* (London [Amsterdam]: Marc Michel Rey, 1768).
44 [P. H. T. Baron d'Holbach], *La Politique naturelle, ou discours sur les vrais principes du gouvernement* (London [Amsterdam], 1773), I, p. 23 and p. 11. See also Holbach, *System of Nature*, p. 221.
45 Holbach, *System of Nature*, p. 143. See also p. 151.
46 Ibid., p. 102. The passage from *Cato's Letters* reads as follows: 'The only way therefore of dealing with mankind, is to deal with their passions; and the founders of all states, and of all religions, have ever done so: the first elements, or knowledge of politics, is the knowledge of the passions; and the art of governing, is chiefly the art of applying to the passions.' J. Trenchard and T. Gordon, *Cato's Letters; or Essays on Liberty, Civil and Religious, and other Important Subjects*, 3rd edn (London: W. Wilkins, 1733), II, pp. 47–8. D'Holbach also expressed the same idea in his *Politique naturelle*: 'The perfection of government would consist in directing the passions of citizens toward the public good. It would be a vain endeavour to try to annihilate them. It would be a vain demand to insist that those who rule men are themselves exempt from passions.' [Holbach], *Politique naturelle*, I, p. 81.
47 Holbach, *System of Nature*, p. 102.
48 For example in *La Politique naturelle*: see below.
49 Holbach, *System of Nature*, p. 107. See also pp. 242 and 249 and *Politique naturelle*, I, pp. 41 and 43.
50 Holbach, *System of Nature*, p. 108.
51 See for example Kors, *D'Holbach's Coterie*. See also, Holbach, *Politique naturelle*, I, pp. 80 and 113. However, it is clear that some readers – not least Frederick the Great – saw more radical potential in his works. On this see Curran, 'Reception of the Works', pp. 123–4.
52 D'Holbach died in 1789.
53 On frequent elections see Trenchard and Gordon, *Cato's Letters*, II, No. 60, pp. 198–9. For the ultimate right of resistance see R. Molesworth, *The Principles of a Real Whig; contained in a preface to the famous Hotoman's Franco-Gallia, written by the late Lord-Viscount Molesworth; and now reprinted at the request of the London Association* (London: J. Williams, 1775), p. 8.
54 Trenchard and Gordon, *Cato's Letters*, II, No. 39, p. 37.
55 Holbach, *System of Nature*, p. 11. See also *Politique naturelle*, I, pp. 48, 60.
56 Holbach, *System of Nature*, p. 105. See also *Politique naturelle*, II, p. 69: 'One is free wherever the laws rule; one is a slave wherever someone is master of the law. One lives under a tyranny wherever the sovereign can commit injustice with impunity.'
57 In this sense, d'Holbach does share something of the republican understanding of liberty. Spitz, 'D'Holbach's Critique of Republican Virtue'.
58 Holbach, *System of Nature*, p. 103. Interestingly, Wickwar suggests that d'Holbach was unusual among pre-revolutionary French thinkers in advocating the right of resistance. Wickwar, *Baron d'Holbach*, p. 193.
59 This work was influenced by the experience of the Maupeou Coup about which d'Holbach was critical. See Curran, 'Reception of the Works', pp. 41–2.
60 [Holbach], *Politique naturelle*, I, p. 70.
61 This is despite Molesworth's rejection of the term 'limited monarchy'. Molesworth, *The Principles of a Real Whig*, p. 7. D'Holbach would not, however, have endorsed the commonwealth appeal to an ancient constitution or the associated sense that the modern world was inferior to the past. See Spitz, 'D'Holbach's Critique of Republican Virtue', pp. 118–19.
62 [Holbach], *Politique naturelle*, I, p. 71.

9

The British origins of Jean-Paul Marat's revolutionary radicalism

Introduction

As with so many aspects of his life, Jean-Paul Marat's ten-year stay in Britain during the 1760s and 1770s subsequently became the focus of rumour and speculation. It was claimed that he had been employed as French master at the famous Dissenting Academy at Warrington, that he had taught tambouring in Edinburgh (where he had been arrested and imprisoned for debt), and even that he had stolen coins and medals from the Ashmolean Museum in Oxford (a crime for which he was supposedly convicted and sentenced to several years' hard labour on the hulks at Woolwich).[1] These stories circulated throughout the nineteenth and twentieth centuries.[2] Not everyone believed them, however, and the last story in particular was rendered questionable by a letter published in Charles Vellay's *La Correspondance de Marat* in 1908. In the letter, which was addressed to a tradesman in England, Marat explained that he was going to the Continent on business and would settle his account on his return in October.[3] It was dated Dover, 11 April 1776 – exactly the time when Marat was supposed to have been in prison in Dublin having been apprehended for the Ashmolean robbery.[4] While a number of commentators remained sceptical about this letter and its supposed disproval of the Ashmolean story,[5] in the 1960s further evidence appeared. In the archives of the Société Typographique de Neuchâtel, Robert Darnton discovered a second letter from Marat – dated Geneva, 14 May 1776 and addressed to Frédéric-Samuel Ostervald of the Société Typographique.[6] As Darnton himself concluded, the letter proves: 'that Marat was with his family in Geneva at the time of the imprisonment of the true robber of the Ashmolean Museum'.[7]

This important discovery has generally been treated as resolving the matter, and subsequent historians appear to have lost interest in Marat's stay in Britain.[8] Yet it was in this period of his life that crucial aspects of Marat's revolutionary thought and persona were first established. It was during his stay across the Channel, in works written in English, that Marat first expressed some of the moral and political views that would come to characterise his mature thought.[9] It was also while in Britain that Marat became involved in political activism for the first time. Moreover Marat, like d'Eon and d'Holbach, was influenced by both the ideas of the English republican tradition and the model of opposition politics offered by Wilkes and his associates.

The Chains of Slavery

Marat wrote a number of works during his time in Britain. These included two medical tracts, several versions of a work of moral philosophy and a novel.[10] However, his best-known work from this period was an anonymously published political pamphlet entitled *The Chains of Slavery*.[11]

The main purpose of *The Chains of Slavery* was to warn its readers about the dangers posed by despotism. Marat demonstrated the means by which princes gradually establish despotic regimes, and he painted a picture of the horrors of despotism. Though published in 1774, he claimed that he had composed the work some time earlier.[12] His decision to publish it that year was prompted by the prospect of the forthcoming general election. His 'Address to the Electors of Great Britain', which prefaced the work, emphasised the importance of the role to be played by the electors and offered detailed advice on the kinds of men they should choose and those they should reject. In this context, the main body of the work was supposed to illustrate the consequences of not adhering to the advice of the 'Address'.

In its aims, content and language, Marat's *The Chains of Slavery* clearly falls within the British commonwealth tradition.[13] As was typical of that tradition, Marat placed particular emphasis on the events of mid-seventeenth-century England. At the end of his 'Address' he warned the people of Britain (in a rhetorical style typical of his later works) not to betray the memory of their forefathers:

> Besides what you owe to your country and yourselves, consider what you owe to posterity.
>
> How careful were your ancestors, although with hazard of their lives, to transmit those rights as entire to their children as they had received them from their fathers. What they did with labour, you may do with ease; what they did with danger, you may do with safety. Will the holy flame of liberty which burnt in their breasts never burn in yours? Will you disgrace the names of your forefathers? Will you not shudder with horror at the idea of injuring your posterity? Is the age of liberty passed away? Shall your children, bathing their chains with tears, one day say, – These are the fruits of the venality of our fathers?[14]

Moreover, he used examples drawn from the period of the English Revolution and republic to illustrate some of the claims he was making. For example, in a footnote to a section in which he criticised the tendency of historians to 'declaim against' popular government, to 'extol the monarchical' and to brand those who throw off the shackles of tyranny as 'rebels' or 'revolted slaves', he referred specifically to the English case: 'and almost all the writers who have mentioned the punishment of Charles I have represented as barbarous parricides those spirited patriots who sentenced that tyrant to death'.[15] One of the few historians whom Marat excused from his criticisms was Catharine Macaulay, and her history of seventeenth-century England was a key source for his work. There is even some evidence to suggest that Marat drew, albeit less explicitly and perhaps even less directly, on the work of at least one seventeenth-century figure. Despite its apparently specific relevance to the elections of 1774, Marat's 'Address to the Electors of Great Britain' has a curious parallel in a pamphlet entitled *Letters of Advice: Touching the Choice of Knights and Burgesses*, which was written by the Surrey poet and political commentator George Wither in 1644.[16]

Echoes of the commonwealth tradition are also evident in Marat's somewhat ambiguous attitude toward the British constitution:

> We never cease boasting of the excellencies of our constitution, and by continually extolling it we are not sensible of its defects, and neglect to reform them.
>
> The constitution of England is, no doubt, a monument of political wisdom, if compared to others; yet it is not so perfect as we are pleased to affirm, nor can it be so, considering its origin and its revolutions.[17]

Marat then went on to examine the defects of the constitution and in particular those 'which still remain'.[18] The features that he emphasised were those noted by the commonwealthmen: the encroachment of royal (executive) power on the legislature; the general corruption and dependence on the Crown (through places and pensions) of the representatives of the nation; and the use of a standing army to enforce the will of the monarch.

The vocabulary employed by Marat was also typical of the commonwealth tradition. The liberty-slavery dichotomy, which lies at the heart of the title of the work, reappears time and again throughout, and indeed, the whole book is concerned with the process by which freedom gives way to servitude. Moreover, there is evidence to suggest that Marat also drew the links between slavery and dependence and between liberty and independence that Quentin Skinner has suggested were typical of this tradition.[19]

Marat also referred repeatedly to the importance of virtue, presenting it as necessary to the maintenance of liberty: 'No constitution maintains itself unaltered but by virtue. If this spring be long unbent, adieu liberty.'[20] Similarly, in the 'Address' he emphasised the need to elect virtuous representatives.[21] Yet, Marat also echoed earlier commonwealthmen in acknowledging the threat posed to virtue by corruption: 'Are the alluring baits of corruption to triumph over your virtue? ... Are the baits of corruption so attractive as not to be overbalanced by the solid advantages tendered by virtue?'[22] Marat certainly believed that government ought to be conducted in the public interest and aimed at securing the happiness of the people.[23] He acknowledged, however, that once in power, even the most virtuous of princes would gradually begin to act in his own, rather than in the public, interest.[24] Nor was the prince alone in this tendency. Even carefully chosen representatives could only be trusted to act on the basis of their own interests and passions: 'When deputies exercise acts of legislation, they seldom make any law which restrains themselves; and often make such as they may turn to their own advantage.'[25] This presented problems especially where the representatives were selected from among a particular class:

> Be it again said, as long as the members that compose the legislature are selected from among one particular class of people, it must never be expected to see them applying themselves to promote common welfare: and like the parliament under Mary, having secured their own possessions, they will be unconcerned for all the rest.[26]

Nor was this only a trait of those in power. Marat believed ordinary people to be just as guilty of acting according to their own interests and particularly according to their own immediate interests: 'Far from being ready to protect the rights of others, every one must have seen his own rights many times flagrantly attacked, before he resolves to defend them'.[27] Thus, for those at all levels of society, self-interest and base passions were the source of all motivation and action: 'All human institutions are grounded on human passions and supported by them only.'[28] In fact, this was not the first time that Marat had engaged in contemporary debates on the thorny issue of virtue, interest and passion.[29]

Marat's moral philosophy

In 1772 Marat had published a work of moral philosophy entitled *An Essay on the Human Soul*.[30] The following year he published a second, longer, work entitled *A Philosophical Essay on Man*.[31] The aim of the *Philosophical Essay* was to demonstrate the reciprocal influence of the soul on the body and of the body on the soul. In the second part of that work, which comprised a revised version of the original *Essay*, Marat set out his belief that self-love is the primary motivating force in human beings: 'self-love, that powerful principle, which irresistibly directs mankind in all their actions, often without being perceived, the source of every passion, and the end to which all our desires are directed'.[32] He went on to explain how this self-love operates:

> When the love of ourselves acts simply in Man, without his comparing himself with others, it is a sentiment prompting him to seek after happiness or pleasure, and to fly from pain.

> When it acts in opposition to the advantage of others, it induces Man to prefer himself to every other consideration and to pursue his own good, even to the prejudice of his friend.[33]

Self-love was behind the passions, which in turn governed all human actions – good and bad: 'The passions are the life of the soul, and the soul of the moral world, [they] impart motion to our faculties, and give activity to every sensible being.'[34] On this basis, Marat challenged conventional assumptions about the relationship between reason and passion: 'Let us leave these philosophers to make passions and reason two contrary principles, and suppose them as opposite in their natures as they please, they will never be able to make calm reason a counterpoise to impetuous desire and strong sentiment.'[35] The only means of restraining the passions was to set them against each other: 'For reason can never counterbalance one sentiment but by its opposite, nor restrain one passion but by a stronger: that is, it must free the soul from one kind of servitude, by subjecting it to another yet more severe.'[36] Among the ancients, the passions had been controlled in this way; with a desire for glory making people behave heroically or virtuously:

> It was the love of glory, which produced those ancient heroes, whose actions so greatly astonish us, *Alexander, Caesar, Gengiscan*. It was the love of glory that made those yet more wonderful men, *Thales, Zeno, Socrates*, sacrifice all the pleasures of life, and pass their days in the painful exercise of the most austere duties
> [...]
> To the same love is to be attributed the incorruptible virtue of *Cato*[37]

The problem in modern times was that the love of glory was no longer a key motivating force. Marat set out this concern most forcefully in his 'Discours adressé aux Anglais' of 1 August 1774:

> [O]ur manners have been poisoned at their source; we no longer have any enthusiasm for heroism, any admiration for virtue, any love for liberty.
> [...]
> Today the art of pleasure is preferred to merit, vain pleasures to useful knowledge. For us a dancer is worth more than a wise man and a joker more than a hero.[38]

A key reason for the corruption of contemporary manners was the inequality that had arisen due to the recent rise of commerce and luxury: 'But since commerce has enriched us, opulence has chased away this kind of behaviour, soon disorders and the whole connection of vices attached to extreme inequality in wealth were born that had been unknown to our fathers.'[39]

Marat was rather pessimistic about the prospects for overcoming these problems, but he did offer two possible solutions. First, the moderns needed to return to the practice of the ancients in constructing a system of manners that would encourage people to behave virtuously and reward them for doing so.[40] Secondly, the inevitable progress of corruption could be slowed, and its worst excesses tempered, if the people constantly watched over their own interests:

> The subjects, in order to maintain their liberty, ought to watch the motions of the ministry with a jealous eye. Men are never so easily undone, as when they suspect no danger; and too great security in a nation is almost always the forerunner of slavery.[41]

This would happen naturally immediately following the establishment of liberty, but as the memory of the former regime became more distant, and as the prince sought to distract the people, so their vigilance would decline:

> In a free government, when care is not taken from time to time to bring back the constitution to its first principles, in proportion as the epoch of its origin becomes remote, the people lose sight of their rights, they soon forget them in part, and afterward retain no notion of them.[42]

As soon as the interests of any one of their number were violated, the people should take action.[43] Marat also advised that the representatives be obliged, through the use of binding mandates, to act according to the interests of the people (who had elected them) rather than according to their own interests or those of the prince:

> The representatives of the people, being intrusted with the interests of the public, ought to enter into an engagement with their constituents: our deputies, when at first admitted into the senate, take, indeed, an oath of fidelity, but in that oath there is not a single word mentioned about the nation.
>
> The representatives of the people ought ever to act according to the instructions of their constituents: but our deputies exercise their delegated power without ever consulting us. When once elected, they take not any more notice of us. We have therefore no hand in the laws enacted by them; and how many times have the resolves of the house been directly opposite to the sentiments of the people they represent? What are then our representatives, but our masters?[44]

The underlying purpose of *The Chains of Slavery* was grounded in Marat's moral philosophy. His aim, as the 'Address to the Electors of Great Britain' made abundantly clear, was to demonstrate to his readers that it was ultimately (if not immediately) in their own interests to curb the advance of despotism, and to stir them to action: 'Gentlemen, the whole nation cast their eyes upon you for redress; but if your heart be shut to generous feelings, and justice to your fellow subjects cannot move you, let your own interest at least animate you.'[45]

It should be clear from this account of *The Chains of Slavery* and *A Philosophical Essay on Man* that Marat's political and moral philosophy was directly in line with the British commonwealth tradition. Indeed it is not an exaggeration to describe *The Chains of Slavery* as a commonwealth text. It is particularly interesting to compare Marat's position with that of d'Holbach. In the realm of moral philosophy the two men adopted similar perspectives – openly embracing neo-Epicurean arguments about happiness being the ultimate goal of society and the advantages to be gained from pitting the passions against each other. There is, however, a difference in their moral views. Where d'Holbach displays an optimistic utilitarian outlook, Marat embraces a pessimistic one. Moreover, whereas d'Holbach placed emphasis on the religious elements of the commonwealth tradition, Marat's focus was with the political.[46] It is also interesting to note that Marat, like d'Holbach, was fascinated by and sympathised with the figure of Wilkes. Moreover, like d'Eon, Marat also drew parallels between Wilkes's exploits and his own, and *The Chains of Slavery* even ended up being used as a weapon in the Wilkite campaign.

Marat and the Wilkite movement

In May 1774 Marat wrote directly, though anonymously, to Wilkes over problems he was facing concerning the publication of *The Chains of Slavery*.[47] The letter was written in French, and began with some discussion of its author's identity. There was a hint that Wilkes might have been able to guess the name of his correspondent, but all that was actually said was that he was not of English birth, but had chosen England for his 'patrie'. Marat went on to express his respect for Wilkes and his cause and to set his own work within the same camp:

> Friend of liberty to the point of enthusiasm, I have followed closely your quarrels with the Minister and his creatures, I have watched with admiration your generous efforts for the public cause, and with distress the triumph of your enemies. Indignant at the violation of the most sacred rights of the nation, I formed a plan to join my weak voice to those of some good patriots and to attack the unjust exercise of power, in a work aimed at unveiling the black webs of tyrants. I have completed this plan, [but] I would perhaps have been better to have first consulted my forces and to have learned that zeal alone is not sufficient to offer a worthy sacrifice on the altar of *Liberty*.[48]

Marat then reinforced the connection between his own patriotic actions and those of Wilkes by describing the attempts by the Ministry to prevent the publication of the work, implicitly drawing parallels between his own treatment at the hands of the authorities and that of Wilkes:

> Not able to suppress my book by force, the public enemies of liberty did so by artifice in condemning it to oblivion from the moment that it saw the light of day. A strange means of oppression, a hundred times worse than open acts of authority, and which was aimed at nothing less than the silent destruction of the liberty of the press![49]

He concluded the letter by asking for Wilkes's assistance:

> I know that you are busy, but ... if love for the patrie fills your heart, please tell me what I can do to foil the cowardly measures of the cabinet. To help me with good advice would be to continue to serve the nation whose respect you well merit. I am ready to receive your advice on whatever day and at whatever time would suit you.[50]

We do not have Wilkes's reply to Marat – if indeed he gave one – but it may have been due to Wilkes that Marat's *The Chains of Slavery* went on to play a role in the Newcastle general election of 1774.[51] Copies of this work were sent to the town where local Wilkites employed them in their campaign against the sitting MPs Sir Walter Calverley Blackett and Matthew Ridley.[52] A letter accompanying one of these copies, which was received by the Company of Bricklayers, even included a direct translation of a passage from Marat's letter to Wilkes.[53]

Wilkes would have been well aware of recent events in Newcastle. Not only did he dine regularly during the early 1770s with his friend George Grieve, who was a leading figure in Newcastle politics,[54] but Grieve had managed to recruit another friend and collaborator of Wilkes, Sergeant Glynn, to act for the guildsmen in their dispute with the town authorities over control of the Town Moor.[55] In the contested election of 1774, the long-standing Tory MP, Blackett, and the son of the sitting Whig MP, Sir Matthew White Ridley, were challenged by two new candidates, Constantine John Phipps and Thomas Delaval.[56] The latter were not only much more sympathetic to the guildsmen's cause in the Town Moor controversy, but unlike Blackett and Ridley they had agreed to sign a series of Wilkite test articles drawn up by the guildsmen.[57]

Significantly, a copy of the Town Moor Act was bound in at the back of the Company of Butcher's copy of *The Chains of Slavery*, suggesting that it was perceived by at least some Newcastle residents as speaking directly to local concerns. Moreover, the 'Address to the Electors of Great Britain' was no doubt seen as a good means of encouraging the electors of the town to vote for Phipps and Delaval rather than for Blackett and White Ridley in the forthcoming election. It is certainly true that the guilds that we know received copies of *The Chains of Slavery* appear to have been directly involved in the Town Moor affair and supporters of Phipps and Delaval at the election.[58]

Interestingly Marat included several references to Wilkes in *The Chains of Slavery*.[59] He praised not only Wilkes himself, but also the Society of the Supporters of the Bill of Rights and Sergeant Glynn.[60] In addition, one of the booksellers listed on the title page was Wilkes's friend Almon, and Almon's *The History of the Late Minority* and his *The Debates and Proceedings of the British House of Commons* were two of the sources used by Marat in writing the work.[61] The references to Wilkes were probably not inserted just to gain favour with him but, rather, were reflections of Marat's own views, since he referred back to his interest in the Wilkes controversies in a letter written in 1789.[62] Moreover, Marat's Wilkite leanings did not escape the attention of his contemporaries. The artist Joseph Farington, who was close to those who were friends with Marat during his stay in England, said of him: 'While he resided in this country, in what related to politicks, he was what was called a Wilkite and was very eager in defending in conversation all opposition to Government'.[63]

The Chains of Slavery and France

Though Marat initially published *The Chains of Slavery* in English and directed it toward British political controversies, he clearly believed that the arguments it put forward were equally applicable in France. It was 1793 before he succeeded in publishing a French translation of the work (though he had been attempting to do so for at least six months), but he had also made use of extracts from it on several occasions during 1789.[64] Marat also drew a direct connection between his activities in England, and particularly *The Chains of Slavery*, and his role in revolutionary France. In a letter addressed to his friend and fellow revolutionary Camille Desmoulins, which appeared in his newspaper in May 1791, he said: 'Open the work that I published in London in 1774 under the title: *The Chains of Slavery*; in reading the preface you will see that sixteen years ago in England I played the same role that I have played in France since the Revolution.'[65] He also reused the epigram of *The Chains of Slavery* (*Vitam impendere vero*) on some of his revolutionary works.[66] What is more significant, however, is that, as Jeremy Popkin has demonstrated, the moral philosophy set out in *A Philosophical Essay on Man* and *The Chains of Slavery* underpinned Marat's mode of operation as a revolutionary journalist.[67] In those works, Marat had implied that people would only take action if their passions were roused and if they were convinced that doing so was in their own interests. This had been the aim behind *The Chains of Slavery* itself – and especially the 'Address to the Electors of Great Britain'. When he embarked on a career as a revolutionary journalist in 1789, Marat adopted the same tactics. His emotive language and emphasis on violence was deliberately designed to rouse the people to action.[68]

Though it was in the context of the Revolution that Marat published a French version of (and extracts from) *The Chains of Slavery*, the passages that were added to the French translation, as Popkin has noted, concerned not the era of the Revolution, but rather the early 1770s.[69] In particular, Marat engaged directly in the debate concerning French history and the nature and origins of France's political institutions, which raged in the late 1760s and early 1770s – and especially in the aftermath of the Maupeou coup.[70] In several chapters that were added to the French edition, Marat offered his own account of the ancient government of the Francs and its corruption over time.[71] Marat's contribution to the debate was distinctive in two particular respects. In the first place, he argued that the cause of the corruption and decline of the original Frankish system lay, at least partly, in the application of a form of government suited to a small warrior people in the context of a large settled state (though he also attributed considerable weight to the ambitions of individual rulers and the dangers arising from them having sole responsibility over executive power).[72] It was because of the size of the state, and the amount of business arising from this, that the nation became unable to assemble and deliberate on each issue, and the prince was able to take advantage of this situation in order to increase his power and ultimately to render it hereditary.[73] There are undoubted echoes here of the idealisation of the kind of small states that were also favoured by Montesquieu, Mably and Rousseau.[74] Secondly, Marat presented neither the *parlements* nor the Estates-General as the direct descendant of the national assemblies of the Franks. The latter was, in his view, merely a later (and inferior) innovation.[75]

Of course, the 1770s were not the first time in eighteenth-century France that these issues had been discussed. As we have already seen, they were of particular concern in the early eighteenth century, and especially among figures who were also exponents of the commonwealth tradition in France, such as Boulainvilliers, Montesquieu and Mably. Indeed, ancient constitutionalism was a central feature of early modern republican writings on both sides of the Channel.

Conclusion

In the case of Marat we unquestionably have an example of an eighteenth-century commonwealthman. In the works that he published in Britain during the 1770s he drew on the moral and political philosophy of the commonwealth tradition. However, Marat's real significance lies not simply in his contribution to the British commonwealth tradition, but rather in the fact that he also applied its ideas and arguments to France. Like d'Eon, Marat noted similarities between the despotic behaviour being exercised by the British government in the 1760s and 1770s (especially in relation to the American colonies and to Wilkes) and that of Louis XV's government – as epitomised by the Maupeou coup. In both cases commonwealth arguments concerning the need to protect liberty against despotism, the tendency of those in power to become corrupt, and the means by which representative assemblies might be used counter the actions of corrupt rulers, appeared to be of particular relevance. Moreover, this was not the only French context to which Marat applied these ideas. Though the additions to the French translation of *The Chains of Slavery* reflect the concerns of the 1760s and 1770s, the work was first published in 1793 in the midst of the French Revolution. The circumstances might have changed dramatically, but Marat clearly believed that commonwealth ideas were equally applicable to, and illuminating of, the revolutionary situation. In this he was not alone, for Marat was just one of a number of revolutionaries who translated or drew upon English republican works and ideas in the context of the French Revolution.

Notes

1 The original source for many of these stories was an article in the *Star* newspaper for 4 March 1793. The article was republished in *Notes and Queries*, 2nd Series, VIII, p. 256 (24 September 1859). However, there is an earlier reference linking Marat to the Ashmolean robbery in Charles-Claude Théveneau de Morande's *Le Courier de l'Europe* for 17 and 24 October 1789. I owe this information to Simon Burrows and details of it will appear in his forthcoming biography of Morande: *A King's Ransom*, which is to be published by Continuum in 2010. See also the series of articles published in the *Monthly Repository* VIII, IX, and X (1813–15) which have been reprinted as *The Warrington Academy* (Warrington, 1957). The latter also mentions the story that Marat had spent some time in Bristol – where he had again been arrested and imprisoned for debt.

2 In addition to the works listed above see *Notes and Queries*, 2nd Series, V, p. 32 (9 January 1858); V, p. 79 (23 January, 1858); VIII, p. 52 (16 July 1859); VIII, p. 93 (30 July 1859); VIII, p. 158 (20 August 1859); X, pp. 214–15 (15 September 1860); 3rd Series, II, p. 317 (18 October 1862); 4th Series, XI, p. 136 (15 February 1873); 7th Series, IX, p. 29 (11 January 1890); IX, p. 78 (25 January 1890); 12th Series, X, pp. 381–4 (20 May 1922); X, pp. 403–5 (27 May 1922); X, pp. 422–6 (3 June 1922); X, pp. 441–3 (10 June 1922); X, pp. 463–5 (17 June 1922); X, pp. 482–4 (24 June, 1922); XI, p. 24 (8 July 1922); XI, p. 53 (15 July 1922); H. Merivale, 'A Few Words on Junius and Marat', in his *Historical Studies* (London: Longman, 1865), pp. 186–203; R. Chambers (ed.), *The Book of Days: A Miscellany of Popular Antiquities*, 2 vols (London and Edinburgh: W. & R. Chambers, 1888) II, pp. 55–6; H. S. Ashbee, *Marat en Angleterre* (Paris, 1891); E. B. Bax, *Jean-Paul Marat: The People's Friend* (London: Grant Richards, 1900) pp. 26–86; S. Phipson, *Jean Paul Marat: His Career in England and France Before the Revolution* (London: Methuen, 1924); L. R. Gottschalk, 'Marat a-t-il été en Angleterre un criminel de droit commun?', *Annales historiques de la Révolution Française* 4 (1927), pp. 111–26; J. M. Thompson, 'Le Maitre, alias Mara', *English Historical Review* 49, 193 (January 1934), pp. 55–73; L. R. Gottschalk, *Jean Paul Marat: A Study in Radicalism* (Chicago and London: University of Chicago Press, 1967) pp. 2–26.

3 J. P. Marat, *La Correspondance de Marat*, ed. C. Vellay (Paris: Librairie Charpentier & Fasquelle, 1908) pp. 1–2.

4 See the *Morning Post and Daily Advertiser*, 9 February 1776, p. 2; the *Gentleman's Magazine*, February 1776, p. 92; March 1776, p. 141; September 1776, p. 432.

5 See in particular Phipson, *Jean Paul Marat*, pp. 129–34 and Thompson, 'Le Maitre, alias Mara', pp. 72–3. For the other side of the argument and a direct attack on Phipson's claims see Gottschalk, 'Marat … criminel de droit commun?'

6 R. Darnton, 'Marat n'a pas été un voleur: une lettre inédite', *Annales historiques de la Révolution française* (1966), pp. 447–50. This article includes a copy of the letter itself.

7 Ibid., p. 448.

8 This period of Marat's life is treated in some detail by two of his most recent biographers, O. Coquard, *Jean-Paul Marat* (Paris: Fayard, 1993) pp. 48–88 and C. Goëtz, *Marat en Famille: La Saga des Mara(t)*, II (Brussels: Pôle Nord, 2001), pp. 11–32, but their accounts are largely based on Marat's own claims and on earlier works.

9 I am not the only person to claim that Marat began to formulate some of his revolutionary political thought while in England. It has also been suggested by Jeremy Popkin in two unpublished papers: J. D. Popkin, 'Jean-Paul Marat's Critique of the National Assembly and the Political Thought of the Old Regime', delivered at the 1989 meeting of the American Historical

Association, and J. D. Popkin, 'Marat and the Problem of Violence in the Revolutionary Era', delivered to the History Department at the State University of New York at Stony Brook in May 1992. I am grateful to Professor Popkin for providing me with copies of these papers and allowing me to cite them. It has also been noted by individuals who are less sympathetic to Marat's views. In 1999 a copy of *The Chains of Slavery* appeared in the sale catalogue of J. Burmeister. It had belonged to the literary critic and Shakespeare scholar Edmund Malone. In a manuscript note on the verso of the half-title page he apparently described Marat as 'that flatigious and execrable monster' 'the French regicide' and he went on 'Here we find the germ and first principles of those detestable doctrines which have now been inculcated from the commencement of the French Revolution, and unless they are constantly opposed by the virtuous part of mankind, will not only destroy the English Constitution, but involve the whole world in anarchy and confusion.' J. Burmeister, *English Books, 1617–1900* (Catalogue 40, January 1999), pp. 27–8. I am grateful to Malcolm Chase for this reference.

10 J. P. Marat, *An Essay on Gleets: wherein the defects of the actual method of treating those complaints of the uretha are pointed out, and an effectual way of curing them indicated* (London, 1775); J. P. Marat, *An Enquiry into the Nature, Cause, and Cure of a Singular Disease of the Eyes* (London, 1776). An original copy of the former is available in the British Library [BL: C.124.g.9]. The two works were reprinted in a single volume in 1891 by J. Blake Bailey, librarian of the Royal College of Surgeons, for private circulation: J. P. Marat, M.D., *Two Medical Tracts*, ed. J. Blake Bailey (London, 1891). [J. P. Marat], *An Essay on the Human Soul* (London, 1772); [J. P. Marat], *A Philosophical Essay on Man: Being an attempt to investigate the principles and laws of the reciprocal influence of the soul on the body* (London, 1773). A French version of this work was also produced: J. P. Marat, *De L'Homme, ou des principes et des lois de l'influence de l'âme sur le corps, et du corps sur l'âme* (Amsterdam, 1775); J. P. Marat, *Les Aventures du jeune comte Potowski*, ed. C. Nicolas-Lelièvre (n.p., 1988).

11 [J. P. Marat], *The chains of slavery: a work wherein the clandestine and villainous attempts of princes to ruin liberty are pointed out, and the dreadful scenes of despotism disclosed. To which is prefixed an Address to the electors of Great Britain, in order to draw their timely attention to the choice of proper representatives in the next Parliament* (London, 1774). A modern, bilingual, edition of the work is also available: J. P. Marat, *Les Chaînes de l'esclavage 1793: The chains of slavery 1774*, ed. C. Goëtz and J. de Cock (Brussels: Pôle Nord, 1995).

12 Marat, *Chaînes*, p. 4167.

13 Keith Baker has described Marat as a classical republican. My aim is to demonstrate that he was, in fact, an exponent of the early modern republican tradition. In addition, where Baker focused on Marat's transformation of the language of classical republicanism in France after 1789, I am more interested in the development of his ideas while in Britain. K. M. Baker, 'Transformations of Classical Republicanism in Eighteenth-Century France', *Journal of Modern History* 73 (March 2001), pp. 32–53.

14 Marat, *Chaînes*, pp. 4182–4.

15 Ibid., pp. 4404–6. Like the British commonwealth writers more generally, Marat did not unambiguously advocate anti-monarchical republicanism. The precise form of government appears to have been less relevant to him than other issues. He was also typical of that tradition in his hostile attitude to Cromwell: see ibid., pp. 4452 and 4488.

16 On Wither see J. Gurney, 'George Wither and Surrey Politics, 1642–1649', *Southern History* 19 (1997), pp. 74–98; D. Norbrook, 'Levelling Poetry: George Wither and the English Revolution, 1642–1649', *English Literary Renaissance* 21 (1991), pp. 217–56 and D. Norbrook, *Writing the English Republic: Poetry, Rhetoric and Politics, 1627–1660* (Cambridge: Cambridge University Press, 1999), especially pp. 87–90, 140–58, 238–42, 351–7 and 384–6. Interestingly, Marat's pamphlet was not the only eighteenth-century commonwealth text that paralleled something by Wither. In 1746 James Burgh published his book *Britain's Remembrancer*. This had also been the title of a work by Wither, published in 1628, and was the name that Wither subsequently adopted for himself. On Burgh see C. H. Hay, 'The Making of a Radical: The Case of James Burgh', *Journal of British Studies* 18 (1979), pp. 90–117.

17 Marat, *Chaînes*, p. 4620. See also p. 4658. Throughout *The Chains of Slavery* Marat wrote as though he were British himself.
18 Ibid., p. 4622.
19 Ibid., p. 4276. See Q. Skinner, 'The Idea of Negative Liberty: Philosophical and Historical Perspectives', in R. Rorty et al. (eds), *Philosophy in History* (Cambridge: Cambridge University Press, 1984), pp. 193–221; Q. Skinner, 'The Paradoxes of Political Liberty', in S. M. McMurrin (ed.), *The Tanner Lectures on Human Values* 7 (Cambridge: Cambridge University Press, 1986), pp. 225–50; Q. Skinner, *Liberty Before Liberalism* (Cambridge: Cambridge University Press, 1998).
20 Marat, *Chaînes*, p. 4252. See also p. 4184.
21 Ibid., p. 4176. See also p. 4632.
22 Ibid., pp. 4180–2.
23 Ibid., pp. 4524, 4528 and 4532.
24 Ibid., p. 4462. See also pp. 4292, 4298, 4308, 4414 and 4532.
25 Ibid., p. 4634.
26 Ibid., pp. 4638–40.
27 Ibid., p. 4362. See also pp. 4230, 4252, 4354 and 4444.
28 Ibid., p. 4420.
29 On Marat's moral philosophy I am indebted to Michael Sonenscher. See M. Sonenscher, 'A Limitless Love of Self: Marat's Grim View of Human Nature', *Times Literary Supplement*, 6 October 1995, pp. 3–4.
30 [Marat], *An Essay on the Human Soul*, see n. 10 above.
31 [Marat], *A Philosophical Essay on Man*. It was reviewed in the *Gentleman's Magazine* 43 (1773), p. 191 and in the *Westminster Magazine* (May 1773), p. 327. A second edition appeared in 1775, printed for H. Setchel, Bookseller, King-Street, Covent-Garden, and in the same year Marat published his French version of the work. Marat, *De L'Homme*.
32 [Marat], *A Philosophical Essay on Man*, I, p. 138.
33 Ibid., I, pp. 138–9.
34 Ibid., I, p. 259.
35 Ibid., I, p. 261.
36 Ibid., I, p. 271. On countervailing passions see: A. O. Hirschman, *The Passions and the Interests: Political Arguments for Capitalism Before its Triumph* (Princeton: Princeton University Press, 1977), pp. 10 and 20–31. Interestingly, in his *Éloge de Montesquieu* Marat claimed that the idea of 'controlling the passions by the passions themselves' could be attributed to Montesquieu. J. P. Marat, *Éloge de Montesquieu*: présenté à l'Académie de Bordeaux, le 28 mars 1785; ed. Arthur de Brézetz (Paris, 1883), p. 48.
37 [Marat], *A Philosophical Essay on Man*, I, p. 252.
38 'Discours adressé aux Anglais le 1 août 1774', in Marat, *Chaînes*, p. 4663.
39 Ibid., p. 4663. Marat also believed that despotic princes furthered this natural process by 'rooting out' the love of glory from among their citizens: 'Princes accordingly lose no opportunity of changing the object of glory. For fame which the public dispenses, they substitute honours which they alone distribute'. Ibid., p. 4280.
40 Significantly Marat saw his own life and actions as underpinned by a love of glory. See Marat, *Journal de la République française*, no.98, 14 janvier 1793, pp. 1–3 as quoted in Coquard, *Jean-Paul Marat*, pp. 35–6.
41 Marat, *Chaînes*, p. 4354. See also pp. 4366 and 4420. Interestingly, Wither had also placed great emphasis on the importance of popular vigilance. See Gurney, 'George Wither and Surrey Politics', p. 83.
42 Marat, *Chaînes*, p. 4522. See also p. 4226.
43 Ibid., p. 4362.
44 Ibid., p. 4630. See also pp. 4182, 4548–50n and 4622–8.
45 Ibid., p. 4182.
46 It should, however, be noted that just as d'Holbach does also make some reference to political

matters and adopts a commonwealth perspective on them, so the brief references to religion in Marat's text suggest that he shared commonwealth views on this issue. See in particular Chapters 42 and 43 of *The Chains of Slavery*, which are entitled 'Of Superstition' and 'Of the Confederacy between Princes and Priests'.
47 Though its veracity is questionable, Marat offered a dramatic account of the writing and publication of *The Chains of Slavery* in a 'Notice' that prefaced the French edition. Marat, *Chaînes*, pp. 4167–75.
48 BL: Add. MS. 30876 f. 174, 'Author of *The Chains of Slavery* to Wilkes, May 1774'.
49 Ibid. In his preface to the French version of *The Chains of Slavery*, Marat gave more detail, claiming that Lord North had bribed the printer, publicists and journalists to stop the work from being advertised. This cannot have been the case, since several advertisements did appear, including one in the *London Magazine* for April 1774 (43, p. 200), one in the *Public Advertiser* for Tuesday 3 May 1774, one in the *Gentleman's Magazine* for May 1774 and one in the *Scot's Magazine* for May 1774 (p. 253). It was also reviewed in the *Monthly Review* in June 1774 (50, p. 491) and, much more favourably, in the *London Magazine* in the same month (43, pp. 286–8).
50 BL: Add. MS. 30876 f. 174.
51 For more detail on this see R. Hammersley, 'Jean-Paul Marat's *The Chains of Slavery* in Britain and France, 1774–1833', *Historical Journal* 48 (2005), pp. 641–60.
52 A notice announcing the arrival of the pamphlets in Newcastle appeared in the *Newcastle Chronicle*, 534 (28 May 1774), p. 2. Moreover, several of these copies are still held among the guild records at the Tyne and Wear Archives, Tyne and Wear Archive Service (TWAS): GU/BR/15, GU/BU/28 and GU/CW/61. A copy also appears to have been sent to the Company of House Carpenters, since their book of Orders refers to the rules concerning the loaning out of the work to Company members, TWAS: GU/HMT/3, p. 18. Copies can also be found in the Special Collections Department of the Robinson Library at the University of Newcastle (Bradshaw 321.6MAR and W321.6.MAR). See also J. Clephan, 'Jean-Paul Marat in Newcastle', *Monthly Chronicle of North-Country Lore and Legend* 1(2) (1887), pp. 1–53, and esp. p. 49.
53 The relevant passage read: 'Not daring to suppress my book by force, they have employed artifice to prevent its being divulged. A strange method of apprehension this, a thousand times worse than open acts of authority and attended with the silent but intire destruction of the liberty of the press unless their clandestine measures be baffled by the influence of true patriots.' TWAS: GU/BR/15.
54 BL: Add. MS. 30866, 'J. Wilkes Diaries (1770–1797)'. According to this source Grieve dined with Wilkes on 5 April, 18, 23, 28 and 31 May 1771; 18, 22, 25, 27 March 1772; 28 March, 1, 3, 9, 26, 30 April, 1 May, 7, 16, 24, 29 June, 3, 5, 10, 15 July 1773; 29 March, 15 June 1774; and on 27 June 1774 he claimed to have dined with 'Grieve's Committee'. I, fols 24, 25; II, fols 2, 24, 25, 27, 28, 29, 37, 40. Grieve was active in both London and Newcastle politics. He was a member of the Society of the Supporters of the Bill of Rights and also the Chairman of the Wilkite Constitutional Club of Durham, Northumberland, and Newcastle. Interestingly, while in France during the Revolution Grieve produced a pamphlet entitled *L'Egalité controuvée ou petite histoire ... de la Du Barry* in which he claimed to be a friend of Marat. See T. R. Knox, 'Popular Politics and Provincial Radicalism: Newcastle upon Tyne, 1769–1785', *Albion* (1979), p. 227; T. R. Knox, 'Grieve (var. Greive), George (1748–1809)' in *Biographical Dictionary of Modern British Radicals*, Vol. I: 1770–1830, ed. J. O. Baylen and N. J. Gossman (Sussex and New Jersey: Harvester, 1979), pp. 198–200 and T. R. Knox, 'Greive, George (1748–1809)', *Oxford Dictionary of National Biography* (Oxford: Oxford University Press, 2004; online edition, January 2008), www.oxforddnb.com/view/article/11578, accessed 1 May, 2008.
55 On the Town Moor affair see [J. Murray], *The Contest: being an account of the matter in dispute between the magistrates and burgesses, and an examination of the merit and conduct of the candidates in the present election for Newcastle upon Tyne* (Newcastle, 1774); R. F. Walker, *The Institutions and History of the Freemen of Newcastle upon Tyne* (Newcastle, n.d.), pp. 74–86; TWAS: GU/CW/15/1, 'Manuscript extracts from Histories of Newcastle, 1426–1845, 2 volumes'; GU/CW/15/2, 'Items of interest on Cordwainers Company, Freemen in general, Town Moor etc.,

Compiled by R. J. Turnbull'; GU/CW/16, 'Manuscript History on the Cordwainers Company by R. J. Turnbull [c.1937]'; and GU/CW/49, 'The Incorporated Company of Cordwainers (historical account) (1877)'. See also D. J. Rowe (ed.), *The Records of the Company of Shipwrights of Newcastle Upon Tyne, 1622–1967* (Gateshead, 1970), 1, pp. 59–63 and 163–4; Knox, 'Popular Politics and Provincial Radicalism', pp. 229–32; T. R. Knox, 'Wilkism and the Newcastle Election of 1774', *Durham University Journal* 72 (1979) and K. Wilson, *The Sense of the People: Politics, Culture and Imperialism in England, 1715–1785* (Cambridge: Cambridge University Press, 1995), pp. 315–73.

56 [Murray], *The Contest*; L. Namier and J. Brooke (eds), *The History of Parliament: The House of Commons, 1754–1790* (London, 1964), I, p. 350. For more detail on Newcastle politics in this period and the connections between local and national politics see H. T. Dickinson, *Radical Politics in the North-east of England in the Later Eighteenth Century* (Durham: Durham County Local History Society, 1979).

57 [Murray], *The Contest*. See also Knox, 'Wilkism and the Newcastle Election of 1774', p. 28. The list of test articles was typical of that originally proposed by the Society of the Supporters of the Bill of Rights in June 1771 and imitated by Wilkites across the country. See I. R. Christie, 'The Wilkites and the General Election of 1774', in his *Myth and Reality in Late Eighteenth-Century British Politics and Other Papers* (London: Macmillan, 1970), pp. 244–59.

58 The Butchers were said to have been an interested party over the Moor. The Bricklayers voted their thanks to the Committee, who acted on behalf of the freemen, and recorded their names in the Company book. The Cordwainers also took an active role in the affair. They contributed toward the expenses, and even commissioned an inscription over the mantelpiece in their hall commemorating the court ruling of 10 August 1773 and recording for posterity the names of the committee members involved. Alongside that plaque hung a portrait of Serjeant Glynn. Namier and Brooke, *History of Parliament*, I, p. 350 (Butchers); TWAS: GU/CW/15/2 (Bricklayers); GU/CW/16 and GU/CW/49 (Cordwainers). Though Phipps and Delaval were ultimately unsuccessful, they did receive considerable support from the Bricklayers, Joiners and Butchers. *The History of Parliament* provides figures for the Butchers and for the building trade as a whole – presumably including both Bricklayers and Joiners. Butchers: Blackett 123, Ridley 114, Phipps 128, Delaval 110; building trade: 121, 121, 157, 138, I, pp. 350–1.

59 Marat, *Chaînes*, pp. 4348–50, 4352 and 4358. There is also a less explicit reference to Wilkes on p. 4632.

60 Ibid., pp. 4348–50.

61 Ibid., pp. 4350n and 4634n. See also p. xxxvii.

62 Marat, *Correspondance*, ed. Vellay, p. 100.

63 J. Farington R.A., *The Farington Diary*, ed. J. Grieg, 2nd edn (London: Hutchinson, 1922), I, p. 24.

64 In January 1789, Marat's journal *Offrande à la Patrie* included a description of the kinds of men who should be chosen as representatives in the forthcoming elections to the Estates General, which was strikingly similar to that offered in his 'Address' of 1774. J. P. Marat, *Oeuvres Politiques, 1789–1793*, ed. J. de Cock and C. Goëtz (Brussels: Pôle Nord, 1995), I, p. 10. The following month his *Supplément de l'Offrande à la Patrie* included a long passage that he admitted came from 'an English work entitled *The Chains of Slavery*'. Marat, *Oeuvres Politiques*, I, pp. 51–52n. See also Coquard, *Jean-Paul Marat*, p. 213. Curiously, the passage that is quoted in fact only appears in the French version of the work in an additional chapter entitled: 'De la guerre étrangère'. Marat, *Chaînes*, pp. 4493–7. Later in the year, in the midst of debates over the form that a new French constitution ought to take, Marat wrote a letter to the president of the Estates-General, which he entitled 'Tableau des vices de la constitution anglaise, destiné à faire éviter une série d'écueils dans le gouvernement que nos députés veulent donner à la France'. The letter was accompanied by a long extract taken from Chapter 60 of *The Chains of Slavery*. On this see Chapter 10 below.

65 Marat, *Correspondance*, ed. Vellay, p. 202.

66 See for example Marat, 'Le Moniteur Patriote' (1789), in *Oeuvres Politiques*, I, p. 56 and 'Lettre

à … sur l'ordre judiciaire (1790)', in *Correspondance*, ed. Vellay, p. 135. The Latin can be roughly translated as 'to spend (lay down) life for the truth' and it comes from Juvenal 4, 91. I am grateful to James Shiel for assistance with the Latin. Interestingly, Rousseau also adopted this phrase as his own motto. See J. Starobinski, 'The Motto *Vitam impendere vero* and the Question of Lying' in P. Riley (ed.), *The Cambridge Companion to Rousseau* (Cambridge: Cambridge University Press, 2001), pp. 365–96.
67 Popkin, 'Marat and the Problem of Violence'.
68 Ibid., pp. 8–9 and 14. Popkin also suggests that Marat interpreted the early years of the revolution in the language of the 1770s. Popkin, 'Jean-Paul Marat's Critique'.
69 Popkin, 'Marat and the Problem of Violence', p. 10; 'Popkin, 'Jean-Paul Marat's Critique', pp. 10–11.
70 He also explicitly criticised Louis XIV and Louis XV. See for example Marat, *Chaînes*, p. 4517n.
71 See in particular ibid., pp. 4201–25 and 4311–29.
72 Ibid., pp. 4201–25.
73 Ibid., pp. 4205–11.
74 See in particular ibid., p. 4217.
75 Ibid., pp. 4319–21. See also Popkin, 'Jean-Paul Marat's Critique', p. 11.

Part IV

English Republicans and the French Revolution

10

Parallel revolutions: seventeenth-century England and eighteenth-century France

Introduction

The French revolutionaries were keen to demonstrate the epoch-changing nature of the events in which they were involved. It was they who invented the term *ancien régime*, in order to distinguish the period before 1789 from that which followed. Similarly, their attempts to draft a new constitution, to change the dating system and calendar, and to rationalise weights and measures were all designed to reflect the fact that the events of 1789 had ushered in a new era.

Historians have generally accepted this sense of 1789 as marking a sharp break with the past. It is still the date at which modern European history is often deemed to have begun, and this fact – combined with the tendency to see the French as the archetypal revolution – seems to have deterred historians from looking for evidence that the French revolutionaries drew on earlier models and ideas. In the case of influences from across the Channel this situation is compounded by both French and British national myths. The French have been keen to present their Revolution as a distinctively French affair – one that exerted an influence abroad, but was not itself the result of foreign influences.[1] At the same time the British have attempted to forget their revolutionary past, and they contrast their own pattern of political evolution directly with the revolutionary model that characterises French history.[2]

Yet, when we look more carefully at the views expressed by contemporaries themselves, the picture seems more complex. Despite their innovative intentions, the revolutionaries did draw parallels with other times and places. There is clear evidence, for example, that they made use of ancient models and ideas, and that they looked to the American Revolution as a source of both inspiration and practical guidance.[3] There were, however, important differences between each of these cases and the French situation, and these differences undoubtedly limited the use that the revolutionaries could make of them. In the first case, there was an awareness of the sheer amount of time that had elapsed since the collapse of the ancient civilisations, and of the huge political, economic and cultural differences between the ancient and modern worlds. In the American case, factors such as the availability of land in America, the relative youth of the country, and the fact that their King had lived over 3,000 miles away, again restricted the applicability of American ideas and practices in France.[4] By contrast, Britain was a country closer in size to France, and there were parallels in the histories and political systems of the two nations. The existing British constitution was of interest to some French revolutionaries, particularly in the first few months of the Revolution. However, it was earlier English models and ideas that proved most influential and enduring.[5] Like the French in the late eighteenth century, the English in the seventeenth had been engaged in combating absolute monarchy and recovering their liberty. Moreover, in doing so they had executed a king and established a republic. Consequently, a number of contemporaries drew a parallel between seventeenth-century English events and those through which the French were living, and suggested that the English experiences – and the ideas generated by them – offered sources of guidance as the French negotiated the complex path of revolution.[6]

The British constitution

It is the group known as the *Monarchiens* who have most commonly been associated with attempts to impose British ideas – and in particular the British constitutional model – in France.[7] Their calls for a constitutional monarchy, a bicameral legislature and an absolute royal veto were certainly reminiscent of key aspects of the British system. Recent scholarship has tended to downplay the anglophilia of this group, and even those who do acknowledge it have suggested that attempts to impose a British-style constitutional monarchy in France came to an end with the votes in favour of a unicameral legislature and a suspensive royal veto in September 1789.[8] Yet, the *Monarchiens* were not the only revolutionaries in the early months of the Revolution to explore the possibility of adopting contemporary British practices. Such proposals were also made by the leading revolutionary the comte de Mirabeau and his friends and associates.

Samuel Romilly, who was close to Mirabeau during the late 1780s, was explicit about his friend's constitutional preferences: 'From the beginning, and when he was the idol of the people, he always had it in view to establish a limited monarchy in France upon the model of the British Constitution.'[9] Elsewhere in his *Memoirs* Romilly substantiated his claim by providing evidence of Mirabeau's attempts to bring British practices to the attention of the French. For example, Romilly described the project that had originally been initiated by the Count of Sarsfield,[10] but which had been taken over by Mirabeau, to produce a French account of the mode of operation of the House of Commons in order to assist the French in deciding on the procedures by which their own Estates-General ought to operate.[11] Sarsfield had originally asked Romilly to procure for him a book on this subject. Since none existed Romilly drew up 'a statement of the Rules of the House of Commons' himself. Sarsfield had begun to translate the work, but had died before completing it. From Sarsfield the papers passed to Mirabeau who, 'fully sensible of the importance of the work, with all expedition, translated and published it'.[12] The interest of Mirabeau and his associates in British practices appears to have persisted even after the votes against the bicameral legislature and the absolute veto in September 1789. In October of that year Romilly received a letter from a friend in Paris, noting that Mirabeau had proposed a law for the suppression of riots that was similar to the English Riot Act, and passing on a request from Etienne Dumont (a friend and collaborator of both Romilly and Mirabeau) for 'an accurate statement of English law on that subject'.[13] Romilly responded immediately. In a letter to Dumont dated 23 October he noted that the Riot Act was useless, but went on to describe other powers held by English justices.[14]

While Sarsfield, Mirabeau and Dumont all appear to have been both keen and active in their attempts to use British constitutional models and legal practices to assist the French in their constitution building, their attempts were not always appreciated by their contemporaries. Referring to his account of the rules of the House of Commons, Romilly said: 'It never, however, was of the smallest use: and no regard whatever was paid to it by the National Assembly'.[15] Romilly's own explanation for this was that: 'The leading members [of the National Assembly] were little disposed to borrow any thing from England.'[16] This view was shared by Dumont. In a letter written to Romilly on 21 June 1789 he declared:

> The French have so much national vanity, so much pretension, that they will prefer all the follies of their own choosing to the results of English experience. Time alone will enlighten them on the absurdities of the police regulations which are in contemplation, and will accustom them to the idea now so revolting to them, of borrowing any thing from your government, which is here repudiated as a reproach to human reason. It is, indeed, admitted, that you have two or three fine laws; but then you have the unwarrantable presumption to assert that you have a constitution.[17]

Yet, given the sources on which some of the opponents of the British constitutional model drew in order to support their claims, it appears that they were not entirely immune to British influences themselves.

On 23 August 1789 Jean-Paul Marat wrote a letter to the president of the Estates-General, which he entitled 'An account of the vices of the English constitution'.[18] He began by pointing out that although that constitution was well regarded, it would not be a good model for the French to follow, since it was corrupted by various vices. He thus saw it as his duty to provide an analysis of the constitution and its problems, which was based on observations he had made during his stay in Britain. Marat's analysis drew heavily on the ideas of British commonwealth writers. Like them, he asserted that the main problem was the direct influence exercised by the king over parliament. Moreover, his explanatory letter was followed by a long extract taken from Chapter 60 of his own commonwealth text, *The Chains of Slavery*.[19] Nine months later Marat still felt the need to press the point. In another letter addressed to the president of the National Assembly he admitted: 'A stay of many years in London put me in a position to know and understand the vices of the English constitution, a constitution that certainly deserves to be admired, though an in-depth examination reduces it to its true value.[20] Similarly, Marat's friend Camille Desmoulins challenged Jean-Joseph Mounier's enthusiasm for the British constitution and his support for an absolute royal veto by citing the criticisms made of them by British patriots and commonwealthmen:

> It is impossible [Mounier] wrote, to know the English Constitution and not be passionate about it! This is not what the English themselves think ... It is wrong that the English are all smitten with the veto. From Milton to Doctor Price our contemporary, their best philosophers and publicists have constantly declaimed against this inversion of principles.[21]

It seems clear that the British constitutional model appealed to French revolutionaries beyond the small circle of *Monarchiens*, and that British practices continued to be of interest even after the votes of September 1789. Moreover, it is also clear that even some of those who did not believe that the French ought to adopt the British model were not averse to drawing on British experiences, works and ideas. In particular, English events of the seventeenth century appeared to offer useful parallels to the contemporary French events.

1689 and 1789

The fact that the outbreak of Revolution in France coincided with the centenary of England's Glorious Revolution rendered it almost inevitable that parallels would be drawn between the two events. It is perhaps also unsurprising that some of the earliest parallels were drawn by figures associated with the Society for Commemorating the Revolution in Great Britain (The Revolution Society). The members of this organisation, many of whom were dissenters, were indeed concerned with remembering and celebrating the Glorious Revolution, but they also believed that it should have gone further than it did, and they campaigned for reform of the political system.

In his *Discourse on the Love of our Country*, delivered to the Revolution Society on the eve of the one hundred and first anniversary of the landing of William of Orange's fleet at Torbay, Richard Price made a number of references to the recently enacted French 'Declaration of the Rights of Man and of the Citizen', implying that its articles embodied principles that were also fundamental to the Glorious Revolution.[22] Moreover, at several points in the speech he drew direct parallels between the two events. For example, in a footnote in which he made reference to Jacques Necker's treatise on French finances, he suggested that the common interest in liberty now shared by Britain and France might have influential results:

> that one of the happy effects of the revolution in that country may be ... such a harmony between the two first kingdoms in the world, strengthened by a common participation in the blessings of liberty, as shall not only prevent their engaging in any future wars with one another, but dispose them to unite in preventing wars every where, and in making the world free and happy.[23]

Similarly, toward the end of the work he yoked together the British, American and French Revolutions: 'After sharing in the benefits of one Revolution, I have been spared to be a witness to two other Revolutions, both glorious.'[24] All three Revolutions had been concerned with establishing civil and political liberty. Moreover the French, like its English predecessor, had instituted a constitutional monarchy.[25]

The parallel between 1688–89 and 1789 also appears to have been important to other members of the Revolution Society. At the same meeting at which Price had delivered his speech, the committee presented a report in which the French Revolution was mentioned, and the Society then agreed to send a congratulatory address to the French National Assembly.[26]

The responses that were received to this Address suggest that it was not only the British who recognised the parallel. In his own response the duc de Rochefoucauld, to whom the Address had been sent for presentation to the National Assembly, noted 'the similarity of ... opinions and ... common enthusiasm for liberty' shared by the two nations.[27] But it was in the letters sent from provincial patriotic societies that the influence exercised by the English model was most clearly enunciated. In his speech to the Patriotic Society of Dijon on 30 November 1789, Monsieur Navier commented:

> Why should we be ashamed, Gentlemen, to acknowledge that the Revolution which is now establishing itself in our country, is owing to the example given by England a century ago?
>
> It was from that day we became acquainted with the political constitution of that island, and the prosperity with which it was accompanied; it was from that day our hatred of despotism derived its energy. In securing their own happiness, Englishmen have prepared the way for that of the universe.[28]

PARALLEL REVOLUTIONS: ENGLAND AND FRANCE 159

Similarly in its response to the Address, the Patriotic Society of Lille admitted:

> [T]hat in politics as in philosophy, you are the instructors and examples of the whole world. It is among you, yes, it is in your favoured isle, that liberty every where attacked and trampled upon by despotism has found a sacred asylum, and if France should obtain that invaluable blessing, she will perhaps be more indebted for it to your nation than to herself; for if we had not been encouraged by your example, and enlightened by your experience, we might yet perhaps have been unable to break those chains under which we were bowed down, and we should still have groaned under that odious yoke (the empire of prejudices and superstition) which tyrannizes over and cramps the faculties of man, enslaves his mind, and degrades his nature.[29]

It is a reflection of just how widespread the sense of a parallel between 1688–89 and 1789 was, on both sides of the Channel, that Edmund Burke went to such lengths to refute it in his *Reflections on the Revolution in France*.

Interestingly, the parallel was invoked once again at the French revolutionary bicentenary celebrations – and from a somewhat unexpected source. Margaret Thatcher insisted that it was the British, rather than the French, who had been the progenitors of the idea of human rights, citing Magna Carta and the Glorious Revolution of 1688–89.[30] In response President Mitterand is said to have pointed out that 1649 constituted a more obvious precedent.[31] Significantly this was also the view adopted by some of Mitterand's predecessors. As the French Revolution developed, the parallel with 1688–89 became less relevant, but that with England's earlier revolution (1640–60) gradually came into play. From the early 1790s onward numerous examples can be found of French revolutionaries noting similarities between their own experiences and English events of the 1640s and 1650s.

The English Revolution 1640–60

It was only in the nineteenth century that the term 'revolution' began to be used by English writers to refer to the period 1640 to 1660. Previously it had been described either as a rebellion or as a civil war and interregnum, with the term 'revolution' being reserved for the events of 1688–89. It is generally acknowledged that it was the French who first used the label, but English scholars have assumed that it was François Guizot in the 1820s who initially applied the term to the earlier period.[32] In fact, describing the events of the 1640s and 1650s as a 'révolution' was commonplace in France from the early 1790s onward. Moreover, the label appears to have been used deliberately so as to draw a parallel between that period of English history and contemporary French experiences. For example, in the preface to the 1791–92 translation of Catharine Macaulay's *History of England*, the direct connection between the two events was explicitly noted: 'Finally, to leave nothing to be desired, the last volume will close with a tableau comparing the English Revolution with that of the French, two revolutions, the first of which enlightened and produced the second which in its turn will produce many others.'[33]

The sense of the parallel was strengthened by the decision in 1792 to put the former Louis XVI on trial. During the debate that preceded that event, allusions were repeatedly made to the example of Charles I.[34] As Jean-Baptiste Mailhe, the spokesman for the Committee on Legislation (which had been asked to consider the legal problems involved in putting Louis on trial) explained: 'Like Louis XVI, Charles Stuart was inviolable, but like Louis XVI he betrayed the country which had placed him on the throne.'[35] Given these similarities, a number of deputies considered how the French could avoid ending up with either a Cromwell or a Charles II. Mailhe's own view was that the English had erred in having the Commons alone take the decision on what should be done with the King. The French could avoid the English fate, he insisted, by allowing the nation as a whole to judge Louis XVI. Charles Morisson used the English example to support his view that Louis should be exiled rather than executed:

> In the place of one head cut off others will appear, and our position will be unchanged. England caused the head of the criminal Charles Stuart to fall upon the scaffold, and yet England is still subjected to a king. Rome, on the other hand, was more generous and merely exiled the Tarquins; and Rome for many years enjoyed the happiness of being a republic.[36]

Interestingly, Thomas Paine, arguing for the same outcome, used the same example, though in a slightly different way:

> I have ever observed that the great mass of the people are invariably just, both in their intentions and in their objects; but the true method of accomplishing an effect does not always shew itself in the first instance. For example: the English nation has groaned under the despotism of the Stuarts. Hence Charles I lost his life; yet Charles II was restored to all the plenitude of power, which his father had lost. Forty years had not expired when the same family strove to re-establish their ancient oppression; so the nation then banished from its territories the whole race. The remedy was effectual. The Stuart family sank into obscurity, confounded itself with the multitude, and is at length extinct.[37]

Though the English precedents were much less frequently cited during the period of Jacobin domination (particularly after war had been declared between the two countries), the parallel with the period 1640–60 was revived again in the aftermath of Thermidor. In 1795, Pierre-François Henry, the translator of Harrington's works, noted: 'The troubles of the French Revolution resemble so closely those of the English Revolution, that those who like to reason from effects to causes [should] not hesitate to study the one so as to better determine the effects of the other.'³⁸ As though following Henry's injunction, in Year VII two works on the English Revolution appeared in French: Antoine Boulay de la Meurthe's *Essai sur les causes qui en 1649 amènerent en Angleterre l'établissement de la république* and Charles Millon's *Histoire de la Révolution et de la Contre-Révolution d'Angleterre*.³⁹

Given that these parallels were recognised by French revolutionaries, it is perhaps not surprising that several of the institutions that tend to be associated with the French Revolution in fact had precedents in its English predecessor. The French revolutionary calendar had been prefigured in the practice of dating events in relation to the outbreak of the Revolution. From as early as 1789, certain works were being dated 'l'an premier de la liberté', and the practice continued on into the 1790s.⁴⁰ From January 1792 it was even adopted by the National Assembly itself. It is perhaps no coincidence that a very similar system had been employed in England during the 1650s when 1648–49 was referred to as 'The First Year of Freedom.'⁴¹

Similarly, two separate Committees of [Public] Safety had been established in England during the Revolution, the first in 1642 and the second in 1659. The former was established on 4 July 1642 and was comprised of key figures from both Houses of Parliament. Its original aim was to try to preserve peace, but once war had broken out it, like its French counterpart, took up the reigns of government. It was eventually replaced, in 1644, by the Committee of Both Kingdoms.⁴² The second Committee of Safety, which was established by the Council of Officers in October 1659, was designed as a small body that would act as a provisional government. It survived only until the re-establishment of the Rump Parliament at the end of December.⁴³

Works of the English republican tradition

No doubt because of the parallels drawn between the events of mid-seventeenth-century England and those of late eighteenth-century France, the outbreak of Revolution also appears to have revived French interest in the works of the English republican tradition. While many of these works were already available in French prior to 1789, most of them were reissued in the months and years that followed.⁴⁴ Bolingbroke's *The Idea of a Patriot King*, Sidney's *Discourses Concerning Government* and Gordon's *Discourses on Tacitus* and his *Discourses on Sallust* all reappeared in the first half of the 1790s, and a new translation of Nedham's *The Excellencie of a Free State* was also published during this period.⁴⁵

At the same time, translations of republican texts that had previously been unavailable in French also appeared. Several of Milton's works were translated in the early months of the Revolution, and although it was 1795 before a full translation of Harrington's works appeared, that year saw not one but two separate translations – one of his political works and the other of his aphoristic works.[46] In fact, even before the appearance of these translations Harrington's ideas were already being discussed in France. Jean-Jacques Rutledge, a leading member of the Cordeliers Club, had been interested in Harrington since the mid-1780s, offering a detailed account of his life and ideas in his newspaper *Calypso ou les Babillards* and comparing him with Montesquieu in a work of 1786.[47] In 1791 Rutledge included lengthy, though unacknowledged, extracts from Harrington's works in his newspaper *Le Creuset* and in 1792 he was behind a draft constitution modelled on Harrington's *The Commonwealth of Oceana* that was submitted to the National Assembly.[48] Nor did Rutledge's endeavours pass unnoticed. In late 1789 a young author named François-Jean-Philibert Aubert de Vitry published a pamphlet entitled *J. J. Rousseau à l'Assemblée Nationale*. The work was particularly concerned with the need to adopt a means of levelling out the economic inequalities that existed in France, and part of the work constituted a 'patriotic dictionary' of authors whose works were relevant to the current situation.[49] Among the authors listed was Rutledge, largely on account of his enthusiasm for Harrington's ideas.[50] Aubert de Vitry claimed that Rutledge had been working for more than twenty years on a book based on Harrington's ideas, and he insisted:

> It will surely not be long in appearing, since we are at last sufficiently mature to read it, since we are happily disposed to profit from the ideas and the *sublime plan* of the friend of the unfortunate Charles I, who will always be regarded by those who know him as one of the most virtuous political writers because he always lived his life according to his principles.[51]

According to Michael Sonenscher, Aubert de Vitry, like Rutledge, was still advocating the ideas of Harrington in 1792–93.[52]

Eighteenth-century commonwealth works were not neglected either. A French version of Macaulay's *History of England* appeared in 1791–92; 1793 saw the publication of the French version of Jean-Paul Marat's *The Chains of Slavery*; during the Directory a member of the Council of Five Hundred, J. L. Chalmel, published a translation of the seventeenth issue of *Cato's Letters*, noting in the preface his intention to translate the rest of the work; and in 1801 Bertrand Barère, the former Jacobin and Thermidorian who only narrowly escaped the guillotine himself, published a translation of Walter Moyle's *An Essay upon the Constitution of the Roman Government*.[53]

These translations, both new and revived, were often accompanied by prefatory material that made clear their relevance to contemporary events. For example, Bolingbroke's *The Idea of a Patriot King*, which was republished in 1790, opened with a message to 'Louis XVI, First Patriot King of the French' in which the editor reminded him: 'that he occupied the most important throne of the universe', 'that he was about to begin reigning over a free, productive and invincible nation' and that he should adopt 'truth' and 'patriotism' as his 'principle ministers'.[54] Writing in rather different circumstances, F. Buisson, the publisher of the 1794 combined edition of Gordon's *Discourses on Tacitus and Sallust*, again acknowledged their contemporary relevance:

> We must take from this work only new light to fortify our love for republicanism, to avoid the errors and the faults of the ancient republicans; to employ our forces well, without abusing them; to conquer the difficulties which do not cease to increase the number of despots and grumblers among us, and to place manners and probity as the order of the day, which could perpetuate among us order, abundance and peace.[55]

Not only were these works available, but there is also evidence that they were read. Reviews of many of the translations appeared in leading journals of the period and once again the reviewers often noted the relevance of these works to the contemporary circumstances. The translation of Nedham's *The Excellencie of a Free State* was reviewed in *Mercure national*, *Journal du Club des Cordeliers* and *Le Moniteur*.[56] All three reviewers noted the contemporary relevance of the work, but the one writing for *Le Moniteur* put it most succinctly: 'Among the political works that have enlightened minds and were destined one day to contribute to the instruction of all people on their true rights, the English distinguish above all the book by Marchamont Needham.'[57] Camille Desmoulins reviewed the translation of one of Milton's works in his journal *Révolutions de France et de Brabant*. He too stressed the importance and relevance of Milton – and especially of his prose works – to the French: 'Milton is little known in France, except as a great poet. By contrast, during his lifetime his reputation was as a great polemical writer and an ardent defender of liberty.'[58] Later in the decade Pierre-Louis Ginguené reviewed the new editions of both Sidney's *Discourses Concerning Government* and Gordon's *Discourses on Tacitus and Sallust* in the journal *La Décade philosophique, littéraire et politique*.[59] Once again Ginguené acknowledged their contemporary relevance. In his review of Sidney he concluded that despite Sidney's flattery of the English, and his prejudices against the French, his work was still useful, and he called for a new translation to be produced to correct and improve on that of 1702. Gordon's work was compared with those of Harrington in a short article by L. Villebrune, the librarian at the Bibliothèque Nationale, which appeared in *Le Moniteur* in Year II (4 July 1794). Villebrune's call for a French translation of Harrington's works was soon heeded, and Guillaume-François-Charles Goupil-Préfelne reviewed the result – Harrington's *Oeuvres Politiques* – also in *Le Moniteur*, in Year IV.[60]

The works and ideas of the English republican tradition were also cited and quoted by revolutionaries in their own works. In 1789 an anonymous pamphlet appeared entitled *Lettre de félicitation de milord Sidney aux Parisiens et à la nation françoise, ou résurrection de milord Sidney. Second coup de griffe aux renards de toute couleur.*[61] The work adopted the premise that Sidney had returned from the dead to counsel the French revolutionaries. While he praised their 'great attempt at liberty', he warned them that their achievements were fragile and urged them to counter the threats they faced – through continual surveillance.[62] Ludlow too was venerated by the French revolutionaries and revivified as a supporter of their campaign, despite the fact that the translation of his *Memoirs* was not republished in France after its appearance in the early eighteenth century. In 1794 there appeared a work entitled *Histoire de la République d'Angleterre d'après les Mémoires d'Edmond Ludlow*. The anonymous author described himself simply as 'un républicain'.[63] The *Memoirs* itself also appears to have still been available in the 1790s. Both Boulay de la Meurthe and Millon made use of it when writing their own works on the English Revolution, and Millon also cited Macaulay's *History*. Finally, Nedham, Harrington, Sidney, Collins and Bolingbroke were all praised by the marquis de Condorcet in his *Esquisse d'un tableau historique des progrès de l'esprit humain*.[64]

The suggestion has even been made that some of the constitutional proposals of the leading revolutionary Emmanuel-Joseph Sieyès owed something to the ideas of Harrington.[65] It was Sieyès's contemporaries who first noticed the similarities between his proposals for dividing the territory and population of France and the ideas set out in Harrington's *The Commonwealth of Oceana*. In his *Mémoirs,* André Morellet challenged the view propounded by Pierre-Louis Roederer and others, that Sieyès was an entirely original thinker, by quoting from an article that had appeared in the newspaper the *Gazette français*. The author of the article had noted that Sieyès was particularly renowned for three ideas: the rights of man, his 'jury constitutionnaire', and the division of France into departments. But he pointed out that the first had been borrowed from the American constitutions, the second had been almost unanimously rejected, and the third had been derived from Harrington:

> Finally, his new division of France, an excellent means of destabilising the monarchy, presents itself to this party as the only means of standing up to the opposition that might spring up in the old provinces, on the part of the former employees of the government ... according to the maxim divide and rule.
>
> There already existed a well-known model of this system, proposed in England in circumstances very similar to those in which we find ourselves.
>
> In Harrington's *Oceana*, which is only the plan of a republic offered to Cromwell, the author divided England in the same manner, suppressing the division into counties. He made districts, precincts and hundreds, which correspond to our departments, cantons and municipalities.[66]

For Sieyès, as for Harrington, dividing the territory and population was an essential means of making popular sovereignty workable in the context of a large nation state. Moreover, Sieyès's local assemblies – like those of Harrington – were expected to perform a dual function, both electing deputies to attend the assembly at the next level and electing officials to administer local affairs.[67]

There are also marked similarities between the system of rotation of office proposed by Sieyès and that devised by Harrington. Though rotation of office had been employed in the Venetian system of government with regard to the Senate, the Council of Ten and other particular offices,[68] it was Harrington who had been the first to propose its introduction within the popular assembly.[69] In this context it served as another means of compensating for the fact that in the large states of the modern world it was not feasible for the popular assembly to be composed of all of the citizens gathered together in a single place. By applying rotation of office to the popular assembly it was at least possible to widen participation and to ensure that a large number of citizens would have the opportunity to attend the assembly at some point during their lives. Harrington's version of the practice was also distinctive in that it incorporated three separate components: limited duration of office for those elected, the replacement of the national legislative bodies by parts rather than at general elections, and a requirement that retiring deputies serve at least a term out of office before becoming eligible for re-election.[70] Thus, Harrington proposed a system in which one-third of the members of each legislative assembly (the Senate and the Prerogative Tribe) would be replaced each year.[71] From the late 1780s, Sieyès was proposing a system of rotation for the legislature that incorporated Harrington's three components.[72] In *Vue sur les moyens* he proposed that the duration of office for deputies be limited to three years; that retiring deputies should then be ineligible for re-election for a further three years in the first instance, and for six years for any subsequent term: 'since public affairs, in the sense used here, ought to be the business of as many people as possible'; and he recommended the practice of annual renewal by thirds.[73] Sieyès reiterated these ideas in a number of later works.[74] Moreover, the discovery of Sieyès's papers has confirmed that he was aware of Harrington's ideas on this issue. Not only does Harrington's name appear in Sieyès's bibliographical list, but on another sheet Sieyès had noted several quotations from *The Commonwealth of Oceana*. One of those quotations was concerned precisely with the practice of rotation of office: 'Le Sénat de Venise ressemble à une Pierre qui roule et qui par sa rotation ne pourra jamais amasser la mousse de quelque intérêt particulier.'[75]

A third constitutional measure, the practice of separating the proposal of laws from their approval, was again directly associated with Harrington (though as in the case of rotation of office his proposals owed something to the Venetian model). He had set out his policy on this in *The Commonwealth of Oceana* through his story of two girls dividing a cake.[76] A similar idea was set out in the draft constitution presented to the Convention by the Commission of Eleven in July 1795.[77] As articles 26 and 27 of Section IV of the draft constitution stated:

> XXVI. The proposition of laws belongs exclusively to the Council of Five Hundred.
>
> XXVII. It belongs exclusively to the Council of Ancients to approve or to reject the propositions of the Council of Five Hundred.[78]

In his speech to the Convention on 2 Thermidor Year III (20 July 1795), in which he responded to the draft constitution, Sieyès praised the different functions given to the *Conseil des anciens* and the *Conseil des cinq cents*, but he proposed that they be replaced by three bodies: the *tribunat*, the *gouvernement*, and the *législature*, with the first two both being capable of proposing laws, while the third body would be responsible for accepting or rejecting them.[79] Despite his insistence on two bodies proposing legislation rather than just one, there were several other respects in which Sieyès's proposal was closer to that of Harrington than was that of the Commission of Eleven. In particular, Sieyès, like Harrington, insisted that the body responsible for accepting and rejecting legislation should be the larger body, whereas the Commission had given this task to the smaller one. Moreover, Sieyès was also closer to Harrington in his account of the mode of operation of the *Législature*. It was a crucial feature of Harrington's system that the legislative body charged with accepting or rejecting the proposed laws was a silent assembly. It was not to discuss the proposed legislation, but simply to vote for or against it. The Commission of Eleven did not adopt this element of Harrington's plan. According to both their draft constitution, and the system that was eventually enacted, both the *Conseil des cinq cents* and the *Conseil des anciens* were allowed to engage in debate. Sieyès went one step closer to Harrington, since he insisted that the *Législature* listen in silence to each proposal, and to the arguments for and against it as presented by the *tribunat* and the *gouvernement*, but he was then prepared to allow the members of the *Législature* the opportunity to debate in private before voting to accept or reject the proposal. This aspect of the process was set out in his constitutional plan of 1799:

> There is therefore debate, there is pleading before the legislative body; it is necessary, therefore, that this body has the attitude and the impartiality of a jury or of a tribunal of judges; it must listen in silence to the two parties.[80]

In fact, the Constitution of 1799 actually came even closer to Harrington's original intention since there the assembly was not even allowed to deliberate in secret.[81] Once again the manuscript evidence confirms that Sieyès was aware of Harrington's ideas on this issue. Another of the passages from Harrington's work that was noted by Sieyès came from the story of the two girls dividing a cake: 'Demandez à ces deux petites filles si celle qui a fait les parts a encore le choix.'[82] Moreover, a description of a bicameral system, which had supposedly been proposed during the English Revolution and which bore a close resemblance to Harrington's model, appeared in *Essai sur les causes qui en 1649 amènerent en Angleterre l'établissement de la république* by Sieyès's friend and collaborator Boulay de la Meurthe.[83]

It should, however, be noted that despite the claims made by several early twentieth-century commentators, this was never more than the borrowing of a few constitutional ideas. The overall purpose and character of Sieyès's constitutional proposals were very different from those of Harrington.[84]

Conclusion

The French revolutionaries may have been keen to suggest that they were creating a completely new era and starting afresh, but they inevitably drew on earlier precedents and ideas both to make sense of the changes taking place around them and to help them to construct workable models for the future. Among the various models and ideas on which they drew, those from across the Channel were particularly important. In the early months of the Revolution the existing British constitution and the example of the Glorious Revolution were cited, but as events moved on it was 1640–60 that offered the most obvious precedent. Moreover, it was not just the institutions and practices of that period that appealed to the French, but also the ideas and constitutional proposals that it generated.

Thanks to the translations and citations of English republican works that had appeared since the beginning of the eighteenth century, the key works and ideas of that tradition were both available and familiar to the French revolutionaries as they set out to recover their own liberty. Indeed, these works and ideas appear to have been well known to revolutionaries from across the political spectrum. Though the passing references explored here are interesting in themselves, there were other revolutionaries whose borrowings from the English republican tradition were both deeper and more extensive.

Notes

1 See for example M. Vovelle (ed.), *Révolution et république: l'exception française* (Paris: Éditions Kimé, 1994) and C. Nicolet, *L'Idée républicaine en France* (Paris: Gallimard, 1982), p. 87.
2 The emergence of this view owed much to Edmund Burke's *Reflections on the Revolution in France* (1790). Yet, it persists up to the present. In an article that appeared in the *Independent* newspaper in 2002, Andreas Whittam Smith declared: 'We [the British] do not recognise a class of intellectuals as such. We withhold the label. And we have no revolutionary tradition to live up to or to inspire us. The British rarely descend on to the streets to advocate political change. Every generation or so, the French do exactly that – in 1789, 1830, 1848, 1870, 1936 and 1968.' Andreas Whittam Smith, 'Trotsky's Legacy is Alive and Well in France Today', *Independent* (25 March 2002). See also Gideon Rachman, 'France Braces itself for a Stiff Dose of Thatcherism', *Financial Times* (8 May 2007).
3 On the reception of ancient ideas in late eighteenth-century France see H. T. Parker, *The Cult of Antiquity and the French Revolutionaries: A Study in the Development of the Revolutionary*

Spirit (Chicago: University of Chicago Press, 1937); C. Mossé, *L'Antiquité dans la Révolution française* (Paris: Albin Michel, 1989); M. Raskolnikoff, *Des Anciens et des modernes* (Paris: Presse Universitaire de Paris-Sorbonne, 1990); M. Raskolnikoff, *Histoire romaine et critique historique dans l'Europe des lumières* (Strasbourg: AECR, 1992); and P. Vidal-Naquet, *Politics Ancient and Modern*, trans. J. Lloyd (Cambridge: Polity Press, 1995). The American influence is reflected in several publications, not least Louis-Alexandre de La Rochefoucauld d'Anville's translation of the State constitutions, which first appeared in 1783 and was reprinted in 1792, and the translation of John Adams's *A Defence of the Constitutions of Government of the United States of America*, which also appeared in 1792. L. A. La Rochefoucauld d'Anville, *Constitutions des treize États-unis de l'Amérique* (Philadelphia and Paris, 1783) and J. Adams, *Défense des constitutions américaines, ou la nécessité d'une balance dans les pouvoirs d'un gouvernement libre* (Paris: Buisson, 1792). On the American model, and the similarities and differences between the American and French republics, see P. Higonnet, *Sister Republics: The Origin of French and American Republicanism* (Cambridge, MA: Harvard University Press, 1988); D. Lacorne, *L'Invention de la république: le modèle américain* (Paris: Hachette, 1991); and for a slightly different perspective, R. Whatmore, 'The French and North American Revolutions in Comparative Perspective', in M. Albertone and A. De Francesco (eds), *Rethinking the Atlantic World: Europe and America in the Age of Democratic Revolutions* (Basingstoke: Palgrave Macmillan, forthcoming). I am grateful to Richard Whatmore for providing me with a copy of this article prior to publication.

4 For a contemporary exploration of the differences between France and America see [F. J. P. Aubert de Vitry], *J. J. Rousseau à l'Assemblée Nationale* (Paris, 1789), pp. 43–8.

5 Significantly the parallels with seventeenth-century England continued to be made well into the nineteenth century. See G. Cubitt, 'The Political Uses of Seventeenth-Century English History in Bourbon Restoration France', *Historical Journal* 50 (2007), pp. 73–95. See also J. R. Jennings, 'Conceptions of England and its Constitution in Nineteenth-Century French Political Thought', *Historical Journal* 29 (1986), pp. 65–85.

6 There were, of course, factors that worked against this model too – not least the long-standing rivalry between the two countries and widespread anglophobia. However, these sentiments did not always inhibit the willingness to look to British models – especially when those models were rooted firmly in the past.

7 On the *Monarchiens* see J. Egret, *La Révolution des notables: Mounier et les monarchiens, 1789* (Paris: Armand Colin, 1950); R. Griffiths, *Le Centre perdu: Malouet et les 'monarchiens' dans la Révolution française* (Grenoble: Presses Universitaires de Grenoble, 1988); and F. Furet and M. Ozouf (eds), *Terminer la Révolution: Mounier et Barnave dans la Révolution française* (Grenoble: Presses Universitaires de Grenoble, 1990).

8 See, for example, K. M. Baker, "Fixing the French Constitution", in his *Inventing the French Revolution: Essays on French Political Culture in the Eighteenth Century* (Cambridge: Cambridge University Press, 1990), pp. 252–305.

9 S. Romilly, *Memoirs of the Life of Sir Samuel Romilly* (London: John Murray, 1840), I, p. 109.

10 The Count of Sarsfield was of Irish extraction and was an associate of Anne-Robert-Jacques Turgot, Adam Smith, John Adams, Jeremy Bentham and others.

11 Romilly, *Memoirs*, I, pp. 101–3.

12 Ibid., I, p. 102.

13 Ibid., I, p. 362. Dumont (and his Genevan associate Jacques-Antoine Duroveray) were themselves committed to the promotion of the British constitutional model in France. See R. Whatmore, 'Etienne Dumont, the British Constitution and the French Revolution', *Historical Journal* 50 (2007), pp. 23–47.

14 Romilly, *Memoirs*, I, pp. 370–1.

15 Ibid., I, p. 102.

16 Ibid., I, p. 103.

17 Ibid., I, p. 354.

18 J. P. Marat, *La Correspondance de Marat*, ed. C. Vellay (Paris: Librairie Charpentier & Fasquelle, 1908), p. 100.

19 On this work see Chapter 9 above.
20 Marat, *Correspondance*, ed. Vellay, pp. 141–2.
21 *Révolutions de France et de Brabant*, ed. C. Desmoulins (Paris, 1789–91), I, p. 125. A few pages later he again cited Milton in response to Mounier. Ibid., I, pp. 129–30.
22 R. Price, *A Discourse on the Love of our Country, delivered on 4 November 1789 at the Meeting-House in the Old Jewry, to the Society for Commemorating the Revolution in Great Britain* (London: T. Cadell, 1789), pp. 12, 21, 38. A copy of the Declaration was also appended to the printed version of Price's speech, preceded by the claim that it: 'contains such an authority for some of the sentiments in the foregoing Discourse, and holds out to the world an instruction on the subject of Civil Government of such consequence, that I cannot help inserting here the following Translation of it'. Ibid., Appendix, p. 5. Price's work was just one example of yet another wave of British commonwealth works that emerged in the 1780s and 1790s. It is interesting to note that the work was almost immediately translated into French, by Louis-Félix Guinement de Keralio, and Price was referred to directly in Théophile Mandar's translation of Marchamont Nedham's *The Excellencie of a Free State*. M. Nedham, *De La Souveraineté du peuple, et de l'excellence d'un état libre*, trans. T. Mandar (Paris, 1790), p. xl.
23 Price, *A Discourse*, p. 30n.
24 Ibid., p. 49. For another example see pp. 13–14.
25 R. Price, *Additions to Dr Price's Discourse on the Love of Our Country, Containing Communications from France Occasioned by the Congratulatory Address of the Revolution Society to the National Assembly of France, with the Answers to Them* (London, 1790), pp. 20 and 24.
26 Price, *A Discourse*, Appendix, p. 13.
27 Price, *Additions to Dr Price's Discourse*, p. 5.
28 Ibid., pp. 14–15.
29 Ibid., p. 18.
30 D. Dhombres, 'Mauvaise humeur britannique Les droits de l'homme ne sont pas nés avec la Révolution française...', *Le Monde* (11 July 1989).
31 See J. Scott, *Algernon Sidney and the Restoration Crisis, 1677–1683* (Cambridge: Cambridge University Press, 1991), p. 108 note 13.
32 See R. C. Richardson, *The Debate on the English Revolution*, 3rd edn (Manchester: Manchester University Press, 1998), p. 87.
33 H. G. comte de Mirabeau, *Histoire d'Angleterre, depuis l'avènement de Jacques Ier jusqu'à la révolution, par Catharine Macaulay Graham, traduit en français et augmentée d'un discours préliminaire contenant un précis de l'histoire de l'Angleterre jusqu'à l'avènement de Jacques I, et enrichie de notes* (Paris, 1791–92), I, p. xvi.
34 Charles I was mentioned in speeches by Jean-Baptiste Mailhe, Charles Morisson, Antoine Saint-Just, Maximilien Robespierre, Pierre-Victurnien Vergniaud and Thomas Paine. See M. Walzer (ed.), *Regicide and Revolution: Speeches at the Trial of Louis XVI* (Cambridge: Cambridge University Press, 1974), pp. 101, 105–6, 118, 124, 133, 205 and 212.
35 Ibid., p. 105.
36 Ibid., p. 118.
37 Ibid., p. 213. It should be noted that not all deputies believed the parallel to be useful. In his speech Robespierre warned his fellow deputies: 'We have permitted ourselves to be led into error by examples from foreign lands which have nothing in common with us.' Ibid., p. 133.
38 P. F. Henry, 'Preface du traducteur', in J. Harrington, *Oeuvres Politiques de Jacques Harrington*, trans. P. F. Henry (Paris, An III [1795]), p. i.
39 A. J. C. J. Boulay de la Meurthe, *Essai sur les causes qui, en 1649, amenèrent en Angleterre l'établissement de la république; sur celles qui devaient l'y consolider; sur celles qui l'y firent périr* (Paris: Baudouin, An VIII); C. Millon, *Histoire de la Révolution et de la Contre-Révolution d'Angleterre ...* (Paris, An VII).
40 A number of examples of this practice can be found. Camille Desmoulins may have been the originator of it, since regular examples can be found among his own published works from as early as 1789, as well as among works published by booksellers that he used (Garnéry, 17

rue Serpente and Imprimerie de Chalon) and among works published by associates of his, especially those associated with the Cordeliers Club.

41 The motto 'In the First Year of Freedom by God's Blessing Restored 1649' appeared on the Great Seal of 1649, while that of 1651 was dated 'The Third Year of Freedom by God's Blessing Restored 1651'. There are also examples of the title pages of works being dated according to the year of liberty. See, S. Kelsey, *Inventing A Republic: The Political Culture of the English Commonwealth, 1649–1653* (Manchester: Manchester University Press, 1997), pp. 93–4 and 101 and D. Norbrook, *Writing the English Republic: Poetry, Rhetoric and Politics, 1627–1660* (Cambridge: Cambridge University Press, 1999), p. 5.

42 A. Woolrych, *Britain in Revolution, 1625–1660* (Oxford: Oxford University Press, 2002), pp. 228 and 274–5.

43 Ibid., pp. 742 and 754–5. It should be noted, however, that Committees of Safety were also established in colonial America from the 1760s, and it is possible that the French got the idea via this route rather than directly from England.

44 For a list of the French translations of English republican works see the Appendix to this book.

45 Henry St. John, 1st Viscount Bolingbroke, *Des Devoirs d'un roi patriote, et portrait des ministres de tous les temps* (Paris: Desenne, 1790); A. Sidney, *Discours sur le gouvernement, par Algernon Sidney, traduits de l'anglais par P.A. Samson: nouvelle édition conforme à cette de 1702* (Paris, 1794); T. Gordon, *Discours historiques, critiques et politiques de Thomas Gordon sur Tacite et sur Salluste, traduits de l'anglois. Nouvelle édition, corrigée* (Paris: F. Buisson, l'An II de la république française une et indivisible [1794]); Nedham, *De La Souveraineté du peuple*, trans. T. Mandar.

46 On the translations of Milton see Chapter 11. Harrington, *Oeuvres politiques*; J. Harrington, *Aphorismes politiques*, trans. P. F. Aubin (Paris, 1795).

47 *Calypso, ou les Babillards*, ed. J. J. Rutledge (Paris, 1784–85), III, pp. 217–25 and 313–59; J. J. Rutledge, *Éloge de Montesquieu* (Paris, 1786).

48 *Le Creuset: ouvrage politique et critique*, ed. J. J. Rutledge (Paris, 1791); [J. J. Rutledge], *Idées sur l'espèce de gouvernement populaire qui pourrait convenir à un pays de l'étendue et de la population présumée de la France* (Paris, 1792). On Rutledge's use of Harrington see: R. Hammersley, *French Revolutionaries and English Republicans: The Cordeliers Club, 1790–1794* (Woodbridge: Boydell and Brewer for the Royal Historical Society, 2005), especially pp. 83–135. See also Chapter 12 below.

49 [Aubert de Vitry], *J. J. Rousseau à l'Assemblée Nationale*, pp. 95–234. For a more detailed analysis of Aubert de Vitry's pamphlet see M. Sonenscher, *Sans-Culottes: An Eighteenth-Century Emblem in the French Revolution* (Princeton and Oxford: Princeton University Press, 2008), pp. 266–73.

50 [Aubert de Vitry], *J. J. Rousseau à l'Assemblée Nationale*, pp. 229–34. Harrington was also referred to at several other points in the work. See p. 191 where he appears alongside Moses, Jesus, Confucius, Penn and Fénelon, and p. 228 where his work is presented as essential to the libraries of *philosophes* alongside those of Pluquet, Xénophon, Epictetus, Marcus Aurelius and William Penn.

51 Ibid., p. 232. Interestingly, one of the epigrams that opened the work was *Vitam impendere vero*, Rousseau's motto, but also the epigram used by Jean-Paul Marat on several of his works. See Chapter 9 above. Aubert de Vitry's interest in Rutledge and Harrington was largely due to their concern with preventing large inequalities in wealth through the use of an agrarian law or its modern equivalent, a land bank. On other matters, not least the nature and workings of representative government, the views put forward in *J. J. Rousseau à l'Assemblée Nationale* were rather different from those developed by Rutledge in his later works. Compare for example ibid. pp. 40–3 with Rutledge's ideas as explored in Chapter 12 below.

52 Sonenscher, *Sans-Culottes*, p. 273.

53 Mirabeau, *Histoire d'Angleterre*. This translation is discussed in detail in Chapter 11. J. P. Marat, *Les Chaînes de l'Esclavage* … (Paris, l'an I [1793]); J. Trenchard and T. Gordon, *Dix-septième lettre de Caton, traduite de l'anglais de Thomas Gordon*, trans. J. L. Chalmel (Paris: Baudouin, n.d.); W. Moyle, *Essai sur le gouvernement de Rome, traduit de l'anglois* [trans. B. Barère de Vieuzac] (Paris: Imprimerie de Marchant l'ainé, an X, [1801]).

54 Bolingbroke, *Des Devoirs d'un roi patriote*, unpaginated dedication.
55 Gordon, *Discours historiques … sur Tacite et sur Salluste*, I, p. vi.
56 *Mercure national et révolutions de l'Europe: journal démocratique*, ed. L. Keralio (Paris, 1791), III, p. 135 (January 1791); *Journal du Club des Cordeliers*, ed. A. F. Momoro (Paris, 1791), Issue 4, pp. 31–4; *Moniteur universel: réimpression de l'ancien Moniteur; seule histoire authentique et inaltéré de la Révolution française; depuis la réunion des états-généraux jusqu'au consulat (mai 1789–novembre 1799)* (Paris: Plon Frères, 1847–79), IV, p. 335.
57 *Moniteur universel*, IV, p. 335. Though the conventional spelling was Nedham, Needham was sometimes used. The significance of Nedham's ideas for the French was also noted by the Scottish judge and writer John Maclaurin, Lord Dreghorn, who argued: 'What we call French Principles, were, by no means, first broached by the political writers of that nation.' Rather than being reflected in Rousseau's *Social Contract*, he believed that the principles of the French Constitution were actually to be found in *The Excellencie of a Free State*. John Maclaurin, Lord Dreghorn, *The Works of the Late John MacLaurin, Esq. of Dreghorn: One of the Senators of the College of Justice* (Edinburgh: Ruthven and Sons, 1798), pp. 173–83.
58 *Révolutions de France et de Brabant*, ed. Desmoulins, I, p. 180. For other references to Milton's works (including some that had not been translated into French) see ibid., IV, pp. 239 and 404 and V, p. 534.
59 *La Décade philosophique, littéraire et politique*, III, An III, pp. 537–44 and IV, An III, pp. 84–95 [Sidney]; III, An III, p. 96 [Gordon].
60 *Moniteur universel*, XXI, p. 123 and XXVII, p. 658.
61 *Lettre de félicitation de milord Sidney aux parisiens et à la nation françoise: ou résurrection de milord Sidney. Second coup de griffe aux renards de toute couleur* (Paris, 1789).
62 French revolutionaries also displayed busts of Sidney. See B. Worden, *Roundhead Reputations: The English Civil Wars and the Passions of Posterity* (London: Allen Lane, 2001), p. 20.
63 *Histoire de la republique d'Angleterre d'après les Mémoires d'Edmond Ludlow l'un des principaux chefs des républicains anglais: contenant la narration des faits qui ont précédé accompagné et suivi ces momens lucides de la nation anglaise* (Paris, l'an II [1794]).
64 J. A. N. Caritat, marquis de Condorcet, *Esquisse d'un tableau historique des progrès de l'esprit humain* (Paris: Editions Sociales, 1971), pp. 190, 209 and 216.
65 See J. H. Clapham, *The Abbé Sieyès* (Westminster: P. S. King & Son, 1912); H. F. Russell Smith, *Harrington and his Oceana: A Study of a 17th Century Utopia and its Influence in America* (Cambridge: Cambridge University Press, 1914), pp. 205–15; *A French Draft Constitution of 1792 Modelled on James Harrington's Oceana*, ed. S. B. Liljegren (Lund: C. W. K. Gleerup, 1932), pp. 44–79; and D. Trevor, 'Some Sources of the Constitutional Theory of the abbé Sieyès: Harrington and Spinoza', *Politica* (1935), pp. 325–42.
66 A. Morellet, *Mémoires inédits de l'abbé Morellet … sur le dix-huitième siècle et sur la Révolution* (Paris: Baudouin, 1822), I, pp. 414–15. The idea that Sieyès borrowed this proposal from Harrington was suggested by Clapham and Liljegren. Clapham, *The Abbé Sieyès*, p. 31; *A French Draft Constitution*, ed. Liljegren, pp. 47–51.
67 Harrington adopted this dual system at every level. See: Harrington, *The Commonwealth of Oceana and A System of Politics*, ed. J. G. A. Pocock (Cambridge: Cambridge University Press, 1992), pp. 78–96. The most explicit account of the dual function in Sieyès's works can be found in his pamphlet: E. J. Sieyès, *Quelques Idées de constitution applicables à la ville de Paris en juillet 1789* (Versailles: Baudouin, 1789), pp. 3–4.
68 See Z. S. Fink, *The Classical Republicans: An Essay in the Recovery of a Pattern of Thought in Seventeenth-Century England* (Evanston, IL: Northwestern University Press, 1945), pp. 31–2.
69 Venice's Great Council was perpetual, being composed of all those deemed to be citizens. Nedham had also hinted at something like this with his idea of 'revolution'. However, he was rather vague as to exactly what it involved. [M. Nedham], *The Excellencie of a Free State. Or, The Right Constitution of a Commonwealth. Wherein all objections are answered, and the best way to secure the people's liberties discovered. With some errors of government and rules of policie* (London: Thomas Brewster, 1656).

70 Harrington, *Commonwealth of Oceana*, p. 33.
71 Ibid., pp. 95–7.
72 It was J. H. Clapham, writing in 1912, who originally suggested that Sieyès had borrowed the idea of rotation of office from Harrington. The claim was subsequently repeated by Liljegren. (Clapham, *The Abbé Sieyès*, pp. 30–2. *A French Draft Constitution*, ed. Liljegren, pp. 46 and 48.) Forsyth questioned this assertion on the grounds that the idea of rotation had been incorporated into some of the American state constitutions and that Sieyès could have borrowed the idea from there. (M. Forsyth, *Reason and Revolution: The Political Thought of the Abbé Sieyès* (Leicester: Leicester University Press, 1987), p. 67). While rotation of office was indeed known and practised in America in both pre- and post-revolutionary regimes, they too appear to have borrowed the idea from Harrington. (Russell Smith, *Harrington and his* Oceana, pp. 152–200). Similarly, Michael Sonenscher has noted that Sieyès could have picked up the idea of rotation from Rousseau. However, Sieyès's conception of the practice is closer to that of Harrington than to many of the American examples or to the references to rotation of office made by Rousseau.
73 E. J. Sieyès, *Views of the Executive Means Available to the Representatives of France in 1789*, in *Sieyès: Political Writings*, ed. M. Sonenscher (Indianapolis, IN: Hackett, 2003), p. 54. See also E. J. Sieyès, *What is the Third Estate?* in ibid., p. 155.
74 *Archives Parlementaires de 1787 à 1860*, ed. J. Madival and E. Laurent, 1st series (Paris, 1789–1914), VIII, p. 597 (7 septembre 1789); A. J. C. J. Boulay de la Meurthe, *Théorie constitutionnelle de Sieyès* (Paris, 1836), p. 21.
75 AN: 284 AP 5–1/1–. 160v. As reprinted in *Des Manuscripts de Sieyès, 1773–1799*, ed. C. Fauré, with J. Guilhaumou and J. Valier (Paris: Honoré Champion, 1999), p. 453. The quotations appear to be from the 1795 French translation. The original can be found in Harrington, *The Commonwealth of Oceana*, p. 160: 'her senate is like a rolling stone (as was said) which never did nor, while it continues upon that rotation, ever shall gather the moss of a divided or ambitious interest'.
76 Harrington, *Commonwealth of Oceana*, p. 22.
77 Andrew Jainchill has suggested that the commissioners perhaps picked up on Harrington's idea via John Adams's *Defense of the Constitutions of the United States of America*, which had been translated into French in 1792. A. Jainchill, 'The Constitution of the Year III and the Persistence of Classical Republicanism', *French Historical Studies* 26 (2003), p. 414. This is entirely plausible, since the section of Harrington's work detailing the practice was copied word for word into Adams's work. Moreover, we know for certain that members of the Commission were familiar with Adams's book. In a speech to the Convention, given on behalf of the Commission on 5 Messidor Year III (23 June 1795), François-Antoine Boissy d'Anglas quoted directly from Adams's work (though he wrongly gave his name as Samuel rather than John). F. A. Boissy d'Anglas, *Projet de constitution pour la République française, et discours préliminaire prononcé par Boissy-D'Anglas, au nom de la commission des onze, dans la séance du 5 Messidor, an III* (Niort: Élies, Year III [1795]), p. 46.
78 Boissy d'Anglas, *Projet de constitution*, p. 92. See also pp. 40–1 where Boissy justifies this decision.
79 *Moniteur universel*, 307, 7 Thermidor, An 3, pp. 1236–1238 and 308, 8 Thermidor An 3, p. 1239. Both Clapham and Liljegren suggested that the other proposal Sieyès made in his speech, the adoption of a *jurie constitutionnaire*, also owed something to Harrington – and in particular to his Academy of Provosts from *Oceana* and the petition that he and his friends presented to Richard Cromwell's Parliament in July 1649. However, any Harringtonian echoes in the *Jurie constitutionnaire* or its successor the *Collège des conservateurs* are rather distant. Clapham, *The Abbé Sieyès*, p. 265; *A French Draft Constitution*, ed. Liljegren, pp. 58–62.
80 Boulay de la Meurthe, *Théorie constitutionnelle de Sieyès*, p. 23. As Albéric Néton put it 'Mais pour éviter l'abus de la tribune, les excès de l'éloquence, les dangers de la réthorique, ce corps devait être muet. C'était un jury, un jury *legislative*. Il devait écouter, en silence, le réquisitoire et les plaidoiries, puis se retirer pour rendre sa sentence.' As quoted in *A French Draft Constitu-*

tion, ed. Liljegren, p. 57. See also *Sieyès: Political Writings*, ed. Sonenscher, pp. xxxi–xxxii.
81 *La Constitution du 22 Frimaire An VIII*, Article 34.
82 AN: 284 AP5–1/1. As reprinted in *Des Manuscripts de Sieyès*, ed. Fauré, p. 452.
83 Boulay de la Meurthe, *Essai sur les causes*, p. 57. In addition, earlier sections of the pamphlet echo Harrington's account of the long-term causes of the events of the mid-seventeenth century. Ibid., pp. 38–41.
84 For the best recent account of Sieyès's thought see M. Sonenscher, 'Introduction' to *Sieyès: Political Writings*, ed. Sonenscher, pp. vii–lxiii and M. Sonenscher, *Before the Deluge: Public Debt, Inequality, and The Intellectual Origins of the French Revolution* (Princeton and Oxford: Princeton University Press, 2007).

11

The comte de Mirabeau and the works of John Milton and Catharine Macaulay

Introduction

The case of the comte de Mirabeau is typical of the more general picture of the influence of British models and ideas during the French Revolution. For the most part, historians have either ignored or downplayed the British influences upon him. Even W. B. Fryer, who devoted an entire article to the subject of Mirabeau's trip to England in the winter of 1784–85, concluded that: 'English influence did not become a major factor on Mirabeau's political career'.[1] This verdict cannot easily be squared with the evidence. Mirabeau's attempt to impose a British-style constitutional monarchy in France, and to introduce other British practices, may not have been well received by his compatriots, but the intention itself was still significant. Moreover, he also drew a parallel between the events of 1640–60 and those of 1789, and oversaw the translation of several English republican works into French.

Mirabeau and the Bowood Circle

Mirabeau's interest in British models and ideas appears to have owed something to his links with members of the 'Bowood Circle' – the group of writers and political activists who gathered around the Earl of Shelburne/Lord Lansdowne in the late eighteenth century.[2] Mirabeau became acquainted with several of these figures during his stay in England in 1784–85. Thanks to a letter of introduction from Benjamin Franklin, he became friendly with Benjamin Vaughan, who in turn introduced him to Lord Lansdowne himself and to Richard Price.[3] At around the same time, one of Mirabeau's Genevan friends, Francis D'Ivernois, introduced him to Samuel Romilly, who became involved in producing an English translation of Mirabeau's French pamphlet against the American Order of the Cincinnati.[4] Mirabeau was then responsible for introducing Romilly to Vaughan, who in turn introduced him to Lansdowne.[5] In return, Romilly acquainted Mirabeau with his Genevan friend Etienne Dumont.[6] Mirabeau dined, conversed and corresponded with these figures until his sudden departure for France on 30 March 1785, and in some cases he kept up his friendship even after he had left.[7]

It was a belief shared by many members of the Bowood Circle that the French and the British could learn much from each other.[8] It is therefore not surprising that members of this group assisted Mirabeau in his attempts to introduce British constitutional practices in France. It was the British members of the group – and especially Romilly – to whom Mirabeau turned for information on British models and institutions, while two of the Genevan members of the circle, Dumont and Jacques-Antoine Duroveray, edited Mirabeau's journal *Le Courier de Provence* in which articles publicising British practices appeared. It is also interesting to note that Mirabeau's *Considérations sur l'ordre de Cincinnatus*, which appeared in 1785, included within it a translation of the work of another member of the Bowood Circle (and commonwealthman) – *Observations on the importance of the American Revolution* by Richard Price. Mirabeau's interest in seventeenth-century English works may also have derived from his Bowood connections since Olivier Lutaud has suggested that it was Romilly who first brought the prose works of Milton to Mirabeau's attention.[9]

Mirabeau's translations of Milton and Macaulay

During 1788 and 1789 Mirabeau published two works that drew heavily on Milton's ideas. *Sur La Liberté de la presse* was a translation of Milton's *Areopagitica*, to which Mirabeau added some editorial material designed to demonstrate the relevance of the work to contemporary events in France. *Théorie de la royauté après la doctrine de Milton* was a French version of Milton's *Pro Populo Anglicano Defensio*, which was preceded by a preface in which a number of Milton's other works were discussed and quoted from (in fact, the whole of the earlier translation of *Areopagitica* was reproduced there).[10]

Mirabeau was also behind the French translation of Catharine Macaulay's eight-volume *History of England*. The idea of translating the work into French was first raised by the Count of Sarsfield in a letter to Macaulay herself in 1777.[11] In a subsequent letter, Sarsfield promised he would: 'find out some man of letters able to do it properly'.[12] Given that after the death of Sarsfield Mirabeau took on at least one of his other projects, it is possible that the task passed from him to Mirabeau.[13] However, Mirabeau supposedly met Macaulay during his time in England, so it is also possible that the arrangement was made directly between them.[14]

Mirabeau died suddenly in April 1791, but had already handed over responsibility for the project to another member of his circle, Charles Guiraudet.[15] Guiraudet was keen to emphasise that the inspiration for the project had come from Mirabeau and that the presentation of it reflected his views. It was even suggested that Mirabeau had corrected the proofs of the first two volumes.[16] In particular, Guiraudet stressed that Mirabeau had seen the relevance of the work to the French in the late eighteenth century: 'Given our circumstances, this is no ordinary work [Mirabeau] said. There exist so many points of contact and connection between these events, these people, and us, that in limiting ourselves to drawing attention to them in footnotes, we will find that we have written the history of two revolutions.'[17]

It followed from this that works produced by the English during their revolution might be of interest to the French during theirs, and this certainly appears to have been the idea behind Mirabeau's translation of Milton's works. Though he admitted in his preface to *Théorie de la royauté* that Milton's prose works were largely polemical, Mirabeau insisted that they touched on important issues that were relevant beyond the context in which they had been written.[18] Thus, Mirabeau's aim was to extract from Milton's works '[t]he political principles drowning in the details of the circumstances and in the verbose erudition of his time'.[19]

Despite Mirabeau's enthusiasm, the works of both Milton and Macaulay posed a potential problem for him, since both authors were tainted with the stain of anti-monarchism. Milton worked for the English republic after the execution of Charles I in 1649, and several of his works explicitly defended both regicide and republic. Similarly, Macaulay's work was generally regarded as a 'republican' history. Given that Mirabeau never wavered in his belief in constitutional monarchy, it may seem odd that he should have chosen to draw upon the works of known opponents of monarchical government. Mirabeau was certainly aware of this problem and was explicit about it at least in relation to Milton.

Though he insisted on the relevance of Milton's works in late eighteenth-century France, Mirabeau acknowledged that there were two aspects of Milton's thought that might be problematic for his French contemporaries. In the first place, Milton had lived 'in a totally religious century'[20] and held firm religious beliefs himself.[21] It was therefore understandable that he had made much use of scripture to support and defend his ideas. Mirabeau's means of dealing with this was straightforward. In addition to warning his readers about Milton's religiosity, he also cut some of Milton's biblical examples. The second aspect of Milton's thought that was problematic for an eighteenth-century French audience was his anti-monarchism. Here Mirabeau's response was more ambiguous. In *Sur La Liberté de la presse* he did not deny this aspect of Milton's thought, but simply insisted that *Areopagitica* was not tainted by it: 'if, in some of his writings, Milton shows himself to be a violent republican, he is in this one, in which he addresses the Parliament of Great Britain, only a peaceful debater'.[22] In *Théorie de la royauté*, however, Mirabeau was not only explicit about Milton's republicanism, but he described – and even quoted from – one of Milton's overtly republican works, *The Readie and Easie Way*.

It would seem that, despite their anti-monarchical associations, Mirabeau considered these works to be useful to him in furthering his own campaign for the implementation of a British-style constitutional monarchy in the early years of the French Revolution. Indeed, Mirabeau's choice of authors known for their anti-monarchism appears to have been deliberate; he seems to have used this aspect of their thought itself as a weapon in his campaign.

Mirabeau's use of Milton and Macaulay

The immediate background to his decision to translate Milton's *Areopagitica* was clearly set out by Mirabeau himself in his preface to the translation. In the context of the King's call for an open and public debate on the form that the Estates-General should take, the ministerial decision to suppress a work crucial to that debate (the *Précis des proces-verbaux des administrations provinciales depuis 1779 jusqu'en 1788*) was deeply disturbing. Mirabeau thus translated and published Milton's work in order to urge the reversal of that decision and the establishment of the liberty of the press.

It is clear, however, that for Mirabeau the liberty of the press was not simply a good in itself. Its real importance lay in its role in securing limited, constitutional monarchy. On Mirabeau's interpretation, Milton had recognised that liberty in one sphere was dependent on liberty in others, and in particular that the liberty of the press was essential to the protection of other liberties. In his translation of *Areopagitica* Mirabeau played up the connection between intellectual and political servitude, adding the following sentences to Milton's text:

> If Rome had maintained freedom of thought, she would never have become the opprobrium of other nations. She would never have submitted to the yoke of monsters who enslaved and debased her, if intellectual servitude had not prepared the way for political servitude.[23]

In his prefatory material Mirabeau was even more explicit. He described a free press as 'not only the palladium of all liberties, but the beacon of government'.[24] He also paraphrased large chunks of a work by another member of his circle, Charles de Casaux's *Questions à examiner avant l'assemblée des États généraux*, in which Casaux had argued that England's free government, prosperity and success were entirely due to the existence there of a free press:

> Remove ... from England, the liberty of the press and in spite of all the resources of its admirable constitution, the ministerial blunders so rare in England will succeed there as rapidly as elsewhere ... and soon this most flourishing nation will be merely an object of pity for all those in whom it excited envy and merited admiration.[25]

Conversely, Mirabeau insisted – still paraphrasing Casaux – that introducing a free press into a despotic nation could bring about a dramatic transformation in the government:

> On the other hand, if you transport the liberty of the press – little by little – to Turkey ... soon ... rich in all the properties of her territory and her immense population, [she] will be more powerful and no less respected than this England so powerful and so respected today.[26]

Clearly this was what Mirabeau hoped would happen in France. In a postscript to the work he noted that, in their ruling of 5 December 1788, the *Paris Parlement* had included a call for the establishment of a free press. This news gave Mirabeau much hope for France's future:

> We will have a constitution since the public spirit has made such progress, such conquests; we will have a constitution perhaps even without great civil disturbances ... we will have a constitution and France will finally reach her destiny.[27]

Mirabeau's translation of Milton's *Pro Populo Anglicano Defensio* was also designed to contribute toward his campaign for the establishment of a constitutional monarchy in France. The relevance of Milton's work toward this end was twofold. In the first place it offered a robust critique of divine-right monarchy. (Chapter Two of the work was explicitly directed toward this end.) In its place it called for popular sovereignty and the rule of law, insisting on their compatibility with monarchical government.[28] The work thus offered to Mirabeau a monarchical response to divine-right theory. Yet while the work accepted the possibility of limited or constitutional monarchy, it also justified not just the execution of Charles I but tyrannicide more generally. Moreover, not only did Mirabeau acknowledge that the central aim of several of Milton's works was the justification of tyrannicide, but also he went so far as to endorse it himself. In his preface to *Théorie de la royauté* he defended the argument of Milton's *The Tenure of Kings and Magistrates* against criticisms by the editor of the *Nouveau dictionnaire historique des grands hommes*. Mirabeau began by quoting the dictionary editor's judgement on *The Tenure*: "[Milton] in that work wishes to prove that a tyrant on the throne is accountable to his subjects, that he can be tried, deposed and put to death. Milton launches other blows against royal authority in many INSOLENT libels." Mirabeau then responded to this judgement: 'I would displease the editor, [since] I think much more insolently than Milton because I believe that even the best kings are accountable to their subjects.'[29] Elsewhere in the preface Mirabeau made his own position very clear. He accepted the execution of Charles I as justified, but he would not endorse the abolition of monarchy that had followed:

> All the world knows that he lost his life on the scaffold, and it is unhelpful that attempts have been made to transform into parricide what was at its foundation a great example of justice ... The great fault committed by the English was not to punish a guilty king, but to proscribe royalty as if it had been complicit in the attacks of those who were invested with it. Just because a magistrate prevaricates in his functions, is it necessary to proscribe magistracy? Undoubtedly not – these are two completely different things and it is important not to confound them. It was not, therefore, necessary to establish a democratic form, incompatible with the time, place and circumstances. It was not necessary, above all, to punish the children of Charles for the errors of their father. It was not necessary to capture and expatriate them while the people suffered patiently as, under the name of protector, an ambitious demagogue usurped the sovereign authority. This was the crime of the English[30]

Despite his caveat, the translation of a work that justified the execution of Charles I was a dangerous move to make in 1789. As someone who saw the parallels between the English and French Revolutions, Mirabeau must have been aware of this. His friends certainly saw the risks. In his *Souvenirs sur Mirabeau* Dumont described how he and Duroveray (who were not involved in producing the translation) became aware of it accidentally through the bookseller Le Jay.[31] They immediately realised the risks:

> After the events of the 5th and 6th of October, the publication of such a book by a member of the national assembly was not only a libel, but an act of high treason ... Duroverai frightened Le Jay to such an extent that he already believed himself in the Châtelet or La Tournelle. He consented to everything we proposed, and we brought the whole edition into the house, where we burned it the same day [though] Le Jay saved about a dozen copies.[32]

Dumont's own explanation as to why Mirabeau published this work was that he was putting himself in a position where he could benefit if the duc d'Orléans succeeded in gaining power.[33] There is undoubtedly something in this, but the evidence suggests that Mirabeau had not completely given up on Louis XVI as yet. Thus his translation of Milton's work was perhaps intended to serve a double function. On the one hand it alerted the duc d'Orléans to Mirabeau's willingness to support him should he come to power, but at the same time the threat of regicide and republic could also be used to warn Louis XVI and those around him of what could happen if they failed to introduce the required political reforms and to accept a limited, constitutional monarchy. Mirabeau, after all, used exactly the same device of warning the King of the consequences of failing to follow his advice in his *Mémoire* of 15 October 1789: 'Several methods present themselves, but there are those which would entail the most terrible evils, and which I only mention to deter the king from a course which would mean certain destruction.'[34]

It is likely that the same intentions lay behind Mirabeau's decision to translate Macaulay's *History*. Given his explicit acknowledgement of the parallel between the events described by Macaulay and those currently being experienced by the French, Mirabeau presumably wanted to use Macaulay's account to demonstrate to the French — including Louis himself — the paths that ought to be taken and those that should be avoided. Mirabeau's hope was that the French could find a short cut from 1640 to 1688 — avoiding the troubles that had faced the English in the intervening years. Offering a detailed account of that period of English history — including the trial and execution of Charles I — was perhaps the best means of convincing his compatriots of the importance of doing so. Thus Mirabeau was able to use the works of Milton and Macaulay in his own campaign to persuade the French to adopt a constitutional monarchy.

The legacy of Mirabeau's English translations

Mirabeau's translations of Milton's works continued to exercise an influence after his death in 1791. However, those who picked up on them did not always acknowledge the subtleties of his original intentions. The second edition of *Sur La Liberté de la presse* appeared in August 1792 in the context of the suppression of royalist works by the authorities.[35] Mirabeau would perhaps have approved of this deployment of the work. He would undoubtedly have been less happy, however, about the subsequent uses to which his translations of Milton were put.

Despite the best efforts of Dumont and Duroveray, some of the copies of *Théorie de la royauté* saved by Le Jay must have got into circulation, because in November 1792 the work was reprinted, by the Council of the Department of Drôme, under the title *Défense du peuple anglais, sur le jugement et la condamnation de Charles premier, roi d'Angleterre*. The timing was deliberate. The title page stated that this was an: 'Ideal work for throwing light on the circumstances in which the French now find themselves'.[36] Charges against Louis had been set out by the Commission of Twenty-Four on 6 November 1792, just a week before the Council of Drôme took the decision to publish the work, and much of the autumn was taken up with debates in the Convention over whether he should be tried and executed. In the prefatory material that accompanied *Défense du peuple anglais* the Council described the background to Milton's original text and went on to explain what they believed to be the value of the work to the French at this time:

> The Council believe that the work of Milton establishes and develops, with as much clarity as solidity, the inalienable rights of the sovereignty of all peoples.

That the spirit that produced it sets alight all hearts with the sacred fire of liberty, that it presents just and wise ideas of royalty, that it successfully combats the ridiculous and barbarous pretensions of these criminal men who, drawing their powers from the ignorance or the weakness of the people, wish to raise themselves above the law and refuse to bow their guilty heads under the sword. That it demonstrates to the partisans of the inviolability of kings that in all times and in all nations, their crimes have been expiated by the scaffold. That it is the duty of administrators to form and nurture public opinion on the great question that concerns the National Convention on the judgement of Louis Capet. That the administrators will be sure to fulfil this essential object by spreading – particularly in the countryside – knowledge of a book that has become very rare, and by the reading of which all French republicans could shrewdly disentangle the connections and analogies that exist between the conduct of Charles Stuart and that of Louis Capet.[37]

In 1793–94 even *Sur La Liberté de la presse* was put to 'republican' ends. This time the agent involved was the radical revolutionary Camille Desmoulins. Desmoulins had worked for Mirabeau, probably on *Le Courier de Provence*, in the autumn of 1789 – precisely the time when Mirabeau was producing *Théorie de la royauté*.[38] Prior to his encounter with Mirabeau, Desmoulins had made no mention in his works of either Milton or the liberty of the press, but in his first work produced after his collaboration with Mirabeau – the newspaper *Les Révolutions de France et de Brabant* – both Milton and the liberty of the press became topics of particular interest to him.[39] Moreover, he appears to have shared Mirabeau's views on the impact that a free press could have on the government of a country. In the forty-fifth issue of *Les Révolutions*, Desmoulins referred to what he claimed was the maxim of an English writer: 'if the liberty of the press could exist in a country in which [there was] the most absolute despotism with all powers united in a single [pair of] hands, it alone would suffice to provide a counter-weight [to it].'[40]

Although Desmoulins already seems to have accepted the powerful and important role that could be played by the liberty of the press when he was producing *Les Révolutions*, it was in his last work – the newspaper *Le Vieux Cordelier* – that he most fully developed his views on this issue. Written at the height of the terror in the winter of 1793–94, *Le Vieux Cordelier* quickly became a vehicle through which Desmoulins launched a thinly veiled attack on what he saw as the increasingly despotic behaviour of the revolutionary government.[41] Once again, Desmoulins's discussion of the liberty of the press in this work bore a close resemblance to that of Mirabeau, in its association of the liberty of the press with the British and the claim that it was a valuable means of defeating despotism and securing political liberty. However, Desmoulins diverged from his former employer in drawing a direct link between the liberty of the press and republicanism: 'What characterises a republican is not the century [or] the government in which he lives, [but] the frankness of his language' and therefore, 'What is it that distinguishes a republic from a monarchy? A single thing: the liberty of speaking and writing.'[42]

Conclusion

It would seem that contrary to Fryer's assertion, British political and constitutional ideas played a fundamental role in shaping Mirabeau's revolutionary politics. Not only did he believe that a constitutional monarchy on the British model represented the best option open to the French in 1789, and work to try to ensure that it was implemented, but he also drew a parallel with seventeenth-century English history and drew on the works of Milton and Macaulay to support his claims.

Mirabeau was not the only French revolutionary to translate and draw upon English republican works during the course of the 1790s. Though the other figures who did so did not share Mirabeau's respect for the British constitutional model, they too believed strongly in liberty and thought that seventeenth-century English works could be used to guide the French both on the kind of post-revolutionary regime that should be implemented and on the best means of doing so.

Notes

1. W. B. Fryer, 'Mirabeau in England, 1784–85', *Renaissance and Modern Studies* 10 (1966), p. 39.
2. On the Bowood Circle see: *An Enlightenment Statesman: Lord Shelburne in Context (1737–1805)*, ed. N. Aston and C. Campbell Orr (Forthcoming).
3. Fryer, 'Mirabeau in England', pp. 62–3.
4. S. Romilly, *The Memoirs of The Life of Sir Samuel Romilly* (London: John Murray, 1840), I, pp. 78–9. Mirabeau was associated with a number of Genevan figures having met them after the failed revolution of 1782.
5. Ibid., I, p. 85.
6. E. Dumont, *Souvenirs sur Mirabeau et sur les deux premières Assemblées Législatives*, ed. M. J. L. Duval (Paris, 1832), pp. 10–11; Romilly, *Memoirs*, I, p. 97.
7. For evidence of Mirabeau dining with Shelburne/Lansdowne see Mirabeau to Mme de Nehra 15 November 1784 as quoted in Fryer, 'Mirabeau in England', p. 63 and Romilly, *Memoirs*, I, p. 84. For evidence of Mirabeau's continuing friendship with Romilly see ibid., I, pp. 96–7 and letters from Mirabeau reprinted in ibid., I, pp. 291–326.
8. D. Jarrett, *Begetters of Revolution: England's Involvement with France, 1759–1789* (London: Longman, 1973).
9. O. Lutaud, 'Des Révolutions d'Angleterre: La Révolution française l'exemple de la liberté de presse ou comment Milton "ouvrit" les etats généraux', Colloque International sur la Révolution française (Clermont Ferrand, 1986), p. 122.
10. Though Mirabeau was undoubtedly behind *Théorie de la royauté* and was the author of the preface, the translation itself was the work of another member of his circle, Jean Baptiste Salaville. Mirabeau's translations of Milton have received some attention: D. M. Wolfe, 'Milton and Mirabeau', *Publications of the Modern Languages Association of America* 49 (1934), pp. 1116–28; 'Mirabeau' in W. B. Hunter et al. (eds), *Milton Encyclopedia* (Lewisburg, 1978–83), V,

148; Lutaud, 'Des Révolutions d'Angleterre'; O. Lutaud, 'Emprunts de la Révolution française à la première révolution anglaise', *Revue d'histoire moderne et contemporaine* 37 (1990), pp. 589–607; A. Thomson, 'La Référence à l'Angleterre dans le débat autour de la république', in M. Vovelle (ed.), *Révolution et république: l'exception française* (Paris: Éditions Kimé, 1994), pp. 133–44; T. Davies, 'Borrowed language: Milton, Jefferson, Mirabeau', in D. Armitage et al. (eds), *Milton and Republicanism* (Cambridge: Cambridge University Press, 1995), pp. 254–71; and C. Tournu, 'Introduction', in *Milton et Mirabeau: rencontre révolutionnaire*, ed. C. Tournu (n.p.: EDIMAF, 2002), pp. 11–54.

11 The Gilder Lehrman Collection on deposit at the Pierpont Morgan Library, The Catharine Macaulay Graham Papers (1763–1830). PML: GLC 1794.23, 'Count of Sarsfield to Macaulay, 16[?] December 1777'. I am grateful to Kate Davies for making copies of these letters available to me.

12 PML: GLC 1794.24, 'Count of Sarsfield to Macaulay, 2 May 1779'. See also GLC 1794.26, 'Madame de Chaumont to Macaulay, 5 July 1778' and GLC 1794.27, 'Madame de Chaumont to Macaulay, 1778'.

13 See Chapter 10 above.

14 B. Hill, *The Republican Virago: The Life and Times of Catharine Macaulay, Historian* (Oxford: Clarendon, 1992), p. 216.

15 Dumont mentions Guiraudet in his *Souvenirs sur Mirabeau* and claims that he was involved with *Le Courier de Provence* for a short while. Dumont, *Souvenirs sur Mirabeau*, pp. 124–5.

16 H. G. comte de Mirabeau, *Histoire d'Angleterre, depuis l'avènement de Jacques Ier jusqu'à la révolution, par Catharine Macaulay Graham, traduit en français et augmentée d'un discours préliminaire contenant un précis de l'histoire de l'Angleterre jusqu'à l'avènement de Jacques I, et enrichie de notes* (Paris, 1791–92) I, p. ix.

17 Ibid., I, p. ix. See also xvi.

18 H. G. comte de Mirabeau, *Théorie de la royauté après la doctrine de Milton* (Paris, 1789), p. ii.

19 Ibid., p. ii.

20 H. G. comte de Mirabeau, *Sur La Liberté de la presse*, in *Milton et Mirabeau: Rencontre révolutionnaire*, ed. C. Tournu (n.p.: EDIMAF, 2002), p. 61.

21 In fact, this view of Milton has recently been challenged. See P. A. Rahe, *Against Throne and Altar: Machiavelli and Political Theory under the English Republic* (Cambridge: Cambridge University Press, 2008), pp. 139–74.

22 Mirabeau, *Sur La Liberté de la presse*, p. 61.

23 Ibid., p. 66. For comparison see, J. Milton, *Areopagitica*, in John Milton, *Selected Prose*, ed. C. A. Patrides (Harmondsworth: Penguin, 1974), p. 204.

24 Mirabeau, *Sur La Liberté de la presse*, p. 85. Mirabeau also quoted Milton's editor Toland on this issue: 'as Toland has rightly observed, the power of censorship in the hands of the prince or his ministers is no better than the inquisition and it is no less dangerous to civil liberty than a standing army'. Mirabeau, *Théorie*, p. xiii.

25 Mirabeau, *Sur La Liberté de la presse*, p. 89.

26 Ibid., pp. 89–90.

27 Ibid., p. 92.

28 J. Milton, *A Defence of the People of England*, in Milton, *Political Writings*, ed. M. Dzelzainis (Cambridge: Cambridge University Press, 1991), see in particular pp. 178–85.

29 Mirabeau, *Théorie*, pp. lxx–lxxi.

30 Ibid., pp. lv–lvi.

31 Dumont, *Souvenirs sur Mirabeau*, pp. 171–2.

32 Ibid., pp. 172–3. Dumont's knowledge of the work appears to be limited, since he describes it simply as a work against royalty, whereas in fact, as I have shown, it could be used to support limited, constitutional monarchy.

33 Ibid., pp. 174–5.

34 'Excerpts from Count Mirabeau's Advice to Louis XVI (1789)' http://personal.ashland.edu/~jmoser1/mirabeau.htm (accessed 23 January 2009).

35 Tournu, 'Introduction', in *Milton et Mirabeau*, p. 22.
36 J. Milton, *Défense du peuple anglais, sur le jugement et la condemnation de Charles premier, roi d'Angleterre*, in *Milton et Mirabeau: Rencontre révolutionnaire*, ed. C. Tournu (n.p.: EDIMAF, 2002), p. 93.
37 Ibid., p. 95.
38 Desmoulins had supposedly written to Mirabeau offering his services in the spring of 1789, but his offer had been rejected. The publication of his pamphlet *La France libre* perhaps made Desmoulins a more appealing prospect, because on 22 September 1789 Desmoulins wrote to his father to say that he had just dined with Mirabeau and that he had been invited to work on his newspaper *Le Courier de Provence*. A week later he wrote again to his father: 'For the past week I have been at Versailles with Mirabeau. We have become great friends, at least he calls me *his dear friend*.' Quoted in J. Janssens, *Camille Desmoulins: le premier républicain de France* (Paris: Librairie Académique Perrin, 1973), p. 185. Dumont also noted Desmoulins's presence at Mirabeau's house in September 1789. Dumont, *Souvenirs sur Mirabeau*, pp. 167–9.
39 Desmoulins's referred to Milton at several points in his newspaper – and he even offered a review of *Théorie de la royauté*. *Les Révolutions de France et de Brabant*, ed. C. Desmoulins (Paris, 1789–91), I, pp. 125 and 180–6, IV, p. 404, V, p. 534.
40 Ibid., IV, p. 261.
41 As is explained in Chapter 12 below, Desmoulins also included within the work long extracts taken from Daudé's translation of Gordon's *Discourses on Tacitus*. For more detail on Desmoulins's *Le Vieux Cordelier* see R. Hammersley, 'Camille Desmoulins's *Le Vieux Cordelier*: a link between English and French republicanism', *History of European Ideas* 27 (2001), pp. 115–32.
42 *Le Vieux Cordelier*, ed. C. Desmoulins (Paris, 1825), p. 133.

12

The Cordeliers Club and the democratisation of English republican ideas[1]

Introduction

The Cordeliers Club, which was established in the spring of 1790, grew out of the Cordeliers District – one of the sixty electoral districts of Paris that had been created to facilitate the elections to the Estates-General.[2] It was one of the most radical of the revolutionary political clubs. The official title of the Club was the *Société des amis des droits de l'homme et du citoyen*, and the Cordeliers presented themselves as intent on ensuring that the radical promises embodied in the *Déclaration des droits de l'homme et du citoyen* were actually fulfilled in practice.[3] Certain members of the Cordeliers Club were calling for a French Republic from as early as 1789, and in 1791 the Club was directly involved in the republican movement that emerged in the aftermath of the King's flight to Varennes. Moreover, the particular version of republicanism favoured by Club members was unusually democratic. In their pamphlets and speeches they combined Rousseau's political theory with ideas drawn from the English republican tradition in order to create one of the first theories of modern democratic government in the Western world.

Rousseau on large state republicanism

On the face of it, Rousseau's political theory would not appear to be easily compatible with that associated with the English republican tradition. In *The Social Contract* Rousseau had suggested that popular sovereignty could only be properly implemented in a small city state where all the citizens could be gathered together in a single place.[4] Moreover, his rejection of representative government led him to some rather scathing observations regarding the English:

> The English people thinks it is free; it is greatly mistaken, it is free only during the election of Members of Parliament; as soon as they are elected, it is enslaved,

it is nothing. The use it makes of its freedom during the brief moments it has it fully warrants its losing it.[5]

Ten years later, however, in his *Considerations on the Government of Poland*, Rousseau himself was forced to consider the means by which a republic might be built in a large, modern, nation state.[6] Perhaps not surprisingly, the view of England (or rather Britain) presented in *this* work was somewhat different. The text includes a number of references to British models and practices, the implication being that the Poles might learn something from them. Moreover, occasionally the observations Rousseau made were explicitly favourable. For example, he referred to the House of Commons to prove that it was possible to tally votes in a large assembly, and he praised the relationship between the peerage and the monarchy in Britain.[7] More often, he cited British practices to demonstrate to the Poles things that they ought to avoid, but even here it is striking that most of his criticisms were similar to those voiced by the British commonwealthmen. Like them, Rousseau was particularly concerned about the influence exercised by the Crown over Parliament, and about the tendency of representative bodies to succumb to corruption:

> The Lawgiver as a body is impossible to corrupt, but easy to deceive. Its representatives are difficult to deceive, but easily corrupted, and it rarely happens that they are not corrupted. You have before your eyes the example of the English Parliament, and, because of the *liberum veto*, that of your own nation.[8]

Moreover, in order to solve the problem of corruption, Rousseau even endorsed the standard commonwealth proposal of frequent elections, alongside the idea of limiting the power of deputies through the use of binding mandates:

> I see two means of preventing this terrible evil of corruption, which turns the organ of freedom into the instrument of servitude.
> The first, as I have already said, is frequent Diets, which by often changing representatives makes it more costly and more difficult to seduce them. On this point your constitution is better than that of Great Britain.
> [...]
> The second means is to require the representatives to adhere exactly to their instructions, and to render a strict account of their conduct in the Diet to their constituents. As regards this, I can only marvel at the negligence, the carelessness, and I dare say the stupidity of the English Nation which, after arming its deputies with the supreme power, adds not a single restraint to regulate the use they might make of it during the entire seven years of their mandate.[9]

This is not to say that Rousseau was, in fact, a commonwealthman in outlook. Apart from anything else, he appears to have remained committed to the importance of genuine civic virtue within a republican polity. But, in *Considerations on the Government of Poland* he was forced to grapple with one of the central questions that had faced the English republican and British commonwealth thinkers: how to create a republic – or a system of government based on popular sovereignty – in a large, modern state.

The Cordeliers and Rousseau

It is clear from their writings that many members of the Cordeliers Club were devoted disciples of Rousseau. His name appears frequently both in works published by individual members and in the Club's official publications. The Club even included among its members René Girardin (formerly René Louis, marquis de Girardin) who had been a close friend of Rousseau. It was Girardin who had offered Rousseau a retreat on his land at Ermenonville in 1778, and who was responsible for producing an edition of Rousseau's collected works after his death. Not surprisingly, Girardin referred extensively to Rousseau's ideas in his own speeches and pamphlets.[10]

The Cordeliers appear to have been convinced by the distinction that Rousseau had drawn between sovereignty (the making of the laws) and government (the execution of those laws), and by his view that the former ought to be exercised by the citizens as a body. They also took more seriously than other revolutionaries Rousseau's opinion that sovereignty should not be represented. While accepting that some delegation of responsibility was unavoidable in a state the size of France, they sought various means by which the delegates (as they preferred to call them) might be kept firmly under the control of their constituents. Rousseau's solution of binding mandates was one of the measures that the Cordeliers adopted,[11] but they also drew on other ideas. Both Girardin and another leading member of the Cordeliers Club – Pierre-François Robert (in a work tellingly entitled *Républicanisme adapté à la France*) – presented the popular ratification of laws as a means of making Rousseauian popular sovereignty workable in a large state.[12] In addition, certain members of the Club also sought solutions to this problem in the works of the English republican tradition.

The Cordeliers and English republicanism: Mandar and Nedham

In the autumn of 1790 the Cordeliers Club member Théophile Mandar published a translation of Nedham's *The Excellencie of a Free State*. Mandar made no reference back to the chevalier d'Eon's 1774 translation of the same work, and he deliberately shaped and supplemented the text so as to demonstrate its relevance to the contemporary situation in France. In particular, he added quotations from other works in order to 'support' Nedham's claims: 'they prove what he has only indicated, and they affirm his reports'.[13]

Central among the other authors on whom Mandar drew was Rousseau. Not only did quotations from Rousseau's works litter Mandar's preface and notes, but the appendix to the second volume contained an entire chapter from *The Social Contract*. The chapter in question was Book III Chapter I in which Rousseau had sought to demonstrate the distinction between legislative and executive power (sovereignty and government). The purpose of including this chapter within the text, Mandar explained, was to demonstrate that this idea – which was generally attributed to Rousseau – had actually been prefigured in Nedham's work.[14]

The way in which Mandar inserted quotations from Rousseau into his translation suggests that he also saw Nedham as providing a solution to the Rousseauian problem of making popular sovereignty workable in a large, populous nation. For example, he inserted the extract from Rousseau's *Considerations on the Government of Poland* on the difficulties involved in conserving liberty in large states (part of which was quoted above) in the midst of Nedham's assertion that frequent elections and the regular replacement of representatives offered a valuable means of preserving liberty:

> FIFTH REASON. Liberty consists in entrusting power to the successive representatives of the people alone;* because this succession is an obstacle to the ambition of individuals, to all the temptations of personal interest.[15]

> *One of the great inconveniences of large states, which most renders liberty difficult to conserve, is that the legislative power can only appear there and can only act, by deputation. This has its disadvantages and its advantages, but the disadvantages win out. The legislature as a body is impossible to corrupt, but easy to deceive. The representatives are difficult to deceive, but easily corrupted – and it is rare that they are not. You have under your eyes the example of the English parliament; and by the free veto, that of your own nation. It is possible to enlighten one who is deluded, but how can one who is for sale be restrained? Without being well informed about the affairs of Poland, I would bet all the world that there is more knowledge in the diet, and more virtues in the dietines.

The implication was clearly that frequent elections and the regular replacement of representatives offered a solution to the Rousseauian problem.

The reviewers of Mandar's works recognised, and appear to have agreed with, the point he was making about Nedham and Rousseau. The reviewer in the *Journal du Club des Cordeliers* endorsed the idea that Nedham's work 'treats admirably the effects of that which the *Genevan* developed the causes'.[16] Similarly, the review in *Le Moniteur* noted, on the basis of Mandar's work, that Rousseau had not invented the idea of the inalienable sovereignty of the people, but had simply reduced to a convenient system that which he had seen in practice in many republican states.[17] Moreover, Mandar himself remained committed to using frequent elections and the regular replacement of delegates as a means of mitigating the problems associated with instituting popular sovereignty in a large state. In his 1793 pamphlet *Des Insurrections* (in which he cited not just Nedham, but also other English republican writers including Harrington, Milton and Sidney[18]) Mandar declared:

> The only means that the people have of maintaining themselves in a state of liberty, and of preventing the fatal consequences of faction and tyranny, are therefore of supporting the power by the successive and regular choice of its representatives; such is the rule that a wise republic prescribes to keep itself free for a long time.[19]

The Cordeliers and English republicanism: Rutledge and Harrington

Mandar was not the only Cordeliers Club member to draw on the writings of seventeenth-century English republicans to overcome the problems associated with establishing a republic in a large state. Jean-Jacques Rutledge drew on the writings of Harrington for precisely the same reason. As was indicated in Chapter 10, Rutledge had long been an admirer of the works of Harrington and had discussed his ideas in two pre-revolutionary works.[20] In the 1790s he returned to Harrington for more practical purposes. Like Sieyès, Rutledge picked up on Harrington's idea of rotation of office.[21] In his newspaper *Le Creuset* he offered an (unacknowledged) translation of the first six chapters of Harrington's aphoristic work *A System of Politics*. His translations of the aphorisms relating to rotation of office were deliberately updated to suit his audience. Aphorisms twenty-two and twenty-three of Chapter 5 of Harrington's work read:

> 22. The ultimate result in the whole body of the people, if the commonwealth be of any considerable extent, is altogether impracticable; and if the ultimate result be but in a part of the people, the rest are not in liberty, nor is the government democracy.
> 23. As a whole army cannot charge at one and the same time, yet is so ordered that every one in his turn comes up to give the charge of the whole army; so, though the whole people cannot give the result at one and the same, yet may be so ordered that every one in his turn may come up to give the result of the whole people.[22]

Rutledge's translation read:

> XIX. The exercise of supreme executive power, residing in the body of the nation, has often, at first glance, appeared impractical. This is what made Montesquieu, and many others before him, believe the introduction of democratic forms to be irreconcilable with a large population and a vast area.

> One can easily agree with these writers, that if the supreme deliberative power belongs only to one part of a large people, the rest effectively cease to be free; and consequently the government will not truly be democratic.

> XX. In truth, it is not possible for an immense army to charge the enemy all at once; but it is easy to conceive that this immense army can be organised in such a way that each of its divisions, that each of its soldiers present themselves in turn – whether to attack or to defend.

> Similarly, though it would be impracticable for a large people, living in a vast area, to take part in the exercise of supreme deliberative power all at once, it would however be possible to make each division and each individual participate, by equal and regular turns; and to establish an order of rotation such that general and common legislation could never be enacted unless it has been consecrated by the people as a whole.[23]

Rutledge also endorsed the moral philosophy of the commonwealth tradition. In his newspaper *Le Creuset* he offered a long discussion of the relationship between reason and passion, which was closely based on Harrington. In the midst of this discussion he declared: 'The passions of man are the motivating force behind all his actions.'[24] Moreover, he also followed Harrington in believing that neither the reformation of manners nor education would provide adequate solutions to this problem, but rather that what was required was the limiting of wide variations in wealth through something like an agrarian law, and the adoption of constitutional mechanisms to ensure that even self-interested behaviour produced virtuous results.

In *Le Creuset* Rutledge explicitly endorsed the idea of an agrarian law.[25] In his view its role was to prevent some citizens from making the laws for all the others.[26] Rutledge also presented a land bank as an alternative means of preventing great inequalities in property. He had originally discussed the idea of a land bank in his *Essais politiques* of 1777.[27] He returned to it during the Revolution when he endorsed the proposal that had been drawn up by Jacques-Annibal Ferrières.[28]

The Harringtonian constitutional mechanisms that Rutledge drew upon in his newspaper included (alongside rotation of office) the separation of the discussion of laws from their acceptance or rejection, and the complex electoral ballot. As Rutledge acknowledged, it was the Venetians who had originally employed these means of controlling and directing the passions:

> But the only certain means of preventing among men the crimes and faults that are the result of a partiality arising from their passions, is to bring into political institutions the combination of relations, such that there is always a veritable lack of moral and material power.
>
> It is Venice where this secret exists; and where it is daily put into practice.[29]

In a series of issues of his newspaper in March 1791, Rutledge described the Venetian system in some detail.[30] He explained how the Senate would debate and propose legislation, but it would then be up to the citizen body at large (in the form of the Grand Council) to accept or reject the proposals. He also offered his readers an account of the Venetian ballot that was based on Harrington's description (and illustration) in *The Commonwealth of Oceana*.[31] This system involved a complicated combination of lot and election, as well as a secret ballot (using coloured balls) in order to choose the candidates for the various political offices. Once chosen the candidates (like the laws) would be subject to ratification by the Grand Council. Rutledge insisted that by these means the problems of corruption and bribery that usually plagued electoral systems could be avoided.

Rutledge also endorsed the religious position of the commonwealthmen, and in particular their belief in the political value of religion and their vision of a society in which liberty of conscience existed alongside a national Church. *Le Creuset* was written in the midst of the religious debate prompted by the attempt to make all ecclesiastical public officials swear an oath of allegiance to the Civil Constitution of the Clergy. Inspired by this debate, Rutledge quoted extracts from Harrington's *A System of Politics* in such a way as to support the Civil Constitution. First he endorsed the importance of religion in a state such as France: 'A nation which is not restrained by the principles of religion, is a crowd of beings without modesty and without morality'.[32] He then went on to argue that under democratic government liberty of conscience had to be guaranteed, since it and civil liberty were inextricably bound up together.

Though he had already done much in *Le Creuset* to demonstrate the relevance of Harrington's ideas to revolutionary France, the proclamation of the first French republic appears to have prompted Rutledge to try to apply Harrington's ideas even more directly to the French situation. As I have argued elsewhere, he was almost certainly the author of a draft constitution, entitled *Idées sur l'espèce de gouvernement populaire qui pourrait convenir à un pays de l'étendue et de la population présumée de la France*, which was presented to the Convention in the autumn of 1792.[33] As the title suggests, the aim of the work was to demonstrate that a system of government based on genuine popular sovereignty could be constructed in the context of a large modern nation state. And, as in *Le Creuset*, the Harringtonian ideas of the agrarian law, rotation of office, the separation of discussion of policy from decision-making and the Venetian ballot were the means by which this feat was to be achieved. However, in this work Rutledge took Harrington's theory of the separation of debating and resolving one step further. Unlike Harrington (and Sieyès), who had envisaged this mechanism operating within a bicameral legislature, Rutledge followed the Venetian model more directly by combining the separation of debate from resolution with the Cordeliers idea of the popular ratification of laws. In *Idées sur l'espèce de gouvernement populaire* it was the legislative assembly that was to debate and propose legislation, but it would then be up to the citizen body at large to accept or reject those proposals.

The Cordeliers and English republicanism: Marat and Desmoulins

Rutledge was not the only Cordeliers Club member to draw on the moral philosophy and religious ideas of the English republican tradition as well as its political theory. It is perhaps no coincidence that Rutledge was a friend and supporter of Marat,[34] whose French edition of *The Chains of Slavery* (which appeared in the spring of 1793) presented his views on these subjects to a French audience.[35] Marat's affiliation with the Cordeliers has often been underplayed in favour of his Jacobin credentials. Yet, not only was Marat a member of the Club, but his revolutionary career began and ended with the Cordeliers.[36] It was the Cordeliers District that had offered Marat protection after he was charged with provoking the popular march to Versailles in October 1789.[37] And, on his death in July 1793, it was the Cordeliers Club that took on the responsibility for organising his funeral, and it was in the gardens of the Cordeliers Convent that he was buried.[38]

Both Rutledge and Marat were also friendly with Desmoulins, whose early commitment to republican government, and interest in Milton and his ideas on the freedom of the press, has already been noted.[39] Like Rutledge and Marat, Desmoulins also appears to have shared the moral philosophy of early modern republicanism. In his newspaper *Révolutions de France et de Brabant* Desmoulins counselled against relying too heavily on the morality and virtue of the people:

> Our legislators must not, therefore, rely on public spirit and morality that do not exist. But I do not despair, on this basis, of the constitution, because I am not of the opinion of those who think that good morals must prepare the way for good laws and that without them a good constitution is only built on sand. It appears to me, on the contrary, that it is up to laws to create morals, and that good laws are the brake on bad morals, that it is this that constitutes the art of the legislator, because, what need would there be for laws if there was morality? And what are laws but the remedy for corruption?[40]

Desmoulins voiced the same idea in his last work *Le Vieux Cordelier*. There he argued that it was not virtue, but the liberty of the press that provided the essential foundation stone of a republic:

> But to return to the question of the liberty of the press, without doubt it must be unlimited; without doubt republics must have as their base and foundation the liberty of the press, not this other base that Montesquieu has given them. [If virtue was the only spring of government, if you suppose all men to be virtuous,

> the form of government is of no importance and all are equally good. Why therefore do we have some governments that are detestable and others that are good? Why do we have a horror of monarchy and cherish republics? It is, one supposes with reason, that men are not all equally virtuous, the goodness of the government must supplement virtue and the excellence of a republic consists precisely in this that it supplements virtue.
>
> ...
>
> This series of simple and incontestable principles renders palpable the error of *Montesquieu*. Virtue is not the foundation of a republic. What does the form of government matter, and what is the need of a republic, if all the citizens are virtuous? But the republic is the supplement of virtue.][41]

Evidently, this passage was intended to challenge the Jacobin notion of a republic of virtue. More specifically it constituted a direct response to Robespierre's discussion of virtue in his speech 'Sur les principes de morale politique', in which he had invoked Montesquieu's idea of virtue as the spring of republican government.[42]

Moreover, like his Cordeliers contemporaries, Desmoulins also drew on the works of the English republican tradition. In support of his attack on the Jacobins and their republic of virtue and terror, in *Le Vieux Cordelier*, he referred to the account of Roman history offered by Tacitus:

> We are now in the midst of a fight to the death between the republic and the monarchy. In this fight it is inevitable that either one or the other will win a bloody victory. But who could object to the triumph of the republic, after having seen the historical evidence left to us by the triumph of monarchy [Who could oppose the republic] after glancing at the debauched and grotesque scenes of Tacitus, that I am going to present to the honourable circle of my subscribers?[43]

What follows is several pages worth of text drawn, not directly from Tacitus, but from Daudé's translation of Gordon's *Discourses on Tacitus*.

The democratisation of the commonwealth tradition

The Cordeliers were unusual among the French revolutionaries in explicitly embracing democratic government from as early as 1790.[44] Their democratic beliefs, and their commitment to Rousseau's ideas, also coloured their attitude toward the English republican texts on which they drew.[45] By likening Nedham to Rousseau and by cutting certain passages from *The Excellencie of a Free State*, Mandar succeeded in making Nedham's work appear more democratic than it actually was. Similarly, Rutledge explicitly presented Harrington's ideas (and the Venetian model on which he had drawn) as democratic.[46] Moreover, he also adapted Harrington's constitutional mechanisms so as to render them better suited to democratic government – as in his amalgamation of Harrington's principle of debate and resolve with the Cordeliers idea of the popular ratification of laws. Thus the Cordeliers engaged in what was effectively the democratisation of the commonwealth tradition.

Conclusion

In many ways the Cordeliers mark the culmination of the early modern strain of republicanism. In their writings a number of ideas that had emerged and been developed earlier in the century were drawn together and put to practical use in the context of the Revolution. Moreover, the Cordeliers radicalised the English republican ideas – developing them beyond the intentions not only of the eighteenth-century commonwealthmen but also of their seventeenth-century predecessors. In particular, by combining Rousseauian and seventeenth-century English republican ideas they reconnected republicanism with anti-monarchism; they cut the commonwealth emphasis on mixed and balanced government – favouring instead the clear separation of legislative and executive power; and they applied what had originally been rather elitist and aristocratic ideas in the service of democracy.

Moreover, in the politics of the Revolution (and especially in the relations between the Cordeliers, the Brissotins and the Jacobins) we see the playing out of the conflict between the various versions of republicanism that had been developed during the course of the eighteenth century. The early modern republicanism of the Cordeliers was developed alongside, and set against, both the modern republicanism of the Brissotins and the ancient-inspired republicanism of the Jacobins.

Notes

1. This chapter builds on arguments that were first developed in my book *French Revolutionaries and English Republicans: The Cordeliers Club, 1790–1794* (Woodbridge: Boydell and Brewer for the Royal Historical Society, 2005). A more detailed account of the political theory of the Cordeliers can be found there.
2. For more detail on the origins of the Cordeliers Club, and its relationship to the Cordeliers District, see ibid., esp. pp. 15–32.
3. It is interesting to note the striking similarity between the official title of the Cordeliers Club and that of the Wilkite Society of the Supporters of the Bill of Rights.
4. J. J. Rousseau, *The Social Contract and Other Later Political Writings*, ed. V. Gourevitch (Cambridge: Cambridge University Press, 1997), p. 110.
5. Ibid., p. 114.
6. For the 'modern' influences on Rousseau see R. Tuck, *The Rights of War and Peace: Political Thought and the International Order From Grotius to Kant* (Oxford: Oxford University Press, 1999), pp. 197–207; P. Riley, 'Rousseau, Fénelon, and the Quarrel between the Ancients and the Moderns', in P. Riley (ed.), *The Cambridge Companion to Rousseau* (Cambridge: Cambridge University Press, 2001), pp. 78–93; and M. Sonenscher, *Before the Deluge: Public Debt, Inequality*

and *The Intellectual Origins of the French Revolution* (Princeton and Oxford: Princeton University Press, 2007), especially pp. 222–53.
7. J. J. Rousseau, *Considerations on the Government of Poland*, in *The Social Contract and Other Later Political Writings* (Cambridge: Cambridge University Press, 1997), pp. 209 and 211.
8. Ibid., p. 201. Interestingly, on p. 204 he used the Wilkes affair as an example of the effects of corruption.
9. Ibid., p. 201.
10. See for example R. Girardin, *Discours de René Girardin sur la nécessité de la ratification de la loi, par la volonté générale* (Paris, [1791]).
11. See for example *Révolutions de France et de Brabant*, ed. C. Desmoulins (Paris, 1789–91), VII, p. 109.
12. Girardin, *Discours de René Girardin*; P. F. Robert, *Républicanisme adapté à la France* (Paris, 1790). Robert's work was reprinted in the aftermath of Louis XVI's flight to Varennes as *Avantages de la fuite de Louis XVI, et nécessité d'un nouveau gouvernement* (Paris, 1791). See also his pamphlet *Le Droit de faire la paix et la guerre appartient incontestablement à la nation* (Paris, 1790). The popular ratification of laws was also defended by other Cordeliers including Desmoulins and Louis de La Vicomterie, and endorsed by the Club as a whole. See *Le Patriot français: journal libre, impartial et national*, ed. J. P. Brissot (Frankfurt-am-Main, 1989), no. 586, p. 285; L. de La Vicomterie de Saint-Samson, *Les Droits du Peuple sur l'assemblée nationale* (Paris, 1791) and L. de La Vicomterie de Saint-Samson, *République sans impôt* (Paris, 1792). For the official endorsement of the idea by the Club as a whole see: Girardin, *Discours de Réné Girardin*, p. 26 and *Journal du club des Cordeliers*, ed. A. F. Momoro (Paris, 1791), p 87.
13. M. Nedham, *De La Souveraineté du peuple, et de l'excellence d'un état libre*, trans. T. Mandar (Paris, 1790).
14. For more detail on this see Hammersley, *French Revolutionaries and English Republicans*, pp. 66–72.
15. Nedham, *De La Souveraineté du peuple*, I, pp. 44–5.
16. *Journal du Club des Cordeliers*, ed. Momoro, p. 34.
17. *Moniteur universel: réimpression de l'ancien Moniteur; seule histoire authentique et inaltéré de la Révolution française; depuis la réunion des états-généraux jusqu'au consulat (mai 1789–novembre 1799)* (Paris: Plon Frères, 1847–79), IV, p. 335.
18. See for example T. Mandar, *Des Insurrections: ouvrage philosophique et politique sur les rapports des insurrections avec la prospérité des empires* (Paris, 1793), p. 211n and pp. 233–6.
19. Ibid., pp. 222–3.
20. *Calypso, ou les Babillards*, ed. J. J. Rutledge (Paris, 1784–85), III, pp. 217–25 and 313–59; J. J. Rutledge, *Éloge de Montesquieu* (Paris, 1786).
21. This was a more sophisticated development of Nedham's notion of frequent elections and the regular replacement of representatives.
22. J. Harrington, *A System of Politics*, in *The Commonwealth of Oceana and A System of Politics*, ed. J. G. A. Pocock (Cambridge: Cambridge University Press, 1992), pp. 279–80.
23. *Le Creuset: ouvrage politique et critique*, ed. J. J. Rutledge (Paris, 1791), I, pp. 293–4 (No. XV, 21 February 1791).
24. Ibid., I, p. 66 (No. IV, 13 January 1791).
25. Ibid., I, pp. 14–15 and 147 (No. I, 3 January 1791 and No. VIII, 1 February 1791).
26. Ibid., I, pp. 14–15 (No. I, 3 January 1791).
27. M. R. C. B. [J. J. Rutledge], *Essais politiques sur l'état actuel de quelques puissances* (London [Geneva], 1777).
28. J. A. Ferrières, *Plan d'un nouveau genre de banque nationale et territoriale* (Paris, 1789). For Rutledge's references to this plan see *Le Creuset*, ed. Rutledge, I, pp. 318–20, 403; II, p. 456 (No. XVI, 24 February 1791; No. XXI, 14 March 1791 and No. XXXXIX, 20 June 1791); [J. J. Rutledge], *Rappel des assignats à leur véritable origine: ou démonstration d'un plagiat dangereux du premier ministre et comité des finances* (Paris, 1790) and [J. J. Rutledge], *Sommaire d'une discussion importante (relative au plan de banque territoriale du modeste M. de Ferrières)* ([Paris], 1790).

29 *Le Creuset*, ed. Rutledge, I, pp. 442–3. (No. XXIII, 21 March 1791).
30 Ibid., I, pp. 416–22, 441–55 and 465–70. (No. XXI, 14 March 1791, No. XXIII, 21 March 1791 and No. XXIV, 24 March 1791).
31 Toland's 1700 edition of Harrington's *Political Works* had included an annotated plan of the Venetian ballot in action, which he had entitled 'The manner and life of the ballot': J. Harrington, *The Oceana of James Harrington, and his other works*, ed. J. Toland (London, 1700). Rutledge included the same plan in *Le Creuset*, under the title 'Assemblée de la république de Venise'. In fact, Rutledge's version is a fainter mirror image of Toland's earlier version, suggesting that he had used it to produce his copy.
32 *Le Creuset*, ed. Rutledge, I, p. 108 (No. VI, 20 January 1791). Harrington's original had read, [A body of people] not led by the religion of the government, is at an inquiet and an uncomfortable loss in itself'. Harrington, *A System of Politics*, in *The Commonwealth of Oceana*, ed. Pocock, p. 274.
33 [J. J. Rutledge], *Idées sur l'espèce de gouvernement populaire qui pourrait convenir à un pays de l'étendue et de la population présumée de la France* (Paris, 1792). Eighty-four copies of the pamphlet were sent to the former mayor of Paris Jérôme Pétion, who was instructed to present one copy to the National Convention and to distribute the others to the departments of the nation. For more detail on this pamphlet see Hammersley, *French Revolutionaries and English Republicans*, pp. 116–35, and *A French Draft Constitution of 1792 Modelled on James Harrington's Oceana*, ed. S. B. Liljegren (Lund: C.W. K. Gleerup, 1932).
34 Rutledge and Marat wrote to each other's newspapers and defended each other there.
35 On the commonwealth character of *The Chains of Slavery*, see Chapter 9 above. It is interesting to note that Marat actually prefigured Cordeliers proposals in that work by placing particular emphasis on the need for vigilance among the population and by calling for binding mandates as well as short terms of office. J. P. Marat, *Les Chaînes de l'esclavage 1793 – The chains of slavery 1774*, ed. C. Goëtz and J. de Cock (Brussels: Pôle Nord, 1995), p. 4630.
36 Owing to the destruction of the records relating to the Cordeliers Club, during the Paris Commune, no official membership list has survived. However, George Robertson constructed his own list on the basis of the sources that are available and Marat's name is included on that list. G. M. Robertson, 'The Society of the Cordeliers and the French Revolution, 1790–1794' (University of Wisconsin PhD Thesis, 1972), Appendix A. See also J. De Cock, *Les Cordeliers dans la Révolution française*, Vol. 1, *Linéaments. Le Lieu. Le District. Le Club* (Lyon: Fantasques éditions, 2001).
37 *Pièces justificatives: exposé de la conduite et des motifs du district des Cordeliers concernant le décret de prise de corps prononcé par le Châtelet contre le sieur Marat, le 8 octobre 1789 et mis à execution le 22 janvier 1790* (Paris, [1790]). For more detail on the Marat Affair see Hammersley, *French Revolutionaries and English Republicans*, pp. 19–20.
38 De Cock, *Les Cordeliers dans la Révolution française*, p. 38.
39 Letters by Rutledge appeared in *Révolutions de France et de Brabant*, and in the autumn of 1789 Desmoulins took over Rutledge's role in defending the bakers of Paris. See C. Desmoulins, *Réplique aux deux mémoires des sieurs Leleu* (Paris, 1789), pp. 12–3. Marat and Desmoulins were also close friends, at least until they fell out over Marat's placard *C'en est fait de nous*.
40 *Révolutions de France et de Brabant*, ed. C. Desmoulins (Paris, 1789–91), VI, p. 612 (No. 78). Interestingly, Desmoulins went on, as Marat had done in his 'Address to the Electors of Great Britain', to stress the importance of making good choices at elections. Ibid., pp. 615–16.
41 *Le Vieux Cordelier*, ed. C. Desmoulins, ed. H. Calvet (Paris, 1936), pp. 237–8. I have used the Calvet edition here because it (unlike the 1825 edition) includes the passage in square brackets.
42 'Now, what is the fundamental principle of democratic or popular government, that is to say, the essential spring which sustains it and which makes it act? It is virtue; I speak of public virtue which made many marvels in Greece and in Rome, and which must produce even more surprising goods in republican France, of this virtue which is nothing but the love of the *patrie* and of its laws.' M. Robespierre, 'Sur les principes de morale politique', in *Oeuvres de Maximilien*

Robespierre, VI–X: Discours, ed. M. Bouloiseau and A. Soboul (Paris, 1950–67), X, p. 353.
43 *Le Vieux Cordelier*, ed. Desmoulins, ed. Calvet, p. 70.
44 On the Cordeliers and democracy see Hammersley, *French Revolutionaries and English Republicans*, especially pp. 45–50.
45 R. Hammersley, 'English Republicanism in Revolutionary France: The Case of the Cordeliers Club', *Journal of British Studies* 43 (2004), pp. 464–81.
46 *Le Creuset*, ed. Rutledge, I, pp. 416–7 (No. XXI, 14 March 1791).

Conclusion

I began this book with a quotation from the marquis d'Argenson's journal, which made clear that republican ideas were already circulating in France by the middle of the eighteenth century, long before the outbreak of the American Revolution or the publication of Rousseau's *The Social Contract*.[1] The immediate source of those ideas was not the models or works of antiquity, but rather those of the English republican tradition. My central argument has been that this strand of early modern republicanism played a significant role in the emergence and domestication of republican ideas in eighteenth-century France, opening the way for and shaping the Revolution.

The French figures considered in earlier chapters not only drew directly on the works and ideas of the English republican tradition, but were also grappling with the same problems, and often adopted similar solutions, to those of their British counterparts. While they were by no means homogeneous in their ideas, it is possible to discern a pattern in the uses made of English republican ideas in France during the course of the eighteenth century.

The Huguenots played a crucial role in bringing English republican works to the attention of a francophone audience through their translations and reviews. Like their Real Whig friends and associates, they believed liberty to be *the* central political value. Many of them also shared the distinctive religious position of their British counterparts. However, the Huguenots presented French-speakers with a relatively radical conception of English republicanism, one that emphasised resistance and opposition over constitution-building. The features that particularly appealed to them in English republican writings were the hostility to tyranny and arbitrary government and the link drawn between political and religious tyranny. Moreover, some Huguenots as residents of the Dutch Republic continued to endorse the anti-monarchical elements of the seventeenth-century tradition.

Among those writers I have discussed who were based in France itself during the first half of the eighteenth century, anti-monarchical republicanism –

where it retained any appeal at all – was an ideal to be admired rather than a model to be followed. In their more pragmatic attempts to reform French absolutism they were closer to the eighteenth-century British commonwealthmen than to the latter's seventeenth-century predecessors. The influence of Bolingbroke – a British commonwealthman who lived for a considerable time in France – was crucial here. Through his links with leading French figures, and via the French translations of his works, Bolingbroke introduced another layer of English republican thought into France. This echoed the Huguenot emphasis on liberty and shared their distinctive religious position, but it was focused more on reform than on resistance; sought to apply republican ideas within a monarchical framework; and laid much more emphasis on the need to take account of the passions and of self-interest when constructing a viable political system. Consequently, this group of French thinkers echoed the Real Whigs in making use of ancient constitutionalism – and in particular the version of French history presented by that sixteenth-century Huguenot resistance theorist François Hotman – to help them devise and justify mixed systems of government that might prove workable in contemporary terms. Not surprisingly, they also interwove the ideas of the Huguenots with those of Bolingbroke. On the one hand, as subjects of the French monarchy they continued to voice Huguenot concerns about tyranny and arbitrary government. On the other hand, as associates of Bolingbroke they were also among the first in France to explore the threat posed by corruption, and like him they placed particular emphasis on the dangers that accompanied the emergence of new financial systems and the associated increase in wealth and luxury.[2] Within this group, Mably holds a central place. While he viewed ancient republicanism as a valued ideal, when it came to the reform of contemporary society he was a committed commonwealthman. Not only did he offer his French audience a comprehensive analysis of the British constitution in commonwealth terms, he also set out a commonwealth reform package for France.

The drawing of parallels between Britain and France became even more common during the second half of the eighteenth century. In France, as in Britain and America, concerns about both tyranny and corruption were revived and extended in light of the events of the 1760s and 1770s. The terminology was brought up to date, however, by the replacement of the outdated word 'tyranny' with Montesquieu's preferred term 'despotism', and by the application of this not just to the monarch but also to his ministers. In France, as in Britain, ministerial despotism was believed to pose as great a threat to liberty as domination by an individual monarch. The works produced on both sides of the Channel during this period also developed a move already made by Mably: a gradual but noticeable shift away from the aristocratic tone of earlier works. Though his own position was complex and ambiguous, Wilkes seems to have played an important role during this period as a bridge between republican theories and political practice, and also between Britain and France. Not only did many of his associates, on both sides of the Channel, become interested in English republican ideas (and in many cases were actually involved in publishing and translating central works from that tradition), but a number of them also appear to have identified with and learnt from Wilkes's own particular method of political activism. While these similarities are undoubtedly important, it is also necessary to acknowledge the differences. In the case of the three francophone associates of Wilkes who were discussed in Part III (d'Eon, d'Holbach and Marat), we find contrasting versions of early modern republicanism. While all three figures shared a preoccupation with civil and religious liberty, a desire to incorporate republican institutions within a monarchical framework and a preference for mixed government, d'Eon's concern with Christian virtue sets him in sharp contrast to both d'Holbach – who took the anticlericalism of the Real Whigs to its logical atheistic conclusion – and Marat – according to whom all human behaviour (even that which appeared virtuous) was unavoidably and intrinsically self-interested.

With the outbreak of the Revolution, the various layers of English republican thought that had been introduced into France during the course of the century suddenly took on a new significance and relevance. In this context, the real value of the English models and ideas was that they provided a kind of road map for the French revolutionaries, one that offered practical solutions to the problems that they faced. As in the 1760s and 1770s, it is striking how broadly these ideas appealed. At one end of the spectrum they were drawn upon by those who wished to implement a British-style constitutional monarchy in France, while at the other extreme they were employed in support of a highly democratic version of French republicanism. Nevertheless, there were important shared concerns. In the first place, all the figures discussed in Part IV were intent upon establishing a regime in which liberty held a central place – and they all acknowledged that this required at least some degree of popular participation in the political system. Secondly, they were particularly exercised by the question of how popular participation might be made workable and meaningful in the context of a large, modern nation state. Since the English republicans of the seventeenth and eighteenth centuries had grappled with this problem themselves, they were ideally placed to offer solutions to the French. The solutions that appealed to the figures discussed here included: freedom of speech, publishing and thought; the establishment of a network of representative assemblies that would integrate local and national systems of government; and the adoption of constitutional mechanisms, such as the rotation of office and the division of political functions, in order to control and direct the (inevitably) self-interested behaviour of individual political agents at all levels of the system. Clearly, this version of revolutionary republicanism was distinctive from (and at several points during the 1790s in direct opposition to) both the modern commercial model of the Girondins and the ancient-inspired variant favoured by the Jacobins. Moreover, members of the Cordeliers Club were particularly important in that they marked the culmination of early modern republicanism, taking the ideas in a sharply democratic direction.

Thus it is clear that from the early eighteenth century, when the Huguenots first introduced English republican works into the francophone world, through to the Revolution, when ideas taken from those works were put into practice and used to legitimise and shape the new regime, this English-inspired strain of republicanism exercised a considerable influence in France. In large part its appeal was that it offered a more practical alternative to ancient republicanism. Unlike their ancient counterparts, English republicans had addressed the crucial question of how republican forms, institutions and mechanisms might be adapted so as to make them applicable in the large nation states of the modern world. In addition, the English ideas were more flexible than those of the ancients. They could be applied in a strongly monarchical and aristocratic context, as in the writings of Bolingbroke and Boulainvilliers, but they proved equally effective in support of the staunchly anti-monarchical and democratic ideas of the Cordeliers. Similarly, they could be associated not only with the neo-Stoic moral philosophy that had traditionally been allied to republican political thought, but also with the neo-Epicurean ideas that became more influential during the course of the eighteenth century.

This account of the role played by early modern republicanism in eighteenth-century France has implications for our understanding of the republican tradition more generally. In the first place, it complicates existing conceptions of the process by which republican ideas emerged and developed in eighteenth-century France. In particular, it challenges any simple binary division into classical and modern republicanism, demonstrating that there were at least three distinct strands of republican thought being developed in France during the course of the eighteenth century. Moreover, while it is possible to identify three versions of revolutionary republicanism that correspond to these strands, many revolutionaries mixed elements from two or more of them. Thus a proper understanding of eighteenth-century French republicanism, including its revolutionary variants, requires a comprehensive knowledge of each of the three forms of republican thought on which they drew.

Secondly, this account ought to lead scholars to question the validity of the conventional tendency to study republicanism solely within national contexts. It is undoubtedly useful to build up a picture of English, Dutch, American or French republicanism, and to focus on the features that distinguished them from each other. However, when adopted too single-mindedly, this approach tends to result in significant blind spots. On the one hand, it has encouraged the homogenisation of those national traditions and the downplaying of the important differences and disagreements among republicans operating within each national context. On the other hand, it has meant that the similarities between republican thought in different countries have been neglected. There has also been a tendency to emphasise diachronic influences at the expense of equally important synchronic ones. In the French case the national focus has led to the neglect of an entire strand of republicanism which played a crucial role in the development of French political thought during the course of the eighteenth century. The national focus has also meant that the cosmopolitanism of republicans, and the importance of their transnational connections, have been under appreciated. Though my focus here has been on the transfer of ideas between Britain and France, the nationalities represented among the key figures discussed include English, Irish, Scottish, Welsh, Dutch, French, German and Swiss. Moreover, Dutch, Polish and American contexts have also had some role to play. Republicanism was a pan-European, indeed a pan-Occidental, phenomenon in the seventeenth and eighteenth centuries. If we are to understand it properly then we must approach it in this way.

Finally, this study has implications for the way in which republicanism is understood and defined. The emphasis has conventionally been on the singular rather than the plural. Even where national differences are given emphasis, there is a tendency to write of 'Republicanism' as 'A Shared European Heritage' rather than recognising the variety of forms it has taken.[3] One effect of this has been the tendency to define 'republicanism' in terms of a set of fixed criteria – among which anti-monarchism has often been taken to be axiomatic.[4] While this approach has the advantage of simplicity and neatness, it forces us to exclude from the republican canon several figures who, in all other respects, clearly belong to it. It has also led to much debate about individuals who appear to have adopted an anti-monarchical position in certain works, or at certain points in their career, while embracing monarchy in other works, or at other times. Ultimately, this approach fails to take account of the practical contexts and how these can differ in significant ways. It implies that, for the most part, republicans could only have existed in certain times and places – those in which there was some value in expressing anti-monarchical sentiments and in which doing so in public would not result in arrest and imprisonment or execution for treason. It also excludes the numerous examples of attempts to blend republican and monarchical ideas from the story of republicanism. Yet, as the French case explored here demonstrates, there was much scope for switching from anti-monarchical to monarchical republicanism and back again as the circumstances allowed or dictated.

One solution to this problem has been to suggest that it is not a commitment to anti-monarchism that is *the* fundamental criterion which distinguishes republicans from non-republicans, but rather adherence to a particular moral philosophy based on reason and virtue. This approach has been particularly common among those scholars who have worked on English republicanism in the period before the mid-seventeenth century.[5] However, this is no more satisfactory as a way of defining 'republicanism' than the alternative. It too would involve excluding the commonwealthmen (along with Harrington and Machiavelli) from the republican canon.

Yet to go the other way and suggest that anti-monarchism and a moral philosophy based on reason and virtue have nothing to do with the republican tradition seems equally problematic. Given this, I suggest that the problem lies less in the criteria themselves than in the assumption that republicanism can be defined on the basis of a specific set of essential criteria at all. Republicanism should be treated not as a fixed tradition, but rather as analogous to a living language, containing distinct varieties. As such, it was shaped and adapted by those who drew on it in order to fit their circumstances and to deal with the particular problems they were facing at particular times and in particular places. Like many other words therefore, the meaning of 'republicanism' can perhaps best be understood via Ludwig Wittgenstein's notion of family resemblances.[6] Wittgenstein challenged the conventional view that all terms do, or should, connote a set of qualities common to all the things they denote. Rather he suggested that their meaning is better understood in terms of complex patterns of resemblance. As he explained, with reference to his concept of 'language games':

> Instead of producing something common to all that we call language, I am saying that these phenomena have no one thing in common which makes us use the same word for all, – but that they are *related* to one another in many different ways. And it is because of this relationship, or these relationships, that we call them all 'language'.[7]

By adopting this approach to the definition of 'republicanism' it would be possible to think in terms of each variant or form of republicanism sharing some things in common with some others, without requiring them all to share a single set of core, defining features.

The seventeenth and eighteenth centuries constitute a remarkably fertile, but also a particularly complex, period in political and intellectual history. Many key political concepts of the modern world were transformed into a form that we recognise today at this time. This study has focused on one such concept – republicanism – and has been designed to convey the complex and multidimensional evolution of the set of ideas and practices to which it refers, in one corner of Europe, during this period. In doing so it has demonstrated some of the relationships that linked the English Revolution of the mid-seventeenth century to the Enlightenment and also to the French Revolution. It has also emphasised the profound and essential connections between the republic of letters and the re-emergence of republican notions of governance as ideals and forms of practice.

Notes

1. R. L., Voyer de Paulmy, marquis d'Argenson, *Journal et mémoires du marquis d'Argenson*, ed. E. J. B. Rathery (Paris: Mme Veuve Jules Renouard, 1856–67), VI, pp. 464 and 320. See the Introduction above.
2. Of course, the South Sea Bubble had a French parallel in the Mississippi schemes of France's Scottish Finance Minister John Law.
3. M. van Gelderen and Q. Skinner (eds), *Republicanism: A Shared European Heritage*. Vol. 1: *Republicanism and Constitutionalism in Early Modern Europe*. Vol. 2: *The Values of Republicanism in Early Modern Europe* (Cambridge: Cambridge University Press, 2002).
4. Q. Skinner, *Liberty Before Liberalism* (Cambridge: Cambridge University Press, 1998). See also B. Worden, 'Republicanism, Regicide and Republic: The English Experience', in van Gelderen and Skinner (eds), *Republicanism*, I, pp. 307–27.
5. M. Peltonen, *Classical Humanism and English Republicanism, 1570–1640* (Cambridge: Cambridge University Press, 1995); D. Norbrook, *Writing the English Republic: Poetry, Rhetoric and Politics, 1627–1660* (Cambridge: Cambridge University Press, 1999); J. Richards, *Rhetoric and Courtliness in Early Modern Literature* (Cambridge: Cambridge University Press, 2003). Jonathan Scott also offers a useful account of the importance of this element within republican thought, while acknowledging that it was not embraced by all seventeenth-century republicans: J. Scott, *Commonwealth Principles: Republican Writing of the English Revolution* (Cambridge: Cambridge University Press, 2004).
6. On this aspect of Wittgenstein's thought see H. Khatchadourian, 'Common Names and "Family Resemblances"', in G. Pitcher (ed.), *Wittgenstein: The Philosophical Investigations* (London and Melbourne: Macmillan, 1968), pp. 205–30; G. Lackoff, *Women, Fire and Dangerous Things* (Chicago: University of Chicago Press, 1987), Chapter 2; and R. J. Fogelin, 'Wittgenstein's critique of philosophy', in H. Sluga and D. G. Stern (eds), *The Cambridge Companion to Wittgenstein* (Cambridge: Cambridge University Press, 1996), pp. 50–8.
7. L. Wittgenstein, *Philosophical Investigations*, trans. G. E. M. Anscombe (Oxford: Basil Blackwell, 1978), p. 31e.

Appendix
French translations and reissues of English republican works, 1652–1801

1652	Milton, *Eikonoklastes, ou réponse au livre intitulé Eikon Basilike, ou le portrait de sa sacrée majesté durant sa solitude et ses souffrances* (London)
1694	Molesworth, *État présent de Danemarc par lequel on voit le fort & le foible de cette couronne* (London)
1694	Molesworth, *Mémoires de M. Molesworth, envoyé de Sa Majesté Britannique à la cour de Danemarc l'an 1692* (Nancy)
1695	Molesworth, *Mémoires de M. Molesworth, envoyé de Sa Majesté Britannique à la cour de Danemarc l'an 1692* (Nancy)
1695	Molesworth, *État du royaume de Danemark, tel qu'il étoit en 1692* (Amsterdam)
1695	Molesworth, *Extrait d'un livre intitulé 'État du royaume de Dannemarck, tel qu'il étoit en 1692'* (Amsterdam) [translation of chapters 7 and 8]
1697	Molesworth, *Mémoires de Mr. Molesworth, dans lesquels on voit l'état du royaume de Danemark, tel qu'il étoit en l'an 1692* (Paris)
1699	Ludlow, *Mémoires d'Edmond Ludlow*, trans. P. Marret, vols 1 and 2 (Amsterdam)
1702	Sidney, *Discours sur le gouvernement*, trans. P. A. Samson (The Hague)
1705	Molesworth, *Mémoires de Mr. Molesworth, dans lesquels on voit l'état du royaume de Danemark, tel qu'il étoit en l'an 1692* (Paris)
1707	Ludlow, *Nouveaux Mémoires d'Edmond Ludlow*, trans. P. Marret, vol. 3 (Amsterdam)
1709	Shaftesbury, *Lettre sur l'enthousiasme*, trans. P. A. Samson (The Hague)
1714	Molesworth, *État présent du royaume de Danemarc, par lequel on voit le fort et le faible de cette couronne* (Paris)
1715	Molesworth, *État présent du royaume de Danemarc, par lequel on voit le fort et le faible de cette couronne* (Paris)
1732	Molesworth, *État présent de Danemarc* (Amsterdam)
1739	Bolingbroke, *Essai d'une traduction des dissertations sur les partis qui divisent l'Angleterre*, trans. E. de Silhouette (London)
1742	Gordon, *Discours historiques, critiques et politiques sur Tacite*, trans. P. Daudé (Amsterdam)
1745	Shaftesbury, *Principes de la philosophie morale; ou Essai de M. S*** sur le mérite et la vertu*, trans. D. Diderot (Amsterdam)

1749	Gordon, *Discours historiques, critiques et politiques sur Tacite*, trans. P. Daudé (Amsterdam)
1750	Bolingbroke, *Lettres sur l'esprit de patriotisme, sur l'idée d'un roy patriote et sur l'état des parties qui divisoient l'Angleterre*, trans. C. de Thiard comte de Bissy (London)
1751	Gordon, *Discours historiques, critiques et politiques sur Tacite*, trans. P. Daudé (Amsterdam)
1751	Shaftesbury, *Philosophie morale réduite à ses principes, ou Essai de M. S*** sur le mérite et la vertu* (Venice)
1752	Bolingbroke, *Lettres sur l'histoire*, trans. J. Barbeu du Bourg (Paris)
1754	Bolingbroke, *Mémoires secrets de mylord Bolingbroke sur les affaires d'Angleterre*, trans. J. L. Favier (London) [translation of *Letter to Sir William Windham*]
1754	Bolingbroke, *Testament politique de milord Bolingbroke, ou considérations sur l'état présent de la Grande-Bretagne* (London) [translation of *Some Reflections on the present state of the nation*)
1754	Bolingbroke, *Réflexions politiques sur l'état présent de l'Angleterre* (Amsterdam) [translation of *Some Reflections on the present state of the nation*, bound in with a translation of Hume's political discourses]
1755	Locke, *Du Gouvernement civil, où l'on traite de l'origine, des fondemens, de la nature, du pouvoir et des fins des sociétés politiques*, trans. J. Rousset de Missy (Amsterdam) [translation of the *Second Treatise of Government*]
1755	Sidney, *Discours sur le gouvernement*, trans. P. A. Samson (The Hague)
1759	Gordon, *Discours historiques et politiques sur Salluste*, trans. P. Daudé (Geneva)
1762	Gordon, *Discours historiques et politiques sur Salluste*, trans. P. Daudé (Geneva)
1767	Trenchard and Gordon, *De L'Esprit du clergé*, trans. d'Holbach (London [Amsterdam]) [translation of *The Independent Whig*, vols 1 and 2]
1767	Gordon, *De L'Imposture sacerdotale*, trans. d'Holbach (London [Amsterdam]) [includes a translation of *Apology for the danger of the Church* and of *The Creed of an Independent Whig*]
1768	Trenchard, *La Contagion sacrée, ou histoire naturelle de superstition*, trans. d'Holbach (London [Amsterdam]) [claims to be a translation of *The Natural History of Superstition*]
1768	Toland, *Lettres philosophiques*, trans. d'Holbach (London [Amsterdam]) [translation of *Letters to Serena*]
1769	Trenchard and Gordon, *De La Tolérance*, trans. d'Holbach (London [Amsterdam]) [includes a translation of several issues of *The Independent Whig*, vols 3 and 4]
1771	Bolingbroke, *Pensées de Milord Bolingbroke, sur différens sujets d'histoires, de philosophie, de morale* (Amsterdam)
1774	Nedham, *De L'Excellence d'un état libre*, trans. d'Eon de Beaumont in his *Les Loisirs du chevalier d'Eon de Beaumont* (Amsterdam)
1775	Marat, *De L'Homme, ou des principes et des lois de l'influence de l'âme sur le corps, et du corps sur l'âme* (Amsterdam)

1784	Bolingbroke, *Testament politique de Milord Bolingbroke, écrit par lui même, ou considerations sur l'état présent de la Grande-Bretagne* (London)
1788	Milton, *Sur La Liberté de la presse*, trans. Mirabeau (London) [translation of *Areopagitica*]
1789	Milton, *Théorie de la royauté après la doctrine de Milton*, trans. J. B. Salaville on behalf of Mirabeau (Paris) [translation of *Pro Populo Anglicano Defensio*]
1789	Molesworth, *Extrait d'un livre intitulé 'État du royaume de Dannemarck, tel qu'il étoit en 1692'* (Amsterdam) [translation of chapters 7 and 8]
1790	Bolingbroke, *Des Devoirs d'un roi patriote, et portrait des ministres de tous les temps* (Paris)
1790	Nedham, *De La Souveraineté du peuple, et de l'excellence d'un état libre*, trans. T. Mandar (Paris)
1790	Price, *Discours sur l'amour de la patrie, prononcé, le 4 novembre 1789*, trans. L. F. Guinement de Keralio (Paris)
1791	Milton, *Théorie de la royauté après la doctrine de Milton*, trans. J. B. Salaville on behalf of Mirabeau (Paris)
1791	Harrington, *Le Creuset: ouvrage politique et critique*, trans. J. J. Rutledge (Paris) [includes lengthy extracts from *A System of Politics*]
1791–92	Macaulay, *Histoire d'Angleterre, depuis l'avènement de Jacques Ier jusqu'à la révolution*, trans. Mirabeau and Guiraudet (Paris)
1792	Milton, *Défense du peuple anglais, sur le jugement et la condamnation de Charles premier, roi d'Angleterre* (Valence)
1793	Marat, *Les Chaînes de l'esclavage* (Paris)
1794	Gordon, *Discours historiques, critiques et politiques de Thomas Gordon sur Tacite et sur Salluste*, new edition, but based on the translation by Daudé (Paris)
1794	Sidney, *Discours sur le gouvernment ... nouvelle édition conforme à celle de 1702*, trans. P. A. Samson (Paris)
1795	Harrington, *Oeuvres politiques de Jacques Harrington*, trans. P. F. Henry (Paris)
1795	Harrington, *Aphorismes politiques*, trans. P. F. Aubin (Paris)
1795–99	Trenchard and Gordon, *Dix-septième lettre de Caton*, trans. J. L. Chalmel (Paris)
1801	Moyle, *Essai sur le gouvernement de Rome*, trans. B. Barère (Paris)

Bibliography

N.B. Square brackets indicate the author of a work that was first published anonymously

Primary sources

Manuscript sources

GREAT BRITAIN

British Library, London (BL)

Add. MSS 4281–9 Desmaizeaux Papers
Add. MSS 30865–96 Correspondence and papers of John Wilkes, MP
Add. MS. 32750 f. 527 Letter from P. A. Samson to H. Walpole (1727)
Add. MS. 36128 f. 76 Peter Augustus Samson, Denization

Huguenot Library, London (HL)

A1/1 Minutes of the Court's Quarterly and Extra-Ordinary Meeting, 1718–1779
E2/12 Daudé, Pierre: original codicil, signed and sealed 8 September 1733, to his will of August 1733 and receipt for £200 bequest
M2/11/1–7 Papers concerning the Daudé bequest

John Rylands University Library, Manchester (JRL)

Christie Collection, 3. f. 38 English-language manuscript version of Toland's *Adeisidaemon* and *Origines Judaicae*

National Library of Scotland, Edinburgh (NLS)

3419, f. 40 Letter from viscount Bolingbroke to the abbé Alary, 1722

The National Archives, London (TNA)

PRO/30/24/20 Shaftesbury Papers, Letters between Anthony Ashley Cooper, third Earl of Shaftesbury and Benjamin Furly
Prob 11/766, ff. 66–7 Will of Peter Augustus Samson
Prob 11/656 Will of Pierre Daudé senior

Prob 11/809 Will of Pierre Daudé junior
SP78/184 Secretaries of State: State Papers Foreign, France, Arrangements for printing and publishing the 'Analyse'

Tyne and Wear Archives Service (TWAS)

GU/BR Guild Records: Bricklayers
GU/BU Guild Records: Butchers
GU/CW Guild Records: Cordwainers
GU/HMT Guild Records: House Carpenters

University of Leeds, Brotherton Library (ULBL)

Brotherton Collection, d'Eon papers

THE NETHERLANDS

Special Collections Department, Library of the University of Leiden (UoL)

March. Prosper Marchand Papers

THE UNITED STATES

The Pierpont Morgan Library (PML)

Gilder Lehrman Collection (GLC)
The Catharine Macaulay Graham Papers (1763–1830)

Newspapers/journals

Bibliothèque britannique, ou histoire des ouvrages des savans de la Grande-Bretagne (1733–47)
Bibliothèque raisonnée des ouvrages des savans de l'Europe (1728–53)
Calypso, ou les Babillards, ed. J. J. Rutledge (Paris, 1784–85)
The Craftsman, ed. Caleb d'Anvers [Bolingbroke et al.] (London: R. Francklin, 1731–37)
Le Creuset: ouvrage politique et critique, ed. J. J. Rutledge (Paris, 1791)
La Décade philosophique, littéraire et politique (1794–1807)
Gazetier cuirassé: ou anecdotes scandaleuses de la cour de France, ed. C. Théveneau de Morande (1772), pp. 16–20
Gentleman's Magazine
Histoire des ouvrages des savans, ed. H. Basnage de Beauval (1687–1709)
Journal britannique, ed. M. Maty (January/February 1750)
Journal du Club des Cordeliers, ed. A. F. Momoro (Paris, 1791)
London Magazine (1774)
Mercure national et révolutions de l'Europe: journal démocratique, ed. L. Keralio (Paris, 1791)
Moniteur universel: réimpression de l'ancien Moniteur; seule histoire authentique et inaltéré de la Révolution française; depuis la réunion des états-généraux jusqu'au consulat (mai 1789–novembre 1799) (Paris: Plon Frères, 1847–79)
Monthly Repository, 8, 9 and 10 (1813–15)
Monthly Review (1774)
Morning Post and Daily Advertiser, 9 February 1776

Newcastle Chronicle (1774)
Notes and Queries
Nouvelles de la république des lettres, ed. P. Bayle (March 1684)
Nouvelles de la république des lettres, ed. J. Bernard (1699–1710)
Le Patriot français: journal libre, impartial et national, ed. J. P. Brissot (Frankfurt-am-Main, 1989 [1789–93])
Public Advertiser (1774)
Révolutions de France et de Brabant, ed. C. Desmoulins (Paris, 1789–91)
Scot's Magazine (1774)
Le Vieux Cordelier, ed. C. Desmoulins (Paris, 1825 [1793–94])
Le Vieux Cordelier, ed. C. Desmoulins, ed. H. Calvet (Paris, 1936 [1793–94])
Westminster Magazine (May, 1773)

Printed primary sources

Adams, J., *Défense des constitutions américaines, ou la nécessité d'une balance dans les pouvoirs d'un gouvernement libre* (Paris: Buisson, 1792)

Akenside, M., *Pleasures of Imagination: A Poem in Three Books* (London, 1744)

Archives Parlementaires de 1787 à 1860, eds J. Madival and E. Laurent, 1st series (Paris, 1789–1914)

Argenson, R. L. de Voyer de Paulmy, marquis d', *Considérations sur le gouvernement ancien et présent de la France* (Amsterdam: Rey, 1764)

Argenson, R. L. de Voyer de Paulmy, marquis d', *Journal et mémoires du marquis d'Argenson*, ed. E. J. B. Rathery (Paris: Mme Veuve Jules Renouard, 1856–67)

Argenson, R. L. de Voyer de Paulmy, marquis d', *Mémoires et journal inédit du marquis d'Argenson* (Paris: P. Jannet, 1857–58)

[Aubert de Vitry, F. J. P.], *J. J. Rousseau à l'Assemblée Nationale* (Paris, 1789)

Autographes de Mariemont, ed. M. J. Durry (Paris, 1955–59)

Boissy d'Anglas, F. A., *Projet de constitution pour la République française, et discours préliminaire prononcé par Boissy-D'Anglas, au nom de la commission des onze, dans la séance du 5 Messidor, an III* (Niort: Élies, Year III [1795])

[Bolingbroke, Henry St John, 1st Viscount], *Remarks on the History of England* (London: R. Francklin, 1743)

Bolingbroke, H. St John, 1st Viscount, *Letters on the Study and Use of History* (London: A. Millar, 1752)

Bolingbroke, H. St John, 1st Viscount, *Reflections Concerning Innate Moral Principles* (London, Bladon, 1752)

Bolingbroke, H. St John, 1st Viscount, *Works of the Late Right Honourable Henry St John, Lord Viscount* Bolingbroke (London, 1809)

Bolingbroke, H. St John, 1st Viscount, *Political Writings*, ed. D. Armitage (Cambridge: Cambridge University Press, 1997)

Bolingbroke, H. St John, 1st Viscount, *Mémoires Secrets de Mylord Bolingbroke sur les affaires d'Angleterre*, trans. J. L. Favier (London, 1754)

Bolingbroke, H. St John, 1st Viscount, *Des Devoirs d'un roi patriote, et portrait des ministres de tous les temps* (Paris: Desenne, 1790)

Bolingbroke, H. St John, 1st Viscount, *Lettres historiques, politiques, philosophiques et particulières de Henri Saint-John, Lord Vicomte Bolingbroke, depuis 1710 jusqu'en 1736* …, ed. Grimoard (Paris: Dentu, 1808)

Boulainvilliers, H. comte de, *Histoire de l'ancien gouvernement de la France, avec XIV Lettres historiques sur les parlements où états généraux* (Amsterdam and The Hague, 1727)

Boulainvilliers, H. comte de, *An Historical Account of the Antient Parliaments of France, or States-General of the Kingdom. In Fourteen Letters*, ed. C. Forman (London: J. Brindley, 1739)

Boulainvilliers, H. comte de, *La Vie de Mahomed* (London [Amsterdam]: P. Humbert, 1730)

Boulay de la Meurthe, A. J. C. J., *Essai sur les causes qui, en 1649, amenèrent en Angleterre l'établissement de la république; sur celles qui devaient l'y consolider; sur celles qui l'y firent périr* (Paris: Baudouin, An VIII)

Boulay de la Meurthe, A. J. C. J., *Théorie constitutionnelle de Sieyès* (Paris, 1836)

Burke, E., *Select Works of Edmund Burke, Volume 3: Letters on a Regicide Peace* (Indianapolis: Liberty Fund, 1999)

[Carey, L., viscount Falkland and J. Colepeper], *His Majesties Answer to the Nineteen Propositions of Both Houses of Parliament* (London, 1642)

Chauffepié, J. G. de, *Nouveau Dictionnaire historique et critique pour servir de supplement ou de continuation au dictionnaire historique et critique de Mr. Pierre Bayle* (Amsterdam, 1750)

Cicero, *De Republica*, trans. C. Walker Keyes (Cambridge, MA and London: Harvard University Press and William Heinemann, 1977)

Collins, A., *A Discourse of Freethinking* (London, 1713)

Condorcet, J. A. N. Caritat, marquis de, *Esquisse d'un tableau historique des progrès de l'esprit humain* (Paris: Editions Sociales, 1971)

Constant, B., 'The Liberty of the Ancients Compared with that of the Moderns', in Constant, *Political Writings*, ed. B. Fontana (Cambridge: Cambridge University Press, 1988), pp. 309–28

Constitution du 22 Frimaire An VIII

Cooper, A. A., 3rd Earl of Shaftesbury, *A Letter Concerning Enthusiasm, to My Lord ****** (1708), in *Characteristicks of Men, Manners, Opinions, Times*, 4th edn (London, 1727), I, pp. 3–55

Cooper, A. A., 3rd Earl of Shaftesbury, *Lettre sur l'enthousiasme*, trans. P. A. Samson (The Hague: T. Johnson, 1709)

D'Alembert, J. et al. (eds), *Encyclopédie, ou dictionnaire raisonnée des sciences, arts et des métiers, par une société des gens de lettres* (Stuttgart, 1967)

D'Eon de Beaumont, *Les Loisirs du chevalier d'Eon de Beaumont ancien ministre plénipotentiaire de France, sur divers sujets importans d'administration, &c. pendant son séjour en Angleterre* (Amsterdam, 1774)

Desmoulins, C., *Réplique aux deux mémoires des sieurs Leleu* (Paris, 1789)

Diderot, D., *Principes de la philosophie morale; ou Essai de M. S*** sur le mérite et la vertu*, ed. J. Assézat and M. Tourneux. Accessed via gallica, http://gallica.bnf.fr/ on 17 December 2008

Diderot, D., *De la Suffisance de la religion naturelle*, ed. J. Assézat and M. Tourneux.

Accessed via gallica, http://gallica.bnf.fr/ on 17 December 2008
Dreghorn, John Maclaurin, Lord, *The Works of the Late John MacLaurin, Esq. of Dreghorn: One of the Senators of the College of Justice* (Edinburgh: Ruthven and Sons, 1798)
Dumont, E., *Souvenirs sur Mirabeau et sur les deux premières Assemblées Législatives*, ed. M. J. L. Duval (Paris, 1832)
Farington, J., *The Farington Diary*, ed. J. Grieg, 2nd edn, Volume I (London: Hutchinson, 1922)
Favier, J. L., *Conjectures raisonnées sur la situation de la France dans le système politique de l'Europe*, in *Politique des cabinets de l'Europe, sous les règnes de Louis XV et de Louis XVI* (Paris: Buisson, 1794)
Ferrières, J. A., *Plan d'un nouveau genre de banque nationale et territoriale* (Paris, 1789)
A French Draft Constitution of 1792 Modelled on James Harrington's Oceana, ed. S. B. Liljegren (Lund: C. W. K. Gleerup, 1932)
Girardin, R., *Discours de René Girardin sur la nécessité de la ratification de la loi, par la volonté générale* (Paris, [1791])
Gordon, T., *An Apology for the Danger of the Church* (London, 1719)
Gordon, T., *Priestianity: or a view of the disparity between the Apostles and the modern inferior clergy* (London, 1720)
Gordon, T., *The Creed of an Independent Whig* (London, 1720)
Gordon, T., *The Works of Tacitus With Political Discourses Upon That Author*, 3rd edn (London, 1753)
Gordon, T., *A Cordial for Low Spirits: Being a collection of curious tracts. By Thomas Gordon, Esq.*, ed. R. Baron (London: Wilkson and Fell, 1763)
Gordon, T., *Discours historiques, critiques et politiques sur Tacite, traduits de l'anglois de Mr Th. Gordon*, trans. P. Daudé (Amsterdam: François Changuion, 1751)
Gordon, T., *Discours historiques, critiques et politiques de Thomas Gordon sur Tacite et sur Salluste, traduits de l'anglois. Nouvelle édition, corrigée* (Paris: F. Buisson, l'An II de la république française une et indivisible [1794])
Harrington, J., *The Oceana of James Harrington, and his other works*, ed. J. Toland (London, 1700)
Harrington, J., *A Discourse Upon This Saying: The Spirit of the Nation is not yet to be trusted with Liberty; lest it introduce Monarchy, or invade the Liberty of Conscience*, in *The Oceana and Other Works of James Harrington*, ed. J. Toland (London, 1737), pp. 601–9.
Harrington, J., *The Commonwealth of Oceana and A System of Politics*, ed. J. G. A. Pocock (Cambridge: Cambridge University Press, 1992)
Harrington, J., *Oeuvres politiques de Jacques Harrington*, trans. P. F. Henry (Paris, An III [1795])
Harrington, J., *Aphorismes politiques*, trans. P. F. Aubin (Paris, 1795)
Histoire de la république d'Angleterre d'après les Mémoires d'Edmond Ludlow l'un des principaux chefs des républicains anglais: contenant la narration des faits qui ont précédé accompagné et suivi ces momens lucides de la nation anglaise (Paris, l'an II [1794])
Historical Manuscripts Commission, *Reports on the Manuscripts of the Marquess of Downshire, preserved at Easthampstead Park, Berks* (London: HMSO, 1924), Volume I: Papers of Sir William Trumbull, Part II.

Holbach, P. H. T., baron d', *Les Plaisirs de l'imagination: poème en trois chants, par M. Akenside*; traduit de l'anglais (Amsterdam and Paris: Arkstée et Merkus and Pissot, 1759)

[Holbach, P. H. T., baron d'], *De L'Esprit du clergé* (London [Amsterdam]: Marc Michel Rey, 1767)

[Holbach, P. H. T., baron d'], *De L'Imposture sacerdotale* (London [Amsterdam]: Marc Michel Rey, 1767)

[Holbach, P. H. T., baron d'], *La Contagion sacrée, ou histoire naturelle de la superstition* (London, [Amsterdam]: Marc Michel Rey, 1768)

[Holbach, P. H. T., baron d'], *Lettres philosophiques* (London [Amsterdam]: Marc Michel Rey, 1768)

[Holbach, P. H. T., baron d'], *De La Tolérance* (London [Amsterdam]: Marc Michel Rey, 1769)

[Holbach, P. H. T., baron d'], *La Politique naturelle, ou discours sur les vrais principes du gouvernement* (London [Amsterdam], 1773)

Holbach, P. H. T., baron d', *Catalogue des livres de la bibliothèque de feu M. le Baron d'Holbach* (Paris: De Bure, 1789)

Holbach, P. H. T., baron d', *Christianity unveiled; being an examination of the principles and effects of the Christian Religion* (New York, 1795)

Holbach, P. H. T., baron d', *The System of Nature: Volume One*, trans. H. D. Robinson, ed. M. Bush (Manchester: Clinamen Press, 1999)

Hollis, T., *Memoirs of Thomas Hollis*, ed. F. Blackburne (London, 1780)

Junius, F., *Letters of Junius*, ed. J. Cannon (Oxford: Oxford University Press, 1978)

Lassay, marquis de, *Relation du royaume des Féliciens, peuples qui habitent dans les terres australes; dans laquelle il est traité de leur origine, de leur religion, de leur gouvernement, de leurs moeurs, & de leurs coutumes*, in *Recueil de différentes choses, par M. le Marquis de Lassay* (Lausanne: Marc-Michel Bousquet, 1756)

Lettre de félicitation de milord Sidney aux parisiens et à la nation françoise: ou résurrection de milord Sidney. Second coup de griffe aux renards de toute couleur (Paris, 1789)

Levier, C., *Catalogus Librorum Bibliopoli Caroli Levier* (The Hague, 1735)

Locke, J., *Du Gouvernement civil, où l'on traite de l'origine, des fondemens, de la nature, du pouvoir et des fins des sociétés politiques par L.C.R.D.M.A.D.P*, [J. Rousset de Missy] (Amsterdam: J. Schreuder and P. Mortier, 1755)

Ludlow, E., *Memoirs of Edmund Ludlow Esq ...* (London, 1720–22)

Ludlow, E., *Memoirs of Edmund Ludlow ...* (London: A. Millar; D. Browne and J. Ward, 1751)

Ludlow, E., *Nouveaux Mémoires d'Edmond Ludlow ...*, ed. P. Marret (Amsterdam: P. Marret, 1707)

Mably, G. Bonnot de, *Observations sur les Grecs* (Geneva, 1749)

Mably, G. Bonnot de, *Principes de morale*, in *Collection complète des oeuvres de l'Abbé Mably* (Paris: Desbrière, L'An III de la République (1794–95)), X.

Mably, G. Bonnot de, *Du Cours et de la marche des passions dans la société*, in *Collection complète des oeuvres de l'abbé de Mably* (Paris: Desbrière, L'An III de la République (1794–95)), XV.

Mably, G. Bonnot de, *Entretiens de Phocion sur le rapport de la morale avec la politique* (Paris, 1797)

Mably, G. Bonnot de, *Des Droits et des devoirs du citoyen*, ed. J. L. Lecercle (Paris: Marcel Didier, 1972)

Mandar, T., *Des Insurrections: ouvrage philosophique et politique sur les rapports des insurrections avec la prospérité des empires* (Paris, 1793)

[Marat, J. P.], *An Essay on the Human Soul* (London, 1772)

[Marat, J. P.], *A Philosophical Essay on Man: Being an attempt to investigate the principles and laws of the reciprocal influence of the soul on the body* (London, 1773)

[Marat, J. P.], *The chains of slavery: a work wherein the clandestine and villainous attempts of princes to ruin liberty are pointed out, and the dreadful scenes of despotism disclosed. To which is prefixed an Address to the electors of Great Britain, in order to draw their timely attention to the choice of proper representatives in the next Parliament* (London, 1774)

Marat, J. P., *An Essay on Gleets: wherein the defects of the actual method of treating those complaints of the uretha are pointed out, and an effectual way of curing them indicated* (London, 1775)

Marat, J. P., *De L'Homme, ou des principes et des lois de l'influence de l'âme sur le corps, et du corps sur l'âme* (Amsterdam: Marc-Michel Rey, 1775)

Marat, J. P., *Les Chaînes de l'esclavage…* (Paris, l'an I [1793])

Marat, J. P., *Éloge de Montesquieu: présenté à l'Académie de Bordeaux, le 28 mars 1785*, ed. Arthur de Brézetz (Paris, 1883)

Marat, J. P., *Two Medical Tracts*, ed. J. Blake Bailey (London, 1891)

Marat, J. P., *Les Aventures du jeune comte Potowski*, ed. C. Nicolas-Lelièvre (n.p., 1988)

Marat, J. P., *Les Chaînes de l'esclavage 1793: The chains of slavery 1774*, eds C. Goëtz and J. de Cock (Brussels: Pôle Nord, 1995)

Marat, J. P., *Oeuvres Politiques, 1789–1793*, eds J. de Cock and C. Goëtz (Brussels: Pôle Nord, 1995)

Marat, J. P., *La Correspondance de Marat*, ed. C. Vellay (Paris: Librairie Charpentier & Fasquelle, 1908)

Millon, C., *Histoire de la Révolution et de la Contre-Révolution d'Angleterre* (Paris, An VII)

[Milton, J.], *The Readie and Easie Way to establish a free commonwealth; and the excellence thereof compar'd with the inconveniencies and dangers of admitting Kingship in this Nation*, 2nd edn (London: Printed for the Author, 1660)

Milton, J., *The Works of John Milton, Historical, Political and Miscellaneous* (London: A. Millar, 1753)

Milton, J., *Areopagitica*, in John Milton, *Selected Prose*, ed. C. A. Patrides (Harmondsworth: Penguin, 1974), pp. 196–248

Milton, J., *A Defence of the People of England*, in Milton, *Political Writings*, ed. M. Dzelzainis (Cambridge: Cambridge University Press, 1991), pp. 49–254

Milton, J., *Eikonoklastes, ou réponse au livre intitulé Eikon Basilike, ou le portrait de sa sacrée majesté durant sa solitude et ses souffrances* (London: G. Du Gard, 1652)

Milton, J., *Défense du peuple anglais, sur le jugement et la condamnation de Charles premier, roi d'Angleterre*, in *Milton et Mirabeau: rencontre révolutionnaire*, ed. C. Tournu (n.p.: EDIMAF, 2002), pp. 97–158

Mirabeau, H. G., comte de, *Théorie de la royauté après la doctrine de Milton* (Paris, 1789)

Mirabeau, H. G., comte de, *Histoire d'Angleterre, depuis l'avènement de Jacques Ier jusqu'à* la révolution, par Cathatine Macaulay Graham, traduit en français et augmentée d'un discours préliminaire contenant un précis de l'histoire de l'Angleterre jusqu'à l'avènement de Jacques I, et enrichie de notes (Paris, 1791–92)

Mirabeau, H. G., comte de, *Sur La Liberté de la presse*, in *Milton et Mirabeau: rencontre révolutionnaire*, ed. C. Tournu (n.p.: EDIMAF, 2002), pp. 55–92.

Mirabeau, H. G., comte de, 'Excerpts from Count Mirabeau's Advice to Louis XVI (1789)', http://personal.ashland.edu/~jmoser1/mirabeau.htm (accessed 23 January 2009)

Molesworth, R., *An Account of Denmark, as it was in the year 1692*, 5th edn (Glasgow: R. Urie and Company, 1745)

Molesworth, R., *The Principles of a Real Whig; contained in a preface to the famous Hotoman's Franco-Gailia, written by the late Lord-Viscount Molesworth; and now reprinted at the request of the London Association* (London: J. Williams, 1775)

Montesquieu, C., *Correspondance de Montesquieu*, eds F. Gebelin and A. Morize (Paris: Librairie Ancienne Honoré Champion, 1914)

Montesquieu, *Catalogue de la bibliothèque de Montesquieu*, ed. L. Desgraves (Geneva: Droz, 1954)

Montesquieu, C., *The Spirit of the Laws*, eds A. Cohler, B. Miller and H. Stone (Cambridge: Cambridge University Press, 1989)

Montesquieu, C., *Pensées, Le Spicilège* (Paris: Robert Laffont, 1991)

Morellet, A., *Mémoires inédits de l'abbé Morellet ... sur le dix-huitième siècle et sur la Révolution* (Paris: Baudouin, 1822)

Moyle, W., *An Essay Upon the Constitution of the Roman Government*, in *The Works of Walter Moyle Esq* (London: Darby &c., 1726)

Moyle, W., *Essai sur le gouvernement de Rome, traduit de l'anglois* [trans. B. Barère de Vieuzac] (Paris: Imprimerie de Marchant l'ainé, an X [1801])

[Moyle, W. and J. Trenchard], *An Argument, Shewing, that a Standing Army is inconsistent with A Free Government, and absolutely destructive to the Constitution of the English Monarchy* (London, 1697)

[Murray, J.], *The Contest: being an account of the matter in dispute between the magistrates and burgesses, and an examination of the merit and conduct of the candidates in the present election for Newcastle upon Tyne* (Newcastle, 1774)

[Nedham, M.], *The Excellencie of a Free State. Or, The Right Constitution of a Commonwealth. Wherein all objections are answered, and the best way to secure the people's liberties discovered. With some errors of government and rules of policie* (London: Thomas Brewster, 1656)

Nedham, M., *The Excellencie of a Free State*, ed. R. Baron (London: A. Millar and T. Cadell, 1767)

Nedham, M., *De La Souveraineté du peuple, et de l'excellence d'un état libre*, trans. T. Mandar (Paris, 1790)

Neville, H., *Plato Redivivus: Or, A Dialogue Concerning Government, Wherein by Observations drawn from other Kingdoms and States both Ancient and Modern, an Endeavour is Used to Discover the Present Politick Distemper of our own with the Causes, and Remedies*, 3rd edn, in *The Oceana of James Harrington, Esq; and his other works ...* (Dublin, 1737)

Pièces justificatives: exposé de la conduite et des motifs du district des Cordeliers concernont le décret de prise de corps prononcé par le Châtelet contre le sieur Marat, le 8 octobre 1789 et mis à exécution le 22 janvier 1790 (Paris, [1790])

Price, R., *A Discourse on the Love of our Country, delivered on 4 November 1789 at the Meeting-House in the Old Jewry, to the Society for Commemorating the Revolution in Great Britain* (London: T. Cadell, 1789)

Price, R., *Additions to Dr Price's Discourse on the Love of Our Country, Containing Communications from France Occasioned by the Congratulatory Address of the Revolution Society to the National Assembly of France, with the Answers to Them* (London, 1790)

Robert, P. F., *Le Droit de faire la paix et la guerre appartient incontestablement à la nation* (Paris, 1790)

Robert, P. F., *Républicanisme adapté à la France* (Paris, 1790)

Robert, P. F., *Avantages de la fuite de Louis XVI, et nécessité d'un nouveau gouvernement* (Paris, 1791)

Robespierre, M., *Oeuvres de Maximilien Robespierre, VI–X: Discours*, eds M. Bouloiseau and A. Soboul (Paris, 1950–67)

La Rochefoucauld d'Anville, L. A., *Constitutions des treize États-unis de l'Amérique* (Philadelphia and Paris, 1783)

Romilly, S., *The Memoirs of the Life of Sir Samuel Romilly* (London: John Murray, 1840)

Rousseau, J. J., *The Social Contract and other later political writings*, ed. V. Gourevitch (Cambridge: Cambridge University Press, 1997)

[Rutledge, J. J.], M. R. C. B., *Essais politiques sur l'état actuel de quelques puissances* (London [Geneva], 1777)

Rutledge, J. J., *Éloge de Montesquieu* (Paris, 1786)

[Rutledge, J. J.], *Rappel des assignats à leur véritable origine: ou démonstration d'un plagiat dangereux du premier ministre et comité des finances* (Paris, 1790)

[Rutledge, J. J.], *Sommaire d'une discussion importante (relative au plan de banque territoriale du modeste M. de Ferrières)* ([Paris], 1790)

[Rutledge, J. J.], *Idées sur l'espèce de gouvernement populaire qui pourrait convenir à un pays de l'étendue et de la population présumée de la France* (Paris, 1792)

Samson, P. A., *Histoire du Règne de Guillaume III* (The Hague, 1703–4)

Sidney, A., *Discourses Concerning Government* (London: A. Millar, 1763)

Sidney, A., *Discours sur le gouvernement, par Algernon Sidney, ... traduits de l'anglois par P. A. Samson* (The Hague, 1702)

Sidney, A., *Discours sur le gouvernement, par Algernon Sidney, traduits de l'anglais par P. A. Samson: nouvelle édition conforme à celle de 1702* (Paris, 1794)

Sieyès, E. J., *Quelques Idées de constitution applicables à la ville de Paris en juillet 1789* (Versailles: Baudouin, 1789)

Sieyès, E. J., *Des Manuscripts de Sieyès, 1773–1799*, eds C. Fauré, with J. Guilhaumou and J. Valier (Paris: Honoré Champion, 1999)

Sieyès, E. J., *Sieyès: Political Writings*, ed. M. Sonenscher (Indianapolis: Hackett, 2003)

Swift, J., *Lettres de Mr le Chevalier G. Temple, et autre Ministres d'état, tant en Angleterre que dans les paies étrangers*, trans. P. A. Samson (The Hague, 1711)

Toland, J., *The Militia Reform'd; or an easy scheme of furnishing England with a constant land force, capable to prevent or to subdue any forein Power; and to maintain perpetual Quiet at Home, without endangering the Publick Liberty* (London: John Darby, 1698)

Toland, J., *Letters to Serena* (London, 1704)
Toland, J., *Dissertationes Duae: Adeisidaemon et Origines Judaicae* (The Hague, 1708/9)
Toland, J., *Nazarenus: or Jewish, Gentile, and Mahometan Christianity*, 2nd edn (London, 1718)
[Toland, J.], *The Danger of Mercenary Parliaments* (London, 1722)
Trenchard, J., *The Natural History of Superstition* (London, 1709)
Trenchard, J. and T. Gordon, *The Independent Whig: or, a defence of primitive Christianity, and of our ecclesiastical establishment* ... 6th edn (London, 1732)
Trenchard J. and T. Gordon, *Cato's Letters; or Essays on Liberty, Civil and Religious, and other Important Subjects*, 3rd edn (London: W. Wilkins, 1733)
Trenchard, J. and T. Gordon, *Dix-septième lettre de Caton, traduite de l'anglais de Thomas Gordon*, trans. J. L. Chalmel (Paris: Baudouin, n.d.)
Voltaire, *Letters Concerning the English Nation* (Oxford: Oxford University Press, 1994)
Walpole, H., *An Honest Diplomat at The Hague: The private letters of Horatio Walpole 1715–1716*, ed. J. J. Murray (Bloomington, IN: Indiana University Press, 1955)
Walpole, H., *Memoirs of the Reign of King George the Third*, ed. D. Le Marchant (London: Richard Bentley, 1845)
Walzer, M. (ed.), *Regicide and Revolution: Speeches at the Trial of Louis XVI* (Cambridge: Cambridge University Press, 1974)
Wilkes, J., *The History of England from the Revolution to the Accession of the Brunswick Line* (London, 1768), in *The Works of the Celebrated John Wilkes, Esq; formerly published under the title of The North Briton, in three volumes* (London, n.d.), I, pp. 3–34.
Wilkes, J., *The Correspondence of the Late John Wilkes*, ed. J. Almon (London: Richard Phillips, 1805)
Wittgenstein, L., *Philosophical Investigations*, trans. G. E. M. Anscombe (Oxford: Basil Blackwell, 1978)

Secondary sources

Works of reference

Biographical Dictionary of Modern British Radicals, Vol. 1, 1770–1830, ed. J. O. Baylen and N. J. Gossman (Sussex: Harvester Press, 1979)
Oxford Dictionary of National Biography, ed. H. C. G. Matthew and B. Harrison (Oxford: Oxford University Press, 2004; online edn), www.oxforddnb.com/

Other published sources

Acomb, F., *Anglophobia in France, 1763–89: An Essay in the History of Constitutionalism and Nationalism* (Durham, NC: Duke University Press, 1950)
Appleby, J. O., *Liberalism and Republicanism in the Historical Imagination* (Cambridge, MA: Harvard University Press, 1992)
Armitage, D., 'A Patriot for Whom? The Afterlives of Bolingbroke's Patriot King', *Journal of British Studies* 36 (1997), pp. 397–418
Ashbee, H. S., *Marat en Angleterre* (Paris, 1891)

Aston, N. and C. Campbell Orr (eds), *An Enlightenment Statesman: Lord Shelburne in Context (1737–1805)* (forthcoming)

Bailyn, B. (ed.), *Pamphlets of the American Revolution, 1750–1776* (Cambridge, MA: Harvard University Press, 1965)

Bailyn, B., *The Ideological Origins of the American Revolution*, rev. edn (Cambridge, MA: Belknap Press, 1992 [1967])

Baker, K. M., *Inventing the French Revolution: Essays on French Political Culture in the Eighteenth Century* (Cambridge: Cambridge University Press, 1990)

Baker, K. M., 'Transformations of Classical Republicanism in Eighteenth-Century France', *Journal of Modern History* 73 (2001), pp. 32–53

Barrell, R. A., *Bolingbroke and France* (Lanham, MD: University Press of America, 1988)

Bax, E. B., *Jean-Paul Marat: The People's Friend* (London: Grant Richards, 1900)

Beckwith, F., 'The *Bibliothèque Britannique*, 1733–47', *The Library: Transactions of the Bibliographical Society* 12 (1931), pp. 75–82

Berkvens-Stevelinck, C., '*Les Chevaliers de la Jubilation*: Maçonnerie ou libertinage? A propos de quelques publications de Margaret C. Jacob', *Quaerendo* 13 (1983), pp. 50–73 and 124–48

Berti, S., 'The First Edition of the *Traité des trois imposteurs*, and its Debt to Spinoza's *Ethics*', in M. Hunter and D. Wootton (eds), *Atheism from the Reformation to the Enlightenment* (Oxford: Clarendon, 1992), pp. 183–220

Brandon-Schnorrenburg, B., 'The Brood Hen of Faction: Mrs Macaulay and Radical Politics, 1767–75', *Albion* 11 (1979), pp. 33–45

Broome, J. H., 'Bayle's Biographer: Pierre Desmaizeaux', *French Studies* 60 (1955), pp. 1–17

Broome, J. H., 'Pierre Desmaizeaux, journaliste: les nouvelles littéraires de Londres entre 1700 et 1740', *Revue de littérature comparée* 29 (1955), pp. 184–204

Buranelli, V., 'The Historical and Political Thought of Boulainvilliers', *Journal of the History of Ideas* 18 (1957), pp. 475–94

Burmeister, J., *English Books, 1617–1900* (Catalogue 40, January 1999)

Burrows, S., *Blackmail, Scandal, and Revolution: London's French libellistes, 1758–92* (Manchester: Manchester University Press, 2006)

Campbell, P., 'The Language of Patriotism in France, 1750–1770', *E-France: An On-Line Journal of French Studies* 1 (2007), pp. 1–43 www.reading.ac.uk/e-france/Campbell%20%20Language%20of%20Patriotism.htm.pdf

Carrithers, D., 'Not So Virtuous Republics: Montesquieu, Venice and the Theory of Aristocratic Republicanism', *Journal of the History of Ideas* 52 (1991), pp. 245–68

Cash, A. H., *John Wilkes: The Scandalous Father of Civil Liberty* (Newhaven and London: Yale University Press, 2006)

Chambers, R., *The Book of Days: A Miscellany of Popular Antiquities*, 2 vols (London and Edinburgh: W. & R. Chambers, 1888)

Champion, J. A. I., *The Pillars of Priestcraft Shaken: The Church of England and its enemies, 1660–1730* (Cambridge: Cambridge University Press, 1992)

Champion, J., *Republican Learning: John Toland and the Crisis of Christian Culture, 1696–1722* (Manchester: Manchester University Press, 2003)

Childs, N., 'New Light on the Entresol, 1724–1731: The Marquis de Balleroy's "Histoire

Politique de l'Europe"', *French History* 4 (1990), pp. 77–109

Childs, N., *A Political Academy in Paris, 1724–1731:The Entresol and its Members* (Oxford: Voltaire Foundation, 2000)

Christie, I. R., 'The Wilkites and the general election of 1774', in his *Myth and Reality in Late Eighteenth-Century British Politics and Other Papers* (London: Macmillan, 1970), pp. 244–59

Clapham, J. H., *The Abbé Sieyès* (Westminster: P. S. King & Son, 1912)

Clark, A., 'The Chevalier d'Eon and Wilkes: masculinity and politics in the eighteenth century', *Eighteenth-Century Studies* 32 (1998), pp. 19–48

Clark, A., *Scandal: The Sexual Politics of the British Constitution* (Princeton and Oxford: Princeton University Press, 2004)

Clephan, J., 'Jean-Paul Marat in Newcastle', *Monthly Chronicle of North-Country Lore and Legend* 1(2) (1887), pp. 1–53

Conlin, J., 'Wilkes, the Chevalier d'Eon and the "Dregs of Liberty": an Anglo-French Perspective on Ministerial Despotism, 1762–1771', *English Historical Review* 120 (2005), pp. 1251–88

Coquard, O., *Jean-Paul Marat* (Paris: Fayard, 1993)

Cubitt, G., 'The Political Uses of Seventeenth-Century English History in Bourbon Restoration France', *Historical Journal* 50 (2007), pp. 73–95

Darnton, R., 'Marat n'a pas été un voleur: une lettre inédite', *Annales historiques de la Révolution française* (1966), pp. 447–50

Davies, K., *Catharine Macaulay and Mercy Otis Warren: The Revolutionary Atlantic and the Politics of Gender* (Oxford: Oxford University Press, 2005)

Davies, T., 'Borrowed language: Milton, Jefferson, Mirabeau', in D. Armitage, A. Himy and Q. Skinner (eds), *Milton and Republicanism* (Cambridge: Cambridge University Press, 1995), pp. 254–71

Deane, S., *The French Revolution and Enlightenment in England, 1789–1832* (Cambridge, MA and London: Harvard University Press, 1988)

De Cock, J., *Les Cordeliers dans la Révolution française*, Vol. 1, *Linéaments. Le Lieu. Le District. Le Club* (Lyon: Fantasques éditions, 2001)

Dedieu, J., *Montesquieu et la tradition politique anglaise en France: les sources anglaises de l'esprit des lois* (Geneva: Slatkine Reprints, 1971 [1909])

Dhombres, D., 'Mauvaise humeur britannique: les droits de l'homme ne sont pas nés avec la Révolution française...', *Le Monde* (11 July 1989)

Dickinson, H. T., *Bolingbroke* (London: Constable, 1970)

Dickinson, H. T., *Radical Politics in the North-east of England in the Later Eighteenth Century* (Durham: Durham County Local History Society, 1979)

Dumas, Judge, 'Huguenot History Written in the Portraits and Pictures at the French Hospital', *Proceedings of the Huguenot Society of London* 14 (1929–33), pp. 326–32

Dziembowski, E., *Un nouveau patriotisme français, 1750–1770: La France face à la puissance anglaise à l'époque de la guerre de Sept Ans*, Studies on Voltaire and the Eighteenth Century 365 (Oxford: Voltaire Foundation, 1998)

Echeverria, D., *The Maupeou Revolution: A Study in the History of Libertarianism: France, 1770–1774* (Baton Rouge, LA: Louisiana State University Press, 1985)

Egret, J., *La Révolution des notables: Mounier et les monarchiens*, 1789 (Paris: Armand Colin, 1950)
Egret, J., *Louis XV et l'opposition parlementaire, 1715–1774* (Paris: Armand Colin, 1970)
Ellis, H. A., 'Genealogy, History, and Aristocratic Reaction in Early Eighteenth-Century France: The Case of Henri de Boulainvilliers', *Journal of Modern History* 58 (1986), pp. 414–51
Ellis, H. A., *Boulainvilliers and the French Monarchy: Aristocratic Politics in Early Eighteenth-Century France* (Ithaca and London: Cornell University Press, 1988)
Fink, Z. S., *The Classical Republicans: An Essay in the Recovery of a Pattern of Thought in Seventeenth-Century England* (Evanston, IL: Northwestern University Press, 1945)
Flammermont, J., 'J.-L. Favier: sa vie et ses écrits', *La Révolution française* 36 (1899), pp. 161–84, 258–76 and 314–35
Fletcher, D. J., 'The Fortunes of Bolingbroke in France in the Eighteenth Century', *Studies on Voltaire and the Eighteenth Century*, ed. T. Besterman, 47 (Geneva, 1966), pp. 207–32
Fletcher, D. J., 'Bolingbroke and the Diffusion of Newtonianism in France', *Studies on Voltaire and the Eighteenth Century*, ed. T. Besterman, 53 (Geneva, 1967), pp. 29–46
Fletcher, D. J., '*Le Législateur* and the Patriot King: A Case of Intellectual Kinship', *Comparative Literature Studies* 6 (1969), pp. 410–8
Fogelin, R. J., 'Wittgenstein's Critique of Philosophy', in H. Sluga and D. G. Stern (eds), *The Cambridge Companion to Wittgenstein* (Cambridge: Cambridge University Press, 1996), pp. 50–8
Fontana, B., *The Invention of the Modern Republic* (Cambridge: Cambridge University Press, 1994)
Force, P., *Self-Interest Before Adam Smith: A Genealogy of Economic Science* (Cambridge: Cambridge University Press, 2003)
Forsyth, M., *Reason and Revolution: The Political Thought of the Abbé Sieyès* (Leicester: Leicester University Press, 1987)
Fryer, W. B., 'Mirabeau in England, 1784–85', *Renaissance and Modern Studies* 10 (1966), pp. 34–87
Fukuda, A., *Sovereignty and the Sword: Harrington, Hobbes and Mixed Government in the English Civil Wars* (Oxford: Oxford University Press, 1997)
Furet, F. and M. Ozouf (eds), *Terminer la Révolution: Mounier et Barnave dans la Révolution française* (Grenoble: Presses Universitaires de Grenoble, 1990)
Furet, F. and M. Ozouf (eds), *Le Siècle de l'avènement républicain* (Paris: Gallimard, 1993)
Gibson, A., 'Ancients, Moderns, and Americans: The Republicanism-Liberalism Debate Revisited', *History of Political Thought* 21 (2000), pp. 261–307
Gilbert, F., review of *The Machiavellian Moment*, in the *Times Literary Supplement* (19 March 1976), pp. 307–8.
Gill, M. B., 'Shaftesbury's Two Accounts of the Reason to Be Virtuous', *Journal of the History of Philosophy* 38 (2000), pp. 529–48.
Goëtz, C., *Marat en Famille: La Saga des Mara(t)*, II (Brussels: Pôle Nord, 2001)
Goldie, M., 'The Civil Religion of James Harrington', in A. Pagden (ed.), *Languages of Political Theory in Early Modern Europe* (Cambridge: Cambridge University Press,

1987), pp. 197–224
Goldie, M., 'The English system of liberty', in M. Goldie and R. Wokler (eds), *The Cambridge History of Eighteenth-Century Political Thought* (Cambridge: Cambridge University Press, 2006), pp. 40–78
Goldsmith, M. M., 'Liberty, Virtue, and the Rule of Law, 1689–1770', in D. Wootton (ed.), *Republicanism, Liberty, and Commercial Society, 1649–1776* (Stanford: Stanford University Press, 1994), pp. 197–232
Gottschalk, L. R., 'Marat a-t-il été en Angleterre un criminel de droit commun?', *Annales historiques de la Révolution Française* 4 (1927), pp. 111–26
Gottschalk, L. R., *Jean Paul Marat: A Study in Radicalism* (Chicago and London: University of Chicago Press, 1967)
Grieder, J., *Anglomania in France, 1740–1789: Fact, Fiction and Political Discourse* (Geneva: Droz, 1985)
Griffiths, R., *Le Centre perdu: Malouet et les 'monarchiens' dans la Révolution française* (Grenoble: Presses Universitaires de Grenoble, 1988)
Gurney, J., 'George Wither and Surrey Politics, 1642–1649', *Southern History* 19 (1997), pp. 74–98
Gwynn, R. D., *Huguenot Heritage: The History and Contribution of the Huguenots in Britain* (London: Routledge & Kegan Paul, 1985)
Haag, M. M., *La France Protestante; ou, vies des protestants français* (Paris: Joël Cherbuliez, 1861)
Haitsma Mulier, E., *The Myth of Venice and Dutch Republican Thought in the Seventeenth Century* (Assen: Van Gorcum, 1980)
Haitsma Mulier, E., 'The Language of Seventeenth-Century Republicanism in the United Provinces: Dutch or European?' in A. Pagden (ed.), *The Languages of Political Theory in Early Modern Europe* (Cambridge: Cambridge University Press, 1987), pp. 179–95
Hammersley, R., 'Camille Desmoulins's *Le Vieux Cordelier*: A Link between English and French Republicanism', *History of European Ideas* 27 (2001), pp. 115–32
Hammersley, R., 'English Republicanism in Revolutionary France: The Case of the Cordeliers Club', *Journal of British Studies* 43 (2004), pp. 464–81
Hammersley, R., *French Revolutionaries and English Republicans: The Cordeliers Club, 1790–1794* (Woodbridge: Boydell and Brewer for the Royal Historical Society, 2005)
Hammersley, R., 'Jean-Paul Marat's *The Chains of Slavery* in Britain and France, 1774–1833', *Historical Journal* 48 (2005), pp. 641–60
Harvey, S. and E. Grist, 'The Rainbow Coffee House and the Exchange of Ideas in Early Eighteenth-century London', in A. Dunan-Page, *The Religious Culture of the Huguenots, 1660–1750* (Aldershot: Ashgate, 2006), pp. 163–72
Hay, C. H., 'The Making of a Radical: The Case of James Burgh', *Journal of British Studies* 18 (1979), pp. 90–117
Higonnet, P., *Sister Republics: The Origins of French and American Republicanism* (Cambridge, MA: Harvard University Press, 1988)
Hill, B., *The Republican Virago: The Life and Times of Catharine Macaulay, Historian* (Oxford: Clarendon, 1992)

Hirschman, A. O., *The Passions and the Interests: Political Arguments for Capitalism Before its Triumph* (Princeton: Princeton University Press, 1977)

Hope Mason, J., 'Individuals in Society: Rousseau's Republican Vision', *History of Political Thought* 10 (1989), pp. 89–112

Houston, A. C., *Algernon Sidney and the Republican Inheritance in England and America* (Princeton: Princeton University Press, 1991)

Hunter, W. B. et al. (eds), *Milton Encyclopedia* (Lewisburg, 1978–83)

Israel, J., *Radical Enlightenment: Philosophy and the Making of Modernity, 1650–1750* (Oxford: Oxford University Press, 2001)

Jacob, M. C., 'John Toland and the Newtonian Ideology', *Journal of the Warburg and Courtauld Institutes* 32 (1969), pp. 307–31

Jacob, M. C., *The Radical Enlightenment: Pantheists, Freemasons and Republicans* (London: George Allen & Unwin, 1981)

Jacob, M. C., 'The Knights of Jubilation: Masonic and Libertine. A Reply', *Quaerendo* 14 (1984), pp. 63–75

Jacob, M. C., 'In the Aftermath of Revolution: Rousset de Missy, Freemasonry, and Locke's *Two Treatises of Government*', in *L'Età dei lumi: Studi storici sul settecento Europea in onore di Franco Venturi* (Naples: Jovene Editore, 1985), I, pp. 487–521

Jainchill, A., 'The Constitution of the Year III and the Persistence of Classical Republicanism', *French Historical Studies* 26 (2003), pp. 399–436

Janssens, J., *Camille Desmoulins: Le Premier Républicain de France* (Paris: Librairie Académique Perrin, 1973)

Jarrett, D., *Begetters of Revolution: England's Involvement with France, 1759–1789* (London: Longman, 1973)

Jennings, J. R., 'Conceptions of England and its Constitution in Nineteenth-Century French Political Thought', *Historical Journal* 29 (1986), pp. 65–85

Jones, C., *The Great Nation: France from Louis XV to Napoleon* (Harmondsworth: Penguin, 2002)

Karsten, P., *Patriot-Heroes in England and America: Political Symbolism and Changing Values over Three Centuries* (Madison, WI: University of Wisconsin Press, 1978)

Kates, G., *Monsieur d'Eon is a Woman: A Tale of Political Intrigue and Sexual Masquerade* (New York: Basic Books, 1995)

Kates, G., 'The Transgendered World of the Chevalier/Chevalière d'Eon', *Journal of Modern History* 67 (1995), pp. 558–94

Kelsey, S., *Inventing A Republic: The Political Culture of the English Commonwealth, 1649–1653* (Manchester: Manchester University Press, 1997)

Keohane, N. O., 'Virtuous Republics and Glorious Monarchies: Two Models in Montesquieu's Political Thought', *Political Studies* 20 (1972), pp. 383–96

Keohane, N. O., *Philosophy and the State in France* (Princeton: Princeton University Press, 1976)

Khatchadourian, H., 'Common Names and "Family Resemblances"', in G. Pitcher (ed.), *Wittgenstein: The Philosophical Investigations* (London and Melbourne: Macmillan, 1968), pp. 205–30

Knox, T. R., 'Popular Politics and Provincial Radicalism: Newcastle upon Tyne, 1769–1785', *Albion* (1979), pp. 224–41

Knox, T. R., 'Wilkism and the Newcastle Election of 1774', *Durham University Journal* 72 (1979), pp. 23–37
Kors, A. C., *D'Holbach's Coterie: An Enlightenment in Paris* (Princeton: Princeton University Press, 1976)
Kramnick, I., *Bolingbroke and His Circle: The Politics of Nostalgia in the Age of Walpole* (Ithaca and London: Cornell University Press, 1992 [1968])
Lackoff, G., *Women, Fire and Dangerous Things* (Chicago: University of Chicago Press, 1987)
Lacorne, D., *L'Invention de la république: le modèle américain* (Paris: Hachette, 1991)
Leigh, R. A., 'Jean-Jacques Rousseau and the Myth of Antiquity in the Eighteenth Century', in R. R. Bolgar (ed.), *Classical Influences on Western Thought, AD 1650–1870* (Cambridge: Cambridge University Press, 1971), pp. 155–68
Livesey, J., *Making Democracy in the French Revolution* (Cambridge, MA: Harvard University Press, 2001)
Lowenthal, D., 'Montesquieu and the Classics: Republican Government in *The Spirit of the Laws*', in J. Cropsey (ed.), *Ancients and Moderns: Essays on the Tradition of Political Philosophy in Honor of Leo Strauss* (New York: Basic Books, 1964), pp. 258–87
Lurbe, P., 'Matière, nature, mouvement chez d'Holbach et Toland', *Dix-huitième siècle* 24 (1992), pp. 53–62
Lutaud, O., 'Des Révolutions d'Angleterre: La Révolution française, l'exemple de la liberté de presse ou comment Milton "ouvrit" les etats généraux', Colloque International sur la Révolution française (Clermont Ferrand, 1986), pp. 115–25
Lutaud, O., 'Emprunts de la Révolution française à la première révolution anglaise', *Revue d'histoire moderne et contemporaine* 37 (1990), pp. 589–607
Maier, P., 'John Wilkes and American Disillusionment with Britain', *William and Mary Quarterly*, 3rd ser., 20 (1963), pp. 373–95
Marshall, J., *John Locke, Toleration and Early Enlightenment Culture* (Cambridge: Cambridge University Press, 2006)
Marshall, P. D., 'Thomas Hollis (1720–74): The Bibliophile as Libertarian', *Bulletin of the John Rylands University Library of Manchester* 266 (1984), pp. 246–63
Merivale, H, 'A Few Words on Junius and Marat', in his *Historical Studies* (London: Longman, 1865), pp. 186–203
Mossé, C., *L'Antiquité dans la Révolution française* (Paris: Albin Michel, 1989)
Namier, L., and J. Brooke (eds), *The History of Parliament: The House of Commons, 1754–1790*, Vol. 1 (London, 1964)
Nelson, E., *The Greek Tradition in Republican Thought* (Cambridge: Cambridge University Press, 2004)
Nicolet, C., *L'Idée républicaine en France* (Paris: Gallimard, 1982)
Norbrook, D., 'Levelling Poetry: George Wither and the English Revolution, 1642–1649', *English Literary Renaissance* 21 (1991), pp. 217–56
Norbrook, D., *Writing the English Republic: Poetry, Rhetoric and Politics, 1627–1660* (Cambridge: Cambridge University Press, 1999)
Ozouf, M. and F. Furet, 'Two Historical Legitimations of Eighteenth-century French Society: Mably and Boulainvilliers', in F. Furet (ed.), *In the Workshop of History* (Chicago: University of Chicago Press, 1984), pp. 125–39

Parker, H. T., *The Cult of Antiquity and the French Revolutionaries: A Study in the Development of the Revolutionary Spirit* (Chicago: University of Chicago Press, 1937)

Peltonen, M., *Classical Humanism and English Republicanism, 1570–1640* (Cambridge: Cambridge University Press, 1995)

Phipson, S., *Jean Paul Marat: His Career in England and France Before the Revolution* (London: Methuen, 1924)

Pocock, J. G. A., 'Machiavelli, Harrington and English Political Ideologies in the Eighteenth Century', *William and Mary Quarterly*, 3rd ser., 22 (1965), pp. 549–83

Pocock, J. G. A., *The Machiavellian Moment: Florentine Political Thought and the Atlantic Republican Tradition* (Princeton: Princeton University Press, 1975)

Pocock, J. G. A., 'The Machiavellian Moment Revisited: A Study in History and Ideology', *Journal of Modern History* 53 (1981), pp. 49–72

Pocock, J. G. A., 'Catharine Macaulay: Patriot Historian', in H. Smith (ed.), *Women Writers and the Early Modern British Political Tradition* (Cambridge: Cambridge University Press, 1998), pp. 243–57

Pocock, J. G. A., 'Afterword', in *The Machiavellian Moment: Florentine Political Thought and the Atlantic Republican Tradition* (Princeton: Princeton University Press, 2003 [1975]), pp. 553–83

Postgate, R., *That Devil Wilkes* (London: Dobson Books, 1956 [1930])

Rachman, G., 'France Braces itself for a Stiff Dose of Thatcherism', *Financial Times* (8 May 2007)

Rahe, P. A., *Republics Ancient and Modern: Classical Republicanism and the American Revolution* (Chapel Hill, NC: University of North Carolina Press, 1992)

Rahe, P. A., *Against Throne and Altar: Machiavelli and Political Theory under the English Republic* (Cambridge: Cambridge University Press, 2008)

Raskolnikoff, M., *Des Anciens et des modernes* (Paris: Presse Universitaire de Paris-Sorbonne, 1990)

Raskolnikoff, M., *Histoire romaine et critique historique dans l'Europe des lumières* (Strasbourg: AECR, 1992)

Reesink, H. J., *L'Angleterre dans les périodiques français de Hollande, 1684–1709* (Paris, 1931)

Richards, J., *Rhetoric and Courtliness in Early Modern Literature* (Cambridge: Cambridge University Press, 2003)

Richardson, R. C., *The Debate on the English Revolution*, 3rd edn (Manchester: Manchester University Press, 1998)

Ries, P., 'Robert Molesworth's "Account of Denmark": A Study in the Art of Political Publishing and Bookselling in England and on the Continent Before 1700', *Scandinavica* 7 (1968), pp. 108–25

Riley, P. (ed.), *The Cambridge Companion to Rousseau* (Cambridge: Cambridge University Press, 2001)

Robbins, C. A., *The Eighteenth-Century Commonwealthman: Studies in the Transmission, Development, and Circumstance of English Liberal Thought from the Restoration of Charles II until the War with the Thirteen Colonies* (Indianapolis, IN: Liberty Fund, 2004 [1987, 1959])

Robbins, C. A., 'The Strenuous Whig, Thomas Hollis of Lincoln's Inn', in B. Taft (ed.),

Absolute Liberty: A Selection from the Articles and Papers of Caroline Robbins (Hamden, CT: Archon Books, 1982), pp. 168–205

Robbins, C. A., 'Library of Liberty: Assembled for Harvard College by Thomas Hollis of Lincoln's Inn', in B. Taft (ed.), *Absolute Liberty: A Selection from the Articles and Papers of Caroline Robbins* (Hamden, CT: Archon Books, 1982), pp. 206–29

Robertson, J., *The Case for the Enlightenment: Scotland and Naples, 1680–1760* (Cambridge: Cambridge University Press, 2005)

Rodgers, D. T., 'Republicanism: The Career of a Concept', *Journal of American History* 79 (1992), pp. 11–38

Rogers, D. D., *Bookseller as Rogue: John Almon and the Politics of Eighteenth-Century Publishing* (New York: Peter Lang, 1986)

Rosenblatt, H., *Rousseau and Geneva: From the* First Discourse *to the* Social Contract, *1749–1762* (Cambridge: Cambridge University Press, 1997)

Rowe, D. J. (ed.), *The Records of the Company of Shipwrights of Newcastle Upon Tyne, 1622–1967*, Vol. 1 (Gateshead, 1970)

Rudé, G., *Wilkes and Liberty: A Social Study of 1763 to 1774* (Oxford: Clarendon, 1962)

Russell Smith, H. F., *Harrington and his* Oceana: *A Study of a 17th Century Utopia and its Influence in America* (Cambridge: Cambridge University Press, 1914)

Salmon, J. H. M., *The French Religious Wars in English Political Thought* (Oxford: Clarendon, 1959)

Sandrier, A., *Le Style philosophique du baron d'Holbach* (Paris: Champion, 2004)

Savage, G., 'Favier's Heirs: The French Revolution and the *Secret du Roi*', *Historical Journal* 41 (1998), pp. 225–58

Scott, J., *Algernon Sidney and the English Republic, 1623–1677* (Cambridge: Cambridge University Press, 1988)

Scott, J., *Algernon Sidney and the Restoration Crisis, 1677–1683* (Cambridge: Cambridge University Press, 1991)

Scott, J., *England's Troubles: Seventeenth-Century English Political Instability in European Context* (Cambridge: Cambridge University Press, 2000)

Scott, J., *Commonwealth Principles: Republican Writing of the English Revolution* (Cambridge: Cambridge University Press, 2004)

Scott, J., 'What Were Commonwealth Principles?', *Historical Journal* 47 (2004), pp. 591–613

Sgard, J. (ed.), *Dictionnaire des journaux, 1600–1789* (Paris: Universitas, 1991)

Sgard, J., M. Gilot and F. Weil (eds), *Dictionnaire des journalistes (1600–1789)* (Grenoble: Presses Universitaires de Grenoble, 1976)

Shackleton, R., 'Montesquieu, Bolingbroke, and the Separation of Powers', *French Studies* 3 (1949), pp. 25–38

Shackleton, R., *Montesquieu: A Critical Biography* (Oxford: Oxford University Press, 1961)

Shalhope, R. E., 'Towards a Republican Synthesis: The Emergence of an Understanding of Republicanism in American Historiography', *William and Mary Quarterly* 29(1) (1972), pp. 49–77

Shalhope, R. E., 'Republicanism and Early American Historiography', *William and Mary Quarterly* 39(2) (1982), pp. 334–56

Shklar, J., Review of *The Political Works of James Harrington*, in *Political Theory* 6 (1978), pp. 558–61

Shklar, J. N., 'Montesquieu and the New Republicanism', in G. Bock, Q. Skinner and M. Viroli (eds), *Machiavelli and Republicanism* (Cambridge: Cambridge University Press, 1990), pp. 265–79

Simon, R., *Henry de Boulainviller: historien, politique, philosophe, astrologue, 1658–1722* (Paris: Boivin [1941])

Skinner, Q., 'The Principles and Practice of Opposition: The Case of Bolingbroke versus Walpole', in N. McKendrick (ed.), *Historical Perspectives: Studies in English Thought and Society in Honour of J. H. Plumb* (London: Europa Publications, 1974), pp. 113–28

Skinner, Q., *The Foundations of Modern Political Thought. Vol. 2: The Age of Reformation* (Cambridge: Cambridge University Press, 1978)

Skinner, Q., 'The Idea of Negative Liberty: Philosophical and Historical Perspectives', in R. Rorty, J. B. Schneewind and Q. Skinner (eds), *Philosophy in History* (Cambridge: Cambridge University Press, 1984), pp. 193–221

Skinner, Q., 'The Paradoxes of Political Liberty', in S. M. McMurrin (ed.), *The Tanner Lectures on Human Values* 7 (Cambridge: Cambridge University Press, 1986), pp. 225–50

Skinner, Q., *Liberty Before Liberalism* (Cambridge: Cambridge University Press, 1998)

Sonenscher, M., 'A Limitless Love of Self: Marat's Grim View of Human Nature', *Times Literary Supplement*, 6 October 1995, pp. 3–4

Sonenscher, M., *Before the Deluge: Public Debt, Inequality and the Intellectual Origins of the French Revolution* (Princeton and Oxford: Princeton University Press, 2007)

Sonenscher, M., *Sans-Culottes: An Eighteenth-Century Emblem in the French Revolution* (Princeton and Oxford: Princeton University Press, 2008)

Sullivan, V. B., *Machiavelli, Hobbes, and the Formation of a Liberal Republicanism in England* (Cambridge: Cambridge University Press, 2004)

Thomas, P. D. G., *John Wilkes: A Friend to Liberty* (Oxford: Oxford University Press, 1996)

Thompson, J. M., 'Le Maitre, alias Mara', *English Historical Review* 49, 193 (January 1934), pp. 55–73

Thomson, A., 'Le *Discourse of Freethinking* d'Anthony Collins et sa traduction française', *La Lettre clandestine* no. 9 (2000), pp. 95–116

Tomaselli, S., 'The spirit of nations', in M. Goldie and R. Wokler (eds), *The Cambridge History of Eighteenth-Century Political Thought* (Cambridge: Cambridge University Press, 2006), pp. 9–39

Tombs, R. and I., *That Sweet Enemy: The French and the British from the Sun King to the Present* (London: William Heinemann, 2006)

Topazio, V. W., *D'Holbach's Moral Philosophy, its Background and Development* (Geneva: Institut et Musée Voltaire, 1956)

Torrey, N. L., *Voltaire and the English Deists* (New Haven, CT: Yale University Press, 1930)

Tournu, C., 'Introduction', in C. Tournu (ed.), *Milton et Mirabeau: rencontre révolutionnaire* (n.p.: EDIMAF, 2002), pp. 11–54

Trevor, D., 'Some Sources of the Constitutional Theory of the abbé Sieyès: Harrington and Spinoza', *Politica* (1935), pp. 325–42

Tuck, R., *The Rights of War and Peace: Political Thought and the International Order From Grotius to Kant* (Oxford: Oxford University Press, 1999)

Van Gelderen, M., *The Political Thought of the Dutch Revolt, 1555–1590* (Cambridge: Cambridge University Press, 1992)
Van Gelderen, M. and Q. Skinner (eds), *Republicanism: A Shared European Heritage*. Vol. 1: *Republicanism and Constitutionalism in Early Modern Europe*. Vol. 2: *The Values of Republicanism in Early Modern Europe* (Cambridge: Cambridge University Press, 2002)
Van Kley, D., *The Religious Origins of the French Revolution: From Calvin to the Civil Constitution, 1560–1791* (New Haven, CT: Yale University Press, 1996)
Venturi, F., *Utopia and Reform in the Enlightenment* (Cambridge: Cambridge University Press, 1971)
Venturino, D., 'Un prophète "philosophe"? Une *Vie de Mahomed* à l'aube des lumières', *Dix-huitième siècle* 24 (1992), pp. 321–31
Vercruysse, J., *Bibliographie descriptive des écrits du baron d'Holbach* (Paris: Lettres modernes, Minard, 1971)
Vicomterie de Saint-Samson, L. de la, *Les Droits du Peuple sur l'assemblée nationale* (Paris, 1791)
Vicomterie de Saint-Samson, L. de la, *République sans impôt* (Paris, 1792)
Vidal-Naquet, P., *Politics Ancient and Modern*, trans. J. Lloyd (Cambridge: Polity, 1995)
Viroli, M., 'The Concept of *Ordre* and the Language of Classical Republicanism in Jean-Jacques Rousseau', in A. Pagden (ed.), *The Languages of Political Theory in Early Modern Europe* (Cambridge: Cambridge University Press, 1987), pp. 159–78
Viroli, M., *Jean-Jacques Rousseau and the "Well-Ordered Society"* (Cambridge: Cambridge University Press, 1988)
Vovelle, M. (ed.), *Révolution et république. L'exception française* (Paris: Éditions Kimé, 1994)
Wade, I. O., *The Clandestine Organization and Diffusion of Philosophic Ideas in France from 1700 to 1750* (Princeton: Princeton University Press, 1938)
Walker, R. F., *The Institutions and History of the Freemen of Newcastle upon Tyne* (Newcastle, n.d.)
The Warrington Academy (Warrington, 1957).
Whatmore, R., *Republicanism and the French Revolution: An Intellectual History of Jean-Baptiste Say's Political Economy* (Oxford: Oxford University Press, 2000)
Whatmore, R., 'Etienne Dumont, the British Constitution and the French Revolution', *Historical Journal* 50 (2007), pp. 23–47
Whatmore, R., 'The French and North American Revolutions in Comparative Perspective', in M. Albertone and A. De Francesco (eds), *Rethinking the Atlantic World: Europe and America in the Age of Democratic Revolutions* (Basingstoke: Palgrave Macmillan, forthcoming)
Whittam Smith, A., 'Trotsky's Legacy is Alive and Well in France Today', *Independent* (25 March 2002)
Wickwar, W. H., *Baron d'Holbach: A Prelude to the French Revolution* (London: George Allen & Unwin, 1935)
Wilson, K., *The Sense of the People: Politics, Culture and Imperialism in England, 1715–1785* (Cambridge: Cambridge University Press, 1995)
Wokler, R., *Rousseau* (Oxford: Oxford University Press, 1995)
Wokler, R., 'Rousseau and his Critics on the Fanciful Liberties we have Lost', in R.

Wokler (ed.), *Rousseau and Liberty* (Manchester: Manchester University Press, 1995), pp. 189–212

Wolfe, D. M., 'Milton and Mirabeau', *Publications of the Modern Languages Association of America* 49 (1934), pp. 1116–28

Wood, G. S., *The Creation of the American Republic, 1776–1787* (Chapel Hill, NC: University of North Carolina Press, 1969)

Woolrych, A., *Britain in Revolution, 1625–1660* (Oxford: Oxford University Press, 2002)

Wootton, D. (ed.), *Republicanism, Liberty, and Commercial Society, 1649–1776* (Stanford: Stanford University Press, 1994)

Wootton, D., review of *Republicanism: A Shared European Heritage* in *The English Historical Review* 120 (2005), pp. 135–9

Wootton, D., 'The True Origins of Republicanism: The Disciples of Baron and the Counter-Example of Venturi', in M. Albertone (ed.), *Il repubblicanismo moderno: L'idea di republicca nella riflessione storica di Franco Venturi* (Naples: Bibliopolis, 2006), pp. 271–304

Worden, B., 'Introduction' to E. Ludlow, *A Voyce from the Watch Tower, V: 1660–1662* (London: The Royal Historical Society, 1978), pp. 1–80

Worden, B., 'Classical Republicanism and the Puritan Revolution', in H. Lloyd-Jones, V. Pearl and B. Worden (eds), *History and Imagination: Essays in Honour of H. R. Trevor-Roper* (London: Duckworth, 1981), pp. 182–200

Worden, B., 'The Commonwealth Kidney of Algernon Sidney', *Journal of British Studies* 24 (1985), pp. 1–40

Worden, B., 'English Republicanism', in J. Burns and M. Goldie (eds), *The Cambridge History of Political Thought, 1450–1750* (Cambridge: Cambridge University Press, 1991), pp. 443–75

Worden, B., *Roundhead Reputations: The English Civil Wars and the Passions of Posterity* (London: Allen Lane, 2001)

Worden, B., 'Whig History and Puritan Politics: the *Memoirs* of Edmund Ludlow Revisited', *Historical Research* 75 (2002), pp. 209–37

Worden, B., 'Introduction' to M. Nedham, *The Excellencie of a Free State* (Indianapolis, IN: Liberty Fund, forthcoming)

Wright, J. K., *A Classical Republican in Eighteenth-Century France: The Political Thought of Mably* (Stanford: Stanford University Press, 1997)

Wright, J. K., 'Mably and Berne', *History of European Ideas* 33 (2007), pp. 427–39

Unpublished sources

Briggs, E. R., 'The Political Academies of France in the Early Eighteenth Century; with Special Reference to the Club de l'Entresol, and to its Founder, the Abbé Pierre-Joseph Alary' (University of Cambridge PhD Thesis, 1931)

Broome, J. H., 'An Agent in Anglo-French Relationships: Pierre Des Maizeaux, 1673–1745' (University of London PhD Thesis, 1949)

Champion, J., '*Some Forms of Religious Liberty*: Political Thinking, Ecclesiology and Freedom in Early Modern England', unpublished paper, 2008

Champion, J., '"The Forceful, Full, Energetic, Fearless Expression of Heretical

Thoughts": Rethinking Clandestine Literature and the European Reading Public, 1680–1730', unpublished paper, 2008

Curran, M., 'The Reception of the Works of the Baron d'Holbach in France, 1752–1789' (University of Leeds PhD Thesis, 2005)

Fletcher, D. J., 'The Intellectual Relations of Lord Bolingbroke with France' (MA Thesis, University of Wales, 1953)

Henry, N. O., 'Democratic Monarchy: The Political Theory of the Marquis d'Argenson' (Yale University PhD Thesis, 1968)

Popkin, J. D., 'Jean-Paul Marat's Critique of the National Assembly and the Political Thought of the Old Regime', delivered at the 1989 meeting of the American Historical Association

Popkin, J. D., 'Marat and the Problem of Violence in the Revolutionary Era', delivered to the History Department at the State University of New York at Stony Brook in May 1992

Robertson, G., 'The Society of the Cordeliers and the French Revolution, 1790–1794' (University of Wisconsin PhD Thesis, 1972)

Index

absolute monarchy 2, 17, 33, 39, 55, 65, 66, 71, 77, 106–7, 155, 199
agrarian law 20, 190, 191
Akenside, Mark 124
   Pleasures of Imagination 124
Alary, Pierre-Joseph 64, 69–70
Almon, John 105, 106, 144
America 2, 4, 33, 95, 100, 101, 102, 103, 114, 115, 117, 146, 155, 199
American republicanism 2, 4, 6, 7, 33, 201
American Revolution 6, 33, 95, 100, 102–3, 154–5, 158, 164, 198
Amsterdam 39, 40, 126
ancient constitution 67, 91, 145–6, 199
ancient republicanism 3, 6, 8, 78, 79, 86–9, 94, 124, 133, 194, 199, 201
   see also classical republicanism
anticlericalism 17, 18, 56, 68, 90, 103, 126–7, 129, 133, 200
anti-monarchism 1, 43, 95, 113, 116, 176, 177, 194, 198, 201, 202–3
Argenson, René-Louis de Voyer de Paulmy, marquis d' 1, 2, 69, 71, 72, 198
   Considérations sur le gouvernement ancien et présent de la France 71, 73
   Mémoires 1, 71
Aristotle 23
Ashmolean Museum, Oxford 137
atheism 123, 127, 128, 129, 133, 200
Athens 91
Aubert de Vitry, François-Jean-Philibert
   J. J. Rousseau à l'Assemblée Nationale 162
Autri, comte d' 70

Bailyn, Bernard 100
Baker, Keith Michael 5, 6, 86
balanced constitution
   see mixed constitution
Barère, Bertrand 162
Baron, Richard 102–3, 113
Basnage de Beauval, Henri 36
   Histoire des ouvrages des savans 36–7
Bayle, Pierre 34
   Dictionnaire Historique et Critique 37
   Nouvelles de la république des lettres 35–6
Beaumont, Christophe de (Archbishop of Paris) 89
Bernard, Jacques 36, 37, 38, 43
   Nouvelles de la république des lettres 36, 41, 42, 43, 45
Bernard, Jean-Pierre 37
Berti, Silvia 42
Bibliothèque angloise 39
Bibliothèque britannique 37, 40, 43
billets de confession 89
binding mandates 142, 186, 187
Blackett, Sir Walter Calverley 144
Böhm, Michel 38
Bolingbroke, Henry St John, viscount 8, 54–79 *passim*, 89, 90, 118, 130, 164, 199, 201
   Craftsman, The 55, 72, 75
   Dissertation upon Parties, A 54, 56, 57, 58, 59, 65
   Idea of a Patriot King, The 59, 73, 89, 117, 161, 162–3
   Letters on the Study and Use of History, 105
   Letter to Sir William Windham 118

On the Spirit of Patriotism 59, 89
Reflections Concerning Innate Moral Principles 56, 73
Reflections upon Exile 59
Remarks on the History of England 55, 57
Some Reflections on the Present State of the Nation 59, 90
Boulainvilliers, Henri de 5, 6, 60, 64–9, 71, 78, 91, 126, 146, 201
 Histoire de l'ancien gouvernement de la France 66, 68
 Lettres historiques sur les parlements 66
 Vie de Mahomed, La 68
Boulanger, Nicolas 126
 Antiquité dévoilée 126
Boulay de la Meurthe, Antoine 167
 Essais sur les causes 161, 164, 167
Bowood Circle 174–5
Brewster, Thomas 113
Brissotins 194, 201
British commonwealthmen 7, 8, 14–27 *passim*, 33, 37, 44, 54–60 *passim*, 64, 65, 66, 67, 68, 69, 72, 73, 74, 78, 89–91, 94–5, 100–1, 102–4, 104–7, 110, 112, 124, 125, 127, 131, 132, 133, 138–9, 142, 143, 146, 157, 162, 175, 186, 187, 194, 198, 199
 see also Real Whigs
British constitution 2, 15, 23, 57, 58, 70, 71, 72, 73–9, 90, 94, 118, 132–3, 139, 155–7, 167, 174–5, 177, 178, 182, 199, 200
Broglie, Charles-François, comte de 118
Broome, J. H. 36–7
Brutus, Junius 26, 105
Buisson, F. 163
Burgh, James
 Political Disquisitions 103
Burke, Edmund 123
 Letters on a Regicide Peace 118–19
 Reflections on the Revolution in France 159

Carey, Lucius, viscount Falkland
 His Majesty's Answer to the Nineteen Propositions 77
Casaux, Charles de
 Questions à examiner 177–8

Catholicism 18, 33, 41
Chalmel, J. L. 162
Champ de Mai, Assembly 66
Champ de Mars, Assembly 66, 67
Champion, Justin 17, 26–7
Changuion, François 40
Charlemagne 65, 66, 68, 91
Charles I (King of England) 77, 105, 125, 139, 155, 160, 162, 176, 178, 179, 180, 181
 see also Stuarts
Charles II (King of England) 160, 179
 see also Stuarts
Charles Martel 65, 67
Chauffepié, Jacques Georges de
 Nouveau Dictionnaire historique et critique 37
Chavignard de Chavigny, Anne-Théodore 60
Chevaliers de la Jubilation 34, 38, 54
Choiseul, Etienne François de 117, 119
Church 18, 24, 55–6, 90, 127, 133, 191
Cicero 55, 114
 De Republica 114
Civil Constitution of the Clergy 191
civil liberty *see* political liberty
civil religion 24
classical republicanism 4, 5–6, 69, 86, 123, 201
 see also ancient republicanism
Club de l'Entresol *see* Entresol Club
Colepeper, John
 His Majesty's Answer to the Nineteen Propositions 77
Collins, Anthony 17, 34, 37, 38, 39, 56, 125, 164
 Discourse of Freethinking, A 39
commerce 4–5, 6, 87, 141
Committee of Public Safety 161
Committee of Safety (1642–44) 161
Committee of Safety (1659) 161
commonwealthmen 79, 86–95 *passim*, 130, 131, 133, 139, 142, 146, 147, 157, 186, 193–4, 199, 203
 see also British commonwealthmen
 see also early modern republicanism
community of goods 87, 88
Company of Bricklayers of Newcastle 144
Company of Butchers of Newcastle 144

INDEX

Condorcet, Marie-Jean-Antoine-Nicolas de Caritat, marquis de
   Esquisse 164
Constant, Benjamin
   'De la liberté des anciens comparée à celle des modernes' 86, 94
Convention (French) 166, 180, 181, 191
Cooper, Anthony Ashley, third earl of Shaftesbury 17, 24, 34, 35, 37, 40, 45, 124
   Inquiry Concerning Virtue 45, 89, 125
   Letter Concerning Enthusiasm 38, 39, 42, 45
Cordeliers Club 162, 185–94 *passim*, 200–1
Cordeliers District 185, 192
corruption 6, 17, 19–22, 23–4, 44, 45, 56, 58, 66, 67, 68, 72, 78, 87, 88, 90, 91, 92, 94, 100–1, 103, 106, 107, 110, 116, 118, 119, 127, 131, 133, 138, 139–42, 146, 157, 186, 188, 191, 192, 199
Cotes, Humphrey 105
Council of the Department of Drôme 180–1
   Défense du peuple anglais 180–1
Crell, Jan
   Junii Bruti Poloni 127
Cromwell, Oliver 113, 160, 164, 179

Darnton, Robert 137
Daudé, Pierre 40, 42, 89, 193
Décade philosophique, La 163
Declaration of the Rights of Man and of the Citizen 158, 185
Dedieu, Joseph 34, 74
De Hondt, Pierre 37, 40
deism 7, 17, 40, 42, 68, 72
De la Court, Johan and Pieter 19
Delaval, Thomas 144
democracy 5, 23, 26, 57, 67, 70, 72, 91, 94, 179, 185, 189–90, 191, 193–4, 200, 201
D'Eon de Beaumont, Charles Geneviève Louis Auguste André Timothée, chevalier 110–20, 123, 138, 143, 146, 187, 200
   Lettres, mémoires et négociations particulières 111
   Loisirs, Les 112, 114–16, 117
Desmaizeaux, Pierre 34, 36–7, 38, 40, 42, 45
Desmoulins, Camille 145, 157, 181–2, 192–3
   Révolutions de France et de Brabant 163, 181, 192
   Vieux Cordelier, Le 181–2, 192–3
despotism 5, 7, 8, 88, 89, 106, 107, 110, 111, 112, 115, 116, 117, 119, 138, 142, 146, 158, 159, 160, 163, 181, 199
   see also tyranny
De Witt, Johan 34, 43
D'Holbach, Paul Henri Thierry, baron d' 123–33, 138, 143, 200
   Christianisme dévoilé 126
   Contagion sacrée, La 126
   De La Cruauté religieuse 127
   De La Tolérance 127
   De L'Esprit du clergé 126
   L'Imposture sacerdotale 126
   Lettres philosophiques 128
   Politique naturelle, La 132–3
   Système de la nature 126, 127, 128, 129, 130–1, 132
Diderot, Denis 89, 125
   Pensées philosophiques 125
   Principes de la philosophie morale 89, 125
D'Ivernois, Francis 174
Dumont, Etienne 156, 174, 179, 180
   Souvenirs sur Mirabeau 179
Durand, David 54
Duroveray, Jacques-Antoine 175, 179, 180
Dutch Republic 33, 34, 35, 36, 38, 39, 40, 43, 44, 65, 71, 198
Dutch Republicanism 3, 19, 43, 44, 201

early modern republicanism 6–8, 69, 94, 116, 124, 126–33 *passim*, 146, 192, 194, 198–202
   see also commonwealthmen
Edinburgh 137
Election (General) of 1774 138, 144
Encyclopédie 37
English constitution *see* British constitution
English republicanism 2, 3, 7, 8, 14–27 *passim*, 36, 37, 43, 45, 75, 78, 89, 102–4, 106, 107, 110, 112, 113–14, 118, 119, 120, 123, 124, 125, 132, 138–9, 143, 155, 161–7, 167, 174–6, 177–80, 182, 185, 187–94 *passim*, 198–201, 203

see also British commonwealthmen
see also Real Whigs
English Revolution (1640–60) 1, 2, 104, 105, 113, 138–9, 155, 159–61, 164, 166, 167, 174, 176, 179, 180, 203
Enlightenment 3, 7, 45, 203
Entresol Club 60, 64, 69–73, 78
equality 87, 88
Erastianism 18, 24, 56
Estates-General (French) 70, 90, 91, 146, 156, 177, 185
Eugene of Savoy, Prince 35

Falkland, viscount, *see* Carey, Lucius
Farington, Joseph 145
Favier, Jean-Louis 118, 123
Ferrières, Jacques-Annibal 190
Financial revolution 57, 58, 59
Fletcher, Dennis 54, 64, 73, 74
Fontana, Biancamaria 4
Francs 65, 66, 67, 91, 145–6
Franklin, Benjamin 174
Frederick the Great (King of Prussia) 117
freedom *see* liberty
free speech 16, 100, 131, 181–2, 200
    see also liberty of the press
freethinkers 40, 42, 68, 72, 123, 124, 125, 126
    see also deism
French constitution 65, 67, 145, 156, 178
    1795 166
    1799 166
French republicanism 3–8, 86, 123, 185–94 *passim*, 198–202 *passim*
French Revolution 4, 5, 6, 7, 8, 45, 86, 118, 119, 123, 145, 146–7, 154–94 *passim*, 198, 200–1, 203
French revolutionary calendar 154, 161
frequent elections 25, 58, 90, 113, 131, 165, 186, 188–9
    see also Parliaments: frequent
Fritsch, Gaspard 38
Fronde 34
Fryer, W. B. 174, 182
Furly, Benjamin 34, 37, 38

Garrick, David 124

Gazette français 164
Geneva 4, 137
George I (King of Britain) 60
George III (King of Britain) 101
Ginguené, Pierre-Louis 163
Girardin, René 187
Girondins *see* Brissotins
Glorious Revolution (1688–89) 1, 2, 25, 26, 41, 44, 54, 58, 90, 105, 155, 157–9, 167, 180
Glynn, John 102, 144
Gordon, Thomas 17, 21, 22, 37, 40, 41, 42, 74, 103, 124, 127
    Cato's Letters 14, 15, 21, 22, 24, 130, 162
    Cordial for Low Spirits, A 103
    Independent Whig, The 18, 124, 126, 127
    Priestianity 17–18
    Works of Sallust, The 39, 40, 44, 45, 89, 124, 161, 163
    Works of Tacitus, The 16, 17, 19, 39, 40, 42, 44, 45, 89, 90, 124, 161, 163, 193
Goupil-Préfelne, Guillaume-François- Charles 163
Greeks 56, 74, 76, 87, 104, 118, 141, 154–5
Grenville, George 101
Grieve, George 144
Guerchy, Claude-Louis-François Régnier, comte de 117
Guiraudet, Charles 176
Guizot, François 159

Hague, The 37, 38, 39, 42
Hampden, John 105
Harrington, James 18, 19, 22, 24–6, 36, 37, 41, 43, 55, 57, 66, 67, 68, 71, 72, 74–8, 91, 106, 114, 131, 160, 161–2, 163, 164–7, 189–92, 193–4, 203
    Commonwealth of Oceana, The 20–1, 23, 24, 25, 44, 74, 75, 78, 113, 124, 162, 164–7, 191
    Discourse Upon this Saying, A 23
    System of Politics, A 17, 189–90, 191
Hénault, Charles-Jean-François 69
Henry, Pierre-François 160
Histoire de la République d'Angleterre 164
Hobbes, Thomas 19, 20, 116
Hohendorf, George, baron de 35

Holland *see* Dutch Republic
Hollis, Thomas 102–6 *passim*, 113, 114, 117, 124
Horne, John 104
Hotman, François 199
    Franco-Gallia 14, 16, 67
Huguenots 6, 8, 33–45 *passim*, 54, 65, 67, 198, 199, 201
Hulme, Obadiah
    Historical Essay on the English Constitution, An 103
Hume, David 103

inequality 73, 87, 141, 162, 190

Jacob, Margaret 39, 54, 65
Jacobins 78, 86, 87, 160, 181, 192, 193, 194, 201
Jacobites 17, 44, 54
James II (King of England) 41
    see also Stuarts
Jansenism 89
Jaucourt, Louis, chevalier de 37
Johnson, Thomas 39, 42
Journal du Club des Cordeliers 163, 188

Kates, Gary 112
Kearsley, George 105

land bank 190
Lansdowne, marquis of *see* Petty, Sir William
Lassay, marquis de
    Relations du royaume des Féliciens 70–1, 72, 73
Lastre d'Oby, Pierre-François 70
Le Clerc, Jean
    Bibliothèque universelle et historique 36
Leiden University 34, 124, 125
Le Jay (French bookseller) 179, 180
Lettre de félicitation de milord Sidney 163–4
Lévesque de Champeaux, Gérard-Claude 72
Levier, Charles 38, 39, 42
liberty 1, 2, 7, 16–18, 19, 23, 25, 26, 27, 41, 42, 43–4, 55–6, 59, 66, 71, 75, 76, 77, 86, 87, 88, 90, 91, 92, 100, 101, 102, 103, 105, 106, 107, 110, 112, 113, 115, 116, 119, 124, 131, 138, 139, 141, 142, 143, 146, 155, 158, 159, 161, 163, 164, 167, 177, 181, 182, 185, 186, 188, 189, 198, 199, 200
    neo-Roman 16, 55
    political 5, 7, 16–17, 27, 33, 35, 42, 55, 71, 76, 78, 105, 124, 158, 181, 191, 200
    of the press 25, 101–2, 143, 177–8, 181–2, 192–3, 200
    religious 7, 16, 17–18, 27, 33, 35, 42, 55, 72, 105, 124, 191, 200
Livesey, James 4–5
Locke, John 41, 43, 114
    Two Treatises of Government 39, 89
London 34, 37, 40, 55, 102, 104, 110, 111, 112, 118, 126, 145, 157
London Evening Post 117
Louis I (the Pious) 66, 68
Louis XIV (King of France) 1–2, 33, 35, 41, 44, 55, 65
Louis XV (King of France) 2, 89, 106–7, 111, 116, 117, 118, 119, 146
    Séance de la Flagellation 106
Louis XVI (King of France) 116, 160, 162–3, 179–81
love of glory 93–4, 130, 131, 141
Ludlow, Edmund 34, 36, 41, 43, 164
    Memoirs 17, 37, 39, 41, 43, 44, 103, 164
Lutaud, Olivier 175
Luttrell, Henry Lawes 101
luxury 5, 59, 73, 87, 88, 90, 92, 141, 199
Lycurgus 87, 88, 92, 94
Lysander 87

Mably, Gabriel Bonnot, abbé de 5, 6, 8, 86–95, 124, 146, 199
    Des Droits et des devoirs du citoyen 87, 88, 90–1
    Du Cours et de la marche des passions 92, 93
    Entretiens de Phocion 92, 93, 94
    Observations sur les Grecs 87
    Principes de morale 92–3
Macaulay, Catharine 104–5, 110, 112, 139, 175–6, 180, 182
    History of England 103, 104, 112, 139, 160, 162, 164, 175–6, 180
Machault d'Arnouville, Jean-Baptiste de 89

Machiavelli, Niccolo 19, 20, 116, 119, 203
  Discourses, The 118
  Prince, The 116
Mailhe, Jean-Baptiste 160
Mandar, Théophile 187–9, 193
  Des Insurrections 189
Marat, Jean-Paul 5, 6, 137–47, 156–7, 192–3, 200
  Chains of Slavery, The 137, 141, 142, 143, 144, 145–6, 157, 162, 192
  Discours adressé aux Anglais 141
  Essay on the Human Soul, An 140–3, 145
  Philosophical Essay on Man, A 140–3, 145
Marchand, Prosper 36, 38, 39, 54
  Dictionnaire historique 42
Marret, Paul 39, 43
materialism 126, 128
Matignon, Marie-Thomas-Auguste-Goyon, marquis de 69
Maupeou, René-Nicolas-Charles de 107, 117, 119
Maupeou Coup 101, 107, 145, 146
Mazel, David 39
Mercure national 163
Mercurius Politicus 113
militia 16, 24–5, 67, 90
Millon, Charles
  Histoire de la Révolution 161, 164
Milton, John 18, 19, 25, 36, 37, 103, 114, 124, 157, 161, 163, 175–82 passim, 189, 192
  Areopagitica 175–7, 180, 181
  Eikonoklastes 34
  Pro populo anglicano defensio 34, 105, 175–6, 178, 179, 180
  Readie and Easie Way, The 17, 177
  Tenure of Kings and Magistrates, The 178
Mirabaud, Jean-Baptiste 126
Mirabeau, Honoré Gabriel Riqueti, comte de 155–6, 174–82
  Considérations sur l'ordre de Cincinnatus 174, 175
  Courier de Provence, Le 175, 181
  Sur La Liberté de la presse 175–7, 180, 181
  Théorie de la royauté 175–9, 180, 181
Mitterand, François 159
mixed constitution 23–7, 44, 57–9, 66, 67, 70–2, 73, 75–6, 77, 78, 94, 131, 132–3, 194, 199, 200
modern republicanism 4–5, 6, 194, 201
Molesworth, Robert 16, 17, 37, 67, 102
  Account of Denmark, An 39
  Principles of a Real Whig, The 14–15, 18, 23, 26, 67
Monarchiens 155, 157
monarchomach theorists 34
monarchy 7, 8, 15, 17, 19, 23, 24, 26, 27, 43, 55, 57, 65, 66, 67–8, 70–2, 73, 75–6, 77, 78, 87, 88, 94, 113, 115, 116, 117, 118–19, 131, 132, 133, 139, 140, 155, 158, 174, 176, 177, 178, 179, 180, 181–2, 186, 193, 194, 198–9, 200, 201, 202
Moniteur, Le 163, 188–9
Montesquieu, Charles Louis de Secondat, baron de 2, 5, 6, 8, 64, 73–8, 86, 115, 119, 124, 146, 162, 189, 192–3, 199
  Considérations sur les causes de la grandeur des Romains 74, 118
  Pensées 75
  Spicilège 75
  Spirit of the Laws, The 74–8
moral philosophy 7, 19–22, 44–5, 56–7, 68–9, 72–3, 91–4, 95, 116, 129–31, 133, 138, 140–3, 190–1, 192–3, 199, 201, 203
  see also passions
  see also self-interest
  see also virtue
Morellet, André 164
Morisson, Charles 160
Mounier, Jean-Joseph 157
Moyle, Walter 17, 18, 37, 91
  Argument, Shewing, that a Standing Army is inconsistent with a Free Government, An 16, 25
  Essay Upon the Constitution of the Roman Government, An 21, 24, 74, 162

Naigeon, Jacques-André 128
National Assembly (French) 156, 157, 158, 161, 162, 179
  see also Estates-General
  see also Convention
Necker, Jacques 158

Nedham, Marchamont 18, 19, 114, 116, 164, 188, 193
    Excellencie of a Free State, The 103, 112, 113–15, 119, 161, 163, 187–9, 193
Nelson, Eric 74
neo-Epicureanism 22, 57, 91, 92–3, 95, 129, 130, 133, 142, 201
neo-Stoicism 22, 57, 91, 92–3, 95, 129, 201
Netherlands, The, *see* Dutch Republic
Neville, Henry 18, 91
    Plato Redivivus 21, 26, 102
Newcastle Town Moor 144
Nicolet, Claude 3–4
Nivernais, Louis-Jules Mancini-Mazarini, duc de 111
nobility 65, 66, 67, 68, 71, 91
Nouveau dictionnaire historique des grands hommes 178
Numa 24

Orléans, Louis-Philippe-Joseph, duc d' 179
Ostervald, Frédéric-Samuel 137

Paine, Thomas 160
Palfrey, William 100
Panaetius 114
Paris 34, 40, 89, 92, 107, 125, 185
Paris Parlement 69, 89, 91, 106–7, 126, 178
parlements 70, 89, 91, 101, 106–7, 117, 119, 146
Parliaments
    frequent 16, 17, 58, 106
    redistribution of parliamentary seats 106
Pascal, Blaise 19
passions 7, 19–22, 27, 56–7, 59, 68, 73, 75, 88, 92, 93, 94, 129, 130, 131, 133, 139–43, 145, 190–1, 199
Patriotic Society of Dijon 158–9
Patriotic Society of Lille 159
patriotism 104, 110, 117, 119, 125, 143, 163
Patriot King 59, 117, 162–3
Peace of Paris (1763) 101
Peace of Ryswick (1697) 24, 35
Pepin (Pippin) 65, 68
Petty, Sir William, earl of Shelburne and marquis of Lansdowne 174–5

Phipps, Constantine John 144
placemen 16, 24, 33, 58, 90, 106, 139
Pocock, John Greville Agard 2–3, 5, 16
Polybius 21, 23, 68, 91, 114
Pompadour, Jeanne-Antoinette Poisson, madame de 117
Popkin, Jeremy 145
popular ratification of laws 187, 191, 194
popular sovereignty 164, 178, 180, 185, 187, 188, 189, 190, 191, 200
Praslin, Gabriel de Choiseul-Chevigny, duc de 117
Price, Richard 157, 174
    Discourse on the Love of our Country 158
    Observations on the importance of the American Revolution 175
Protestantism 33, 35, 41, 42, 44, 45
    see also Huguenots
Public Advertiser 110

Rahe, Paul 19
Rainbow Coffee House, London 54
Ramsay, Andrew Michael, chevalier 72
Real Whigs 14–27 *passim* 33–45 *passim*, 54–60 *passim*, 65, 67, 102, 123, 126, 128, 133, 198, 199, 200
    see also British commonwealthmen
religion 7, 18, 24, 38, 56, 68–9, 72, 73, 90, 118, 123–9 *passim*, 131, 133, 143, 176, 191, 192, 198, 199
Rennes Parlement 106
representative government 4, 100, 107, 113, 116, 117, 119, 132, 139, 142, 146, 165, 185–7, 188–9, 200
republicanism 1–8 *passim*, 14, 15, 27, 34, 43, 55, 56, 70–1, 73, 74, 76, 77, 78, 79, 86, 87, 88, 103–4, 113, 116, 118–19, 129, 131, 163, 177, 179, 181–2, 186–7, 189, 192–3, 194, 198–204 *passim*
republican tradition 1–8 *passim*, 14, 19, 22, 23, 27, 44, 56, 64, 86, 91, 123, 129, 201–4
revocation of the Edict of Nantes (1685) 33
Revolution Society 157–9
Rey, Marc Michel 126
Ridley, Matthew 144
Ridley, Sir Matthew White 144

right of resistance 25, 33, 44, 131, 132, 198
Riot Act 156
Robbins, Caroline 7, 15–16, 33, 35, 106
Robert, Pierre-François 187
   Républicanisme adapté à la France 187
Robespierre, Maximilien 5, 6, 86, 193
Rochefoucauld, François duc de la 19, 21
Rochefoucauld d'Enville, Louis-Alexandre, duc de la Roche-Guygon et duc de la 158
Roederer, Pierre-Louis 164
Roman Republic 24, 25, 70, 88, 91, 104, 114, 116, 118, 141, 154–5, 160, 177
Romilly, Samuel 155–6, 174–5
   Memoirs 125, 155–6
Romulus 24
rotation of office 165, 189, 190, 191, 200
Rousseau, Jean-Jacques 5, 6, 86–7, 124, 146, 185–7, 188, 193, 194
   Considerations on the Government of Poland 87, 186–7, 188
   Social Contract, The 86–7, 185, 188, 198
Rousset de Missy, Jean 39, 42, 43, 89
rule of law 16, 17, 23, 55, 71, 72, 131, 132, 178
Rutledge, Jean-Jacques 162, 189–92, 193–4
   Calypso ou les Babillards 162
   Creuset, Le 162, 189–91
   Éloge de Montesquieu 77, 162
   Essais politiques 190
   Idées sur l'espèce du gouvernement populaire 162, 191–2

Saige, Guillaume-Joseph 5
Saint-Hyacinthe, Claude Thémiseul de 54
Saint-Just, Louis-Antoine 6
Samson, Pierre Auguste 38, 41, 42, 43–4, 89, 124
   Histoire du Règne de Guillaume III 38, 39, 41, 42, 43
Sarsfield, Count of 155–6, 175
Saumaise, Claude
   Defensio regia 34
Sawbridge, John 103
Saxons 26, 57–8
Scipio 114
Scott, Jonathan 17, 19

Secret du roi 111, 118
self-interest 7, 19–22, 23–5, 27, 45, 56–7, 59, 68, 73, 93–4, 129, 130, 131, 133, 139–43, 145, 188, 190, 199, 200
self-love *see* self-interest
Seven Years War 89, 111
Shackleton, Robert 74
Shaftesbury, third earl of, *see* Cooper, Anthony Ashley
Shelburne, earl of, *see* Petty, Sir William
Shklar, Judith 78
short terms of office 25
Sidney, Algernon 15, 19, 25, 34, 41, 44, 55, 74, 105, 106, 114, 163–4, 189
   Court Maxims 34
   Discourses Concerning Government 36, 37, 38, 39, 41, 42, 44, 89, 102, 106, 124, 161, 163
Sieyès, Emmanuel-Joseph, abbé 5, 164–7, 189, 191
   Constitutional plan of 1799 166
   Vues sur les moyens 165
Skinner, Quentin 3, 16, 123, 139
Société des amis des droits de l'homme et du citoyen, see Cordeliers Club
Société Typographique de Neuchâtel 137
Society for Commemorating the Revolution in Great Britain *see* Revolution Society
Society of the Supporters of the Bill of Rights 101, 104, 106, 144
Sonenscher, Michael 6, 162
Sparta 87, 88, 91, 92, 94
Spitz, Jean Fabien 123
Standing Army Controversy 17, 24
Stuarts 19, 26, 58, 160
Swift, Jonathan
   Letters written by Sir W. Temple 38

Tacitus 16, 17, 40, 76, 193
Thatcher, Margaret 159
thèse nobiliaire 65, 70, 71, 73
thèse royale 65, 70, 71, 73
Tindal, Matthew 56, 125
Toland, John 17, 22, 24, 34, 35, 36, 37, 38, 39, 40, 56, 102, 105, 113, 124, 125
   Adeisidaemon 38, 39

Danger of Mercenary Parliaments, The 16–17, 24
Letter From an Arabian Physician, A 39
Letters to Serena 126, 128
Life of John Milton, The 102
Militia Reform'd, The 25
Oceana and Other Works of James Harrington, The 26–7, 36, 37, 102
Origines Judaicae 38, 39, 42
toleration 18, 90, 126, 127–8
Tombs, Robert and Isabelle 117
Torcy, Jean-Baptiste Colbert, marquis de 60, 69
Traité des trois imposteurs 38, 42, 65
Treaty of Ryswick *see* Peace of Ryswick
Trenchard, Jean 14, 17, 21, 37, 126, 127
    Argument, Shewing, that a Standing Army is inconsistent with a Free Government, An 16, 25
    Cato's Letters 14, 15, 21, 22, 24, 130, 162
    Independent Whig, The 18, 124, 126, 127
    Natural History of Superstition, The 126
Trumbull, William 55
tyranny 17, 18, 19, 24, 25, 41, 42, 44, 45, 55, 57, 66, 68, 87, 102, 113, 115, 116, 139, 143, 178, 189, 198, 199
    see also despotism

Vane, Henry 19
van Gelderen, Martin 3, 123
Van Twedde, John 34
Vaughan, Benjamin 174–5
Vellay, Charles 137
Venice 21, 25, 91, 165, 190–1, 193

Venturi, Franco 2–3, 6
Verteillac, Thibaud de La Brousse, comte de 70
vigilance 25, 58–9, 94, 142, 164
Villebrune, L. 163
Villette, Marie-Claire de Marcilly, marquise de 60, 64, 69
virtue 5, 6, 19–22, 23–4, 27, 45, 56–7, 59, 72, 73, 75, 91, 93, 94, 104, 115, 116, 119, 127, 129, 131, 139–43, 186, 190, 192–3, 200, 203
Voltaire, François Arouet de 2, 60, 64, 115

Wade, Ira 65
Walpole, Horace 103
Walpole, Horatio 38, 44
Walpole, Robert 44, 59, 60
Warburton, William 56, 73
Warrington Academy 137
Whatmore, Richard 4–5
Wilkes, John 8, 100–7 *passim*, 110, 112, 119, 123, 124–5, 138, 143–5, 146, 199–200
    History of England 105, 106
    North Briton, The 101, 105, 107
Wilkes, Polly 105, 107, 112
William III (King of England) 17, 24, 26, 41, 43, 105, 158
William of Nassau 41–2
Wither, George
    Letters of Advice 139
Wittgenstein, Ludwig 203
Worden, Blair 17
Wright, Johnson Kent 5–6, 86

Lightning Source UK Ltd.
Milton Keynes UK
UKOW06f0905210216

268774UK00004B/79/P